PRAISE FOR *Find the Perfect College for You*

"Rosalind Marie and Claire Law have crafted a unique and impressive volume that can serve readers who want to use personality type as one of the tools for understanding and choosing a college."

—*Charles Martin, Ph.D., author of*
Looking at Type: The Fundamentals and Looking at Type and Careers

"This book is long overdue! At last two premier experts have combined qualitative research and their decades of experience with matching students with the right colleges to produce an insightful guide for students, parents and guidance counselors.

"In today's economy, mistakes can be costly, and parents are looking for a sure strategy to match their student to a college that fits them.

"Hats off to these two—They hit the bull's-eye!"

—*George de Lodzia, Ph.D., Emeritus Professor*
of Business Administration, University of Rhode Island

"The idea that applying to college should be about a 'great match' rather than a prize to be won has thankfully, entered into common thought. Yet how to divine a great match has been unclear—until now. Through this book, Marie and Law have brought scientific research and understanding of personality, motivation and learning into the mix in a way that offers new insights to students and parents as well as counseling and admission professionals."

—*Mark H. Sklarow, Chief Executive Officer, Independent Educational Consultants*
Association

"Students, their parents and their advisors will gain from the insights provided here. This is new and valuable college planning territory. Take a look. These pages take college planning to a new level."

—*Steven R. Antonoff, Ph.D., Certified Educational Planner,*
Antonoff Associates, Inc.

"This book presents a proven, effective tool for the job of finding a college! Each one of our high school seniors has been able to pick their major and find a college by working through this process. What a relief!"

—*Lori Pohly, parent, Huntsville, AL*

FIND *the* PERFECT COLLEGE *for* YOU

82 Exceptional Schools That Fit Your Personality and Learning Style

ROSALIND P. MARIE
and C. CLAIRE LAW

Find the Perfect College for You: 82 Exceptional Schools That Fit Your Personality and Learning Style
Third Edition By Rosalind P. Marie and C. Claire Law

Published by SuperCollege, LLC
2713 Newlands, Belmont, CA 94002
www.supercollege.com

Credits: Cover: TLC Graphics, www.TLCGraphics.com. Design: Monica Thomas
Layout: The Roberts Group, www.editorialservice.com

Trademarks: All brand names, product names and services used in this book are trademarks, registered trademarks or tradenames of their respective holders. SuperCollege is not associated with any college, university, product or vendor.

Disclaimers: The authors and publisher have used their best efforts in preparing this book. It is sold with the understanding that the authors and publisher are not rendering legal or other professional advice. The authors and publisher cannot be held responsible for any loss incurred as a result of specific decisions made by the reader. The authors and publisher make no representations or warranties with respect to the accuracy or completeness of the contents of the book and specifically disclaim any implied warranties or merchantability or fitness for a particular purpose. The accuracy and completeness of the information provided herein and the opinions stated herein are not guaranteed or warranted to produce any particular results. The authors and publisher specifically disclaim any responsibility for any liability, loss, or risk, personal or otherwise, which is incurred as a consequence, directly or indirectly, from the use and application of any of the contents of this book.

ISBN13: 978-1-61760-039-5

Manufactured in the United States of America
10 9 8 7 6 5 4 3 2 1

Library of Congress Cataloging-in-Publication Data
Marie, Rosalind P.
 Find the perfect college for you : 82 exceptional schools that fit your personality and learning style / Rosalind P. Marie, C. Claire Law. -- Third edition.
    pages cm
 Includes index.
 Summary: "A comprehensive approach to selecting a college that is in tune with a student's learning style, this guide offers a personalized, psychology-based approach to selecting the perfect university. With accessible tables and simple descriptions of campuses and majors, college bound students and their parents will find self-assessments and suggestions for 82 well-known colleges"-- Provided by publisher.
 ISBN 978-1-61760-039-5 (paperback)
 1. College choice--Psychological aspects--United States. 2. Personality. I. Law, C. Claire. II. Title.
 LB2350.5.M344 2014
 378.1'61--dc23
                                    2014013958

Susan J. Bigg
Educational Consultant
Who saw bright futures

ACKNOWLEDGEMENTS

We would like to thank all the parents and students who selected our approach to college planning over the years and our readers. We are thankful for our publisher, SuperCollege, who supported our vision and continues to help us bring it into the collegiate public square. Our admiration and gratitude goes out to the twentieth century psychologists, Carl Jung, Katharine Briggs and Isabel Briggs Myers, whose research influenced us lastingly and remains our constant inspiration while advising high school students. We salute the educators in American Universities and Colleges, their yeomen's job now is to inform and envision a robust America without division and with leaders who honor all of her citizens and all of her history.

NOTE FROM THE AUTHORS

This book was born out of the authors' personal experience while advising college-bound students. Our philosophical perspective strongly points to starting the process by helping students better understand themselves through assessments, interest inventories and personal interviews. With those emerging student profiles we call upon our knowledge of individual campuses and their unique academic and social environments. Throughout each advising session, telephone discussion and meeting with student and family we seek to match and interface the student personality preferences and learning style with college and universities that support and appeal to those student profiles. We set out to capture that advising process in this book and elected to enter our individual, subjective views of college campuses into a qualitative research design.

Over the period of ten years, we consulted with professional educators and psychologists to develop and move forward with the methodical framework that resulted in this book. Our observations and advising are heavily based upon and follow much within the theories of student development and environmental theories which encompass the physical and social environment. The research and theories of Alexander Astin, 1962, 1968; and Astin and Holland, 1961; Holland (1973) and Myers (1980), Michelson, 1970; Moos, 1979, Pascarella, 1985; Stern, 1986; Strange, 1991 and Kurt Lewin, (1937) have influenced our work in this book. The *Myers Briggs Type Indicator*®, emanating from Jungian Psychological theory, is the foundation of our college advising process and lays the fundamental groundwork for this book.

CONTENTS

THE COLLEGES

As you will come to understand, there is much depth and perspective in this book. We thank you for investing time and energy moving through the written words and sometimes demanding concepts. Remember, however, that this book is not a field directive. We want the best for you as you may take direction from its pages. It is a privilege to enter your life and we do so with suggestions, not mandates. Ultimately your parents and you have the credentials to determine the right college and the right educational major.

Do These Situations Look Familiar?

"My son is in high school and we were hoping that he would get interested in going to college. He visited his college friends on campus and did take the ACT, but now he doesn't want to talk about it."

"Sarah dropped her iPad on the kitchen table on the way to the fridge, and said, 'I'm not going to apply to that college. None of my friends are going there.'"

"Tristan is a top student at a very strong independent school. Each semester as grades come out, his place in the class rank seems to draw energy away from exploring colleges, he has his mind set on a couple of really tough universities to get into."

"Andrew has done very well in the sciences in high school, but with two A's in pottery and a 1st place in local competition, he is focused on art colleges now. How can we encourage his earlier interest and excitement for biology and math?"

"Karlee attends a private school of our religious denomination. She says she wants to go to a public state university. We want to keep religious colleges in the mix. How can she evaluate the differences and then make her decision?"

"Jason, our son, wants to go to a college that we really cannot afford. We would like him to look at a few other similar schools that are less costly. He is willing but how can he expand the college search?"

"Leah is a very good student in her class and she will be the first to attend college in our family. She has been offered good scholarships at two different colleges. She is unsure which to select. How do we help her?"

These are fairly common scenarios in families of college-bound high school students. This innovative book presents a new way to talk about colleges. Those conversations that are stuck can be reintroduced in new directions. The concepts in this book offer a fresh, personal perspective using the student Personality Type as the key.

CHAPTER 1

WHAT'S IN THIS BOOK?

The College Search

Starting the search for the right college can be both exciting and unsettling for families. Students are about to start an unfamiliar journey. Parents may or may not have much experience with the new college application process. Over the years, family, friends and neighbors have been good sources for help. Visits to the bookstores were a good bet for help too. Now parents and students find themselves back in the aisles or on the internet, but this time searching for College Guides. There are many books to choose from with observations and statistics about selecting a college.

So why would you choose this book? Because it is the *only* college book that matches the student Personality Type in reference to the Myers-Briggs Type Indicator® with the teaching philosophies at colleges and universities.* You will be able to use a proven method that highlights the specific learning style associated with each of the different Personality Types. Our book offers this original perspective for students, parents and high school guidance counselors because the focus is on the student learning style primarily and the college descriptions secondarily.

Within these pages you will find 82 of our favorite colleges that run the gamut from the most selective to more or less open admission. By following our planning suggestions throughout the search, parent and student will begin to recognize differing learning environments. You will then be able to match Student Personality Type and learning style with the colleges you visit. As you do this, you can add a few colleges that we suggest for your Type to your starter list. The value in doing this is to confidently add new colleges for serious consideration and time consuming campus visits. At the same time, the process can lead you to drop others. As you understand more about learning style and how it plays out in the lecture halls and classes, you will also more accurately assess colleges that are not listed in this book.

Personality Type

So exactly where does this Personality Type research come from and how reliable is it? The concept grew out of the work of early 20th century psychologists Carl Jung and Katherine Briggs with her daughter, Isabel Myers who developed a complex theory of human personality and the concept of personality preferences. Their understanding of human personality was put to practical use during World War II when GIs were successfully assigned to work tasks based on their answers to questions developed by Myers. Those questions, updated to reflect modern society, are in constant use today, in business, government and education. Our book highlights the career fields favored by each of the sixteen personality types as identified in decades of research. We then recommend the educational majors and minors that prepare undergraduates for those fields. We have found that high school students like to talk about majors surfaced by this research for their type and are less interested in talking about others.

In Chapters Two and Three you will explore and then uncover the likely student Personality Type**. With this selection, you can get started using our book to expand or slim down your college list. In the process you will become quite knowledgeable about three powerful tools in college planning. They are the student learning style, educational majors favored by each Personality Type and the college environments. We highlight each of these three tools as they appear on the individual college campuses. They are the heart and soul of our book.

Learning Style

Learning style is so important because it frees the student to be more creative and more open to exploration if they are in a learning environment that works for them. The learner is quickly motivated when there is a good match between the college educational approach and their individual learning style. Undergraduate college students use a lot of emotional and intellectual energy in the classroom to understand information presented by the professor. The student who is taking in knowledge with their preferred learning style can focus wholly on the subject at hand. The student who is not so well matched to the learning style is doing two things: learning the information and then rearranging it into ways that can be remembered and utilized. Therefore, the student who learns best by working with others in pairs or small teams learns quickly and soundly if the professor requires student teams. The undergraduate who learns best by mulling over ideas in their mind without interruption learns well if the professor relies heavily on reference documents at the library or online. These two study methods utilize two of the eight potential learning preferences that make up a student's learning style. The primary use of our book is matching the student learning preference with the colleges that support them through educational practices in and out of the classroom.

Exploring Educational Majors

How many times have we heard about college undergrads who don't know what to declare for their major in the last two years of college? How many times have we heard from graduates who languish after college graduation because their degree has little relation to the job they want? A proven way to avoid this is to take advantage of the research that identifies occupations favored by each of the Personality Types. In our book, we recommend majors and minors that pair up with the preferred occupations of each Personality Type as archived in MBTI® career research. Our second powerful planning tool therefore is the 1,300 short descriptions of majors and minors presently being offered on campuses across the nation. Once again, this is the only book that connects the dots between personality preference and educational majors. It is a great tool for most high school students who are undecided. For those who have a major in mind, our specific suggestions give complementary studies for a minor or concentration that also appeals to student Personality Type.

College Physical and Social Environments

Our concept of identifying Personality Type and learning style at the colleges is unique, yet, there is also the more familiar and obvious campus social culture to consider when choosing a college. It is best introduced through the Social and Physical Environment sections found in each of the 82 college descriptions. Together they comprise the third powerful tool in our book.

Both the social and physical environments have strong influence in shaping the shared values, beliefs and behaviors of the student body. Social psychologists such as John Holland describe how certain people shape a social environment and are attracted to like-minded individuals. Lawrence Kohlberg, also a social psychologist, offers a foundation for understanding the development of college student morality. Research by pioneers such as these two theorists has influenced key practices in collegiate environments like the Honor Code. Environmental psychologists, such as Kurt Lewin, describe how the physical attributes can also shape specific behaviors. This is addressed in the next chapter.

You would witness the Person Environment Theories in action when students march for or against climate controls. Individuals on any particular campus tend to be like-minded, and would likely hold similar views or at least be sympathetic with each other on the growing divisions within our polyglot American culture. These important theories helped frame our observations of the illusive nature of campus social life that is so important during college selection.

82 Colleges

So why did we select these 82 colleges as a 'primer' for matching learning style and Personality Type with college environment? *The simple answer is because these 82 colleges have very cohesive and well-crafted educational environments.* These colleges are consistently on target with their educational beliefs. They put their understanding into action every day, each semester. They have administration and faculty perspectives that fit a clear cluster of types among the 16 learning styles. These 82 colleges translate their beliefs into a cohesive curriculum and residential life. The core courses required for graduation harken back to the philosophy of their founders. The course curriculum is notable for what it offers and what it does not offer. The undergraduate time spent on and off campus, in internships or study abroad trips, reflects how the administration and faculty view acquiring knowledge. The option to double major or combine a single major with other minors reflects the administration's view of society's needs in the workforce. The advising for post-graduation options points to how the college expects its graduates to contribute to society. All of these reflect and support specific learning styles and define educational culture on the campus. This is why we selected these 82 excellent colleges.

Three Powerful Tools

The solid match between undergraduate student and college can launch the young adult into their first professional position with personal satisfaction and success. Learning style, best fit majors and minors and social/physical environment are three powerful tools used to find the right college. Yes, they are not quickly absorbed, but the advising method as presented in this book capitalizes on them. It lays out the basic concepts and hundreds of specific examples that you can access by tables or by reading the individual college reviews. We hope you will agree.

*Myers-Briggs Type Indicator®, MBTI® and Myers-Briggs® are trademarks or registered trademarks of the MBTI® trust, Inc., in the United States and other countries.

**www.mbticomplete.com is recommended by the Association of Psychological Type as the official website for completing the MBTI® survey online.

CHAPTER 2

THREE POWERFUL TOOLS VIEWED IN ACTION ON COLLEGE CAMPUSES

In this chapter, we present a layman's description of Personality Type with learning style, the benefits of exploring educational majors through personality preferences and key features of the physical and social environments.

Why is this important information to have? As a high school student, you can recognize your personality preferences and honor them. Your personality preferences typically lead to behavior and actions that are repeated almost daily. In this way through elementary, middle and high school you developed strengths and predictable style. We suggest that you use this valuable self knowledge to move ahead into college with confidence. Even though your choice may be very different than those of your friends, you can feel secure about your decision to enter a particular university or community college. Do this by taking time to discover and honor your personality preferences.

So what are those behaviors and actions that you repeat almost daily? Think about how often you changed up the hallways you used to get to the next class. Did you take a different route to catch more friends you've missed during the week? What was your reaction to a teacher who said the test would be an essay? Did you wish it would be fill-in-the-blank? If an uncle tells a personal story about playing on a baseball team decades ago, does it help you with your teammates? Or bore you a bit? Are you disappointed when your fave frozen waffles are missing and frozen breakfast perogies along with tamale breakfast bars is what you find in the freezer Saturday morning? These examples point backward to the student's personality preferences that are in play every day in the high school classroom and will show again in college lecture halls.

We are going to take the forward approach in this book. We will alert you to the environmentally-focused college campus in the mountains that makes hiking mandatory, or to a college located near others that often results in students being able to cross-register. We remind the reader that colleges with independent founders often explore morals and beliefs through their courses and in the classroom. Contrast this with the solitude of the public university that sticks to the subject content in their lecture halls. We know that you probably lean to learning sciences by detail/facts or by ideas/concepts. We will remind you to honor your preference for learning and understand how it will impact your college years. We know that all students lean toward four of eight learning preferences. This knowledge adds a personal foundation to the college search and helps answer that nagging question - Why you are choosing to go to *that* college.

Personality Type and Learning Style in College

Yes, each Personality Type has its own characteristic learning style. The learning style can be thought of as how each individual takes in information and retains it for use. There are eight distinct preferences in combination that determine Type and learning style. Most college campuses honor and support certain of these eight preferences. Colleges develop teaching strategies over decades that favor some of the eight preferences over others. In this way, they honor some Learning Styles over others. Very few campuses successfully honor and support all eight of the learning styles associated with Personality Type. In our observations, we typically found that colleges serve a range of two to four distinct preferences quite well through their educational practices, curriculum and academic philosophies. We identified compatible Personality Types for each of the 82 colleges in this book with this information and other factors, following the tenets of qualitative research.

OK, lets get more specific. The eight preferences called out above are organized into four pairs. An individual student can be one or the other within each pair but not both. Therefore, each student will have four and only four preferences that make up their Personality Type. The student may 'borrow' the opposite preference for an assignment or a particular course, but it will never become their preferred preference or change their learning style.

Extravert and Introvert Learning Styles

College students with the Extravert preference would like professors who require frequent participation or teaming with other students on projects anywhere on campus. The opposite choice is the student with the Introvert preference. They would like coursework that requires iPad research in their room or a quiet nook and reading a list of selected journals on reserve at the library. These are examples of educational practices that honor two prefer-ence opposites: Extraverts (E) and Introverts (I). Each of us has a preference for one of these, but not both. Most colleges have educational features that serve both of these preferences. However, some colleges lean toward one or the other.

Sensing and Intuitive Learning Styles

The next pair of preferences includes the Sensing (S) preference and the In-tuitive (N) preference. The Sensing student prefers to learn by collecting all the facts and then arriving at a conclusion. The needs of this Sensing student would be met in a college freshman course like "Introduction to Experimen-tal Biology." This would likely be taught in a step by step, building block approach through lab techniques. On the other hand, a freshman course like "Foundations in Biology" that probably starts first with the theories cen-tral to understanding life on earth meets the needs of the Intuitive learner. This Intuitive learner likes to get the big picture first and then discover the facts. A student will have either the preference for Sensing courses or Intuitive courses, but not both.

Colleges may offer both types, sensing and intuitive courses. Sensing and Intuitive preferences are the predominant preference pair that underlies col-legiate academic philosophies. Colleges tend to lean heavily toward one or the other: Sensing or Intuition. Educational practices influenced by these two preferences interface with all majors and minors as well as some extracur-ricular activities.

Thinking and Feeling Learning Styles

The third pair of preferences includes students with a Thinking (T) prefer-ence and students with a Feeling (F) preference. Objective analysis and logic rule within the preference for Thinking. A college emphasizing this prefer-ence would lean more toward analytical and precise subject matter. Advisors would encourage undergraduates to explore career fields. On the other hand, a college that mentors and advises with an orientation for the Feeling prefer-ence would emphasize humanistic content and career exploration by defining personal beliefs and values. Educational advising influenced by the Feeling preference would call attention to values and beliefs during an open-ended discussion between professor and student.

Many college courses are quite grounded in objective analyses as a pre-ferred way to acquire knowledge which reflects the Thinking preference. A lesser number of colleges heavily emphasize exploratory, values driven cur-riculum. The reader should know that each of these opposite learning prefer-ences can lead to an exceptionally fine education. Colleges have historically leaned toward the Thinking preference. As society is changing with emphasis on relativist values, we have observed that colleges are offering more content and curricula through the lens of the Feeling preference. Students will be one or the other of these two opposite preferences.

Judging and Perception Learning Styles

The last set of preferences is that of Judging (J) and Perception (P). Again, an individual undergraduate student is one or the other of these preferences. The student who likes a course syllabus that is well organized with a list of to-do's and clear cut-offs for grades favors the learning style of the Judging preference. The undergraduate who likes just a paragraph on the course objective at the start of the class, leans toward the Perceiving learning preference style. College professors often utilize a little of both of these orientations in how they organize the course objectives. However, the college administration policies outlined in the catalogs often lean toward one preference or the other. It will be reflected in the requirements for graduation, the regulations for residential housing, registration, research participation and more. These two tend to influence both the social and academic life on the campus.

College Educational Majors and Minors and the Best Personality Fit

As noted in Chapter One, there are preferred occupations for each of the sixteen Personality Types. Many decades of research with the MBTI® instrument support the connection between personality and occupation*. It is our position that the student who is familiar with their Type's preferred careers/occupations will have a clearer, chartered path through their four collegiate years. The value of this book is to identify educational majors and minors that lead to those preferred careers and occupations.

Within these pages, the reader will find their Personality Type matched to specific majors at over half of the colleges that are reviewed. The purpose of each short description is to pique the interest of the high school student and encourage the exploration of that educational major or minor. We strongly recommend that over time all students read through each of the educational majors listed for their Personality Type. Listed by page number in chapter 6, there are about fifty various majors recommended for each Type. That exercise alone will likely trigger new ideas about how to evaluate other colleges.

The individual description is not intended to be a directive for declaring a major at that college. Rather, it is one of the powerful tools in this book that will help high school students start to think about the purpose of their collegiate education. In this way, a student could read about a major recommended at College A that looks good on the college website. Yet that very major could be at College B, taught in the same way at a similar campus, and closer to home. Or perhaps a student might like the looks of a major at College C listed under a different type but with two of the same preference letters in their Type. It is important to be flexible in your use of the 1,500 major recommendations on these pages.

College Physical Environment

The environment is what you experience when you first visit a college campus. You scan the campus landscape and the views, flower beds, trees and buildings. Some buildings are easily recognizable icons. You notice how the undergraduates dress. You hear the sounds of city noise traveling across the campus. You hear what students are talking about. You feel the energy level across the campus on the day of your visit. Everyone notices the environment in some way. We believe that two features of the environment are particularly important for making the right college selection. They are the physical and the social environments.

Because colleges are aware that building layouts and floor plans actually influence students, new buildings are configured with specific goals for student behavior. Residence halls built after 2005 often form a sort of village community where students can easily socialize. They include mini conference spaces to study with laptops connected to the college servers. Most new residence halls are likely to be suite-style apartments with a common living room. Semi-circular classrooms with smart boards are spaces that encourage discussion among students and professor. New student centers with lots of couches, multiple study nooks and snack locations encourage students to sit and read while friends finish the indoor climbing wall. Over a cup of coffee some will seize the opportunity to discuss the upcoming exam. Many colleges have also elected to build professional level theaters and music practice rooms with high quality acoustic stage and sound equipment. Students who might otherwise drop their musical instrument after the close of the football season may take up their flute again with new awareness of music's connection to math theory.

As colleges use physical space across the campus in new ways, professors are moving their offices into the residence halls. Upperclass students are given their own offices within the department. This is especially attractive to students who want to continue a discussion that started in class. It increases student options during free time when not sitting in lecture halls. These changes are supported by the theories of twentieth century psychologists, from Kurt Lewin (1936) to Alexander Astin (1984) and George D. Kuh (2004). Their research examined the effects of campus environments identifying variables that keep students more engaged on campus.

Taken as a whole the Environmental Press influences how students spend their free time. The House System originating at Oxford and Cambridge Universities in England forms intellectual communities within the university, serving just about every need of students, from elegant dining to academic and social mentoring. If a student is at a university with the House System, they will identify more with their residence hall than the university itself. Yet other campuses may require off campus semester study, diminishing the insular campus environment and encouraging interaction and identity outside of the collegiate bubble. The "city drain" can also take students away from on-campus activities. Most large American cities are multi-cultural and students will quickly experience competing values and beliefs in action on our sidewalks. However, colleges located adjacent to American suburbs don't "drain." Suburban neighborhoods are quiet and empty during the working week encouraging social interaction to remain on campus. Along with academic work, these variables associated with college location will very much impact student learning and experience.

College Social Environment

The social environment describes the many experiences other than academic study at a particular college. Sometimes they may be identified as Extracurricular. When we visit colleges we note individual activity and groups that seem to color the social scene. By describing the social environment we offer the reader another lens to understand the differences between campuses that otherwise seem similar. At some colleges the grading policies generate competition while at others it's "all for one and one for all." While each student is unique, they are still members of the whole student body, and they influence one another. Along with the administration policies, structure, restrictions and rules, they define the college social environment.

While assessing college social environments we relied on the work of another prominent social psychologist, John Holland, who proposed career clusters based on the simple concept that birds of a feather flock together. The Holland Typography®, used in high schools across the country, was adapted to ACT's® World of Work Map. Holland's work predicts that artistic individuals are attracted to those who, like themselves, want to see creative, original results from their efforts. These artistic students together influence and agitate for an open, exploratory curriculum. So they may seek out a college where little or no connection is drawn to today's economic scene. In capturing the nature of the social environment for our readers, we often looked at the list of student clubs and closely read the student newspapers and the bulletin boards in libraries and dining halls. They pointed to what the whole student body experienced and requested during the semester.

Each of these defining physical and social features is important in that they melt together like a cake, once it is baked, to comprise the campus culture and environment. They are critical because students need to know before they apply to college whether they like chocolate, caramel or vanilla cake.

With a little help from the concepts in this book, families will learn to recognize the physical and social press of the environment. Parents and students can now evaluate these environments as they follow along on the campus tour.

In the next chapter, we offer an exercise that allows parents or students to choose their four preferences that form a Personality Type.

* The MBTI® instrument has been the subject of hundreds of research projects studying the links between personality type and different aspects of life. The Center for Applications of Psychological Type™ (CAPT®) maintains the largest single collection of research about the MBTI® instrument in the world. (In the 1940s and 1950s, Isabel Briggs Myers first recorded her research notes on thousands of index cards, which are now part of the archives at the University of Florida in Gainesville, Florida.) www.capt.org

CHAPTER 3

UNCOVER YOUR PERSONALITY PREFERENCES AND TYPE

With a basic understanding of the eight preferences from Chapter 2 you can move forward by making a choice on four scales. When you make your selection within each of these four pairs you will identify your likely Personality Type. At the same time, we recommend students formally complete the MBTI® assessment. It will likely improve your ability to use the book confidently and definitely will give you a heads up on self knowledge. Most counselors, psychologists, high school guidance counselors and educational consultants can administer the survey. Ask around because you may have access even without extra fees. However, you can also take the MBTI® on line at www.mbticomplete.com.

Now, as you start utilizing Personality Type in the college selection process it is important to remember that any student can find success at any college. Adaptability, capability, strength of high school academics, motivation and other factors come into play. Yet students who know their Personality Type are more likely to visit and hone in on campuses that really fit them. Read the following four sections and take a guess on which of the eight preferences feels the most like you.

Extraversion and Introversion

The first scale is between Extraversion and Introversion. Please read and react to the information below. Which one sounds more like you? Which has more of your behaviors? Which describes you better?

Extraversion, referred to as (E), appeals to those high school students who want to socialize with a large group of friends, from casual acquaintances to middle and best friends. The social butterfly gets energized by meeting many people and being involved in clubs and extracurricular activities. Extraverts are the first to say hello in the hallway and one of the first to raise their hand in class, volunteering to give answers. They could be attracted to the dance team, the mock trial or student council. Extraverts are often visible in activities, sports and projects and they are familiar to teachers and staff in the high school. They like to be expressive conversationalists, often using their hands for gestures. Extraverts are usually chatting on their smart phone and sometimes getting in trouble for chatting in class too. Their Facebook pages have a lot of info. Easy to know, extraverts often think out loud and quickly throw their personal thoughts into the classroom discussions.

Introversion, referred to as (I), appeals to those high school students who want to have a few, select friendships. Introverts could possibly lose interest and enthusiasm in some of the rah-rah high school activities like pep club. Yet, the math team or cross country team meet the Introvert's needs because they involve others, but nevertheless are mostly an individual effort. They rely on their own gathering of information and reflect with care and time as they reach conclusions or act on information. Texting is an ideal way to connect with friends. They have a short Facebook page or maybe not one at all. They enter the hallway without taking up a lot of room or gesturing, possibly absorbed in conversation with a classmate or a teacher. Introverts prefer to do homework alone. Outside of their closer friends, they typically communicate with a few other students once in a while. Art class may appeal to them because they can express themselves without excessive conversation. Introverts ponder and pause before voicing their opinions in class often seeking a deeper explanation than the teacher provides.

Which of these two sounds like you?	
❏ **Extraversion**	❏ **Introversion**

Sensing and Intuition

Sensing, referred to as (S), students love to study subjects that have a practical connection to the world. They use structure to assure that their facts are categorized and correct. They like step by step directions and feedback that is definite and measurable. Sensors in high school prefer not to have many open ended questions from the teacher that require guesswork or interpretation. This preference learner tends to like subjects such as earth or life sciences and physics. Their memory is an asset that helps them get good grades on fill in the blank and matching quizzes in high school. They follow instructions accurately. They are first class observers of what they can see, hear and smell.

Generally speaking, they are not looking for hidden meanings. So when they text message it will be descriptive with facts and times. If a teacher does not move rapidly through the material or jump around, these students will get a solid understanding of the subject. Sometimes it is a struggle to get the whole concept from a lesson. Sensors might challenge a teacher if the facts in a lesson plan don't jive with their knowledge of reality. They can be good at athletics because they focus on today's game, tuning all their senses to the sport during the play. They are present and attending, happy with the organized teacher who covers what they need to know.

Intuition, referred to as (N), students prefer to explore theoretical information and abstract knowledge. They are driven by possibilities. They love to develop big ideas and random thoughts researching on their iPads. They are imaginative, global learners who appreciate the big picture and are disinterested in the nitty-gritty details. Intuitive students are able to see beyond the information presented by the teacher during the class period. They anticipate the subject matter and look forward to the next chapter. They can miss important details. They may not be looking or listening in class at any moment. They like to read books that have heroes or fantasy orientations or anything else that stretches the imagination. They rely on their hunches and can build connections between seemingly unrelated topics. These students like to add to the information presented in class. They are future oriented and would like the model United Nations if their high school should offer it. They like a teacher who moves along quickly and offers choice in doing homework assignments. Intuitive students are ready to move on to new material and will automatically connect it to earlier knowledge. They prefer variety and new materials in the classroom; it brings excitement and interest to sequentially-based knowledge.

Which of these two sounds like you?	
❏ Sensing	❏ Intuition

Thinking and Feeling

Thinking, referred to as (T), students are analytical, logical and place greatest importance on the knowledge offered in the classroom. They often enjoy analyzing ideas and information with an objective point of view. They try to bring a "cause and effect" clarity to a free-roaming, off-task class discussion. They need logical principles and order. Thinkers would respond well to a teacher who presents complex issues without emotion and focuses on the underlying foundation. These students would not respond well to a teacher who tells stories about their own life experience as a way to bring understanding to the subject. Thinkers can simmer down a complicated problem because of their ability to logically organize complex situations. They can examine an event from the outside. Their precise conversation can even seem like a critique, yet it originates from the need to objectively square up what they know. Occasionally, their logic can rule over more gentle viewpoints that rely on instinct or intangible information. Students with the Thinking preference really expect and focus on fairness through order in the high school administration. They are motivated by assignments and accomplishments that lead to an objective report or grade. They like the high school website if it is up to date.

Feeling, referred to as (F), students often place the greatest importance on the personal connections with the teacher and other students in the classroom. They gain energy through their friendships. They are aware of others' feelings. Those with this preference can seem diplomatic, capable of sizing up situations and able to avoid stepping on toes if needed in the situation. They find something to appreciate in most of their friends and not-so-friends. They need harmony at home and in the high school social groups in order to function well. The Feeler brings human stories to the subject and likes teachers who bring their life stories into the classroom. They shine with appreciation when the teacher compliments their contribution. Small group work in the class is a hit with them. They are supportive of their friends and would like each and every friend to support them in return. They would like pages on the high school website to highlight individual students rather than activities and schedules. They can be very persuasive in both academic and extracurricular activities if they choose because they understand the emotional needs of others. They will notice if the high school principal pays attention to the energy and needs of the student body as well as the lunchroom dust ups and grades.

Which of these two sounds like you?	
❏ **Thinking**	❏ **Feeling**

Judgment and Perception

Judgment, referred to as (J), students like to plan their week, their school day and other activities in advance. Their day follows a routine if possible. As high school students, they usually like to finish their homework, closing the book, figuratively and literally. Those of this preference see homework and class assignments as immediate business that should be completed. They expect teachers to be consistent and clear in grading class work. After they have made a decision about class schedules, electives or extracurricular clubs to join, they are confident and are not likely to second guess that decision. Arriving at a decision may be an uncomfortable process. They like well organized, purposeful teachers in the classroom. They often arrive at class on time. They quickly end rambling conversations on their smartphones. Their iPad screen and files will be well organized. They don't run out of gas on the way to school or show up late at after-school-jobs. They like high school administrators who are consistent and ensure a predictable calendar of activities from year to year. If the parking lot empties quickly with two exits during sophomore and junior year, it doesn't need a third exit, rearranging the lanes, in senior year to see if it can be done faster.

Perceiving, referred to as (P), students like to gather information and explore at length and without deadlines or time limits. Perceiving students value the unknown. They are comfortable while considering the alternatives in a decision, needing to examine them for a good while. After the decision is made, they may still ponder the other options they did not choose. They appreciate a high school teacher who responds positively to second viewpoints or alternative viewpoints. They enjoy spontaneity in the classroom and like the discovery method to understand complicated ideas. Chances are good this student will have tardies over the semester. Arriving late is connected to their reluctance to close down and finish a conversation in the halls. Homework is turned in late sometimes. Most of the time, homework is started at the last minute. There is often room for improvement in their work if only there was more time to pursue their latest thought. This student will always appreciate the teacher or administrator who changes it up, brings in some new material or adds excitement to the biology lab or traditional pep rally in high school.

Which of these two sounds like you?	
❑ **Judgement**	❑ **Perceiving**

Did you have trouble making a decision with any of the four? Let us remind you that taking the MBTI® with a professional or online can help with your indecision. But for now you can mark each of your four choices with an indicator of how strong you felt that the preference letter fit you. Was your choice a slight fit, moderate fit or a clearly defined fit? These descriptions are called Clarities. Write your preference clarity next to each of your four chosen letters in the box below. For example an ESFP would write: Extraversion - Clear, Sensing - Moderate, Feeling - Slight, Perception - Definite. It is OK to be just 51 percent sure of your choice. However, if you are truly divided between a pair, then select the preferences, I, N, F, or P with a slight clarity so that you can move forward.

Extraversion (E)	Introversion (I)
Sensing (S)	Intuition (N)
Thinking (T)	Feeling (F)
Judgment (J)	Perception (P)

Now that you have your four preferences identified, circle your likely Personality Type on grid below.

ISTJ	ISFJ	INFJ	INTJ
ISTP	ISFP	INFP	INTP
ESTP	ESFP	ENFP	ENTP
ESTJ	ESFJ	ENFJ	ENTJ

You will find this same chart with each of the 82 college descriptions. If your selected preference is shaded then it is a college well suited to your Type. If your Personality Type is next to one of the shaded, selected Types then there are considerable features at the campus that should appeal to you also.

In the next chapter, you can read your Personality Type's typical learning experience with math, English, science and history in the high school classroom. It is our experience that the descriptions in Chapter 5 are likely to be helpful in confirming your Type Preference. If you are slight on a particular preference, read both of those Personality Type experiences in the high school classroom. For example, read both ENTP and ESTP if you are slight on the Sensing - Intuition scale.

*Students can also formally confirm their selections in this chapter by completing the MBTI® assessment. It is available through a large number of professionals from psychologists to educational consultants or through www.mbticomplete.com.

CHAPTER 4

DESCRIPTION OF PERSONALITY TYPES IN HIGH SCHOOL

Each of the sixteen Personality Types is the focus of this chapter. To illustrate the Personality Types, they have been summarized specifically to reflect students in the junior year of high school. The sixteen descriptions highlight how each Personality Type relates to the four core courses, math, English, science and history, in high schools across America. The reader will find that each of the sixteen types reacts differently to the core subjects based on their preferred learning style. Yet it is also important to note that the teacher's own Personality Type plays into the way the material in the course is delivered. If you have a teacher who is really influencing your like or dislike of a subject, compare the write up in this chapter to the same subject but in an earlier year, perhaps sophomore or freshman year.

ENFJ Learning Style in High School

English: English is likely to be a favorite subject. A teacher who presents literary figures along with the reasons for their behavior in the novel is a favorite. This type can read between the lines and understands the motivations of the characters in novels like *Robinson Crusoe*. They often love to participate in class. They must have harmony in the class to feel positive and will actively participate in discussion where values are front and center. If the teacher plays favorites and allows the class to become divided for any reason, this type will shut down. The teacher who encourages study groups will appeal to this type.

Math: A teacher who assigns nightly homework in precalc and covers the answers the next day in class really works for this type. These daily exercises will help this student meet their personal goals within the semester precalc curriculum. The teacher who actually assigns a grade or a point value to daily or weekly work will gain their appreciation. Teachers will get a thumbs up if they offer markers or milestones that track completion and academic progress throughout the semester. Teachers who only give periodic tests will get a thumbs down because this type likes to know where they are at in the class.

History: This type will probably like history, but may not get the best grade because sometimes they let their personal opinions count more than the facts. The teacher who brings out the human interest in historical narratives really plays to their learning style. The teacher who devotedly follows the chronology or focuses on the objective reasons for a war may not get their approval. They might view the Pilgrims' perilous Atlantic crossing through the survivor's tales and emotional scars. They are much less interested in the actual year that the Pilgrims landed than the drama of it all.

Science: The ENFJ will like a science teacher who assigns projects that require outside work with other classmates. They especially like anatomy classes because they are connected to human health. The "knee bone connected to the leg bone" makes for the orderly, structured way they prefer to learn. The teacher who acknowledges their skill and ability to be a team player will best develop this student's potential. The teacher who assigns technical lab reports that only require recording observations will be hard for this type. Daily or weekly quizzes centered on data will also not appeal to this type if it is the primary method for the final grade.

ENFP Learning Style in High School

English: English is likely to be a favorite subject. This type likes teachers who help them clarify their ideas. They will enjoy just about any novel, short story, or poem the teacher assigns. They really like to have a personal relationship with their teachers. The English teacher is likely to appreciate this type's quick mind and solid ability to identify human emotions in the literature. As a result, the teacher might encourage participation by this type for help inspiring class discussions and ultimately become a friendly mentor or counselor. The ENFP will happily offer insightful comments if they actually read the assignment on time. Typically doing homework at the last minute, they may drag their feet on actually capturing those insightful comments on a paper. They are likely to get a B or a C in this subject if the teacher does not help them out.

Math: This type likes teachers who use humor and variety in the class, but also stick to the lesson plan and always explain the steps within each problem. This student gets the overall nature of the formula, but because they miss the details, the steps must be pointed out to them. This student is a big picture learner and loves the teacher who can teach with an imagination which stimulates the class. The teacher who scores big for this type makes time for informal problem solving and fun during class.

History: Teachers will get the best work from the ENFP if the homework assignment directly matches the information presented in class. The teacher who enthusiastically talks about Bismarck and Germany gets their attention and will get the best work from this type by assigning a paper that follows the classroom discussion to be turned in within the next few days. The teacher who speaks about Bismarck in class but changes the topic for homework that night will discourage this type. Variety in the assignment and extra credit projects are welcomed by this type.

Science: This student likes teachers who start with the adult insect to explain the process of metamorphosis in biology. The remaining steps in the process should have some fun and negotiation. A teacher who allows for a self-designed project will definitely please them. This type likes "minds-on" and "talking it out" with others rather than solo, pencil and paper, observational reports. They relate to the spoken word, especially if the teacher has developed a personal relationship with the class. Short answer, projects and verbal reports best reveal this type's knowledge in chemistry versus multiple choice and fill-in-the-blank.

ENTJ Learning Style in High School

English: The ENTJ likes a teacher who is fair and rewards students who turn in homework on time and gives extra credit for lengthier reports. They are curious and like complex literature but also want it to be related to reality. They would like biographies and literature that explains how great minds and important figures came to be. They like a teacher who encourages a lot of classroom discussion. They like to speak up and will raise their hands to relay the continuous ideas that come into their head during class.

Math: This type wants to be right and often likes precalc because there is a clear and finite answer to each problem. A math teacher who organizes a little competition between student groups will score a touchdown with this type. They like to do problems that others may not be able to complete. They like to invent their own way of working a math problem calling on their broad understanding of the formula. They will take the time to explore different solutions to get the same right answer. If the teacher is organized when presenting new material, the ENTJ will rise to the task.

History: This student will like history if the teacher can present the subject through class projects like dramatic reenactments, oral presentations and class discussions. A teacher who would assign team projects and offer a chance to lead a project would be a favorite. This type will not like a teacher who primarily uses a lecture format to teach history. At the same time, they do like an orderly, chronological march throughout the semester and appreciate a teacher who reminds them if they seem to be missing important details in their search for the big picture.

Science: The ENTJ likes the way chemistry, biology and physics teachers give the class a structured, sequential outline at the beginning of a segment or chapter. The ENTJ will be interested in learning facts and objective information about the brain if the teacher uses ferrets or gerbils to illustrate the application of that knowledge. They may dislike the physics teacher who passes up this type of experiment that offers the opportunity to use insight. Memorizing facts and cramming to cover one more chapter before the semester ends gains their dislike.

ENTP Learning Style in High School

English: This type likes the fact that literature is open to many interpretations. The ENTP explores the possible motives and reasons why a protagonist may act in a certain way. Poems are also something that triggers their imagination. They will like teachers who invite student discussion and include multiple points of view. They will not like teachers who do not deviate from a structured interpretation of book. The ENTP can deal with opposing points of view. When this type has an assignment, such as writing a book review, they are not likely to make an outline. They will like a teacher who gives multiple short stories or poems to read, as opposed to a teacher who stays on one novel all semester. Teachers may find that this student's original interpretation of a poem is not clearly supported in writing and find it difficult to assign a "C" to the most original paper turned in.

Math: The ENTP may have a hard time following the formulas and prescribed teaching in precalculus because there is little room for creativity. However, the teacher who shows different approaches to solving a problem will pique their interest. The teacher who gives an open-ended math test, such as "tell how you would build a bridge using math formulas" will be their favorite. If the teacher only offers one kind of math exam all year long, it could become the tedious, ho hum class of the day. The ENTP quickly tires of rules and could make careless, small mistakes. They tend to prefer conceptual math, where they can apply new ways of solving problems.

History: This student likes a fascinating teacher who ties in past events with today's world. They like to read and teach themselves. The teacher who speaks of the numbers of horses and soldiers and hours involved in the battle of Gettysburg will lose this type. The teacher who speaks of Lee's battle plan and Grant's hunches will have them raising their hands to join in with their unique opinions. On a test, they are likely to miss the starting date of the Phoenician wars but the reasons for it will be understood by them. For that reason, an essay test in history is preferable to a multiple choice test.

Science: The ENTP loves asking questions, figuring out how scientists discovered a new vaccine and knowing why milk is best drunk when pasteurized. Teachers in the subject of biology who really ask the "why" questions are favored by the ENTP. The teacher who makes them work hard to memorize the species and specific functions of cells is not a favorite. The teacher who gives students ten chemicals in the lab and rewards the student who made the most compounds brings out the best of their creative learning style.

ESFJ Learning Style in High School

English: This student will like the teacher who requires a chapter to read in the assigned novel and then follows it with a quiz, all the better if this is done on a weekly schedule that is predictable. The ESFJ does not like teachers who skip around and grade with different methods. They do not appreciate surprise assignments or quizzes. This student's written reports however, will likely be well-prepared and reveal more insight into the material presented in class. If the literature is about values and compassion, their own passion for helping others will shine through because of their own, often deeply held values. This type will not mind a lecture on the various types of poetic cadence and will take detailed notes.

Math: This ESFJ likes to use graphic calculators because of the step-by-step sequences. Teachers who use this as a primary tool will be appreciated by this student. Typically very responsible and earnest, this student will remain on task during difficult algebraic explanations. The ESFJ could ask for clarification on behalf of the class. They are going to be a full participant in the classroom and could be very helpful to fellow students who are less willing to acknowledge their confusion. But no matter how far behind the class or an individual student gets, the ESFJ will be socially appropriate and not likely to disrupt the class or give up.

History: This type will often put forth their ideas in class discussions because they quickly recognize and appreciate facts. They will be well informed and freely share that information to help others in the class reach the same conclusions. They appreciate the teacher who gives them compliments and will do better when they receive positive comments about their work. Their clarity of thinking will shine when the teacher keeps the lessons concrete. They like that practical movement toward the knowledge expected for the coming tests and quizzes. They do not appreciate abstract, theoretical possibilities that require making assumptions about history. They will gladly help other students in the class.

Science: The ESFJ is likely to understand and appreciate the formulas because they can be demonstrated. In other words, this could be the favorite subject during the class day. Concrete concepts and application of those ideas is a favorite activity at which they often excel. Their lab work is very thorough and their lab grades may improve their overall subject grade. Mastering the individual concepts of meticulous lab work is their specialty, and they could earn the highest lab average in the class because of this. They like to work with their peers in a group in the classroom, preparing for the next day's lab experiment.

ESFP Learning Style in High School

English: The ESFP is very social and often gregarious, they may enjoy literature that describes social conventions such as *The Great Gatsby*. They usually support social traditions and may not appreciate literature with an abstract, philosophical bent. A highly detailed book that describes the social scene well will really bring the story alive for this type. Literature that defies social conventions may offend their sense of values. They could shine giving an oral book report on a subject in which they are interested. Their preference for step-by-step learning will allow them to give a sound, thorough report that other students may learn from and come to appreciate.

Math: This type does well with a structured math presentation, and they will especially learn well from applied math lessons that relate to a real situation. They will need those frequent spontaneous energy bursts sometimes to get through the semester in abstract algebra. If the teacher is organized and personable, the teacher will bolster this student's confidence in acquiring and mastering the math work. The teacher gets a thumbs up who regularly encourages discussion of the math problems while the class together works out the answer. Plotting, graphing and geometric designs make sense to them. Classroom management that discourages active discussion or allows one or two students to frequently provide the answers won't work for this type. Follow through with after class assignments and practice may be difficult for them because it is a solo activity and may not necessarily be fun.

History: This student will do well with a history curriculum that allows for hands-on activities like dramatic reenactments or interactive videos. Group activities, such as poster sessions for history day, where this type can study with others, will really bring history alive and pique their interest. They will prefer history taught through significant historical figures versus the traditional chronological time and events approach. They can be fascinated by the lives of people. They could become anxious if they are not encouraged by teacher and this could happen because they are typically sensitive. They are likely to procrastinate on turning in assignments unless they are passionate about the topic. Remembering specific facts and historical details is often a gift of this type who typically does not like highly abstract concepts.

Science: This type will like the teacher who presents the theory of radioactivity through Marie Curie's own research. Science must be connected with reality and purpose for this type. The hands-on nature of environmental science could be a favorite subject, especially if the teacher takes the class to the river to test water samples. They need a certain framework to assignments but also need some elbow room to test and try out their own ideas. The teacher who takes the lab outside of the classroom to identify rocks, collect and identify plants, find animal traces and monitor atmospheric instruments should make this student very happy. Group work and student pairing for class assignments is satisfying because of the personal relationships.

ESTJ Learning Style in High School

English: Papers will be written clearly in a journalistic style, handed in on time without any wandering sentences. The typical literature studied in the classroom is likely to be somewhat mysterious to them such as *Beowulf*. Nevertheless, they will persevere and remain on task in reading the entire assigned list of books. They will also give their opinion in class especially if the book blends facts with a good story, like *The Da Vinci Code, Nickel and Dimed: On Making it in America* or detective novels. The teacher who centers a reading list on books like *Beloved* by Toni Morrison may activate the impatience of this type because the story line is metaphorical. They will not easily suspend their disbelief to move along with a story line that intertwines fantasy with reality.

Math: Where order reigns and the teacher is well-prepared and follows a predictable, sequential lesson plan the ESTJ will likely appreciate the class and the teacher. They prefer clarity in explanations of math work. They will want to be sure that they are right or present themselves well prior to raising their hands to ask a question or give an answer. Yet they will speak up even if they are alone in their opinion. They will not feel comfortable revealing a lack of understanding. They prefer tangible results so ongoing problems with answers the next day is not their favorite way to learn. They will appreciate being asked to mentor other students, if requested by the teacher. They gravitate toward finite math because solving the equations will yield correct or incorrect answers and their strong observational skills will identify small mistakes along the way.

History: Since these students are impressed by proven knowledge, history is likely to make perfect sense to them. This tradition bound type likes the straight forward, historical records because they are factual events without hypothetical queries, and history offers fewer opportunities for abstraction than other subjects in high school. The ESTJ student can sit and learn from a dry presentation of the topic if it includes concrete examples. Clear expectations and homework assignments are preferred by this student. Conversely, abstract or opinionated teachers could possibly energize the student who would ask for clarification in a respectful and appropriate way. Typically, they will turn reports in on time, follow through with homework and take a leadership position in the class.

Science: They tend to like this subject because they are learning something useful and real to them. Opinions, interpretations and nebulous ideas are rarely interfaced in the high school science classrooms, so this student is more comfortable with this quantifiable subject. There is no room for argument on how mitosis occurs or at what temperature water boils. The ESTJ's attention for detail, conscientious approach and willingness to take charge helps them excel in the lab assignments. They respect the teacher who presents this subject traditionally, with a syllabus and well-organized. They also enjoy being publicly recognized for good work in the classroom because competence is an important milestone for them. The teacher who gives this independent learner the responsibility to lead others will find an enthusiastic student leader because leadership is valuable to them.

ESTP Learning Style in High School

English: This type will like literature which emphasizes, describes and is grounded in the physical environment, real things and people. The teacher who assigns reading that is primarily abstract and emotional in its story line will not hold the attention of this student. Hemingway's *Old Man and the Sea* and readings of Mark Twain are right up their alley. Homework that emphasizes variety in assignments and subject matter helps them stay engaged with abstract literature. Their contribution in class discussion is often summarizing or expanding on earlier comments so that the lesson can move forward. They're appreciative of the multiple points of view in literature and really enjoy the films and videos that illustrate the novel they are reading.

Math: The concepts involved in higher math such as precalc can give this student pause and possibly stump ESTP who has previously done well in understanding discrete math and concrete problems. Their typical strength of collaborating with other students is not often seen in math. High math requires and rewards mastering the abstract concepts embedded within the formulas. The math teacher who brings in practical, real world examples of the math problems will make inroads with this student.

History: History may be the favorite subject of the school day if the teacher uses project-based activities such as documentaries, pictorial exhibits and dramatizations that liven up and add variety to this fact-based discipline. They could be strong contributors in class discussion because their recall of historical facts is a comparative strength in the typical history class. They find historical figures to be compelling if the teacher offers study methods that physically engage their senses. Curiosity is a very real learning tool for this type. Written assignments will likely avoid the 'would have, could have, should have' line of reasoning. They prefer instead to prove their understanding of the subject by revealing a logical thread without unnecessary theory.

Science: This student is likely to prefer the days spent in the lab verses the days spent in listening to lecture and preparation. They will be comfortable with lab partner assignments that include three to four students over the typical two assigned to an experiment because they are often gregarious. They are likely to be the enthusiastic member of the group and will move the experiment forward if it stalls, even if it requires a blunt direct comment from them. They prefer to experiment informally and explore with the least fuss and muss. The teacher who leans too heavily on book and lecture will garner their disfavor. Visible, concrete results, often a part of high school sciences, give them a chance to excel through active, direct and assertive participation.

INFJ Learning Style in High School

English: This student could be quiet and unassuming about this subject that really speaks to their hearts, but they are shy about revealing this to others because they are private people. They do not like a teacher who would call on them, unless they raised their hand with a carefully thought out answer. They like a teacher who understands that they are listening and are on task, even if they do not speak out in class and answer questions. They may especially do well in a home schooling experience for a year or two because they need time and quiet to process their thoughts and prefer to teach themselves. Idealism and heroism such as is portrayed in *The Perfect Storm* by Sebastian Younger will appeal to this type.

Math: The INFJ prefers a teacher who is very well prepared. The teacher who offers a steady, even presentation of the big picture and the theory that underlies the numbers gets their respect. An equation will make more sense to this type even if it is not plotted on a graph because they can picture it intuitively. They thrive on careful analysis and the freedom to search for their own math solutions. They are independent learners and may need gentle guidance from a teacher to get back on the right track. They rely on their insights about math to be correct, but will ask a question of the teacher to confirm that they have the right answer.

History: This type is usually fascinated by this subject. They are excited to learn how the colonies came together to form a union. An assignment that required a full length examination of John Calvin would be right up their alley. Calvin is a complex figure and clearly impacted the pilgrim's motivation. INFJ would love to examine the Puritan ethic. They prepare very well for all history tests even if the teacher doesn't teach to their style. This student loves to read and will do extra credit for the learning itself.

Science: They will do well in this subject. They will thrive with a demanding teacher who requires the students to be organized, good with time management and planning a semester project and the accompanying paper, projects and reports. They will relate positively, through reason, to certain science issues like sustainability unless their personal belief system does not support that view. If they make a small error in judgment during a project or lab and the teacher calls attention to it, they will take it personally and be really hurt because of their high standards.

INFP Learning Style in High School

English: The INFP does well in class because INFP is usually interested in literature. They probably are avid readers of the *Harry Potter* series because it is richly metaphorical and depicts relationships and human values. They may also like science fiction books that stimulate their curiosity. They easily take on additional reading that is not required for class. They may find it hard to tear themselves away from a favorite novel. Their interests in literature range far and wide. They write their best papers when inspired and the topic relates to their own beliefs. They want the teacher to appreciate and compliment their work as well as coach and mentor them.

Math: In class, the INFP may be deeply invested in learning if math is taught in general concepts rather than preplanned, linear lessons and repetitive homework problems. For example, the INFP likes to know how the story of how Mr. Pythagoras discovered the Pythagorean Theorem, and how this can be applied to understanding how the universe works. A teacher who is always rational, objective and to the point, who doesn't let emotion enter the class discussion, may be upsetting to the INFP.

History: They like to use their inquisitive mind while working or studying solo. They typically like history if there is stimulating discussion in class and it is not abrasive or argumentative. Lectures might be considered boring, especially if it's a monologue by the teacher. INFP seeks to understand reasons for wars and is likely to look for a universal reason that explains all conflict. They prefer harmony in the classroom and will dislike a teacher who cannot earn the respect of the class. They may have trouble finishing their history report because the details can bog them down. The teacher who provides structure with some wiggle room does well with this student.

Science: This type sometimes gets bored with studying traditional biology or physics. They want science to relate to the human experience. The study of light and lenses make more sense to them if the teacher talks about people who suffer from cataracts. INFP needs broad concepts and big pictures first to spark the interest otherwise they may not incorporate the facts which they receive as too monotonous and boring. INFP would rather write about metamorphosis and life cycle in a short answer test rather than fill in a list of stages on a matching test.

INTJ Learning Style in High School

English: The INTJ loves the teacher who is competent and knows their literature. They would not like a teacher who accepts multiple interpretations of a novel. They want the teacher and class to settle on the best and most accurate interpretation that can survive the INTJ's analysis and critique. They do not like a teacher who moves from novel to short story to a poem in one lesson plan on a whim. They like an organized, logical review of each assigned reading.

Math: They challenge the teacher because they are quiet and learn privately. They often avoid group assignments and choose not to volunteer answers. They will complete math homework almost with resignation because the formulas do not give them freedom with the outcome. Sometimes they work so hard in trying to perfect the answers on their take-home precalc exams that they get down on themselves. Generally, INTJ is comfortable in the math classroom. This subject utilizes INTJ's love for analysis. Solving a problem is like getting to the finish line, an important milestone for this type.

History: This type will challenge the teacher's position on the Vietnam War. They like a teacher who will allow them to ask pointed questions. They ask questions to learn about the subject. They risk being not liked by the teacher and possibly others in the class because they learn by challenging the views presented in history classes. A teacher who follows the textbook interpretations regularly is not their favorite. They like a teacher who presents history in conceptual frameworks that encourage student insight.

Science: This student finds that teachers who start with the big picture in chemistry or physics are right up their alley. They are ok with missing a few of the steps and details because they will fill in the gaps later. Some teachers may like it when the INTJ challenges a few of their statements. They like a teacher who moves quickly through the chemistry chapters verbally explaining and highlighting required concepts for the upcoming AP exam. INTJ has an inner vision of how chemistry composes the world. The teacher syllabus must interface with the INTJ's vision.

INTP Learning Style in High School

English: The INTP may be reticent to speak up although they have may have an opinion. INTP can get very absorbed in a novel if it interests them. If the short story or poem does not interest them, they are likely to get bored. If the novel includes puzzles, mysteries, riddles or science fiction it is a winner as far as they are concerned. They connect the unrelated hints and clues to find the solution.

Math: This student is often on the honor roll. They may shine in precalculus because they have the thinking power to hang in there and get the abstract theory behind the formulas. They are likely to enjoy the derivatives in higher level calculus. They really can tap in the coordinates and numbers on their handheld T-83 graphic calculator. They like this little instrument. For those who do not like math, their tendency to overlook details may trip them up on exams. Their uneven surges of energy could drain their overall effort. If the teacher negotiates with this student on the grading to include math problems that seem to be riddles, then INTP's impressive concentration kicks in.

History: Teachers that connect historic events with current problems and policy will really get INTP to pay attention. If teachers dwell on event upon event to build a chronological timeline, they are likely to lose this type. INTPs may not get appreciation by the teacher because they can become totally absorbed in connections between the past and future, with little bearing on current class discussion. History may be a favorite or a loathed subject depending on the teacher's approach. This type may come across as skeptical in their questioning as they explore and satisfy their exceptional curiosity.

Science: This type likes the pure science that teachers talk about in the classroom, and they can listen and learn while moving a concept around in their head. They may actually enjoy or not enjoy the lab experiments. They certainly don't care for the group and collaboration often assigned by the science teachers. They will shine at memorizing the formulas and enjoy the complexity of the problems in science. Sometimes they become so absorbed in their lab work that they lose sense of time and place.

ISFJ Learning Style in High School

English: The teacher who is clear and highlights the moral issues helps them figure out the various shades of gray in the story line. They will be comfortable reading Jane Austin's *Sense and Sensibility* because it is pretty straight forward yet deals with common family issues. This author feeds the type's compulsion to make mental scrapbooks, rich with people details. ISFJ will be paying very close attention to everything said in the class so that they can be accurate in forming their judgments. They value the establishment and social conventions more often than not because it helps them know where they stand. Inferences made by students or the teacher in class may not be understood or accepted because they hear things literally. However, they are not likely to speak up and challenge the teacher or fellow students.

Math: Their usual mastery of the facts and their great work ethic will let them shine in the more sequential math tasks. The nature of abstract concepts in math may frustrate and wear them down so that test grades could be inconsistent sometimes. They complete all of their homework ahead of time even at the expense of play. They will like a teacher who applies the Pythagorean Theorem to figure out distance, which is a practical, hands-on concept for this type. They will like the teacher who offers a familiar routine to the lesson plan throughout the school year. They don't like to be rushed. The security of an orderly classroom that is evenly paced is very helpful to them.

History: Studying history through the social and human side is a favorite way to get into this subject. They can bring history alive, for themselves, by wondering what historical figures thought and believed at that time. They will even pass judgment on the morals or decisions made by those historical persons. Only when they ask will the teacher find out that the ISFJ has some unique and interesting insights. If a history teacher includes historical dramas in the course, they will make it easy for ISFJ to learn. Teachers who approach history in terms of facts, dates and events are less liked by this type, especially if the teacher calls attention to them in class.

Science: Mastering the facts in the sciences and then devising practical applications in the lab will be a natural and preferred learning experience for them. They will like the definite outcomes of experiments which leave little to guess about. Experimental teaching in the labs will work well for them if the teacher gives specific direction and identifies what is the end result of the lesson. ISFJ have their exceptional observation and retention skills. They are likely to be the best prepared lab partner and conscientiously accept responsibility for the exercise.

ISFP Learning Style in High School

English: The ISFP likes a teacher who is crisp and direct in discussing the storylines in literature and avoids shades of grey morality. What really drains this type's reserve is drawn-out explanations and hypothetical insights into what an author might have meant by a certain phrase or poem. In this high school class, ISFPs would rather watch a Shakespearian play on DVD first, and figure out the rest on their own. Usually, ISFP in English class hesitates before contributing opinions. They want to please the teacher. They are just as happy to observe rather than to propose an interpretation that they fear might be farfetched.

Math: This type appreciates the clarity of this subject. However, because they are not assertive and prefer to remain unnoticed, they could fall through the cracks if they don't have a caring teacher who coaches them along. They will put in extra effort if math interests them. They are cautious until they feel supported by the teacher at which time they can become energized in the classroom. Math teachers who don't seem personally interested in the students will not be their favorite. The precalc teacher should give examples of practical nature when presenting formulas to this type. The teacher who injects humor into the class lesson or is willing to make a game out of learning math could be their favorite.

History: This student is likely to excel and enjoy history if the teacher encourages them to informally come up with their own interpretations of the facts and events. They appreciate a teacher who pauses and gives the class enough time to process new information and their individual thoughts. If the history topic really piques their interest, they will go all out and turn in a seven page report. They will excel at a project that requires cut and paste historical mosaics. On history day, they will use posters to illustrate historical figures, complete with pictures and illustrations of clothing and dwellings. The teacher who notices them in a personal manner will be a favorite.

Science: They really understand and learn from those labs where there are animal samples and skeletons and specimens. Learning comes easier to them this way. They will learn from film or video presentations about the natural life cycles and the chemistry involved in those cycles. Sometimes the teacher does not understand their informal, impulsive interest in learning. At the same time, these students do not appreciate the big picture, relying instead on memorization of the facts. A teacher who pairs them up with another socially sensitive, down-to-earth student will get ISFPs best work.

ISTJ Learning Style in High School

English: This type will be suspicious of the many possible meanings to a metaphor. The inferential reasoning required to interpret literature could be a riddle to them. Deep inside they don't trust all the positions and interpretations because in their view, only one is correct. They will listen quietly, not complaining, and likely not reveal their discomfort with the open-ended and exploratory class discussion. They are likely to write clearly, with organization and free of flowery prose. They do well with book reports gathering factual information that would support a position. They could submit well written papers and call on their previous knowledge of grammar and English structure that they learned and enjoyed via drills in earlier school years. ISTJs want to reach the learning objectives set by the teacher and if they don't get this in class they will sort it out later by themselves.

Math: They are able to grasp the theory and concepts in advanced math by building up their math knowledge sequentially over the years. Math takes advantage of their logic-based approach and so they can solve complex problems especially if the teacher is clear about the foundational steps. They will pay attention to formulas presented on the board with intense concentration especially if there are graphs, tables and illustrations involved. They will accurately pinpoint errors that they identify. On math quizzes and tests there will be no small careless mistakes. When they are solving equations they will remember to use the right laws of properties and numbers.

History: They will be accurate on dates and facts with reports they turn in on time. If the history teacher assigns a wide-ranging topic that is not broken down into a clear outline, they will not like it. They will like the class if the teacher offers the material in an organized fashion and sequentially leads to the big picture. The ISTJs make for very good students, carefully observing and following the teacher's directions. They don't want to call attention to themselves so they appreciate the teacher who acknowledges their due diligence quietly. They are keen observers of what is. Their excellent memory is like the hard drive in a computer. Group work is not their favorite way to learn because ISTJs will step in and finish what others did not complete. As a result of doing this heavy lifting, they become aggravated. When it comes to answering questions in class, they will be thoughtful with a planned answer. Sometimes the conversation will have moved on to another point and they will not volunteer that thought they were preparing. The teacher will often come to know this student's mastery of the subject through their written work.

Science: Biology, chemistry or environmental sciences are enjoyable because they allow for logic and reasoning to arrive at a definite conclusion. These sciences move toward the big picture typically after introducing facts and information followed by a building block sequence. ISTJ likes this approach. Hands-on lab work will provide them an opportunity to demonstrate their competency and awareness of safety issues. They will not blow up the lab. Through their senses, they are very grounded in the lab assignment. Occasionally, they will volunteer to do a demonstration, taking responsibility for carrying the experiment to the end and making sure it gets done. They won't forget to come back to the lab to shake up the vial or check up on the growth.

ISTP Learning Style in High School

English: This type will prefer literature that is in a journalistic style of writing: what, where, when and how. This satisfies their need to know what makes things tick. They will like clearly descriptive essays, short stories and novels about what is, in the non-fiction category. If the teacher prefers novels with high emotional content and allegory this student will likely be turned off. They are likely to find themselves out of synch with the English class during poetry study. However they might like the haiku poetry because of its short, clear presentation with more concrete words. The teacher who is touchy feely and highly creative will be a puzzle to them. This student is likely to be passive in class and if the teacher requires participation, the grade could suffer.

Math: They usually like this subject, especially finite math like algebra I, statistics and geometry. They are often orderly, paying attention to detail, and carefully print their numbers on the page so they won't make mistakes. They will adore math teachers who present lessons clearly. There are two types of answers, right and wrong, and this student is likely to willingly retrace their steps if they made a mistake. The shortcuts in math formulas and most efficient proof to verify the correct answer is like duck soup for the ISTP. They like the objectivity of math. The sequential, step-by-step teacher will keep the attention of this student. The occasional math teacher who gets lost in their own presentations is not going to work for this student because they crave clarity. Math helps this type understand technical material which is what they are really interested in.

History: The teacher who presents this subject with emphasis on facts in categories and logical classifications will be a favorite teacher and likely to get this student to raise their hand in class. A teacher who covers the chapter with multisensory learning tools like video, graphs, posters, maps and text will allow ISTP to look for that practical thread that pulls it together. For that reason it may take the teacher several months or perhaps the semester to understand what this student has to offer to the class discussion. A teacher who flavors their history with social, religious or political random threads will not be their favorite. If the history topic piques their curiosity, they will want to know the material clearly and objectively as it relates to their present circumstances.

Science: They are likely to shine in physics, chemistry, biology and earth science because these subjects impact their lives today. This type really enjoys the many hands-on experiments and learning assignments, like dissection, because these make practical things clearer and are basically like play. The classification and systems of science are very appealing to them. Enjoying and excelling in their observations of experiments, ISTPs are likely to become participants and leaders in this class. Their papers and written work will highlight the accumulative, factual nature of the sciences. It is likely they will be engrossed by class projects.

CHAPTER 5

THE COLLEGE DESCRIPTIONS

The reader will find our three powerful tools for finding the perfect college contained in each of the following campus descriptions. We suggest starting out by reading several of the 50 or so majors we recommend for you. It will not be difficult since they are about 4 to 5 sentences each and their page number is found in Chapter 6 (pages 378-385). In this way you will become familiar with your preferred learning style. You will get a feel for many of the subjects taught in college with the teaching methods that work best for you. You will take a very large jump forward in self-knowledge with this exercise.

Next, pick out four or five colleges and read their entire descriptions including all of the major recommendations. It is important to realize that a college identified for your Personality Type preference lists six or eight other majors too. The major we recommended for your Type is intended only to be a sign post. It calls attention to the overall college which has a good number of academic methods that fit your learning style. That is true because colleges themselves do not have Personality Types. They usually offer somewhere between 50 and 100 majors taught with all eight preferences listed below. Their academic philosophies tend to lean in four of these eight preferences and we selected those colleges that most closely associate with your four preferences. So please, if you are med school bound, don't get hung up with our major recommendation for a degree in Asian languages. Rather, if you are an ESFJ, take a close look at the majors we recommended for ESTJ, ESFP and ENFJ if they are shaded. In each case, you share three of their favored learning preferences.

As you continue to become familiar with the book, pay close attention to the bolded words in the Physical and Social Environment descriptions. They call out defining features of the campus. In the MBTI compatibility section you will see reference in italicized form like (S) for sensing. Those letters identified within the sentence are predominant preferences on the campus in our opinion. The eight preferences listed below and their description are a quick reference to use while reading the compatibility section.*

As you approach high school graduation, we hope you have a good feel for several new educational majors and will look forward to exploring them at the college that you attend. We hope you will recognize your learning style and select educational studies and professors who are in tune with your preference. Most of all, we hope you will find direction to the perfect college through self-knowledge.

E—Extraversion
Focus on the outer world of people and things

I—Introversion
Focus on the inner world of ideas and impressions

S—Sensing
Focus on the present and concrete information gained from the five senses

N—Intuition
Focus on the future, with a view toward patterns and possibilities

T—Thinking
Form decisions on logic and on objective analysis of cause and effect

F—Feeling
Form decisions primarily on values and on subjective evaluation of person-centered concerns

J—Judging
Prefer to have things settled and tend to plan and follow an organized approach to life

P—Perceiving
Prefer to keep options open and tend to follow a flexible and spontaneous approach to life

* Copyright CPP, Consulting Psychologists Press, Inc., 3803 E. Bayshore Road, Palo Alto, CA 94303

AGNES SCOTT COLLEGE

Office of Admission
141 East College Avenue
Decatur, GA 30030
Website: www.agnesscott.edu
Admissions Telephone: 800-868-8602
Undergraduates: 861 Women

Physical Environment

Agnes Scott College is located a few miles from the center of Atlanta, in Decatur, a very cosmopolitan and welcoming suburb. The vibrant pace of the capital infuses energy and opportunities into the lives of the women at this college. The public metro line, MARTA, starts at the airport and makes the city accessible. Students stop at the Decatur station to get to the Agnes Scott campus or travel to and from an internship in the city. A few blocks from campus there are vibrant small businesses and boutiques. There are coffee shops that make comfy study spots off campus. The Starbucks and Java Monkey often appeal to students who want their latte while reviewing the umpteenth chapter of Organic Chemistry before a final exam.

Once on campus, the 100-acre treed setting feels quiet, cool and comfortable. The campus was established around the 1900s and has a mix of collegiate architecture and Victorian-style buildings. It has a deep **sense of history**. In 1886, Agnes Scott College started out as the Decatur Seminary for Women and certain buildings have a clear spiritual feel, especially Main Hall and Rebekah Scott Hall, connected by a charming outdoor passageway. These were the first buildings on campus. Some of today's students may still have future seminary aspirations.

The academic buildings are located on a long rectangular stretch of land that ends with a pond, used for researching birds and wildlife and their habitat. Many women here are **ecologically-minded.** Five of the oldest buildings and faculty residences were retrofitted to reduce their ecological footprint and won the SEEA Sustainability Energy Award in late 2013. The weather in Atlanta is warm most of the year, and so swimming and tennis are two very popular sports at Agnes Scott College. Many "Scotties" participate in Division III sports, including popular lacrosse.

Social Environment

Scotties like to learn, to express the truth and to make the world a better place for everyone. They accept the Honor Code which allows them to schedule their exams when they want to take them. Scotties are encouraged to think **honorably**. This is part of the Agnes Scott experience. The college takes in high school graduates and expects them to become a force in society. Most Scotties relate strongly to helping others while taking care of themselves as well. There is an implicit sense that excessive stress should be avoided. They may join the meditation group, go to the dance studio for yoga or attend light-hearted, inspiring lectures given on campus by authors like Niel Gaiman. Niel delightfully dealt with Lucifer in his award-winning comic book genre, *Sandman*. Many Scotties become active in volunteer efforts, others join the Women in Business Club. The administration seeks a wide variety of women. As a result, some are looking for that classic liberal arts education, others for liberal arts with an exposure to business, some for the pre-med and pre-teacher education, others still for the sciences that emphasize resource utilization as well as the broad offerings in the performing and visual arts on this campus.

Some undergraduates are members of academic honor organizations such as **Phi Beta Kappa** and Dana Scholars. Religious organizations, like the Baptist Campus Ministry and Jewish Student Association, are well-received by the student body and include several other Judeo-Christian denominations. Undergraduates are very involved on campus and assert themselves in a collaborative manner. **Leadership** is valued by the entire community with students taking a stand on current issues from politics to ecology. Their clubs and organizations function to benefit the entire college campus. They actively make their views known in the school paper. The process of becoming is important along with the end goal. Scotties believe in themselves, and so they are able to assert themselves, to **speak out for the purpose** of making improvements, whether in their life at the college or in society. They do so actively yet avoiding the most radical of positions. Bright, competent, mindful women graduate from Agnes Scott.

Compatibility with Personality Types and Preferences

Undergraduates at Agnes Scott College are often activist in their approach to learning. The women come to this campus to secure professional skills and gain entry into the marketplace. The student body might define competency as expertise within a field. Competency is also defined as communication and persuasion to enact new processes (P) in a discipline. Undergraduates look to traditions but embrace change here. Faculty and administration follow a similar trajectory. Most areas of study are familiar, traditional (J) subjects found at liberal arts colleges, yet, there is a strong program to interface students with fast-paced Atlanta. Neither students nor professors shy away from the dynamic enterprise of this rapidly growing city.

The directional factors that propel this small, unique women's college in the 21st century seem to center on justice and access. Religious tradition and faith, originally the centerpiece in founding Agnes Scott College, have found their voices through study of these contemporary American issues (E). Students are accepting of ideas that encompass the unknown (N). Graduates expect to become actively engaged with their communities. They anticipate opportunities to solve tomorrow's problems. They expect to bring talent and leadership to the table for this purpose. Agnes Scott graduates are measured and confident at the same time.

In the following listing of college majors it is important to remember that students can fit into any college and can be successful in any major. We have found that the Personality Types below fit very well at this college. The course-of-study

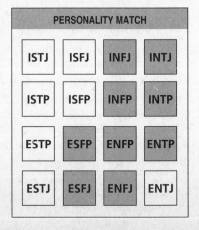

PERSONALITY MATCH

ISTJ	ISFJ	INFJ	INTJ
ISTP	ISFP	INFP	INTP
ESTP	ESFP	ENFP	ENTP
ESTJ	ESFJ	ENFJ	ENTJ

chosen for each Personality Type corresponds to MBTI® research and is presented as one of many examples favorable for that type.

INFP likes to ponder and examine their own values and those of others. This habit is going to be an asset at Agnes Scott. The campus is a blend of modern day American social currents and traditions of past years. It is an environment in which diverse social viewpoints are welcomed. INFP will take notice and appreciate this. The minor in **Educational Studies** prompts discussion about the best ways to develop leadership with moral content for the divisive environments increasingly found in the public school classrooms of this decade.

INFJ is very inclined to follow their beliefs into a profession or work setting and often it is one that helps or cares for others. They have a passion for understanding the human condition, theirs and others. The faculty at Agnes Scott College offers a major or minor in **Religious Studies** that reveals the foundations of religions across the world. Spirituality naturally lends itself to introspection and INFJs prefer to mull their thoughts over with others as they incorporate observations into personal beliefs. Never fear, INFJ is more than up to the challenge of discernment within the department's course offerings that reflect the smorgasbord of spirituality found in many American liberal arts colleges today.

INTJ will likely enjoy the very abstract nature of studying **Biology** at Agnes Scott College. Students approach studies in this major through the lens of process, advanced technology and evolution. Very little is static in the curriculum, and facts are accumulated to find their way into the big picture. Courses in biology at this college require a great deal of intuition in addition to the sweat equity associated with comprehending basic, essential biological processes. The department offers a selection of courses across this growing discipline from evolution, genetics and ecology to botany. It is ideal for INTJ to study biology in this manner.

INTP is drawn to the impossible, well at least the hard-to-understand. The degree in **Physics** should suit INTPs for this reason. The labs and the intense logical reasoning within this science are comfortable arenas for this type. The unknown, at least unseen, nature of the physics generates plenty of abstraction. They have tolerance to dwell on the process within this discipline of physics. But they will not dwell much on the resultant loud bangs, hissing sounds or clouds of unpleasant odors. Again, this is just right for INTP who wants to focus on the how-it-happened rather than the after-the-fact collection of hisses, bangs and odors.

ESFP is often coordinated. This combined with their penchant for entertaining others, including themselves, points to the Agnes Scott major in **Dance.** The college offers an enviable selection of courses in this department. They include lesser known dance concepts such as Laban that present movement as an art form. The curriculum includes a balance of dance forms, dance history, techniques and expression. ESFP will appreciate the versatility of study within this degree at Agnes Scott as well as the career options for performance, teaching and possibly choreography after graduation.

ENFP often desires freedom and intellectual space to pursue their ideas. Business environments that offer this will bring out the entrepreneurial spirit in this type. The degree in **Economics** at Agnes Scott College allows ENFPs to study economic theory and application through the big picture lens. The type's insight and creativity is very helpful with the abstract nature of courses focused on resource allocation.

Spontaneous and enthusiastic, with little patience for getting bogged down, their participation will be positive in college and on the job in the dynamic world of finance.

ENTP can look to the **Mathematics** major to take advantage of their strengths. Mathematics professors are actively connecting math with the power that this discipline brings to society and humankind. ENTP is all about these kinds of very large concepts. Given an inclination for math, ENTP will be willing to declare one of the three math majors offered by the creative faculty in this department. Along the way, any number of interesting applications and careers will fly through the ENTP's active mind. It is likely to give them entry to important work environments and mathematical research applied to improving everyday life.

ESFJ and the **Chemistry** major at Agnes Scott is a duo that can work. The department is focused on practice and development in research design. It is a hands-on experience course of study that is very practical. The major prepares graduates for entrance into medical diagnostic specialties, teaching or pharmaceuticals. Each of these fields can bring ESFJs together directly with those in need of their knowledge and skills. Agnes Scott actively includes experimental research design in their curriculum. This approach often requires collaboration with others and conscientious follow through. Both of these are characteristic strengths of the ESFJ.

ENFJ could be quite happy with the quality and variety of course work in **English** offered at Agnes Scott College. A broad study of literature is excellent training ground for understanding human motivation. Reading between the lines comes naturally for ENFJs as well as analysis of literature. This same set of abilities could also come in handy at discerning social media's influence on emerging literature. Polished and decisive, they will likely move into the world of authorship with confidence.

AMERICAN UNIVERSITY

Office of Admissions
4400 Massachusetts Avenue, NW
Washington, DC 20016
Website: www.american.edu
Admissions Telephone: 202-885-6000
Undergraduates: 6,970; 2,818 Men, 4,152 Women
Graduate Students: 1,433

Physical Environment

Located in the northwest part of the nation's capital, American University takes advantage of its location to observe **Washington DC politics**, the media and socio-economic issues affecting our nation and the world. The campus architecture features many square and rectangular cement buildings that remind us of government structures. The lawns between the buildings are free of flower beds and other frills, except for the occasional bench. The university, increasingly mindful of its historic place in Presidential history, has elected to cancel demolition of the East Quad Building site dedicated by President Dwight D Eisenhower in 1957. The nation's capital invites serious-minded students interested in understanding **substantive issues** that can be acted upon. Politics and history are substantially intertwined at American University. In this setting, undergraduates may be wearing business attire to classes that start after 5:30 pm when adjunct professors in government, non-profits and world organizations are available to lecture.

There are seven residence halls on the main campus. Themed housing is a strong feature at this university and reflects the interests of the student body as well as the university's curriculum. Residential Community Clusters allow 6-18 like-minded students to live together in the dormitory and pursue learning associated with academic objectives. The university's newest building houses the **School of International Service.** Its mission is "waging peace" and undergraduates may be admitted directly as freshmen to this prestigious school. The McKinley building has a striking new addition scheduled for completion in 2014 which will house the School of Communication with a media innovation lab. Since the Washington DC media streams fanciful stories daily, there will be no shortage of video to study for fact and fantasy in this new facility. American University does not fight or ignore **the pull of the city**.

Social Environment

Students who fit in well at American University are **independently motivated** and can achieve their goals. They are not shy and typically take advantage of all that American U and Washington DC have to offer. They will participate in events around the capital, from attending political debates to demonstrations. Students' goals are usually connected with journalism, government, political science and national and international politics.

Undergraduates often come with established leadership skills. They start establishing their network with fellow students hailing from all corners of the world.

Students find a very strong curriculum in foreign languages here. It is easy to seek off-campus venues to become proficient in their chosen language. Many take advantage of courses in the international service programs and school of communication offerings while still majoring in traditional subjects. AU is for students who like to study democracy and most other subjects in a **practical way**, such as analyzing a system of ballot collection. They want to visit historic monuments, attend rallies and report on media events.

In the dorms, students create a home away from home as they forge relationships by introducing themselves to others on their floor. Sports at AU don't monopolize the social scene nor do they define the school spirit. AU is a Division 1 member of the Patriot's League. It has no football but the Eagles basketball and volleyball teams are sufficient to keep fans entertained. It is likely that undergraduates will meet many international students whose family is connected in someway with the nation's capitol, be it taxi driver or **foreign embassy** staff officer.

Compatibility with Personality Types and Preferences

American University is adjacent to the strategic and cultural diplomatic neighborhoods of Washington, DC. For all educational purposes, there is a permeable boundary between this university and the power offices in DC. Prospective students are alerted to the fact that professors often have positions in policy-making throughout the government. The faculty and staff assertively take advantage of their proximity to the nation's capitol. The university has a long-established network which it activates on behalf of its undergraduate students.

Happy students at American University can't wait to step foot in the office (E) of their first internship. Many of these positions are within the halls of the congressional offices but the city also hosts hundreds of national offices for business and other enterprises. Students are exposed to multiple worldwide ethnicities by venturing into the city for entertainment. The American University curriculum is designed for those with a passion plus a driving need to accomplish (J). Those drawn to this university are pretty sure of their convictions. Most desire a career track at international policy levels or within U.S. governmental departments that play across the international scene. Starting out as freshmen they search out the major or minors that move them toward their interests in policy, politics, business, communication, social science, etc. Prior to graduation, students will have well-explored and likely settled in on a career goal (S) such as campaign manager or nonprofit executive. Their international perspectives are refined through the university's academic philosophies and the amazing international presence in the nation's capitol.

In the following listing of college majors it is important to remember that students can fit into any college and can be successful in any major.

PERSONALITY MATCH			
ISTJ	ISFJ	INFJ	INTJ
ISTP	ISFP	INFP	INTP
ESTP	ESFP	ENFP	ENTP
ESTJ	ESFJ	ENFJ	ENTJ

We have found that the Personality Types below fit very well at this college. The course-of-study chosen for each Personality Type corresponds to MBTI® research and is presented as one of many examples favorable for that type.

INTJ is compelled to privately generate new concepts and ideas. The Bachelor of Science degree in **Economics** at American University with an emphasis in theory will be ideal for this type. The coursework is rich with options for theoretical interpretation. It has multiple points of entry to determine an economic perspective. INTJs will take this as an invitation to develop their own scenarios as they carefully grasp information presented in class lectures. This type can do both at once.

ISTP is attracted to facts, details and information that have a practical use. The degree in **Anthropology** at American University has a reality-based focus which suits ISTPs who ordinarily shy away from this abstract field. Looking a few layers deeper, ISTPs realize the discipline has the potential to be an excellent fit. The archeologist, in a subfield of anthropology, searches for hard, specific clues that could reveal much about an ancient city or culture. It is a strongly featured discipline within the department at American University. Internships and work experience in national research libraries such as the Smithsonian and National Museum of American History offer ISTPs the reality base they prefer.

ISTJ is going to like the looks of the minor in **Justice**. At American University, the curriculum leans heavily toward the policy of dealing with crime and deviance across the nation. Coursework focuses on public government functions as it seeks to address systemic corruption in society. ISTJ is practical in their daily work habits and attitudes. They honor fairness and following procedure, and each of these characteristics is quite desirable for a civil service career in justice. ISTJs understand that supporting the criminal justice system is also protecting and serving the community. It is all very appealing to this type who is often dependable and conservative by nature.

INTP can be drawn to mathematics if their endeavors can be used as a tool to solve problems. Considering this, INTP will like a degree such as American University's **Applied Mathematics.** This type is always thinking, always defining and analyzing subjects of interest to them. Undergraduates in this math degree can follow their interests and bring the power of math analysis to research in important national agencies—all within walking or subway stop distance. The National Archives would present tons of options for a research design. This type would probably also enjoy looking at the rare, historical math volumes in the university archives. This collection will surely spark a few minutes of INTP thought about the lives of those earlier mathematicians.

ESTP could go for the **Law and Society** degree at American University because this type has the ability to meet others and quickly establish a working rapport. ESTPs will also find fascinating options for co-op and internships across the DC governmental agencies. This type's desire to learn in a fast-paced, experiential environment affords them the possibility to troubleshoot or bring about a settlement through their skilled negotiation. At American University there is a balance between academic study and hands-on experience. The curriculum is ideal for those desiring to go on to law school and it offers an American as well as international perspective in legal studies. As a result, ESTPs may also explore and could pursue international legal careers.

ESFP is well suited for the 24-hour news cycle. The degree in **Public Communication** at American University is chock-full of arguably the best foundation courses. ESFPs need only to turn on the computer or TV to study the government releases moving across the airwaves in this capital. ESFPs live and work in the present day and the current week. They are not inclined to give much attention to the distant future. Instead, they superbly pick up on what is going on around them, not missing a beat. They typically relay that observation with enthusiasm and social finesse. This degree—at this university—for this type—is a stellar choice.

ENTP loves to look into the future with other interested students and a professor who is willing to listen. The degree in **Computational Science** offers the complexity and rewards that suit their leadership style. Speculation is an ENTP's forte, so the larger and more abstract the organizational problem, the more the solution calls for their forte and computer modeling. The curriculum here requires application within the natural sciences, social sciences or engineering. The nation's capital is a marketplace for organizational problems and this is just the challenge ENTP loves.

ESFJ is most often the cheerleader for an organization. They reliably pull for the team rewarding both the fans and players for their participation. Students in the elementary classroom thrive with a teacher who so rewards and appreciates traditional effort and duty. The degree in **Elementary Education** at American University has an exceptionally fine program for future teachers. Undergraduates will spend considerable time observing and practice teaching in urban and suburban DC schools. The ethical emphasis for public educators in our society to empower and enlighten the next generation is a focus of American's curriculum. Very social, almost always pleasant, ESFJs bring stability and caring to their classrooms, yet it will be their curiosity about others that might draw them into educational research.

ESTJ wants to live the responsible and sensible life—in the dorm, in college classes and thereafter. Order is a need and usually a talent for this type. Take charge ESTJs would enjoy the precise nature of the scientific courses in the medical health fields. The Bachelor of Science in **Health Promotion** is bolstered with strategic internships in DC, perhaps with the Department of Health and Human Services. ESTJs will find the interdisciplinary nature of the curriculum helpful because of the regular exposure to specializations within the broad health field. The degree also leaves open the door for graduate work in medical research. The university sponsors research in human performance with a state of the art laboratory that focuses on diagnostic practices.

ENTJ with a political passion quickly recognizes that American University has several degrees tailored specifically for their strengths and interests. The degree in **Political Science** has a rich and unique curriculum. Unusual courses in the curriculum include Ancient Political Thought that examines the world of Socrates, Plato, Aristotle and ancient Roman law not from the philosophical perspective but from political, civic views. Metropolitan Politics covers the political nature of the city with its suburbs rather than the social nature of the city. ENTJs are power players themselves and would not shrink from the deterministic nature of this discipline. The Peace and Conflict Resolution semester held at American University will also help ENTJ prepare for a career in politics or government.

AMHERST COLLEGE

P.O. Box 5000
Amherst, MA 01002-5000
Website: www.amherst.edu
Admissions Telephone: 413-542-2328
Undergraduates: 1,817; 931 Men, 886 Women

Physical Environment

The beautiful Amherst campus spreads out over 1,000 acres, overlooking the Holyoke mountain range of western Massachusetts. Students enjoy the sweeping views and use the many hiking trails. Plants and well-aged trees on the campus create a similar garden feel as at Emily Dickinson's nearby home. Some of the Amherst students are drawn away from their books by this type of **literary setting**. Another nostalgic venue came with renovation of the old powerhouse that was converted recently for student use.

The heavy feel of the traditional, permanent red brick buildings across the campus is at odds with the curriculum which regularly evolves. However, an easy architectural escape from red bricks and Amherst's plainer, new architecture is the charming, artsy town of Amherst right outside their door. A few undergrads will be attracted to the hustle and bustle of social activates at the large state university in town also. A small number of undergraduates take the shuttle bus to the other campuses for courses that cross register with the **Five College Consortium.**

Social Environment

Amherst College is an ideal setting for students who like to be big fish in a small pond and love to learn. There are many **talented equals** on this campus, and yet all are noticed. They are interested in almost everything, they learn to become proficient at problem solving and they easily draw **logical conclusions**. They have the ability to discern what is missing and are likely to question agendas such as Amherst's Colloquium on American Founding Fathers. It now seems to feature topics on marriage and the Middle East in 2013, despite its name and original purpose. International perspectives infuse most if not all of the curriculum on campus with faculty coming from around the globe. It is not uncommon to see American exceptionalism questioned as a valid concept within courses such as The War of 1898: US Empire in the Caribbean and Pacific.

The heavy **academic rigor** required for study on this campus channels the social life of the student body, composed primarily of high school valedictorians. Comfortable in the **world of ideas**, these bright and self-directed students form a vibrant and diverse community of leaders. Amherst students are comfortable socializing across varied social and economic backgrounds as well as addressing pluralistic issues. This shapes their perspectives as they chart their individual course of liberal studies. Amherst students can be super-studious and **intense,** even overly-invested in their studies. Yet they tend to also be efficient at finding time to analyze the broad issues facing the world's future. Reality is never far from their thoughts or this campus.

Undergraduate students here arrived as freshmen with outstanding academic qualifications and individual accomplishments.

Compatibility with Personality Types and Preferences

With its orderly approach to offering a unique and wide ranging curriculum, Amherst appeals to personalities that are comfortable with structure and accountability (J). At the same time, there is a wide, free range of choice within the pathways of any particular major or course of studies. A personality that prefers to rationally analyze (T) will appreciate the foundation courses typically found in each discipline. They afford the tools to tackle that complex interdisciplinary subject matter of upper class course work. Students with a love of facts and details (S) will find this strength helps them with the 'accountability' piece and the sheer academic production that will be required at this most selective liberal arts college.

Students on this campus learn by lively discussion and free exchange of ideas. They equally converse with each other and faculty. They observe, read, discuss, observe some more, read some more and exhaustively survey the foundations within a discipline. Then there is an internal mandate within the undergraduate student body that each individual will analyze the heck out of that foundational information, the point of this analysis being to plumb the depths and to create new knowledge, to synthesize a personal understanding.

The administration and faculty believe this process takes place primarily on campus. The libraries, coffee shops, dormitories, lecture halls and professor's offices are all fair game for learning locations. Basically at Amherst learning occurs anywhere that is sufficiently free of distractions which could sidetrack the student from reaching the most comprehensive understanding of their discipline. Undergraduates must master their own major as well as develop a significant understanding outside of their declared discipline. On the journey through this reasoned learning environment, students receive sufficient, occasional reminders of the difficult world that awaits them on graduation. Their open, wide-ranging academic experience at Amherst College mirrors cross cultural influences upon policy and practice in unsettled, dynamic America.

In the following listing of college majors it is important to remember that students can fit into any college and can be successful in any major. We have found that the Personality Types below fit very well at this college. The course-of-study chosen for each Personality Type corresponds to MBTI® research and is presented as one of many examples favorable for that type.

ISFJ with a spiritual bent will like the **Religion** major at Amherst College. This very caring and attentive type will find the structure they need to comfortably work with their advisor in this abstract field. Three areas are required for mastery that allow undergraduates to successfully pursue graduate study.

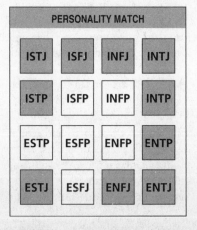

PERSONALITY MATCH

ISTJ	ISFJ	INFJ	INTJ
ISTP	ISFP	INFP	INTP
ESTP	ESFP	ENFP	ENTP
ESTJ	ESFJ	ENFJ	ENTJ

They are precise knowledge of one particular religion, general knowledge of a second religion and the skills for prescient research in this historical discipline that strikes at the heart and soul of mankind. The department offers coursework with a strong grounding in Judeo-Christian spirituality.

ENTP will be attracted to the **Law, Jurisprudence and Social Thought** major. They like to jump into difficult, wide-ranging discussions that have few finite truths. In the course titled Law, Speech and the Politics of Freedom, Amherst students attempt to make sense of the multiple interpretations of the words 'free,' 'speech' and 'speaker.' With those in place they move on to define dangerous, anarchic, politically correct speech and public discourse. It is all to understand critical components of modern day civilizations.

INTJ with a penchant for mathematics will probably make room in the schedule for **Philosophy of Mathematics**. This course explores the three philosophies of math that evolved in the 20th century—logicism, intuitionism and finitism. This personality preference is great at mulling over the possibilities privately, in their mind, as they stroll across a quadrangle to dinner. Perhaps during dessert they will come up with an experimental algorithm for pushing math philosophy forward into new purposes for the 21st century.

ENFJ finds that no matter what major they select, their idealism will be honored in the **Five College African Studies Certificate Program**. It complements any major selected at Amherst. Diplomatic and ideal, ENFJs would could happily work for organizations providing services on the African continent. Improving and focusing on community and generating basic human services come naturally to this type.

INTP can become absorbed in the **Physics Department** approach to the major. Their course offerings delve into the past, recreate landmark experiments by masters such as Faraday, allow students to discover the results and interface their observations with the current and emerging theories in physics today. New technology in laser application and photonics is clearly something that would appeal to this curious, flexible, deep-thinking type.

INFJ could conclude that **Architectural Studies** at Amherst College leads to a career focused on human needs. The design and function of our workplace buildings, neighborhoods and our homes is gaining more attention through the sustainability movement. This type will find the solitude and underlying theory that accompanies studying design for human habitation very appealing. They will have little trouble defending and advocating for their architectural designs. The major is offered through the Five College Consortium.

ISTP might like the **Film and Media Studies** major. The courses which explore film and video are compelling and allow this technical personality preference to delve into the digital techniques producing the moving image. Marching to their own drummer, ISTPs want freedom to create an individualized program of study. Amherst College is more than supportive since film and video courses appear throughout the curriculum such as the Weimar Cinema: The Golden Age of German Film found in courses listed by the German department.

ESTJ will be on time to make the required early declaration in the **Neuroscience** major at Amherst College. This type understands and approves of preplanning with a goal. The elbow grease and interdisciplinary nature of the courses in this major work perfectly as preparation for post graduate study in medicine, law and the sciences. ESTJs can see the sense in the well-structured, somewhat foundational and somewhat novel work required in this major.

ISTJ could find that **Psychology** at Amherst is going to work because of the academic depth and breadth in the department. ISTJs like to become masterful in their selected courses. It is not surprising that the alpha to omega is covered by the Amherst curriculum in this fast-evolving field. Courses reach into the study of memory, the psychology of leadership, rigorous research methods and more. The way psychology is taught at Amherst is ideal for this type because of the extensive exposure and preparation to successfully pursue the PhD level of studies. ISTJs find research in the psychological discipline rewarding because of its precise nature.

ENTJ will appreciate the extraordinary breadth and currency of the curriculum offered through the **Economics** department at Amherst. From game theory to the economics of poverty to the nuts and bolts of micro and macroeconomics, the faculty and courses present a sweeping look at this complex discipline. ENTJs rarely shy away from complexity or large concepts. In fact, they thrive on elements inherent to demanding social movements within our society. Studying the human weave between politics, policy and resources is likely to compel young, energetic ENTJs.

BATES COLLEGE

23 Campus Avenue
Lewiston, ME 04240-6098
Website: www.bates.edu
Admissions Telephone: 207-786-6000
Undergraduates: 1,769; 836 Men, 933 Women

Physical Environment

Bates College is located in the Lewiston area, about 35 miles north of Portland. These are former mill-towns that grew on the banks of the river during the industrial revolution. Although most students stay on campus during the weekend, there are restaurants and malls within a short distance where students buy top quality winter clothing and gear. There are many opportunities for **outdoor recreation** and students participate and compete in regional alpine and cross-country skiing. Students like hands-on experience and utilize the **coastal Maine environment** to conduct chemistry and geology research, learning first hand with nature. The 109-acre Bates campus is surrounded by a residential neighborhood with a very small lake in the center. Fondly called "**the puddle**," students **skate and play hockey** during wintertime on it while others sit warmly within the glass-fronted academic buildings watching the entertainment. The architecture is a mixture of modern and historic buildings. The Dining Commons hall, a starkly modern building, has multi-story windows with pretty views of the alumni walk and the trees on campus. Plans call for the familiar Chase Hall, an old, well-worn facility that felt soft and warm in comparison to the new architecture on campus, to regain its place on campus as a contemporary student center. Along with new dormitories slated for completion in 2016, Bates continues to nicely define spaces with the outdoors in sight and mind. The Hedge - Williams Project furthers Bates academic philosophy by providing social learning spaces designed for faculty and students to informally cross paths.

Creative students are drawn to the Olin Arts Center, by the pond, which has an art museum, a theater and music and fine arts studios. The sofas and lounge areas add a comfortable feel to this building for the eclectic, imaginative Bates student.

Social Environment

Bates students are somewhat **different from one another**. They arrive on campus with surprisingly varied interests and an insatiable curiosity. They are seekers. They don't exactly follow the status quo. They leave high school personas behind and become socially and intellectually driven students in an alternative style. Those students who were into intellectual Goth or Anime in high school find that on this campus they are embraced and accepted for their open and unique artistic qualities. On the edge of being ironic, students here are comfortable criticizing the day to day rhythms of daily life, even to their professors with whom they become close. Students often drip with **tongue in cheek humor**, as they comment on politically correct currents often apparent at selective liberal arts colleges in America today.

While students may have bought into traditional or conventional social activities in high school, here they want to do something new, different. They look to craft an exciting, intellectually rigorous course of study that shapes their beliefs and time on campus. Students appreciate using their **fine-tuned writing** and computing skills. There is a certain sense of relaxation in students here, who are laid-back, comfortable in their skin and free to be what they want. There's also a spiritual thread across the curriculum and the students seek to apply moral principles to what they learn. They **examine their purpose in life**. Students embrace the ideals of freedom and equality. The majority of undergraduates are service-oriented and volunteer in local, state, regional and/or national venues. Bates undergrads voice their individuality from the get go with most of them opting not to submit SAT scores which isn't mandatory at this campus that is pleasing to those who march to a discordant tune once in a while.

Compatibility with Personality Types and Preferences

Bates College is bold. The B equals Bold **X** Bates². In many ways it is like a formula, a straight-forward campus. The administration is likewise. Few collegiate curriculums bring attention to Catholicism's role copying ancient documents, otherwise lost to history, during the medieval period in northern Europe. The students also are on the cutting edge of straight-forward. Unconventional and grounded, Bates undergraduates are in your face if you care to stand in front of them. They are confident in their edginess (P). The courses of instruction here are very interesting. One could say the courses are bold too. The titles keep your eyes glued to the catalog page: Roller Coasters - Theory, Design and Properties, Crusader Art and Architecture, Frontier and Border in US Literature. The above are offered in addition to traditional coursework for the degrees in math, classics and American Studies. Humor must be a staple in the coffees here.

The faculty and administration have constructed numerous service learning options (F) and tied these together with moral perspectives. It's a win-win situation because so many of the students are involved in service work. The campus environment seems devoted to the future (N). As a result, the compelling nature of the learning environment is to construct a better future. Bates undergraduates look to the present world conditions with a discerning eye. They travel through their undergraduate studies to gain a personal platform of knowledge, skills and finesse. It is their goal to enter the evolving marketplace of career fields on graduation with a knowing, disciplined look at the future.

In the following listing of college majors it is important to remember that students can fit into any college and can be successful in any major. We have found that the Personality Types below fit very well at this college. The course-of-study chosen for each Personality Type corresponds to MBTI® research and is presented as one of many examples favorable for that type.

ISFP and the major in **Biology** move in tandem together nicely on this campus. This type likes to mix it up outside with activity

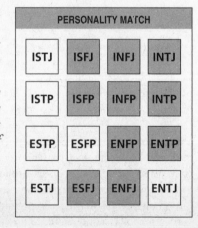

PERSONALITY MATCH

ISTJ	ISFJ	INFJ	INTJ
ISTP	ISFP	INFP	INTP
ESTP	ESFP	ENFP	ENTP
ESTJ	ESFJ	ENFJ	ENTJ

and variety. The courses of instruction here are unconventional with many hands-on labs in the open fields and forests of Maine. The quiet and accepting ISFP will fit well into the unconventional ways. At the same time, this type has a real need to develop their deeply held values. Bates' philosophy of education interfaces with moral perspectives.

INFP might like the **African American Studies** at Bates College. The courses of instruction are particularly rich here. This reflects the administration philosophy which is strongly tolerant, almost, but not quite, Quaker-like. Regardless of ethnicity, the INFP will delight in the depth and breadth of this course of study. On graduation, they would be exceptionally well qualified for organizations pursuing African American perspectives in the work place.

ENFJ has a penchant for the dramatic. This type's fine ability to connect with others could be further fine tuned with Bates major in **Rhetoric.** The undergraduate can select a concentration in theory and criticism or film and television studies. Either way, the ENFJ will naturally excel at presenting information in a way that helps others. The Bates Quimby Debate Council places regularly in competition at the International Debate Education Association.

ESFJ is likely to be concerned by the honest review of American public schools in the course Educating for Democracy. With the Bates 'tell it like it is' approach to social criticism, the course calls attention to alienation within today's voters and our youth also. The minor in **Education Studies** does not shy from the provoking issues in elementary and secondary education. It presents a rich selection of courses for ESFJ who is always curious about others and genuine in helping them move forward.

ENFP would likely excel as a research assistant in academic environments. How about the **American Cultural Studies** as a potential major for this fun-loving type? It is an interdisciplinary program and ENFP gets to pick the exciting courses in each field. Maybe they will register for Story of Things - Introduction to Material Culture, or Gibbons, The Decline and Fall of the Roman Empire. This last book prompts complex conversation about western civilization and American history.

ISFJ will probably appreciate the expansive courses available in the **Religious Studies** major. Emphasis is placed on cultural expressions of faith other than Western civilization and Christianity. Mystic literature, medieval religious practices, Greek and Roman Myths and ancient gods guide the religious studies into a historical and cultural perspective. Reflective and calm, ISFPs will likely gather in this curriculum and quietly construct their spiritual and religious thoughts into a personal, cohesive belief.

INFJ with artistic interests will find the **Art and Visual Culture** major quite desirable. The studies are likely to be dripping with symbolism here. There is a solid inclusion of European arts which are thinly represented at some liberal arts colleges. With this major, the INFJ might move into the world of visual design. This type's independence and creativity will be strong assets for developing public and private events at galleries, museums, corporations and civic associations.

INTJ will find academic roaming room in the **Psychology** major at Bates College. There are four content areas: biological-health, developmental-personality, cognition-emotion and cultural-social. These four allow the undergraduate INTJ to survey the discipline while looking for that exploratory nook within the expanse of human personality. This type likes to ponder and is likely to come up with new avenues for research en route to a PhD in psychology or perhaps neuroscience.

INTP who selected high school math courses with a purpose should look into **Mathematics** at Bates College. The faculty presents this subject with excitement, interest and honest enthusiasm. Though this type doesn't need the extra motivation, the nature of unsolved solutions in math equations will keep INTPs busy searching for patterns and answers throughout their four undergraduate years. Chaotic Dynamical Systems calls out loudly to this type.

ENTP has a pretty deep reservoir of energy for their projects. This type with some talent for numbers will enjoy studying **Economics** at Bates College. With the basics of micro and macroeconomics completed, the ENTP can further focus with the course, International Financial Stability. Charged up by finding ways out of financial crises could become a career for this type!

BELOIT COLLEGE

Office of Admission
700 College Street
Beloit, WI 53511
Website: www.beloit.edu
Admissions Telephone: 608-363-2500
Undergraduates: 1,359; 553 Men, 806 Women

Physical Environment

"You don't voluntarily move to Wisconsin" says a Beloit student who comes from California, however, this is where she felt **compelled to come.** The college is on the Wisconsin-Illinois line and is accessible from the airports of Chicago, Milwaukee and Madison. The city of Beloit is rather quiet, recalling its earlier paper and pulp industry now transitioning to artistic and niche enterprises. The campus is located in a residential neighborhood near the town center. Beloit College was designed by a group of prominent folks from New England and hence it has a northeastern look to its architecture.

Some students live in **special interest houses** around the perimeter of campus mostly in old Victorian and Colonial homes. Rarely larger than 10 students each, they form their own small communities bound by common interests. There are a few Greek houses as well, and they focus on community service initiatives. Most first-year students live in freshman housing. The state of the art science complex was designed around learning laboratories and promotes collaborative work. It is conveniently adjacent to the living, fitness and academic areas of the campus. The Beloit art and anthropology museums offer students a real life experience as curators as well as exhibiting artists. These museums are open to the community and add an intellectual and **artistic influence** to this small community composed of college and city. The Hendricks Center for the Arts is a delight for musicians, dancers and artistic technophiles complete with a lighting design studio.

Social Environment

High school students who moved outside of the conventional high school social groups like Beloit College because here it's perfectly all right to have "your own sort of interests" and to express them in "your own way." Undergraduates here want to continue avoiding tradition. They mostly embrace a **very crunchy and artsy lifestyle** or politically express themselves by leaning to the left of center. The administration follows suit utilizing considerable resources gifted and focused on left of center politics such as the Weissberg Program. Beloit emphasizes international perspectives and curriculum is often directed at seeking knowledge outside of the national experience. Students accept that everyone is honored for their different talents here. A good number choose the vegetarian way.

Some within the community seek harmony and are less likely to strike out in nontraditional directions. They focus on their academic studies. Incoming students might declare a passion for molecular biology and research but quickly change over to political science. The reality is that many students are change-oriented and proud of it. There is a strong desire to live and practice what they learn so they are attracted to advocacy within the campus environment. They support activity like sustainable gardening or establish special interest housing such as the French Slow Food house. Students at their core are **sensitive, caring and searching** for other possible ways of understanding community. The smallness of this community helps them try out and practice those concepts.

The college supports this personal examination by reintroducing familiar content but with completely fresh levels of interpretation. Beloit College is likely to open up many options for students so it's not unnatural for them to change their majors. The town of Beloit in some ways is a traditional in rural America, so the college encourages international studies and travel by these undergrads. The interesting student personalities on campus add their own spice to the educational studies. Graduates look to the world of employment and expect to be productive in their careers, well equipped to support the arts and service organizations within their spheres.

Compatibility with Personality Types and Preferences

Beloit College is dedicated to reasoned learning. While the faculty and administration remain open to many perspectives (P), students are expected to arrive at their own cohesive view of the world. There are many avenues that provide encouragement to examine national and world perspectives for this purpose. Students explore their beliefs through the lens of their academic courses and service to the community both on and off campus. Often topics and extracurricular events at Beloit College will be addressed from a humane point of view (F). Some undergrads become socially active and refine their perspectives into clubs and events that support their views. There is a hands-on, observational approach to the course work. Students move through their educational studies with a measured process, observing, collecting and arranging information into personal meaningful knowledge. The campus academic energy channels this type of analysis in a way that is intense, articulate and caring. Conversations can be free-wheeling and oriented from many directions, but students are definitely reaching for a position throughout their academic studies that will lead to employment and a meaningful career. At Beloit, there is an ever present undercurrent to an individual's purpose in life that translates to careful selection of next semesters courses. Undergraduates tend toward the unknown, less understood subjects because they offer a new filter to understand what they observe. The successful student at Beloit College is one who does not feel bound to a familiar, traditional college major. Rather there is a tension to add in an unexpected elective. There is also commitment to learning with fellow students who are also on their quest to build an individual view of the world. Graduates have a sensitive, reasoned and reflective approach to life's work.

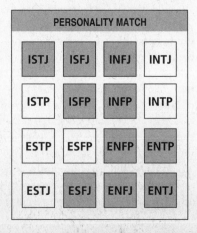

PERSONALITY MATCH			
ISTJ	ISFJ	INFJ	INTJ
ISTP	ISFP	INFP	INTP
ESTP	ESFP	ENFP	ENTP
ESTJ	ESFJ	ENFJ	ENTJ

In the following listing of college majors it is important to remember that students can fit into any college and can be successful in any major. We have found that the Personality Types below fit very well at this college. The course-of-study chosen for each Personality Type corresponds to MBTI® research and is presented as one of many examples favorable for that type.

INFP should find the study of **Geology** appeals to their creativity. The discipline is wide open for specialization and the department faculty nicely surveys all the foundational land forms within the four-year curriculum. This type will become committed to an area of interest that is connected with human development as well. Beloit campus is ideal for interfacing this solid, observable science with human perspectives.

INFJ often brings compassion and idealism to studies. The major in **International Political Economy** suits them well. The department keeps the curriculum flexible. Undergraduates must reach their own perspective of world economies and learn of ways to interface their understanding in the international worlds of business, profit, non-profit and nongovernmental organizations. The department tends toward a holistic approach to international economies. The INFJ is fine with this. They can be creative, caring and proud of their work. All three are pretty important for this type.

ISTJ will find the **Molecular, Cellular and Integrative Biology** major focuses on proposing and probing hypotheses. It is an orderly, structured discovery of what is there for the observer. This is an ideal way for ISTJs to learn. This type is considered and reasoned in their approach to learning and Beloit is a fine collegiate environment for their learning style. Though they are not inclined to be alternative in thinking, the ISTJ will relate to the reasoning process which is so prevalent on this campus. This major will give them a traditional preparation for graduate school in the health sciences.

ISFJ wants to express their convictions in a low key way. This type is also a master at details with a fabulous memory for those details. The major in **Science for Elementary Teaching** at Beloit College is an excellent choice for this type. Their content course work in the biology department approaches learning through analysis of what can be observed. This type's appreciation of fine detail will be such an asset in this precise field. Their inclination to find personal meaning through quiet reflection will be rewarded on this campus of searchers for life's truths.

ISFP will find the art department at Beloit College particularly rich with expansive thinking. The **Studio Art** major is very much connected to process learning. The process of communicating within the art is a focus. Written and oral communication underlies the technical courses in drawing and design. Peer feedback is a regular part of this curriculum as it highlights the message being sent by the artist. Well, that is just swell for ISFP who wants to be a loyal and cooperative member of the community. At Beloit, individual perspectives are encouraged, and feedback will be measured and supportive. Again, this is just swell for ISFP.

ENFP can keep the options open with the unusual major in **Education and Youth Studies** by selecting the Youth and Society track. This concentration prepares students for graduate study in a surprising number of fields: law, social work, mental health, art, coaching, adolescent health services and family research. The ENFP will probably want to sample coursework in most of these. Beloit College requires a full term of field work. ENFP will look on this as an opportunity to select the most interesting research connected with youth services. This type has the vision to align their educational goals with pertinent research of interest to them in the field.

ENTP could be attracted to the major in **Business Economics** at Beloit College. Typically, the core course work required of business majors would not excite ENTP. However, Beloit College combines the fundamentals found in business with economic theory. Add in the touch of required international courses, developing written communication to convey business analysis and the student managed Belmark Associates and you may capture the ENTP imagination.

ESFJ will really like the approach to learning **Chemistry** at Beloit. The department is determined to bring the abstract nature of this field into the labs. Much of the course work is based in inquiry and experimentation using sophisticated instruments found in newer research labs. By replicating recent research designs, students at Beloit follow the chemical pathways through the reactions. The department brings forth those actual experiments to focus on the microscopic behavior of materials. It is a nice companion and contrast to more experimental laboratory foundations. ESFJ will appreciate this practical, real avenue of learning for the detailed yet abstract world of chemistry.

ENFJ has the enthusiasm and energy to work with today's teenagers in middle schools. The department devotes curricula and coursework heavily toward the **Adolescents and Schools** track. ENFJ's will get the classroom experience needed in this field as well as applied concepts in motivation, theory and middle school pedagogy. Their warmth and creativity while problem solving will be in much demand.

ENTJ could really appreciate the foundational approach to the expanding, interdisciplinary field of **Psychology.** This field is growing by leaps and bounds looking to explain human behavior in connection with other more traditional sciences like biology and chemistry. This expansive thinking is exactly what ENTJ does very naturally. This type likes to wrap-it-up after a meaningful exploration of the issue at hand. Not spontaneous by inclination, they will however calculate and skip over information along the way. At Beloit, the major in Psychology will prepare this type to move on to graduate study. It also refines ENTJ's natural ability to reason through human behavioral patterns, ask meaningful questions and arrive at certain positions.

BOSTON COLLEGE

140 Commonwealth Avenue
Chestnut Hill, MA 02467
Website: www.bc.edu
Admissions Telephone: 617-552-3100
Undergraduates: 9,686; 4,572 Men, 5,114 Women
Graduate Students: 4,700

Physical Environment

All it takes is just a walk through the campus of Boston College for most high school juniors and seniors to fall in love with this university. The view from the main entrance is dotted by the mature trees lining the way to the tower of newly remodeled Gasson Hall. In 1913, it was the first classroom building on campus, and students studied "recitation," the art of memorizing and public speaking. The collegiate Gothic architecture is repeated in other buildings such as the Burns Library that houses rare manuscripts and antique books. The campus physically has a **spiritual feel** parallel to the presence of the Jesuit fathers, many of whom teach classes, hold mass services and interact with students.

The football stadium holds over 44,500 spectators and is a popular place for these **sporty students** and alumni who go all out for their teams and have fanned many victories since the football team joined the Atlantic Coast Conference. The Flynn recreation center is also a favorite place for many students who like intramural sports and want to **keep fit**. Stokes Hall, opened in 2013, was designed to increase collaboration between the departments of classical studies, English, history, philosophy and theology. Its striking stone edifice speaks to the importance and solidarity in these abstract disciplines of knowledge. The Boston College campus is surrounded by a mature neighborhood of upscale homes and estates. There is public transportation outside the entrance to upper campus. It's the last stop and turn-around for the T, a trolley that runs down the middle of **Commonwealth Avenue**. It is usually packed with students from other nearby universities, the Boston Common, coffee shops and rental apartments in this popular college town.

In the past fifteen or so years, Boston College has experienced significant enrollment growth in both its undergraduate and graduate programs. There are four distinct campus centers at Boston College, Newton, Brighton and Lower Campuses all with undergraduate housing. Middle Campus is strictly academic. The college provides regular bus service to get back and forth. There are five different bus routes, including a Grocery Shuttle! Getting around Boston demands foot, bus, subway and cars. Students will use all of these and often.

Social Environment

Students at Boston College were high achievers in high school. They carry their ambitions on to college and add an intense and dynamic feel to the classroom and social life. Students from a **Catholic** background are comfortable here, as are others who are open to taking religion as part of the required core of classes. There are many students whose parents graduated from Boston College, although being a legacy is not enough to gain a spot on the admitted list.

Students come to this college to **study and play hard**. Irish and Italian ethnic perspectives run strongly throughout the student body. Social life is active, vibrant and abundant. Students here care about their grades, preparation for a rewarding career and **intend to be successful** on graduation. They take full advantage of the **exceptional career advising** by faculty.

The Jesuit presence on campus sets the tone for tolerance of alternative behavior with an underlying moral foundation. An ethical education is part of the curriculum and student life. **Service to the community** is very important here and virtually no one graduates without having done a considerable amount of work to benefit others in the community. It may be why BC graduates remain a close-knit group of people who support one another up to and after graduation.

Compatibility with Personality Types and Preferences

Boston College with its four undergraduate divisions delineates academic disciplines (T) in a traditional manner for undergraduate students. Students must declare admission to one of four undergraduate divisions on their application: Arts and Sciences, Management, Education or Nursing. This approach to admission typically attracts students who know what academic concentration they intend to pursue (S). However, applicants do not necessarily need to declare a major and they will be considered as applying for the College of Arts and Sciences. In our world that is becoming more cross disciplinary, the college offers a unique advising program that strongly guides students to identify potential careers. This is in opposition to the more common experience of an undergraduate taking a course in one of the social sciences or arts and directly abandoning their earlier intent to major in the physical sciences. At Boston College the advising process occurs throughout four years of education. Through one-on-one discussion with student and professors information is offered for exploration. The greatest advising focus for first year students is through the faculty offering their experience and knowledge. Off campus retreats and programs specifically for students also connect academic majors with potential careers.

The city of Boston plays a large part in the nature of academic advising and career exploration. The city lures prospective students for its limitless activities. Once they arrive on campus as freshmen, the undergraduates live in figurative and literal city noise that permeates their college experience. The frequent trips on the green line to downtown and the excitement of city life must be woven into the traditional academic coursework. The successful Boston College student is one who can balance these two while incorporating spiritual and moral perspectives within their educational studies. Students come with

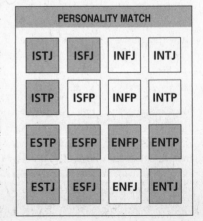

PERSONALITY MATCH

ISTJ	ISFJ	INFJ	INTJ
ISTP	ISFP	INFP	INTP
ESTP	ESFP	ENFP	ENTP
ESTJ	ESFJ	ENFJ	ENTJ

the expectation that values supporting society will be honored, valued and interfaced with their education.

In the following listing of college majors it is important to remember that students can fit into any college and can be successful in any major. We have found that the Personality Types below fit very well at this college. The course-of-study chosen for each Personality Type corresponds to MBTI® research and is presented as one of many examples favorable for that type.

ESTJ will find the **Accounting** concentration at BC very well tuned to organizations, public and private, international and local, that require sophisticated audits. ESTJs approve of accountability and responsibility so this is a natural fit. They are also objective and typically capable of cutting to the heart of matters efficiently. The Carroll School of Management is well resourced and this accounting major will be well complimented by other majors in the school. Socially, ESTJ is likely to summon their no nonsense approach to keep enticing Boston events in balance with academics.

ISTJ after college graduation will not likely mind putting on the professional garb and providing accurate, organized and timely services to the customers. The concentration in **Finance** offers the very opportunities which ISTJs excel at—understanding large organizational system. Boston College offers a solid array of introductory and advanced classes in this important discipline that ever-prepared ISTJs will want and jump right into from the first day of classes. Relying on their sense of loyalty and fabulous memories, they move through the cumulative courses and secure a financial body of knowledge they so need and prize on graduation.

ENTJ will make good use of the concentration in **Corporate Reporting and Analysis**. This type is skilled in leadership and capable of good intuitive observations applied to the near term future. The sequence of courses in this major will prepare often savvy ENTJs to navigate the crucial monetary patterns in financial corporations. Socially, this type will want to be where the action is occurring and that is in the vibrant financial district in downtown Boston during the day and lively suburbs on the weekend.

ENFP might find the **Communication** major at BC very well suited to their style. The curriculum is a solid and somewhat unusual combination of theory and some practical course work. ENFPs are abstract thinkers that need variety. Lectures addressing the theory of how information flows will be enticing for this type. Courses that interface the nuts and bolts of TV productions provide the fun they need too. At BC, discourse on ethics in the media will also rivet ENFP attention. This type will be energized by fun activities in the city, yet will often remain on campus as frequent participants in student life.

ISFJ will appreciate the degree in **Nursing** at BC with so many top-notch hospitals within subway distance. Internships are accessible and this type will appreciate the one-on-one contact with patients. The degree includes a strong curriculum in diagnosing, therapy and ethical issues. The ISFJ with their deeply held personal values will strongly relate to the moral perspectives at this catholic college. There will be ample opportunities for off campus retreats offered to undergraduates for advising. When time permits, this type will step out into Boston life, but only after all other responsibilities are met.

ESFJ can take advantage of the major in **Secondary Education.** Boston's many neighborhoods with different ethnic influences are available for the teaching practicum. This is an exceptionally strong program and the graduate will have a solid grounding in classroom management. Curriculum reflects the difficulties found in American classrooms today. The requirement to double major allows this conscientious type to be thoroughly prepared in the high school classroom. Always a loyal team member, they will support BC through volunteer community service or cheering at the football games.

ENTP will like the flexible nature of the **General Management** program at BC. ENTPs can select two areas from among accounting, information systems, finance, marketing, organization studies or operations technology management. The field research options within the city's financial district are exceptional. With this type of experience, ENTPs with this concentration will have credibility to enter national financial management firms. ENTP vision can be pretty clear when it is resting on accurate information. Their exciting, risk-taking nature also works well in the world of business.

ESFP will call upon their outgoing, enthusiastic style in the **Marketing** concentration at BC. Students practice and incorporate communication theory during the course of studies. Obviously, their talkative nature will be a natural asset. Linking consumer interests to products and services within business organizations is quite enjoyable for ESFP's with an entrepreneurial sense. Totally thorough in its curriculum, BC ensures this graduate understands factors in the research, pricing, managerial accounting and retail buying decisions of the products that they are promoting.

ISTP has the option to pursue employment or research with the **Geological Sciences** major. In either case, ISTPs get to head straight for the labs and practical projects. This type will volunteer to head out to the field with instruments, set them up and live in a tent next to the gadgets until the data is recorded accurately. In respect to Boston social life, they are likely to head into town with a few close friends and show up for the major BC social activities. Otherwise, catch them jury-rigging gadgets in the dorm room.

ESTP and **Operations Management** are a good fit. Competition and fast-paced markets demand across-the-board acumen in manufacturing and service organizations. This type understands the competition and the fast pace. They are excellent at networking and troubleshooting. ESTP is also excellent at pulling together a deal among competing team members. The actual reading and lectures might tax some ESTPs, yet there will be good opportunities to get out into Boston's businesses for outstanding job training. While they are putting in a full day at the office, they will also likely join the office staff for afterhours socializing. The line between learning, working and socializing is intermittent for this gregarious type!

BOSTON UNIVERSITY

121 Bay State Road
Boston, MA 02215
Website: www.bu.edu
Admissions Telephone: 617-353-2300
Undergraduates: 18,206; 7,219 Men, 10,987 Women
Graduate Students: 14,297

Physical Environment

Boston University stretches along Storrow Drive which flanks the Charles River, and the Mass Pike on the south side. Commonwealth Avenue crosses the campus from Kenmore Square on the east side to Babcock Street on the west side by the university track and tennis center. This is a **very urban campus** and students who love it, **love Boston**. University shuttle buses are large, convenient, cool in the summer and offer the warm alternative to walking in chilly winter winds. Nearby Fenway Park, home of the Red Sox, Newbury Street and Kenmore Square attract high school graduates who want to dress with flair and increase their city smarts. Undergraduates **learn to navigate Boston quickly**. When it's sunny and warm, they may go to the "beach," an area by the law school that flanks the Fenway with the heavy flow of cars substituting for the sound of ocean waves.

The university is tightly constrained by the city neighborhoods and highways. It successfully plans renovations and new construction that offer smart, clean environments which negate some of the city grime and congestion. The Sargeant Activities Center holds multiple support offices for undergrads and, of course, is a vertical building, six stories high.

At BU students live in a variety of residence halls. First years often are assigned to the Towers which are classic cinder block dormitories. Then there are four city blocks of impressive brownstones which are much desired by the upper class students. The student village is located next to the sports complex and the ice-hockey arena. It's an 18-story highrise where up to 2,500 students live in apartments. Some upper class students opt to live off campus in Brookline or other nearby areas.

Social Environment

BU students work hard and play hard. They **balance academics with socializing** just about every week. Most were at the top 10 percent of their high school class, learn by collaborating with other students and desire clear cut plans that support realistic goals. Students here are **independent** and manage their lives and activities in this busy and varied environment. There is a need to develop city smarts rather quickly as Boston mirrors many large American cities with comparable crime stats. Students do well to research the course offerings ahead of time and pursue what clearly interests them. Students who take several semesters to declare a major risk lengthening the time to graduate. Once their major is declared, they start to gain a greater sense of community at this very **large** university sporting 32,000 studying within its environs. They can participate in undergraduate research if they collaborate with a professor to submit a grant proposal and secure approval. Students at BU are **go getters**.

At night students might go out into the city with their friends from the dorm, yet the following night, they may join another group of undergraduates for yet a different adventure. They may not know each other by name but there is still a sense of camaraderie. The BU experience is a **smorgasbord of social activity**: living in a certain tower, exercising in the new sports center, cheering for the Terriers, watching a Red Sox game. All of these are part of this dynamic college community.

Compatibility with Personality Types and Preferences

Boston University is for the high energy student who is pumped up by the city's fast pace. However, success takes a lot more than just being attracted to this savvy city. BU students usually have the endurance and sharpness needed to secure an undergraduate degree while juggling lots of alluring and exciting activities (P). At Boston University, the administration clearly directs the students toward self-responsibility with sometimes Byzantine administrative and academic policies. Students are intellectually challenged, recognize the limits of economic reality and are less inclined to charge into activist agendas. The true and valuable bonus of this administration's academic philosophy is academic content without the draining social and political prompts prevalent on many liberal arts campuses today. As a result, undergrads are discerning and familiar working within bureaucratic organization. They navigate the requirements for graduation (S) in the required core courses, divisional studies, concentrations and minors in nine colleges, including a College of General Studies that only offers curriculum for the first two years at BU.

College advising starts with students keeping their Student Link page up-to-date (S). It is supplemented with appointments to the advising center for academic guidance throughout the undergraduate years. The faculty expect a level of maturity that coincides with confidence and intellectual brightness. For those who move through the academic system efficiently, there is the additional reward of acquiring sophisticated urban knowledge. Looking around the campus during any season of the year, you will find exactly these types of students. They are strong students, willing to take a risk, who know what they want in respect to fun and work.

In the following listing of college majors it is important to remember that students can fit into any college and can be successful in any major. We have found that the Personality Types below fit very well at this college. The course-of-study chosen for each Personality Type corresponds to MBTI® research and is presented as one of many examples favorable for that type.

ISTJ makes a good choice with the **Environmental Analysis and Policy** concentration because it is an evolving field, yet one laden with specifics, like quantitative environmental modeling. This works well for ISTJs who will definitely drive policy decisions in the future. This type is comfortable with cataloging facts to memory and then using

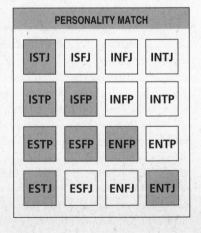

PERSONALITY MATCH

ISTJ	ISFJ	INFJ	INTJ
ISTP	ISFP	INFP	INTP
ESTP	ESFP	ENFP	ENTP
ESTJ	ESFJ	ENFJ	ENTJ

those facts to form decisions with logic. Fortunately, this will work well at Boston University which is rule and policy-oriented.

ISTP will make positive use of the major or minor in **Human Physiology** which only offered at large universities. This degree will provide the gateway for ISTPs to move on to further training in the medical field. Also the school of engineering offers an **Engineering Science** minor focused on biomedical engineering. These two courses of study would likely lead to allied health specialties that require technical expertise and independent analysis of health data. This type is comfortable with spontaneous decisions of a technical nature especially if it involves their fave—machines.

ESTP with knowledge gained from the specialization in **Advertising** at BU could be dynamite in a business setting. Adaptable and spontaneous, they are well suited to this field but will gain needed abilities via the departments required course in Fundamentals of Creative Development. Further advantage would come with Portfolio Development for Advertising. ESTP must be careful to balance their academic studies with the fun excitement of Boston's sidewalks.

ESTJ likes the facts and the tradition associated with teaching science. Science labs are a well known and permanent feature of chemistry that is not going to change. This suits ESTJ and BU offers a program called **Teaching of Chemistry** that fits right into ESTJ views of the world. What high school principal wouldn't be comforted by ESTJ's appreciation of standard operating procedures? Typically conscientious, this type will highly value the common core chemistry courses.

ISFP who works in the field of **Archeology** gets to play outside in the dirt and stick with the facts, essentially the artifacts. Leaving the abstractions and theories to others, this type will enjoy piecing together real finds, and once done move on to the next field! BU's minor in Archeology, not often available outside of large universities, is a hidden gem and strongly supported by the active archeology club.

ESFP is a good bet for a career in physical therapy. BU offers a strong undergraduate degree in **Health Science** for admission to competitive physical therapy graduate programs. This type revels in helping others, especially if it involves repetition of complex skills the ESFP has learned. This degree also offers exploration and entry into emerging health specialty careers other than physical therapy. As medical treatment advances through technology, new careers are opening.

ENFP likes to be creative and the concentration in **Nutritional Science** at BU definitely offers a wide perspective. Nutritionists will be important in the future not only as dieticians, but also as medical professionals, researchers and policy setters. Boston has amazing medical resources from Tufts New England Medical Center to Brigham and Women's/Children's Hospital, plus many more. This environment is designed for the creative, fun-loving ENFP to secure more than one internship while building the social network for further study after graduation.

ENTJ is going to reach for the stars with the degree in **Mathematics Specialty in Statistics** program. They can further blast through the stratosphere, so to speak, by combining this precise major with a minor in Business administration and management. ENTJs have an entrepreneurial side to their personality that nicely mixes with professional positions. Boston will be more than happy to surround ENTJ with the high finance environments that demand mathematical analysis.

BOWDOIN COLLEGE

5700 College Station
Brunswick, ME 04011-8448
Website: www.bowdoin.edu
Admissions Telephone: 207-725-3100
Undergraduates: 1,839; 923 Men, 916 Women

Physical Environment

Bowdoin College is located on the **coast of Maine**, 26 miles from Portland. Brunswick is a quaint town of 20,000 people, with cobblestone streets and many restaurants that are friendly to students. Within a short drive, the college's Coastal Studies Center on Orr Island draws students away from the charm of the campus to participate in geology and marine research. Nearby Freeport, with its designer outlets, attracts students who have a taste for function with fashion in their outdoor clothing. Bowdoin's 225-acre campus includes **forested areas** with walking trails where **athletic** students run or cross-country ski.

Here the nature of the Maine environment attracts students who like to be very physically active. Yet the natural beauty also invites wonder and spirituality. Perhaps it prompted **The College Offer,** a 1906 purpose statement that is currently expanded and now reflects on artistic creation. As the main campus is built around the 1855 Congregational Church it follows that Bowdoin would move forward in 2013 and hire its first director of Religious and Spiritual Life. Two museums of art and modern theatre remind students and faculty daily of human kind's beauty. Almost everyone on this campus is attracted to and loves the **visual and performing arts** even if they are not talented themselves. Performance often tries to infuse **literary and social meaning**.

The issue of sustainability is a thread throughout the administration and curriculum. Discerning students will frequently hear of natural resources projected to diminish in the 21st century. Residing in green residential halls, built with recycled materials, using natural sources of light and heated by geothermal means gives them a unique experience unlike many of their contemporaries at other campuses across the nation. On top of that, dormitories save potable rain water to flush toilets. It all makes sense on the surface.

Social Environment

Eighty-five percent of students are from out of state and bring a strong high school resume hailing from public and independent schools. They are likely to be **creative** thinkers or performers in dance, theatre, music and fine arts. They are accomplished writers and speakers, publishing many **provocative** articles for literary magazines on campus. After all, Henry Wadsworth Longfellow, Nathaniel Hawthorne and Franklin Pierce were in the Bowdoin class of 1825, and we know the rest of their stories. The common denominator here is that students are willing to participate in and support **The Common Good**, not only for Bowdoin but also for the world. The McKeen Center houses the common good program and coordinates student volunteer service and community learning throughout the college.

Though there are no fraternities or sororities, many students belong to outing clubs and are skilled at outdoor sports. Some really identify with the house they were assigned to by Bowdoin in the freshman year. They continue to socialize with that House group where collaborative direction is given by its members for the House cultural activities. Others like to socialize through the clubs that organize primarily around sports, performance and culture activity. Social activities within the traditional dormitories are quite strong also.

Bowdoin students are **bright,** enthusiastic, curious, athletic, artistic and high-achieving. In high school they juggled a heavy academic load with many extracurricular activities. They are thirsty for knowledge, willing to work hard, engage in intellectual discussion and create their own social environment defined as the common good. All resources are at their disposal for this purpose and the Bowdoin Student Government is exceptionally robust. Students typically respect each other's point of view and freely express their emerging opinions which often mirror progressive trends in society. Education is student-centered, faculty do not impose or take center stage. Learning tends to be **non-competitive and collaborative**. Students enjoy each other's talents and gifts whether they are modest or exceptional.

Compatibility with Personality Types and Preferences

Bowdoin College brings to mind the words "laid back" and "intense" at the same time. The Bowdoin undergraduate is in pursuit of acquiring very large, sweeping ideas as they apply to society. It's a demanding endeavor so there is plenty of stress relief in the campus environment starting on Friday night. Faculty question students by making observations of what "is." Student answers could be more complex questions. Bowdoin undergrads become accustomed to ambiguity and discovery as paths to learning (P). It is OK to delay and get lost in the process before a good answer appears, maybe even more than one right answer will surface. This open, intuitive, approach (N) is nicely applied in the study of earth sciences where the interpretation of land forms related to plate tectonics of the Appalachian mountains spreads across curriculum. Students become attuned to purpose, accomplishment and outcome (T). They accept the role of change agent and prefer to do this with others in collaboration. The faculty and administration very much assume that sweeping societal changes are not initiated as solo events, but take a community of committed and knowledgeable individuals working together with a plan. Being connected with others (F) on campus seems to promote a natural brotherhood. Moving forward into their careers with confident expectation is a good description of the Bowdoin students on graduation day.

In the following listing of college majors it is important to remember that students can fit into any college and can be successful in any major. We have found that the Personality Types below fit very well at this college. The course-of-study

PERSONALITY MATCH			
ISTJ	ISFJ	INFJ	INTJ
ISTP	ISFP	INFP	INTP
ESTP	ESFP	ENFP	ENTP
ESTJ	ESFJ	ENFJ	ENTJ

chosen for each Personality Type corresponds to MBTI® research and is presented as one of many examples favorable for that type.

INFJ brings insight to the world of art. The **Visual Arts** major at Bowdoin is wonderfully supplemented by the natural beauty of the Maine coastline and rolling forests and a strong technical curriculum. It will be so enjoyable for this type, often searching for life's meaning, to reach for that technical perfection in a calming landscape that pulls an emotional response from the viewer.

ISTP enjoys seeing direct connection between material, force and movement. The major in **Physics** as offered at Bowdoin is ideal for this type. The course titled Physics of Musical Sound will let them play with recording equipment and speculate on waves and wave propagation. It gives ISTP wiggle room to stay in the laboratories and perhaps take a trip to Orr Island for direct observations.

ENFP may be attracted to the teaching minor in **Education**. The Bowdoin preparation for prospective teachers is exacting and selective. The faculty require much introspection about the meaning of a purposeful life on the part of the prospective student teacher. Schools are viewed within the large context as a national institution. ENFP will relate to this conceptual approach

ENTP is fascinated with power and doesn't mind thinking about moving into power circles. The study of power is well viewed through the lens of Eastern Europe. At Bowdoin, the **Eurasian and East European Studies** interdisciplinary major provides the large pair of glasses in this allegory. Conflict, past and current, in this pivotal part of the world could assure ENTP many opportunities to apply their knowledge in an advisory or consulting role after graduation.

INTP might find the projected interdisciplinary major of **Mathematics and Biology** a reality in Fall 2014 and beyond. It would be sufficiently deep in theory and application to enter the worlds of medical research after graduation. If not available, certainly the student-designed major would be well received in the math department. Prior to graduation, INTP will have puzzled hours over the interfaces.

INTJ and **Mathematics** is a good platform from which this focused personality can launch into the world of advanced studies. At Bowdoin College, math is studied for its pure logic and for its utility for mankind. The course titled "Optimization" teaches the original-thinking INTJ that math formulas are made to solve the world's social problems too. At Bowdoin, this type will be exposed to the idea of using math beyond releasing more statistics and databases. This would be the math department's contribution to Bowdoin's common good.

INFP with a good ear can devote themselves to a career in music. At Bowdoin the **Music** majors often follow one of four tracks: General Music, Music and Culture, Composition and Theory or European and American Music. For the INFP with their penchant for adaptability and insight, the fifth option in a self-designed music major is an alluring choice too. Perhaps they will want to connect music directly with people and the concept of service. It will be INFP who can tie these three together with meaning and utility.

ENTJ is a dynamite consultant in the business world. At Bowdoin, the interdisciplinary major titled **Mathematics and Economics** will allow this hard-charging type to enter into the most selective financial houses and consulting companies. The wide-ranging discourse of this major as related to the linear world of money and math are covered quite nicely. ENTJ smiles with anticipation as they look into their consulting future with this preparation.

ENFJ and **Psychology** makes good sense for this type that is gifted with seeing human potential in individuals and organizations. The Bowdoin College environment is a good fit for this personality preference. Often gifted with a good sense of humor, ENFJ's interaction with clients in therapy will help individuals recognize their weaknesses and strengths.

ISFP often likes careers in the health services field. Their exceptional powers of observation combine nicely with the many practices and techniques involved with diagnosing illnesses. The major in **Biology** at Bowdoin naturally follows the college philosophy to improve the body of knowledge for the "common good." This works for ISFP since they very much want to use their skills while working one-on-one with people. This major will allow ISFP to launch into any advanced medical training.

BRANDEIS UNIVERSITY

Office of Admission
415 South Street
Waltham, MA 02454-9110
Admissions Telephone: 781-736-3500
Website: www.brandeis.edu
Undergraduates: 3,563; 1,550 Men, 2,013 Women
Graduate Students: 2,200

Physical Environment

Brandeis is located on the beltway surrounding Boston, I-95. The commuter rail stop is located near the Brandeis athletic fields on South Street and the university operates its own shuttles into Boston and vicinity. The campus is built on 235 acres of rolling hills, referred to as an **upper and lower campus**. The buildings are modern, rectangular structures, with the exception of the circular theatre building and the **Usen Castle**. The castle is an iconic and striking structure that houses sophomores and is located on a higher elevation overlooking the campus. It also houses Chum's coffeehouse with late night snacks so that all students have access to its sweeping views of downtown Boston. With a softer architectural contrast, the new Mandel Center for the Humanities seems to be purely glass and shining metal with neon light bars suspended in thin air. The new Shapiro Science Center offers a sobering, geometric presence that is akin to its advanced national research laboratories.

There are three distinctive architectural **houses of worship** which visually relay the spiritual egalitarian views that exist on this campus: a Catholic, **Jewish** and Protestant chapel, in addition to a Muslim prayer room. The academic calendar is arranged so as to permit students of all faiths to celebrate their holidays. Although Brandeis is nonsectarian it has deep Jewish heritage. The dining room has a section for kosher dining and another section for American-style food. It's typical to see the interfaith chaplains joining students for lunch on this campus so cognizant of religion and its place in the American community.

Social Environment

The university was founded in 1948 and is named after the first Jewish Supreme Court Justice, Louis Brandeis. It quickly established its research credentials and is considered a top private research institution. Undergraduate research within the academic departments is available and students participate as research assistants to faculty. The Schuster Institute for Investigative Journalism sponsors student research in the area of **worldwide human rights**. Founded in 2004, the Institute also directs its watchful eye on local and national government activity within the United States. Many students volunteer with AmeriCorps and other service organizations. The college does not track the number of students who enroll who are Jewish but the general sense is that approximately half are Jewish.

Even before arriving at Brandeis students understand what it means to respect and support community. The Department of **Student Rights and Community Standards** highlights the Circle of Values, akin to moral precepts and inalienable human rights. Citizenship, respect, civility, integrity, diversity and lifelong learning comprise the six values held across the community and curriculum. All students must reach the intermediate level of proficiency in a foreign language prior to graduation supporting the administration's commitment to understanding the international community.

Students who do well at Brandeis are **investigative, inquiring** and focused. They must handle challenging academics and interface academically with excellent professors in the mentoring process. Many students are interested in becoming medical doctors, veterinarians or lawyers. Approximately 75 percent of students come from outside of Massachusetts. **International** students bring their customs and perspectives to campus contributing to the global feel very much like suburban Boston. Brandeis students look well cared for, comfortable with the preparation they are receiving on this watchful campus for successful careers.

Compatibility with Personality Types and Preferences

Brandeis University is exceptionally accommodating in connecting academic studies with student interest and exploration. The faculty is quite active with their own independent research, but they do solicit students interested in their particular research to join in. There is careful, consistent and practical (S) advising for identifying majors, career tracks, advanced study and research after graduation. University cultural programs and career mentoring are outstanding.

Extracurricular activities and clubs reveal the exceptional interest and study of humane issues (F) in the broadest sense. It is supplemented by the university's strong outreach across the globe. Brandeis admits international students to increase understanding between international cultures through its academic curriculum. The terrorist attack in Mumbai in late 2008 highlighted this significant international perspective within the student body also. Students formed an immediate response including direct support to the devastated overseas Mumbai community. Approximately 10 percent of the student body is foreign national.

Undergraduate students typically develop a personal **ideology** that embraces spirit, body and mind. In fact that is part of the first year orientation curriculum. Students may become passionate about issues and the full Brandeis experience can offer a bright light on multiple disciplines from several perspectives. Undergrads learn through traditional experience in the classrooms, while rational thinking and logic are favorite processes. The faculty, curriculum and research are prodigious. It takes time to comprehend the academic depth of this university (T). It takes several dimensions of time and thought to graduate from this university.

In the following listing of college majors it is important to remember that students can fit

PERSONALITY MATCH			
ISTJ	ISFJ	INFJ	INTJ
ISTP	ISFP	INFP	INTP
ESTP	ESFP	ENFP	ENTP
ESTJ	ESFJ	ENFJ	ENTJ

into any college and can be successful in any major. We have found that the Personality Types below fit very well at this college. The course-of-study chosen for each Personality Type corresponds to MBTI® research and is presented as one of many examples favorable for that type.

INFP could elect to declare the **Studio Art** major at Brandeis University. Their personal vision is drawn out through the encouragement and sensitivity of faculty within this department. There is an underlying theme that requires students to look at art as an expression of their personal motivation and to develop contemporary expressive techniques. INFPs excel at relating their personal beliefs through their creative work. At Brandeis University, both the beliefs and the creativity are expected and nicely combine in this major.

ISTP likes to be efficient with the resources at the disposal of a student team or class project. The major in **Computer Science** at Brandeis University requires coordination and efficiency. ISTPs enjoy team work and controlling chaos if their technical trouble shooting can save the day. Research directed at machine learning will definitely appeal to this techno. The degree in computing here has wide options for focus and ISTP loves the spontaneous nature within this department.

ISTJ will like the historically-based curriculum and the extraordinary course offerings in the **American Studies** major at Brandeis. The curriculum presents this huge, chaotic field with objective structure, encouraging the student to form a foundational body of knowledge that accurately references the American nation. It is significant for its absence of today's trendy political and social filters. The minor in **Legal Studies** is a swell combo with this major. ISTJs will be headed toward a career in justice or law and be very well prepared between these two courses of study.

ISFJ is often a natural leader in the field of education. This type has a comfort level with administrative procedure and attention to detail. Both are desirable for a major in **Education Studies**. The Brandeis degree prepares for graduate study in school leadership and administration. The department directs much focus on the ethical purposes of education. There are many Why and How questions here for ISFJ to ponder. At Brandeis, there will be a watchful eye of the Common Core instituted by the current administration. Little different in purpose than the past national effort, No Child Left Behind, these government directives have come and gone in the past. ISFJ will remain a beacon of human rights regardless.

ISFP has a thoughtful side to their daily habits. The degree in **Environmental Studies** will provide enough rumination for a full-bodied ISFP career. They will get lots of energy being outdoors and being productive with a meaningful environmental student project. The faculty commits to undergraduates exploring the relationship between environmental policy and practice as directed by industry through government directives. Since ISFPs are quite adaptable to change, this dynamic career field is quite suitable.

ESFP more often than not has an affinity for animals. Brandeis University has introductory courses that explore animal behavior. Perception: Human, Animal, and Machine is just one example. In sophomore year, ESFP may elect to apply for an independent interdisciplinary major in **Animal Studies** that combines the fields of psychology, biology and sociology. Graduation may find them in settings where people and animals interact such as zoos, therapy, wildlife preservation or security.

ESFJ definitely is a supporter of family, school and community traditions. It reveals itself in their typical concerned attitudes and their preference for caring professions. The major in **Health: Science, Society and Policy** is an extensive study of health service across all levels of society. This type is typically an effective member within large bureaucracies that deliver services to the public. All ESFJ needs is the foundational knowledge within this curriculum to excel in a public health career. The troubled reorganization of all American health care and its roll out in 2014 will be the source of many assigned papers at Brandeis.

ESTJ likes the idea of a solid, no frills undergraduate degree. ESTJs interested in science will be attracted to the degree in **Chemistry** since it is well-received and appreciated in the job market. ESTJs must determine which focus within this broad degree to follow after graduation. Brandeis University prepares the chemistry graduate for entry to careers in biochemistry, environmental sciences, pharmacology, medicine, dentistry, law or business. If they did not arrive with a major in mind, ESTJ usually struggles to make career decisions early in the undergraduate college years. The colloquia lecture series of visiting professors from other institutes is excellent at Brandeis and just may make that decision a little easier.

ENFJ is a master at oral communication. Words certainly can intrigue this type as tools that carry multiple meanings, some of them persuasive. The major in **Language and Linguistics** has both variety and underlying structure that is appealing to this type. For the ENFJ who can be a computer geek, Brandeis has a nice complementary line of study that connects linguistics with computation. This field has multiple avenues in graduate study from anthropology and sociology to computer science, psychology and beyond. Faculty in the department pursue strong linguistics research from artificial intelligence to mathematical properties of linguistic formation.

ENTJ is one to come up with innovative and logical steps for solving problems. **Neuroscience** offers application for these two ENTJ characteristics. This emerging field is well positioned at Brandeis University for study of the brain through its neural systems. A full complement of faculty research includes chemical, biological, genetic, computational, perceptual, memory, spatial and behavioral lines as applied to the brain. ENTJ likes to be on the leading edge of an evolving career and Brandeis research in this field introduces this undergraduate to a huge array of research and follow on study options.

BROWN UNIVERSITY

45 Prospect Street, Box 1876
Providence, RI 02912
www.brown.edu
Admissions Telephone: 401-863-2378
Undergraduates: 6,117; 2,943 Men, 3,174 Women
Graduate Students: 2,303

Physical Environment

The city of Providence provides a sophisticated and lively environment for Brown students. It's like a mini-Boston minus the hustle and bustle of a large city. City streets like Thayer run through the university area and offer interesting diversions in an **upscale atmosphere**. There's a one screen movie theatre which often runs foreign language films, many recently released from the Cannes film festival. There are internet cafes, ethnic restaurants and street musicians in good weather.

The prominent hill in Providence is home to Brown University along with historical homes and buildings with some on the national register including the first Baptist Church in America from the 1600s. The federal style historic homes speak to social upper class living. The train station is within a few minutes of the university and it connects students with Boston and New York. Prospective bright students with considerable artistic talent are drawn to the possibility of a dual degree from the Rhode Island School of Design, adjacent to Brown's admission office.

Some of the Brown buildings retain the look and feel of the late 1800s and Brown undergraduates like New England's old customs and ways, reminiscent of England which they may have visited. Many of its 235 buildings were built more recently. The large Life Science complex joins the "Walk" an interconnecting network of sidewalks and parks. Landscape architecture and tradition are also enhanced by the Van Wickle wrought iron gate which opens and closes for incoming and graduating students. The many **diverging footpaths** on the campus are representative of the **academic freedom** here. Students drawn to Brown love the possibility of experimenting with courses and enjoy the pleasing physical landscape for its quaint originality as compared to other historic districts across the country. The entire environment speaks to a classy intellectual lifestyle. Students here want to be in the midst of it.

Very much in tune with recent collegiate architecture, the new Granoff Center for the arts contains collaborative spaces for artistic production and reminds one of a toddler's attempt to square up three building blocks, yet gets them off center. It is amusing and delightful to look at. The Metcalf Center for Research provides collaborative space for the cognitive, linguistic and psychological disciplines. The Faunce House Campus Center, with its minimalist feel in design, is enlivened by undergraduates meeting over latte and organic chem quiz questions.

Social Environment

Brown University's founding mission gave license to students studying what they wanted, to the depth they wanted and without taking other "prescribed" classes. As Brown faculty would be first to admit however, change is a constant and today, the open curriculum is interpreted by the individual departments. They can and do identify concentrations by title and course content. Naturally the breadth of courses and content within each is voluminous. That is where the true **Open Curriculum** resides with its appeal and potential. Students identify courses in conjunction with their advisors, meeting the concentrations core curriculum and then indulging their interests within the expansive elective offerings.

Students who love Brown University truly love it. The admission process is rigorous as are the classes. The educational philosophy appeals to these free-thinking, bright students who are as familiar with daydreaming as they are with accomplishment. The faculty expects students to learn from each other and bring new information to the classroom experience. In fact, there is a sense that Brown University is relying on its students to be the trailblazers who will move the common body of knowledge forward. Students here are self-directed to the "nth" degree. They are referred to as Brown's primary resource. Often nurtured by their professors, at times they are **treated as equals** with insights to share. Brown students are genuinely **single-minded** about something, and often they get lost in that "something."

In addition to handling a heavy work load, these students get intensely attracted to niche, original activities. Most will become loyal in friendships by identifying with the themes of love, peace and happiness. Some would have been described as "nerds with a social personality" in high school. Others are children of free thinkers who are identifying with their parents' ideals. There are also conservative-thinking, conventional students here who will be tested in their views. Most are relaxed despite the **heavy academic demands**. Students are likely to collaborate and help each other. With a plurality of individuals, the common denominator is commitment to advancing knowledge. Brown students are oriented to the future. It accommodates their originality well.

For these students who seek to express themselves and explore without limits, the campus is paradise. Brown academic practices tend to support the concept that **knowledge is interconnected and relative**. Undergraduate students come to see that they can and should contribute to the base of knowledge in any field, not just their selected concentration. They are likely to identify present day information as transient in nature. They find less use for ordinary, commonly known facts. Some are very well grounded and become extraordinarily successful. Others choose to apply their expertise and acumen without thought of practical worldly concern.

Compatibility with Personality Types and Preferences

Brown University is a study in diffusion (P). Simply said, there are no hard lines or sharp edges in this intellectual environment. Instead, synthesis, discovery and expansion seem to rule. Students who find Brown University a comfortable place are those who want to see beyond and to the side of what is currently known: the future with support from the past and present only as needed. Their motivation may be intense curiosity, or they may be compelled to help others (F) as the primary way of defining themselves. Regardless of their motivation, these students are willing to jump into the unknown at some level (N) with the confidence that they will surface with personal abilities which will be used productively. They have many personal definitions to nail down in four years. They are likely to search for their own understanding of "productivity." They come expecting to find the academic climate that will welcome these very abstract questions. They are optimistic that their personal connections with people and their intellectual acumen will translate into humanistic accomplishment. They have much less admiration for the practical, expedient world. Rather, Brown students will devote their intellectual energy to learning how to ask the questions. It is almost certain that the answers will expand the body of knowledge in their academic fields.

In the following listing of college majors it is important to remember that students can fit into any college and can be successful in any major. We have found that the Personality Types below fit very well at this college. The course-of-study chosen for each Personality Type corresponds to MBTI® research and is presented as one of many examples favorable for that type.

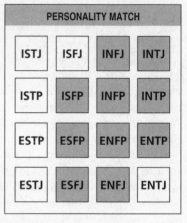

INFJ would potentially find the concentration of **Human Biology** at Brown University a nice play on words. In fact, they might also like the well-paired words, health and disease, which is one of the required themes offered in the curriculum. This type is not likely to accept conventional practice. Their intuition easily kicks in and they will not shy away from the huge health issues facing our nation. Their own idealism can translate into exceptionally fine leadership when they believe in the work at hand.

INTJ is truly a type where still waters run deep. Their friends and associates often are amazed at the originality and depth of their thinking when INTJ chooses to reveal it. The educational philosophies at Brown University will be ideal for this type. During these four years, they will be encouraged and rewarded for revealing their ideas. Although many classmates will be comfortable with the process and the evolving nature of learning, INTJ has the chutzpah to charge on and find the definitive answer. Definitive answers are part of their larger than life visions. So who else to tackle such a revolutionary and intense concentration as **Cognitive Neuroscience**? The additional complexities that occur at freely floating Brown University simply call out louder to INTJ.

ISFP will appreciate the **Visual Arts** concentration at Brown University since a sense of beauty is innately a characteristic of their personality. This warm fuzzy type is quite comfortable communicating through the arts and is likely to be drawn to the hand-crafted, three dimensional pieces that speak through their simplicity. ISFP is very good with the here and now, with what can be seen and touched. It is this preference for the observable that allows them to excel in the fields of design. At Brown, this type will find the encouragement they need to reveal and translate their inner convictions through artistic craftsmanship and design.

INTP doesn't actually believe that problems are insolvable. It is not in their nature to grant you that position. Naturally, they are pretty skeptical. Sometimes it can be a challenge to get them to agree that the sun will come up tomorrow morning, clouds or no clouds. The concentration in **Computational Biology** will give them a proper tool to be skeptical with reason. They are big, long-range thinkers who can deal with the tremendous quantitative information coming from DNA and genetic studies. As they get deeper into the data bits, when many of us mortals would have difficulty recalling what 1 or 0 meant, it is the INTP who stays on track with an internal compass. Theories and innovation mix naturally with their afternoon Coke break.

INFP will find Brown's **Architectural Studies** concentration a possibility to launch a career in Historical preservation. This type likes to bring original and current information to the table. So if others are talking about tomorrow on this campus, this type can quietly speculate on the past. As succeeding generations are exposed to less of our American Presidents and their founding ideas, how better to utilize the National Historic Register than to call attention to their principles in question today at the highest levels of intellectual America? Brown's great openness in curriculum offers this type the autonomy they thrive on when learning. A thesis on American Presidential homes that delineated their political ideology through architecture, such as Jefferson's Monticello, would be an informative read. INFP would be doubly pleased if it sparked a trend to revisit those foundational principles in the figurative and literal sense.

ESFP just knows that once you gather all the information, the solution will reveal itself. Their confidence is ideally suited to Brown's educational perspectives. Neither Brown University nor ESFP are going to get all worked up with worry. They would rather just create and have fun with discovery. So who wouldn't have fun swimming with porpoises? The track in **Marine Biology** within the biology degree offers a narrow exposure to marine life. Yet passionate Brown undergraduate students can craft their experiential education and elective coursework toward the careers they might seek in animal habitation, wildlife conservancy or zoology.

ENFP will find the challenge and excitement that they enjoy in the **Business, Entrepreneurship and Organizations** concentration at Brown University. It includes a really innovative combination of three fields: engineering, sociology and economics. The originality of interfacing these three will keep ENFP's insatiable curiosity satisfied. This concentration requires students to further focus their studies after the foundation courses. It could be the ever original ENFP who graduates Brown University to enter the world of business consulting for profit in a technical field.

ENTP is a thinking machine. Their minds don't often take a break unless they are sleeping. It takes a dynamic mix of courses with a far reaching impact to keep this type from getting restless. The concentration in **Early Cultures** is ideal for this analytical and resourceful type. The faculty in this program alone numbers 40. The resources are indicative of the depth of this concentration which studies the foundation of advanced western civilization. With growing unfamiliarity in the latter, it might be the enterprising ENTP who prompts its reintroduction into public middle and high school curriculums.

ESFJ who has a talent for numbers will want to look at the concentration in **Statistics** at Brown University. The concentration leads to a degree from the School of Public Health. Students develop much awareness and skill with statistical methods applied to research in the social sciences. Tender-hearted ESFJ is going to naturally appreciate the opportunity to apply their newly learned skills to building community. At Brown there will be significant awareness and discussion of national and world service organizations. Which will they apply their newly learned statistical prowess to?

ENFJ can put their ability to see all sides of an argument to good use in the **Education Studies** concentration at Brown University. This type is quite aware of the frequent charge that our schools are underperforming. ENFJ has the extraordinary skills to bring audiences to new perspectives. They are also comfortable with leadership and establish relationships with ease. Brown's concentration in this field will give ENFJ the background to take on critical issues in education. While at Brown, they will seek resolution in their own minds for regional and national problems surrounding the emotional health and education of American children.

BUTLER UNIVERSITY

Office of Admissions
4600 Sunset Avenue
Indianapolis, IN 46208
Website: www.butler.edu
Admissions Telephone: 888-940-8100
Undergraduates: 3,943; 1,590 Men, 2,353 Women

Physical Environment

Butler University is surrounded by the metropolitan suburbs of Indianapolis. The Butler campus occupies 290 acres just five miles north of downtown. The campus is laid out in a triangular shape delineated by the White River at the base. Large banners and signs are common and colorful on the buildings. They call attention to upcoming events and infuse energy across the community. The student body is wild for Division I sports. The Butler Bowl arena propelled the university to the **NCAA national basketball championship** consecutive playoffs in 2010 and 2011. The **Greek houses** on this campus lend extra spirit and organization to the cheering along with Butler Blue II, the university mascot and fine-looking English bulldog. Campus is less than a mile from Broad Ripple Village, known for its diverse entertainment as one of six cultural districts in Indianapolis. The president's house is prominently located on campus and reminds one of the administration's caring, hands-on guidance.

Butler University reflects the temper and culture of the city of Indianapolis, energetic and forward-looking. The university has completed several significant renovations such as the state of the art addition to the **Pharmacy and Health Sciences** building. In 2013, the new Schrott Center for the Arts joined the impressive complex of facilities devoted to the **performing arts** on this campus. Yet the physical environment remains mindful of the student body with indoor passage from building to building during the winter months. Winters are severe and students make good use of the huge Butler Fieldhouse with indoor football and baseball practice fields. Two of the three first-year residence halls are built around a square forming a courtyard in the middle. The inner square is more shielded from the winds and this lends a sense of community for most of the freshmen.

Social Environment

While students like to have fun here, they also strive for academic excellence, tapping out searches on their iPad to supplement course materials. As interested as they are in academics, students are also interested in being trained for jobs and careers. They enjoy **applied learning** and the internships that come with many majors. Faculty focus on practical career advising. Study abroad is also part of the Butler experience, and the college has a campus in Spain as well as other programs. Academically, students at Butler have freedom to explore within **a clear structure** superimposed by the academic practices. Enterprising high school graduates interested in improving their future work options will receive a **solid education** here. Students with learning differences will also find success in this collegiate academic atmosphere.

Those who are undecided about their future can remain undeclared for two years. An advisor is appointed to undeclared students and it is very likely they will graduate on time. The curriculum has something for the artsy folks as well; in fact, students are required to attend six cultural experiences over the four years at Butler. The very **competitive dance and theatre** programs attract those who were in private arts instruction since they were knee high. During a campus visit, they may be surprised at the depth, quality and facilities devoted to the arts. In addition to excellent opportunity to master their crafts they will also benefit from the practical advising that permeates the administration's academic practice. Some will go on to teach while others find performance, management and technical positions with professional theaters and stages across the nation.

Butler University appeals to students who want to join clubs and organizations that draw them together for traditional collegiate activities. Many students come from the Indiana farms with about 40 percent coming from outside of Indiana. Politically, many of these students trend to the conservative side. They are likely to **value religion and tradition**. Their families have 19th century roots, Indiana family histories and more recently Ellis Island 20th century immigrant histories. Honoring the historical American principle of independence receives a warm welcome here.

Compatibility with Personality Types and Preferences

Butler University prepares its graduates for the professional world of work and careers through four years of intentional advising and excellent curriculum in each of the six colleges. Students at Butler University look to their professors for state of the art information (S) within their fields. The administration specifically recruits professional practitioners to function as faculty on campus who then bring their expertise, excitement and reality to the classes. The faculty within the performing arts disciplines are typically retired professional artists. The permeable boundary between Butler's campus and the national and international scene fuels very active off campus learning that is specifically tailored to the undergraduate's major. Individualized academic mentoring is also a strong part of the planned approach to undergraduate education. Interests and talents are viewed holistically for each student and this broadens their career exploration pathways.

At Butler team spirit translates into community building, community strength and individual strength. Students and professors capitalize on this energy. Butler is exceptionally fine in their support for the undecided undergraduate. These undecided undergraduates will find a specialized sequence of courses and advising in each of the colleges. Their exploratory course designations tailor the content and purpose beyond what is usually offered in "Intro to..." courses. Generally, undergraduates here seek out and appreciate guidance from their instructors. This is exactly what the university provides.

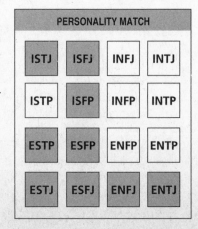

PERSONALITY MATCH

ISTJ	ISFJ	INFJ	INTJ
ISTP	ISFP	INFP	INTP
ESTP	ESFP	ENFP	ENTP
ESTJ	ESFJ	ENFJ	ENTJ

In the following listing of college majors it is important to remember that students can fit into any college and can be successful in any major. We have found that the Personality Types below fit very well at this college. The course-of-study chosen for each Personality Type corresponds to MBTI® research and is presented as one of many examples favorable for that type.

ISTJ often has intense concentration that is a much desired trait in the health sciences. Butler University offers the **Pre-Physician Assistant** program with undergraduate opportunities for admission into the selective College of Pharmacy and Health Sciences. This could really work well for ISTJ with their stability, perseverance and mastery of details. Butler University offers a carefully designed curriculum with considerable exposure to a large variety of medical settings that utilize physician assistants. The guidance is very realistic and focused at Butler University and ISTJs will appreciate this.

ESFP is often able to juggle several projects in the moment. The theater stage is particularly attractive to this type. The ESFP with high school experience and demonstrated talent should look to the majors in **Theater** or **Dance**. Visiting actors and professional performers take up residence at the university. ESFPs are energized by the culture associated with performing arts. The daily work environment is focused on the next performance—the immediate and daily tasks at hand. The college also offers an **Arts Administration** degree in each of these areas for ESFPs who may not prefer to continue performing in front the audience.

ESTJ has the inclination to carefully preplan for a career. The field of Pharmacy definitely requires this type of preplanning which Butler University offers in the **PrePharmacy** major. The department goes above and beyond the general idea of prepharmacy advising. The major directly pairs a clear curriculum and internships with strong academic work required by the undergraduate student. It is likely to lead to the completion of the pharmacy doctorate. There is certain admission to graduate school when milestones in the undergraduate years are passed. ESTJ can work to meet each one knowing that it ultimately leads to admission into pharmacy school.

ISFP has very desirable work characteristics such as loyalty, flexibility and practicality. In certain business environments, this type can anchor the whole organization. At Butler University, with the excellent exploratory programs and courses, ISFPs can become familiar with the corporate and nonprofit business worlds. Encouragement and careful internship selection by the faculty will smooth the way. This type typically searches for opportunities to serve customers with their warm, affirming personalities. The College of Business highlights and enhances these individual strengths in **Exploratory Studies in Business.**

ISFJ really might enjoy the therapeutic speech and language field. At Butler University, the major in **Communication Sciences and Disorders** is designed for successful entry into graduate school. As a speech and language pathologist, ISFJs could help others directly and be a valued member of the school system or hospital rehabilitation department. These are both important values for ISFJs. Providing language therapy at the elementary schools will take advantage of this type's expertise at sequenced routines and unerring accuracy with repetition. Butler University assertively includes these emerging therapies for mentally-impaired youngsters entering school.

ESFJ could excel in the fields that require frequent communication between business and the community. The major in **Strategic Communication: PR and Advertising** at Butler University offers a strong base in experiential learning for ESFJ to excel. This type takes a personal approach to their work and their genuine, friendly ways quickly become an asset. They are also very strong in recalling and utilizing information, rarely getting their facts mixed up. With the experience afforded from the hands-on opportunities, ESFJ could select an entry position in public relations with opportunity to work for established businesses or traditional government agencies.

ESTP is curious and quick to react. They may find a career in the criminal justice system quite desirable. The major in **Criminology** at Butler University includes a solid background in psychology and sociology. ESTPs have the interest in others and enjoy being in the middle of activities with many different types of people. This type is observant and often able to understand the desires of others. At Butler, ESTPs can explore each of the work environments that require criminologists. Ultimately they can settle on the one that suits their adaptability and ability to take in a scene and quickly ascertain the pertinent information.

ENTJ might be quite impressed with the **International Business** major at Butler University. The degree requires foreign language proficiency and this hard-charging type is willing to put in the study and wants to excel. Advantages like conducting financial transactions in a native language would not be lost on ENTJs. They don't mind being a step ahead of the competition. The College of Business Administration has identified selected international business schools for internships. These international, off campus courses will give enterprising ENTJ the global launching pad for a strategic business career.

ENFJ might find the major in **Middle and Secondary Education** ideal at Butler University. There is excellent preparation for teachers here. Undergraduates spend considerable time observing and participating in classrooms prior to actually student teaching. They are paired with master teachers located in the nearby Indianapolis schools. This type could easily find the advanced classes in high school rewarding to teach. American public school classrooms are challenging environments from many perspectives. Responsible and diplomatic, this type would garner support when tackling institutional weaknesses in a school leadership role.

CALIFORNIA INSTITUTE OF TECHNOLOGY

1200 E. California Boulevard MC 1-94
Pasadena, CA 91125
Website: www.caltech.edu
Admissions Telephone: 626-395-6341
Undergraduates: 997; 615 Men, 382 Women
Graduate Students: 1,246

Physical Environment

Cal Tech has an urban campus surrounded by the city-streets of Pasadena. The adjacent neighborhoods pose in a **small town way**, without high-rises, and with shopping and ethnic restaurants nearby. Buildings are designed along the style of Oxford University in England. Students form **self-governing units** in each of the eight dormitories or Houses as they are called. Each has enclosed courtyards, corridors and alley ways, which contribute to a strong sense of privacy and identity. The interior of these residence halls is basic and looks **well-used**. Students cook their own dinners and serve themselves in the basic, utilitarian kitchens.

Many valedictorians and salutatorians get lost in the impressive laboratories. The laboratories in math, physics, astrophysics and geology really appeal to the high school student who was fond of world geography and planetary science in the eighth grade. The scientific facilities are exceptional from electron particle accelerators to the Hale telescope that supports the planetary sciences. Students at the top of their high school class are drawn to Cal Tech's off campus **research facilities** in Hawaii and Peru for astrophysics and planetary sciences. The Linde + Robinson Laboratory for Environmental Science is a stunning renovation of the 1932-era astronomy lab. The new Schlinger Laboratory is dedicated to the discipline of chemistry and the art of engineering.

The **cannon** in front of Fleming house has a history of disappearing, as other technical rival colleges steal it away. It actually made a long trip to their archrival in Massachusetts. Students here take pride in this tradition. They like prankster humor—a throwback to the 1950s—when the cannon was fired for the first time to mark the end of a semester. When not pranking, undergraduates are all wrapped up in their study and discoveries; the campus energy is devoted to knowledge with little precious energy given over to routine life activities.

Social Environment

Cal Tech has a small, very select undergraduate student body highly centered on **the physical sciences**. They collaborate with the larger graduate student body so much so that in the second year of course work, undergraduate students are in some classes with graduate students. These undergraduates are expected to step up their effort and perform at graduate level.

At Cal Tech these exceptional students continue to conduct research in engineering sciences after graduation and so they don't typically intend to become working engineers in the traditional sense. Cal Tech grants only Bachelor of Science degrees at the undergraduate level. The students here would rather unravel a puzzling **theory** than address social conundrums with activist practices. They are future-oriented students who prepare for grad school, likely to be followed by working in the national labs.

They socialize around research and solving problems, **slurping up a late night Boba** while **tackling scientific hypotheses**. Fun has to be involved somehow with technology. The January 1, 2014, Rose Bowl fans were greeted at half time with a 2,000 square foot electronic sign above the stadium. It simply read 'Cal Tech' in Rose Bowl red! Depending on how you look at it, 100 students pulled it off or put it up on the hillside. Collaboration with team members who are very different from one another is the norm. Cal Tech is unusual in many ways. The amenities others absolutely must have, like a PF Chang look-alike in the campus dining commons, is simply absent from this campus. The student body is undemanding in that sense. All students let their imaginations roam, making connections and opening floodgates of ideas from many cultures during **brainstorming** sessions. Students value truth and abide by a strong honor code whereby they can take un-proctored tests whenever they are ready. For the student who is fascinated by the uncharted areas of science and brave enough to follow their hunches, Cal Tech is perfect.

Compatibility with Personality Types and Preferences

California Institute of Technology is more than a university; in reality it is a national and world scientific laboratory resource that also has dormitories for young twenty-somethings, identified as undergraduate students. As such, Cal Tech must regularly communicate with two disparate groups: prospective high school students and world research scientists. They specifically reach out to current high school students who may be good matches for their rather unique learning environment. Analysis (T) is predominant in this campus culture. It is hard to imagine how the extreme and fundamental nature of Cal Tech research could push into scientific discovery without having almost institutionalized the tool of analysis. Of course, innovation and the pull of the unknown (N) has the next place of honor in approaching the daily drill. Cal Tech's mission clearly states that human knowledge is expanded to benefit society by combining research and education. The educational philosophy is more along the lines of a think tank that just happens to have young adults as participating members. It is an institution that prepares its graduates for the world of scientific discovery rather than careers and professions. They are prodigies and an underutilized American resource.

In the following listing of college majors it is important to remember that students can fit into any college and can be successful in any major. We have found that the Personality Types below fit very well at this college. The course-of-study chosen for each Personality Type corresponds to MBTI® research and is presented as one of many examples favorable for that type.

PERSONALITY MATCH			
ISTJ	ISFJ	INFJ	INTJ
ISTP	ISFP	INFP	INTP
ESTP	ESFP	ENFP	ENTP
ESTJ	ESFJ	ENFJ	ENTJ

ISTJ will relate well to the factual and fundamental nature of the **Biology** track option at Cal Tech. With emphasis on the basic life properties, the biology option also allows for flexibility through Cal tech research and elective courses. This type is drawn to practice in the professions. ISTJ will be quite proactive at refining research skills in the undergraduate program at Cal Tech. Entrance to medical research universities will not be far from this undergraduate's daily thoughts.

ISTP is pretty good with numbers and will enjoy the **Economics** option here at Cal Tech. There is a course titled Electricity Market, and it surveys the nature of electricity as a commodity. ISTP will function as the instructor and acquisition catalog in reviewing Warren Buffet's recent purchases in the 'boring' electricity industry. The freedom and autonomy associated with financial success includes 'boring' once in a while. Not inclined to overdo anything, this type understands that boring and efficiency sometimes go together quite well.

ESTP could like the **Business Economics and Management** option since it looks so heavily at strategy within the markets and financial networks. Students apply mathematical formulas such as binomial and Black-Scholes pricing models while studying risky debt. The course in venture capital will appeal to their risk-taking nature. The department's well-grounded courses in accounting and finance may try their patience, however.

ESTJ who looks closely at the **Applied Physics** option will discover practical stuff hidden within. There will be introductory courses on energy sources in labs that fabricate test diodes, transistors and inverters. This approach allows the ESTJ to get the immediate and useful feedback they need to comprehend theory. Fiber optics, microwaves, radiation and X-ray diffraction are all observable first facts for this type.

ENFP won't likely be skeptical when we suggest selecting the **History and Philosophy of Science** option at Cal Tech. This broad-based observation of how science has been applied to mankind's welfare is something that would attract an ENFP. The course in Forbidden Knowledge is both ironic and choc-full of foresight. It addresses cases in history where knowledge has been squashed, such as that of Galileo's experience with our sun-centered galaxy. Currently, NASA's Roy Spencer and his research questioning the validity of global warming will surely be reviewed as an example. Political movements of this decade adopt passionate agendas and the public is left to ponder.

INTJ is comfortable in the world of computers and the **Computer Science** option here requires an original capstone project. The INTJ has a very strong intuitive sense that is not expressed in the company of others. As powerful thinkers, they will likely find it intriguing to study the limits of computing science theory in the course titled Decidability and Tractability. Cal Tech demands rigor and creativity as attributes associated with this course of study. Two adjectives that quickly come to mind when describing this personality type are rigorous and creative.

INTP will find the **Astronomy** major at Cal Tech is designed to be a stepping stone for a career in basic research. The first year course includes a lab introducing astronomical measuring techniques. Yet, INTP enjoys the theory and mystery part of this major. Nevertheless, getting their hands and arms moving in a lab will be a good for this type who may stay in the Ivory Tower a tad too long. There will be plenty of fellow undergrad classmates who will help them with the details in the lab in return for a leg up on some hunch.

ENTP will like the **Political Science** option and its emphasis on predictive methods. Cal Tech brings their powerful penchant for analysis into this social science. ENTP is well suited to find the irony in the course option PS 126 which has changed its name in successive course catalogs from "Political Corruption" to "Business, Public Policy and Corruption" and now to "Business and Public Policy." However, the departments of anthropology and political science picked up the baton with An/Ps 127 simply titled, "Corruption." This type is a power player and mixing in advanced technology would appeal to their restless character.

ENTJ could like the **Chemical Engineering** degree at Cal Tech because of its broad exposure to the use of chemical reactions for energy as well as products. ENTJ will find the connection to both the real and practical that they so appreciate. As this type progresses through undergraduate study at Cal Tech, they will likely respond to their entrepreneurial instincts and also pick up electives in the business, economics and management curriculum.

CARLETON COLLEGE

100 South College Street
Northfield, MN 55057
Website: www.carleton.edu
Admissions Telephone: 507-222-4190
Undergraduates: 2,037; 960 Men, 1,077 Women

Physical Environment

Carleton College is in a small town that is **quaint,** clean and friendly. Northfield's slogan "Home of cows, colleges, and contentment" is well coined. This setting appeals to students who are looking for a safe, **trendy**, artsy environment. The town has a commercial street winding along the river, with lovely old buildings, coffee shops, artisan bakeries, bars and restaurants. A former middle school, renovated and opened as the Weitz Center for Creativity, houses facilities and space for the visual arts. Resident Carleton faculty rotate their offices within this complex to collaborate with each other in the proximity of well-designed space with resource support. October 2011 marked the start up of the college's second wind turbine which feeds into the electrical grid. This bold step in budget commitment cost 1.8 million dollars and performance is projected to be paid off in 12 years by reselling the electricity produced back to the local power company. Intellectual payoff for American cities that may look for valid feedback—immediate. Thank you Carleton.

Carleton students especially like the **long connected buildings** and two new dormitories so that they can walk around in shorts and flip-flops in winter. The center of campus features the original chapel with surrounding buildings in familiar Collegiate Gothic style and some that are throwbacks to the 60s. Carleton has a vibrant **Office of the Chaplaincy** which appeals to many Jewish and Catholic students seeking to be active spiritually during undergraduate years. Worship services and special religious holiday celebrations are posted in the monthly agenda. There are 16 special interest houses that encourage students to explore academic ideas and develop personal ideologies with like-minded people.

Social Environment

Carleton students form an eclectic group, interested in a liberal education that allows them to express their thoughts and form opinions. Students expect a platform for freedom of expression in and out of the classroom. Carleton students prefer **cause-related activities** and seek to assure all are represented. There are the local chapters of international organizations like Engineers Without Borders. Some clubs have a multicultural perspective such as Fellowship in Christ, which seeks to bring differing national and ethnic students together, exploring faith with the New Testament. Many are oriented for fun and entertainment, like the Carleton Anime Society.

Students are **self-absorbed in their education and social life**. Undergrads are not above questioning themselves or their college administration. Sometimes they feel they are overloaded with their trimester class schedule. Editors of the student newspaper speculated that the six-week term breaks have negative effects. They cited losing out on summer jobs snagged in early May by other collegiate undergrads. Yet they also cited the lack of itinerant, six-week jobs in this poor economy. In the classroom they ask imaginative questions, not necessarily looking for definitive answers. Carleton students are **comfortable with questioning** and change is an answer acceptable at Carleton.

All in all, friendships form fast and easily because of similarities and the long winter months. Here students may release their academic tensions in creative ways. Screw Date is a winter pastime that formerly had an edge to it. Now the blind dates combine with classic first night activities across the campus, similar to Boston's First Nights. Previously, the match ups were selected to be mismatches in the comedic sense. Now, with Carleton undergrads' willingness to turn the spotlight on themselves, they changed it up and participation has increased. Yet the favorite winter pastime is the annual faculty vs. student's broomball game on the bald spot. Students are athletic and participate in many sports, this tradition is not likely to change.

Compatibility with Personality Types and Preferences

The Carleton College environment is idealistic and emotionally safe. It facilitates an imaginative learning experience (N). The mentoring relationship between student and professor seems to take on the closeness evident in friends or family. Humor is very much valued on this campus. It serves to promote a comfortable familiarity between faculty and student. In this way, the campus experience encourages the student to shed conventions and attitudes (P) they may have brought with them from high school. The educational philosophy moves toward critical observation (T) of American society. Our country's diverse talents are highly valued by the faculty and administration. Carleton students experience an intense, insular, individualized education that reflects practice and reality in quaint Northfield. Yet the undergraduate student body gathers up strength accumulated in four undergraduate years. They step out smartly but with pause into messy big city, big issues America. Carleton College brings together reason, objectivity, introspection and humor in a learning environment ideal for young thinkers.

In the following listing of college majors it is important to remember that students can fit into any college and can be successful in any major. We have found that the Personality Types below fit very well at this college. The course-of-study chosen for each Personality Type corresponds to MBTI® research and is presented as one of many examples favorable for that type.

ENFP is often the fun-meister on campus. With their flair for the dramatic, they could easily be interested in the **Cinema and Media Studies** major at Carleton. In fact, the course titled Contemporary Global Cinemas says it all. The breadth of this major is truly impressive. These studies could prepare the student with technical expertise and creative

PERSONALITY MATCH			
ISTJ	ISFJ	INFJ	INTJ
ISTP	ISFP	INFP	INTP
ESTP	ESFP	ENFP	ENTP
ESTJ	ESFJ	ENFJ	ENTJ

awareness. Cinema studies are explored by nationality within the Film History sequence of three courses. The subtle humor on campus is surely apparent within this major.

INFJ likes to work with others in small work settings solving the world's problems. This works well for a career in social science. The **Sociology and Anthropology** major is an excellent preparation for graduate studies. The class in Anthropology of Humor is going to help this type chill while being studious simultaneously. Committed and conceptual INFJs have much to offer in this abstract discipline and can benefit from a little lesson in chill at this winter campus.

INFP with talent in art finds a perfect home at Carleton College in the **Art** major. The studio arts department offers a rich selection of handcraft courses that INFP can pursue while expressing personal beliefs through the artistic medium. The Paper Arts course offers a definitive study of dyes, colors and fibers providing a knowledge base that is sought after in specialty shops, museums and high end artifact boutiques. When combined with this type's originality and talent, the artist will not be starving at this Carleton graduate's household.

ENTJ may bring a streak of practicality to this campus and to the studies in the **Psychology** major at Carleton College. This department emphasizes analytic skills and allows ENTJ to pursue the intellectual challenge of understanding complex human behaviors and institutions. The course in Language and Deception will attract this type often possessing of leadership instinct.

INTJ and the major in **Political Science** at Carleton could lead to a professional career in justice. The faculty has an exceptionally fine curriculum that rewards these strong introspective thinkers. The American political canvas is portrayed by accurate historical content and context, notable for its absence of politically correct filters. INTJs would not shrink from the difficult decisions and dilemmas of government service at national and regional levels.

ENTP likes to start up projects or ventures. The concentration in **South Asian Studies** will prepare them for exciting opportunities in the region comprising India, Pakistan, Nepal and Sri Lanka. This part of the world is increasing material consumption as well as manufacturing. Combined with the major in **Economics**, enterprising ENTPs might work for international business concerns looking to expand services in the region. Travels to the other side of our world will help fill up ENTP's bottomless curiosity and imagination.

INTP relates to the word 'concentration' and will likely find Carleton's concentration in **Cognitive Science** a good choice. In fact, they might delight in the comparison of the computer to the human mind as one of the directions this study will point them toward. The nature of careers in the cognitive sciences suit INTP who prefers to reason with technical concepts. Excitement for this type is to find the cutting edge and the sharper the better.

ISTP can handle the precision and concentration needed in the work associated with **Biochemistry**. At Carleton, students study both chemistry and biology as separate fields and then pursue integration through experience and exercises developed by the faculty. ISTP likes technical work and might easily wander into the field of applied medicine in designing, operating or maintaining sensitive medical equipment.

CASE WESTERN RESERVE UNIVERSITY

103 Tomlinson Hall
10900 Euclid Avenue
Cleveland, OH 44106-7055
Website: www.cwru.edu
Admissions Telephone: 216-368-4450
Undergraduates: 4,260; 2,384 Men,1,876 Women
Graduate Students: 4,616

Physical Environment

Case Western Reserve University is located at the cultural center of Cleveland, surrounded by museums, the Cleveland Orchestra's Severance Hall and the Institutes of Art and Music. Students occasionally attend the performances and the more informal arts venues since they are within walking distance. The nearby Little Italy draws students in droves for their favorite foods. The city of Cleveland itself pulls in students who are comfortable with novelty and unusual environments as exemplified by the **Rock 'n' Roll Hall of Fame**, designed by world famous architect I. M. Pei.

CWRU's 550 acres are separated by Euclid Avenue, which is the main throughway. The north side of campus feels younger because it has newer buildings and houses first and second year students. The architecture on north campus is ultramodern. Village at 115 is a seven-building residential complex for upperclass students with many amenities of apartment-style living. The Peter B. Lewis building for business management has rounded walls that appear as if they were melted, topped off with a huge metal bow on the roof. The metal bow gives the building a look as if it were a boxed present left out in the rain. Students study in this creative, **inspirational architecture**. It's easy to see it took guts and imagination to place it on the campus. Yet the light is plentiful inside, and it's clear that the physical space is designed to break down conventional assumptions and enhance productivity.

The south side of campus has a grander, more established feel located on the hill. It houses upperclass students and **fraternities and sororities**. The hospital, engineering and science departments have existed here for a long time and appear very solid in contrast to the north campus architecture. Students are attracted to CWRU because of the **world class research facilities**. The hospital on campus serves the Cleveland community as well as for internships in the many health-related majors. Varied yet cohesive, the architecture on this campus is a metaphor for the inter-disciplinary connections that students make between very different subjects as they move through their undergraduate years at CWRU.

Social Environment

CWRU is great for those students who expect to conduct **mega research**, **love technology** and wander in big city vibrant cultural neighborhoods. Cleveland and this university fulfill each of these expectations and then some. High school valedictorians find a way to keep up the study routine and enliven their social experience in Cleveland's artistic districts. CWRU is also for those who like old-fashioned congeniality. There is solid representation from each of the 50 states and, yes, it is a long flight from Alaska and Hawaii. Most international undergraduates come from South Korea, China and India. Yet another surprise, Lake Erie, offers a visual respite for the undergrads coming from continental land masses surrounded by oceans.

CWRU is pulling in students who have a **practical expectation** of making a positive difference in their chosen career fields. However, they are not out to break the mold and tend to be **traditional** in their dress and political views. Students are attracted to the **exceptional openness** in the course of studies and the many possibilities for research, in all of the "ologies" and human health. Those who prefer a measured and moderate pace in which to study can find this rhythm on campus also. Competition is not the prime motivator. The strong social scene of the city and the vibrant Greek system on campus tend to mediate academic intensity. Many students here are **intellectually confident** and comfortable within their skins. The strong Residential Life programs and living villages on campus take advantage of these characteristics within the student body, translating these strengths into graduate and professional skills

Compatibility with Personality Types and Preferences

Case Western Reserve University and Cleveland are delightful, especially in warm weather. This university maintains the passion of a small liberal arts college for the humanities plus the intellectual rigor and commitment to advanced research in the physical sciences. A major characteristic of the educational philosophy is openness (P), with few intellectual boundaries. CWRU seeks to be a transforming presence in America and the world. It is an exceptional institution that develops and maintains current scientific and cultural knowledge. The role of the CWRU graduate is to seemlessly identify with everyday American enterprise and institutions. In this cooperative manner, CWRU seeks to interface human content and values with technology (F). The university stays quite fluid when it comes to prescribed academic courses. Traditional subjects of study can lead to either a bachelor of arts or a bachelor of science. Students here choose which would be better suited to their future plans after graduation. At CWRU, the traditional academic majors are supplemented with choice electives. The major of anthropology has four concentrations plus a fifth option. That option allows the student to follow their interest with permission from the department. CWRU brims with creativity (N). It is in the academic bulletin of courses, exemplified in the humorous architecture, and unique in their strong support via the Greek Life Office within the Division of Student Affairs. Students at Case Western Reserve will find it very easy to socialize and learn on this campus. The whole campus culture here is fond of connecting logic (T) and free association of ideas. They are familiar with genuine, human concern.

In the following listing of college majors it is important to remember that students can fit

PERSONALITY MATCH			
ISTJ	ISFJ	INFJ	INTJ
ISTP	ISFP	INFP	INTP
ESTP	ESFP	ENFP	ENTP
ESTJ	ESFJ	ENFJ	ENTJ

into any college and can be successful in any major. We have found that the Personality Types below fit very well at this college. The course-of-study chosen for each Personality Type corresponds to MBTI® research and is presented as one of many examples favorable for that type.

ENFJ will find the Bachelor of Arts in **Computer Science** a most pleasant way to prepare for a career in the field. They are not often drawn to such precise fields of study without obvious connections to people. CWRU, with its characteristic openness, invites interface between human kind and the logic in computer science. At CWRU, this type might want to work on seismic detection through computer programming while combining research with the exceptional geology department and its state of the art research labs. Or, since a substantial part of the degree is in electives, perhaps ENFJ will choose the premed sequence. International students of the Pacific Basin on this campus can call attention to the anguish of tsunamis.

ISTP loves mechanical gadgets. With the return to the moon on the distant American horizon, the degree in **Aerospace Engineering** is mighty attractive to this type. CWRU has a strong predisposition for space exploration and the degree is readily focused on vehicles that transition from atmospheric layers to space. CWRU has the amazing technical facilities to do meaningful research at the undergraduate and graduate level. This will keep ISTP smiling while tinkering with the fancy gadgets and thrilled that there is little regimentation in this research environment.

ENTJ has to find innovation within their educational studies and careers to be well satisfied. Although **Civil Engineering** is a traditional field, CWRU threads innovation and discovery throughout the curriculum. Construction Engineering and Management is one of the elective sequence options within this degree. CWRU really prompts its graduates and faculty to start businesses. It will be this type who takes the latest ideas and technology out to the market.

ENTP is just fine with the unusual combination of the major in **Japanese Studies** and minor in **Entrepreneurial Studies**. The fast moving atmosphere of international business always with out-of-the-ordinary flair is very appealing to ENTP. Avoiding routine and structure within a career is important because they are stressed by too much of the familiar. There will be little of that in the Japanese written characters and CWRU starts off with elementary levels emphasizing the 50 kanji characters. At this university, the daunting is possible and this is a type who will not be scared off.

ESFP likes to have a toolbox of skills which they can utilize with expertise. As a dietitian, this type gets to help others in a most direct, beneficial way. The major in **Nutrition** allows ESFP to get personally involved with clients interpreting the tension and conflict that often accompany diets. The state of the art research facilities add extra structure to this degree at the molecular level. At CWRU, there is flexibility in pointing the undergraduate studies toward all the career options from graduate programs to work in the pharmaceutical industry.

ISFP might want to take advantage of CWRU direct admission for first year students to the **Nursing** program. Here students will find policies of encouragement for entering nursing programs at the undergraduate level. The exceptional quality and breadth of this four-year nursing program is another indication of the openness of CWRU educational philosophy. On any one day, ISFP might be in the classroom, Cleveland Clinic, the Center for Bio-informatics, the Multimedia Simulation Center or the cyber café. The world of health care and its many avenues for personal commitment and career paths is going to be well understood by graduates of this university. ISFP appreciates and seeks the professional guidance that is clearly part of the Frances Payne Bolton School of Nursing.

ISFJ often likes to work in the health care environment. The undergraduate degree at CWRU in **Nutritional Biochemistry and Metabolism** is offered as either a bachelor of science or a bachelor of arts. Since this type is meticulous by nature, the exacting requirements in this discipline are fine with them. Reflective ISFJ prefers to have time and not to be rushed or pushed into career decisions. CWRU admission policies are well in tune with and understand the open doors on this campus are designed to peer through while deciding which path to take.

ESTP likes to pull solutions together with no notice, and being spontaneous is in their nature. A **Management** degree with a concentration in finance could seem pretty sensible to them. The reality of the organizational budget can be a springboard to the solution for this type, a masterful negotiator. This major at CWRU fits in nicely with the university's overall interest in transforming society. In this case and this degree, the transformation takes place through entrepreneurial investments. This type is comfortable with the risk and CWRU is primed to teach their graduates how to move forward in the dynamic business world.

ENFP will smile at the idea of combining two rather unusual courses of study while moving forward into a fun, rewarding career track. The double major is encouraged at this university and **Music** combined with **Gerontological Studies** is a distinct possibility for ENFP who likes to motivate others with their own sense of the possible. This type simply must have fun somewhere in their lifestyles and why not at work? Music fits in nicely with the elderly population who is not as rushed and has the time to enjoy it. Can't you see the older faces smiling now?

INFP could find the **Religious Studies** major personally and professionally rewarding. As this type needs to reach out to others in a caring, individualized way, adding the minor in **Gerontological Studies** makes good sense. It allows them to teach and develop spiritual materials for use with the baby boom generation as their golden decades progress. This type very much wants to help others realize their full potential with inspiration. It also allows them to put their powerful reflection toward new and creative services for the aged.

INTP can tailor their own interests into specific studies about the laws of nature at CWRU. This type who loves to ponder will probably arrive on campus with a few thoughts on what they would like to study related to physics. So the **Engineering Physics** degree takes it a step farther for this theoretical type who prefers to work with complex ideas. This degree is right on for INTP since it pairs the biomaterials sequence with the likes of tissue engineering and such stuff.

INFJ who decides to take the degree in **Sociology** at CWRU will be in good shape when it comes to guidance and mentoring for a focus within this broad field. The department emphasizes the connection to health policy and health decline throughout the life course. This type truly wants to affect the well being of others, yet would prefer to do this through an organizational structure. With the current complex governmental directives coming from Washington DC, there will be no shortage of needy elderly citizens struggling to secure basic health services.

INTJ can often have a bit of the artist in them because of their bent for original thinking. There is a nice combination of studies here that will let this creative type run profitably with their imagination. The **Art History** major combined with the **Pre-Architecture** major is a natural at CWRU. The city of Cleveland right outside the doors of the campus is a wonderful study in architecture with its Rock 'n' Roll museum designed by I. M. Pei. One only has to look at the campus buildings recently completed to see how serious this university is about physical design and its daily influence to understand how well-suited this degree on this campus is for INTJ.

THE CLAREMONT COLLEGES

Claremont McKenna College
890 Columbia Avenue
Claremont, CA 91711-6425
Website: www.claremontmkenna.edu
Admission Telephone: 909-621-8088
Undergraduates: 1,260; 660 Men, 600 Women

Harvey Mudd College
31 Platt Boulevard
Claremont, CA 91711
Website: www.hmc.edu
Admission Telephone: 909-621-8011
Undergraduates: 782; 440 Men, 342 Women

Pitzer College
1050 North Mills Avenue
Claremont, CA 91711-6101
Website: www.pitzer.edu
Admissions Telephone: 909-621-8129
Undergraduates: 1,000; Men and Women

Pomona College
333 N. College Way
Claremont, CA 91711-6312
Website: www.pomona.edu
Admissions Telephone: 909-621-8134
Undergraduates: 1,596; 766 Men, 830 women

Scripps College
1030 Columbia Avenue
Claremont, CA 91711
Website: www.scrippscollege.edu
Admissions Telephone:
Undergraduates: 962 Women

Physical Environment

These five premier colleges are the western version of New England's **small prestigious liberal arts colleges.** They live up to that reputation superbly. Within a hundred years they have replicated and branded their identities well short of the three centuries of their peers in the northeast. Each has a particular architecture that drives its own character academically and socially. However, put together, they are more than the sum of the whole.

The physical environment is driven by the warm **southern California weather**, which allows for consistent outdoor activity. Students become strong in their biking skills and skateboarding. They can be seen walking or using mopeds and unicycles to get around. Students are often in summer wear in November as they walk from one campus to the other. Because the colleges are **adjacent to one another**, it's common to have Pitzer students interact with Harvey Mudd students who are located just across the street.

The colleges are located an hour east of Los Angeles. The San Gabriel Mountains are immediately north of the campus. There is a healthy competition among the students to see which campus uses less water in this ecologically fragile environment. Students are attracted to the Claremont campuses where they can pick limes and grapefruit on their way to class.

Pomona College will be sporting the new Millikan Laboratory in 2015 with planetarium, teaching labs, classrooms student research space, faculty labs, lounges and Woo Hooooo....a machine shop.

Claremont McKenna has an expansive interior courtyard that promotes students mingling at the snack bar on the perimeter while others play Frisbee or lay on the grass. The Spanish-style plaza, the Parent Field, is large enough to serve as the **congregation point** for the student population of all the five colleges and is often used for socials. The new Kravis Center solves the previous parking problem and sports a delightful architectural design with glass, water and cantilevered wings. The Mid Quad dormitories of the 50s and 60s are next in the renovation schedule for 2014 and 2015, complete with air-conditioning.

Pitzer College is the most "**artsy**" campus with cartoon panels/vignettes painted on its walls. The 2007 **residential life project,** reminiscent of 1950s and 60s motels constructed along the highways of that era, has a green belt around the perimeter equal to the size of its footprint. Phase II, the East and West Halls, were completed in 2012 and received much praise for energy conservation design. The entire project, designed by committee, seems to reflect the input of many perspectives. Comfy they have to be!

Scripps College is located in the center, surrounded by Harvey Mudd, Pitzer, Claremont McKenna and the graduate university. Scripps boasts a beautiful courtyard surrounded by the dance studio, art museum and theatre arts center lending a **cultural** feeling to this campus. The dorms are furnished with antiques and rugs.

Harvey Mudd takes up a narrow rectangular area on the northern perimeter of the Claremont campuses. The residence halls are located at one end of the Mudd campus and students **skateboard** down to the dining hall and library at the other end. The campus celebrated the opening of the new academic building with collaborative learning in mind and lots of passive daylight strategies. They were a big step up from the utilitarian concrete of the 1950s former learning spaces.

Social Environment

Each of the Claremont Colleges can be viewed with their individual social style and unique values of the student body.

At **Pomona** undergraduates are **high-achieving** students who like to talk, have fun and **relax**. They are **clean-cut** and happy to be at Pomona. They have solid interests in non-academic activities, such as ballroom dancing. What they wear is not important as long as it is comfortable, so there are many jeans and T-shirts, knapsacks, soccer gear and of course, lots of smartphones. The student body consists of a mix of liberals and conservatives. They are interested in discovering various perspectives ranging from the realistic to the imaginative to the outrageous.

Harvey Mudd is the engineering college for the Claremont campus. Those who select the engineering major are comfortable and confident with the broad-based engineering studies. Their team-based approach starts in first the year and it pulls in students who like to **collaborate** and socialize. Ultimate Frisbee is a favorite on this campus. High school students who may have spent their last four years behind a keyboard will grow in their ability to converse and express complex ideas.

Claremont McKenna has a reputation for being the most social of the colleges and hosting the most popular and well-attended parties. Typically, these students are **polished** and sure of themselves. It's no surprise that from Sunday through Friday they are in their room studying intensely, maybe on iPads searching bloomberg.com. The college motto is "Leaders in the Making." The Athenaeum features many prominent speakers. In Fall 2013, multiple Jewish perspectives were offered, along with speakers of Asian religions, notably absent was the Christian perspective. Although it's ok to be academically undecided, many students arrive with specific career goals in mind.

Pitzer students are **sensitive,** some may be bold in appearance but there is a sweet marshmallow somewhere in each of these undergrads. They seek to be in each other's company, supporting causes like the preservation of the declining bumble bee population. But their second love is **food**. Pitzer has the best pasta on campus. But don't ask the Ptizer club Grillmasters, they are into meat. Delightfully **unique** within the Claremont colleges, this campus encourages taking social chances, building friendships and conversing within comfortable architecture a bit like your favorite slippers.

Scripps attracts contemporary, **composed** women who like to express themselves through the dramatic arts, reading and writing. This is a group comfortable with humanistic values focusing on caring for others, absent activist policy agendas. Campus social life is richly supplemented by programs and activities in the Scripps residence halls. This college is the rare and enviable institution that promotes female perspectives within the context of impacting the whole of society as experienced by both female and male citizens.

Compatibility with Personality Types and Preferences

The five Claremont Colleges, collectively known as the Consortium, operate in five different environments with five separate admission offices. Their cultural environments seem to stem from the time period each was founded. They physically sit across the street from each other, sharing the same compact campus space. It is a great combination and it is not surprising that they have an educational fit for all sixteen of the Personality Types. Pomona College with its claim to being first, 1887, and the sponsor to the rest is also the wise granddaddy. Their founders embraced a leadership role and looked far into the future (N). Pomona has an intellectually peaceful environment that stimulates the connection between student and knowledge. In this way, Pomona encourages passion. Scripps College, the women's college of the Consortium, was founded next in the roaring 20s with the liberated ideals of the times. Since then it has developed an educational philosophy that graduates competent (S) women who take their place in society without fanfare. Claremont McKenna is a WWII baby, founded in 1946. While winning is not their motto, the triumph that came with winning that war has seeped into CMC's culture. Leadership is a strong characteristic (T) within this student body which catapults them into dynamic professions. Harvey Mudd, the unique engineering college, moved into a cultural open space at the Claremont institution. In 1955, America was struggling with ever increasing weaponry and technical progress that threatened to spin out of man's control; this is the turbulent vortex that Harvey Mudd competently filled. Their administration brought in the extraordinary emphasis on humanity (F) and put it together with technological disciplines. The youngest in the Consortium, Pitzer College, grew up in the 1960s counter culture and lovingly embraced those ideals. Here it is more than OK to be uncertain (P); in fact, it helps Pitzer students dig deep into the meaning of souls.

In the following listing of college majors it is important to remember that students can fit into any college and can be successful in any major. We have found that the Personality Types below fit very well at this college. The course-of-study chosen for each Personality Type corresponds to MBTI® research and is presented as one of many examples favorable for that type.

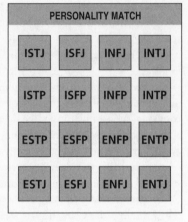

ISTJ can follow their desire to go into civil service positions through the Pomona's **Public Policy Analysis** program. There are 11 concentrations within the program which is usually reserved for senior undergraduate students. However, ISTJ is a workhorse and the **Economics** concentration offers the data points they love. At the same time, Scripps College offers an approach to economics that could work for the lady ISTJ. Intermediate Microeconomic Theory looks at the role of government and this type often appreciates well-delineated roles and responsibilities.

ISTP works well at Pomona College, Scripps and Harvey Mudd because all offer compatible learning environments for this objective type. **Computer Science** at Harvey Mudd mixes experiment, theory and design. The ISTP will be pleased with this degree that blends logic and philosophy in its attempt to harness the dynamic discipline. For example, the course in Artificial Intelligence will include searching, learning and representation within the environment of uncertainty. At Scripps, the **Psychology** major compiles knowledge through observation, participation and experimental investigation. This approach leans toward utility in the field of psychology, perhaps a career in forensic psychology for ISTP?

ESTP at Claremont McKenna might dive into economics through the **Financial Economic Sequence**. The sequence examines the cultural environment of high finance and allows this type to see how their instinctual problem solving can be applied. Harvey Mudd supports a dynamic and exciting trial-and-error approach to learning about the physical world. For this type who pages through the books when necessary, Harvey Mudd has the 'show me' approach that they prefer. In one recent newsletter Mudders called out - Gnarly Waves Equal Gnarly Research. Ok, here's the explanation. There were two Mudders who went surfing over a recent break.

ESTJ at Pomona College could look to the **Molecular Biology** major that offers an interdisciplinary approach. This type does not enjoy interdisciplinary subjects, yet Pomona will bring chemistry and biology together in the senior level, laboratories -- the microscopes will be on. The major would provide excellent access to research and advancement to medical school. The **History** major at Scripps stands up and looks closely at Liberation Theology's impact on the Catholic Faith in Latin America. Should Claremont McKenna's Athenaum invite Pope Francis to address the subject, ESTJ will be there with iPad in hand. Pope Francis or no Pope Francis, the types impersonal objectivity will be an asset in the course. Claremont McKenna offers an **Ethics Sequence** that within the humanistic curriculum also addresses moral principles based on religion.

ISFJ who is interested in **Dance** will find an outstanding program at Scripps. The major assumes that dance is an interdisciplinary major and prepares graduates for a variety of career options such as arts administration, dance therapy and studies in kinesiology. The growing field of linguistics could draw this type in as well. At Pitzer, the **Linguistics** major highlights foundational knowledge and ethnicity in the classrooms. It will be the sensitive, caring ISFJ at Pitzer whose immigrant ancestry is from northern Europe who understands what it means to be ignored within public education's social programming.

ISFP who is inclined toward arts and crafts will be a good match for Pitzer College. At Pitzer, this type will be able to pursue a love of the arts while exploring and defining a successful career path. Perhaps the student will design a **Special Major** with coursework like Mexican Visual Cultures, Sculptural Objects Functional Art, Tropical Ecology with Biostatistics and Natural Resource Management. This student might wander into the national park service, arts administration or nonprofit organizations that promote the art/nature connection. Two of the three required advisors for the Special Major may be off-campus professionals in their fields.

ESFP will find a unique major that could suit them at Pitzer within the science field. The major in **Human Biology** connects the pure sciences with the social sciences and appeals to this friendly, practical type. The program initiative titled Cross Cultural Health and Healing offers study of alternative medicines and may bring forward any number of successful remedies to our medical research institutes after graduation. The **Biology** major at Harvey Mudd offers the semester in environmental sciences at Woods Hole Marine Biological Laboratory in Massachusetts. Here this type can find a wonderful, creative, can do, hands-on laboratory research world that would support many graduate study options.

ESFJ will find the **Religious Studies** is a cooperative program offered by all five colleges together. Approached by interdisciplinary study, it avoids spiritual direction or exploration. It addresses human meaning thru humanistic philosophies. For their needed practical grounding, ESFJ can also pair it with the **Organizational Studies** major at Pitzer. In the five Claremont Colleges environment, this unusual major/minor combination would make for a fun conversation at the coffee house.

INFJ might go for the **Environmental Analysis** Program at Pomona. It will let this type indulge in the art of problem solving as applied to the fields of law, medicine, conservation, global climate, urban planning and resource management. At Harvey Mudd, creativity rules, and the major in **Mathematical Biology** crosses over into evolutionary biology. With a sufficient background and the investigative bent of Mudders, this type could make a real contribution in research graduate studies that support practices in occupational and physical therapies, not to mention kinesiology. At Claremont McKenna, the goal-driven INFJ can get prepared to find solutions to our most difficult societal problems such as terrorism and abusive governments with the **Human Rights, Genocide and Holocaust** studies.

INFP at Harvey Mudd can put their dreaming and conceptual skills to good use by majoring in **Physics.** The major is heavily dependent on experimental or theoretical research and encourages students to follow their hearts. Pomona is the department chair for the **Theater and Dance** major offered by the five colleges. It encourages exploration of the purpose behind entertainment and form. This is particularly true with dramaturgy and mime. Studying Perspectives on Mind and Brain will prove to be rewarding for INFP in the **Linguistics and Cognitive Science** major at Pomona.

ENFP at Pomona College can comfortably look for the big picture in the major **Philosophy, Politics and Economics**. This course of study allows a student to ponder on right and wrong as well as focus on reality. Surely the problem-analyses in this major will get the ideas flowing freely. The **American Studies** major is a five colleges program. It addresses America's complexity and reviews the different methods by which the subject can be approached. At Harvey Mudd, this type will want to take up the interdisciplinary major, **Biological Chemistry**. It is an emerging discipline with amazing new discoveries and will fascinate the ENFP.

ENFJ could study **Science and Management** at Pitzer. This type's hidden flair for marketing will fit nicely into first-hand experience in the business world encouraged by the department. At Claremont McKenna, the student majoring in **Government** could become astute to dangers when international corporations and the national government get together to form policy behind complicit media journalism. This type will select from concentrations dictated by their personal values. Harvey Mudd is a place where the **Chemistry** major could volunteer for the Science Bus to give a demonstration at local elementary schools. At Scripps College, this type could pursue the major in **Art Conservation**. Careers in consulting can appeal to ENFJ who can be passionate while marshaling the necessary financial resources to conserve historic art.

INTJ might look closely at the **Neuroscience** major offered at Pomona College. It includes emerging concepts about the brain with courses like Biological Basis of Psychopathology. At Claremont McKenna, this type would look at the **Economics and Engineering** program, a dual degree with Harvey Mudd. This five-year degree would offer the intensity and the access to a career that would push the edges of building design for human need. At Scripps, the visual resources library holds over 100,000 images available for those majoring in **Art**. This helps the INTJ meet their intense need for finding meaning within the volume and depth of visual culture.

INTP who is interested in the **Psychology** major will like the strong emphasis on the scientific method/theory. The courses typically have laboratories at Pomona. As a result, this psychology degree offers an excellent stepping stone to professional schools in many fields. The **Philosophy** major at Pitzer College should keep this type's desire for deep thinking fairly satisfied with courses like Knowledge, Mind and Existence. At Harvey Mudd, the degree in **Mathematics** will be fun because of great math software programs like Mathematica and Matlab which allow this type to stay up late solving problems.

ENTP often attracted to politics could pursue the **Russian and Eastern European Studies** at Pomona College. Those knowledgeable of the history and ways of the Slavic peoples are in demand. Comfortable in powerful organizations, this type will offer up original interpretations should they enter a career in international politics. Whatever major ENTP might select at Claremont McKenna, it can be complimented with the **Computer Science Sequence**, a strong set of courses designed to give a graduate excellent data analysis skills. The utility of bringing software analysis to a field will definitely make good sense to this type. Harvey Mudd will resonate with the ENTP because optimism in technology and its role in solving human problems that are prevalent throughout all the studies on this campus.

ENTJ should see value in the **Science, Technology and Society** major at Pomona. This type loves the large ideas and global reach of this major. At the same time, this type will be looking to put it to practical use for the future in business, politics or law. Claremont McKenna offers **Legal Studies** as a dual major, paired up to interface with a professional career in other disciplines of the humanities. Among other perspectives, this program option looks at the law as a collection of societal values. The major in **Italian/Italian Studies** is offered only at Scripps College and the Italian Corridor with resident Italian faculty in the dormitory enriches this major. For the ENTJ, the major could lead to a number of artistic enterprises that combine creativity and consulting in the Italian culture.

COLBY COLLEGE

4800 Mayflower Hill
Waterville, ME 04091
Website: www.colby.edu
Admissions Telephone: 800-723-3032
Undergraduates: 1,863; 845 Men, 1,018 Women

Physical Environment

Colby College is built on a hill that **overlooks the town** of Waterville which grew on the banks of the Kennebec River during the industrial revolution. This is an **athletic**, energetic crowd, comfortable with the outdoors, snowboarding at nearby resorts. Students love the Perkins Arboretum, Marston Bog and a bird sanctuary and become **conscientious** about protecting natural environments. The dance majors like to practice on the lawn after the snow has melted and the fields reveal shades of awakening chartreuse. The entire quad is covered with students looking to catch the beginning of their summer tan. Colby's campus architecture is uniform in red brick buildings lined up neatly around the rectangular campus green. It is punctuated by the Miller Library at the very top of Mayflower Hill. Looking out and down from the library offers a vantage point that anchors the campus and one can see the well-used sports fields below.

Students here combine **familiar, conventional** views of civility with the protestant work ethic that embraces hard work and mirrors this traditional **Norman Rockwell** setting. Downtown Waterville feels like a small city, but students essentially remain on campus for the most part. The new BioMass electrical plant is gathering in one national green award after another. Colby stepped out here with a big vision. They use natural compost from surrounding woodlands to fuel their boilers. Realize that Maine remains pretty much forested with a resource not available in many locations. Yet the expanse of this continent needs citizens and forward thinkers in each region to research practical initiatives. Although the adjective 'practical' is still up in the air, Colby will be in the enviable position to host the conference and publish the findings a few decades from now. Bravo Colby.

Social Environment

Colby College students are a smart bunch. They are nattily dressed in seasonal gear and are **high achievers**. Relaxed and sporty, they manage to study, study, study and play at least one club or varsity sport. Colby athletes are successful at national levels. Ice hockey, lacrosse, indoor and outdoor track as well as rowing all scored national placements by Colby undergrads in the last few years.

More than half of the undergrads come from outside New England although a sizeable group claim "just outside of Boston." There is distinct **American metropolitan perspective** at this rural campus, with the campus Jitney that takes runs into Waterville for Starbucks refills. Students here make good use of faculty mentorship and its **extra attention to take academic risks**. The intellectual experience is **guided and structured** with the tutelage of professors. **Collaboration** is the preferred method of study by faculty and students. Study abroad is encouraged as a community service. What about politics? Similar to many colleges, students at Colby tend to be left of center, and question the status quo. However, these students are likely to also value familiar values of order and predictability as they explore current, cultural and social perspectives. The new Multi-Faith Council at Colby seeks to bring faith and spirituality into campus discussions over the evident division growing in pluralistic American society. The administration and the graduates look for the advantage of education to positively impact the communities in which they will work and live. Similar to their Biomass energy experiment, Colby College academic philosophy seeks to capitalize on available resources within present human understanding and reach.

Compatibility with Personality Types and Preferences

Colby College presents a steady educational journey through four years of exacting undergraduate collegiate studies. The administration and faculty expect that students will gain "a broad acquaintance with human knowledge." The Colby College approach to learning seems sequential (S), orderly and often project-based or discovery-based and is known as the Colby Plan. The administration highly integrates the concepts of teaming into campus cultural events as well as course offerings. Colby undergraduates utilize numerous avenues to learn about the beliefs and values of cultures other than their own. Students, for the most part, expect and appreciate the sensitive, empathic views (F) toward world cultures and national ethnicities.

The 360 Plan reflects Colby's admirable, broad presentation of American history and culture as emphasized across the undergraduate experience. The Founding Fathers belief in individual effort protected by freedom from government is explored and presented with contemporary cultural perspective. American culture is also presented through its deficiencies and missteps over the decades. At Colby, these are identified as resolvable. The curriculum, academic practices and methods often highlight the process of consensus, collaboration and majority agreement. Advocacy is viewed as a viable option and it follows that positions can be translated into governance through education and community regulation. In many ways, stewardship drives this campus culture as Colby students seek personal and career directions that can also address inequity.

In the following listing of college majors it is important to remember that students can fit into any college and can be successful in any major. We have found that the Personality Types below fit very well at this college. The course-of-study chosen for each Personality Type corresponds to MBTI® research and is presented as one of many examples favorable for that type.

ISFJ with fine organizational ability is the perfect type for careers in research and could excel as a curator in natural history and science museums. The major in **Science, Technology and Society** at Colby is an ex-

PERSONALITY MATCH			
ISTJ	ISFJ	INFJ	INTJ
ISTP	ISFP	INFP	INTP
ESTP	ESFP	ENFP	ENTP
ESTJ	ESFJ	ENFJ	ENTJ

cellent preparation for this work and it lets ISFJ make important contributions. As they often prefer they can do this and remain behind the scenes with meticulous preparations.

ESFP often loves animals and can prepare for entry into the veterinary sciences with a concentration in **Cell and Molecular Biology/Biochemistry.** The options after graduation would include graduate study for veterinarian, vet techs and numerous positions with animal reserves and zoos. As more species seem to be moving toward endangered status, there will be increasing efforts to reintroduce them. The ESFP who has this coursework on their resume will find it has much value in this emerging field.

ESTP will like the looks of the concentration in **Financial Markets**. The faculty promotes internships and the capstone experience across public and private business enterprises. The course Intro to Financial Decision Making is a short January term survey of personal finances. In this course, astute ESTP will observe the allocation decisions others make with their credit cards. It is an unusual opportunity that supplements the overall study of finance with an atypical psychological lens.

ISFP often times likes to help others, offering services that are delivered through professional groups or organizations. The concentration in **Neuroscience** at Colby College is an excellent preparation for addiction counselors or therapists. The course Biological Basis of Behavior will be a good start for ISFP to explore the helping professions for future career options, especially in substance abuse services.

ENFJ will identify with a minor in **Human Development** since it will provide a good preparation for careers attractive to this type in child welfare services. ENFJ wants to improve the quality of life for others and will enjoy the flexibility that this minor offers for future and concurrent educational studies. Colby curriculum in this discipline is exceptionally focused on issues of justice and prejudice with less coursework on methodologies in teaching.

ESTJ who is attracted to numbers will benefit from a minor in **Mathematics** at Colby. It would not be unusual for this type to find themselves drawn to leadership positions on campus and after graduation. With a minor in mathematics, the ESTJ will likely rise to increasing levels of management over the course of a career. This minor with its strong offerings in both pure and applied math allows the ESTJ to gather solid experience with formulaic numbers. All the better to confidently move on to national research institutions at executive levels, especially if paired with a science major at Colby.

ESFJ is often interested in the community, and this type's natural ability to reduce tension in conflicted situations suggests moving into careers that serve the public. The **Economics** minor at Colby College offers a good deal of flexibility to direct studies toward a student's interest. This minor can offer the foundational courses for an independent major that centers on **Health Studies** and draws courses from biology, anthropology and global studies.

COLGATE UNIVERSITY

13 Oak Drive
Hamilton, NY 13346
Website: www.colgate.edu
Admission Telephone: 315-228-7401
Undergraduates: 2,860; 1,324 Men, 1,526 Women

Physical Environment

Colgate University is located in **rural,** central New York, in the small town of Hamilton. After students exit from I-90, they see expanses of farmlands, silos and cows. The Colgate campus is built on a hill and the library gives the impression of a castle surrounded by water and well-tended fields. Students here develop **international perspectives** because over half of them study abroad. Financial awards apply to off-campus study trips and these students take advantage of it. Faculty-led research trips are a key component of Colgate's reach out and beyond the campus.

Weather-hardened students love the Trudy Fitness Center and the hikes up and down the hill. They make light-hearted videos of snow adventures on campus. Arriving first year students march up the hill led by faculty and the honor society with torches in hand. Four years later, graduates march down the hill with torches that are tossed into a huge bonfire. The senior class then celebrates one last time together. This campus community is **tight-knit.**

Campus enthusiasm is high for their Division I sports. Within walking distance of the campus there are frat houses and townhomes and apartments for senior undergraduates. The administration announced the campaign for a new athletic facility that will house soccer, hockey and lacrosse. The astronomy and physics curriculum receives national awards with basic laboratories and equipment. It speaks to the robust intellectual commitment resident on campus.

Social Environment

Clubs, clubs, clubs define the highly extroverted nature of students on this campus. Leadership, community service and cultural explorations are high on the list of extracurricular activities for all Colgate students. These undergraduates use Colgate as a lab in which to try out their leadership skills. They are able to juggle many activities while getting good grades. They are attracted by the quality of **academic advising.** Faculty participating in national research may or may not hold current day views on hot button subjects. Professors seem to represent a range of political thought on this campus. This is somewhat unusual at liberal arts colleges in America today, yet gives these undergrads a heads up.

Many students love it here because they have a deep affection for the liberal arts. They find it easy to satisfy the core curriculum requirements and enjoy the many inter-disciplinary courses. **Imaginative** students are attracted by these classes. Logically-minded students are equally attracted to the new science complex.

Nearly half of the students join a fraternity or sorority after their first year, providing more options to develop leadership and planning abilities. Football games are both athletic and social events where many friends cross paths.

Compatibility with Personality Types and Preferences

Colgate University is defined and stands out by its educational atmosphere. It is exceptional in the sense of the relationship (F) between student and faculty in the advising process. Here faculty prompt student originality, discovery and creativity. Administration practice at Colgate fosters independence over group action. Many, if not most, non-academic resources are offered without attached social perspectives. At Colgate support seems to translate into academic courage, so one finds less emphasis on learning centers and tutoring. Students pursue their studies and interests with little political interface from the college pedagogy. It results in exceptional openness, relying on students to precisely think and interpret what they experience. In 2014, the Brothers Annual Speaker will feature Cornel West and Chris Hedges. These two intellectuals are severe critics of current governmental policy and practice. Their message is strident and challenging to process. The Colgate education is characterized by this intensity, originality and modified risk taking. It leads to independent thinkers ready to function across national and global settings. It pushes each student to reach within and outside of Colgate, to build knowledge in their chosen major. In this way, the Colgate experience supports exploration (P) followed by analysis (T). Just ask the Colgate community about raising Colgate's awareness with number the 13 on twitter.

In the following listing of college majors it is important to remember that students can fit into any college and can be successful in any major. We have found that the Personality Types below fit very well at this college. The course-of-study chosen for each Personality Type corresponds to MBTI® research and is presented as one of many examples favorable for that type.

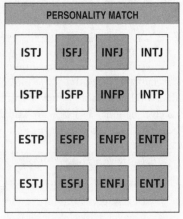

ISFJ will enjoy the orderly nature of the study of **Linguistics.** The minor in this discipline at Colgate offers a strong introduction to the many facets of language studies. Undergraduates write original computer programs to analyze verbal data. This type will apply their meticulous attention and comfort with details to the project.

INFJ could quickly justify the **Peace and Conflict Studies** major at Colgate as a great preparation for a graduate degree. The INFJ really resonates with this topic and also is always ready for a challenge. This research-based major offers three areas of concentration: collective violence, human security and international social justice. Working with others in harmony and yet persuading them toward a common good is a true skill of this type.

INFP often wants to contribute to a cause that they believe in passionately. If they have a scientific bent and toleration for math, the **Environmental Economics** major at Colgate could be a happy find. The study of the environment easily lends itself to passion and the answers are complex and varied. Combined with economics, this major can keep INFP intensely busy reflecting on their values while preparing to sally forth and save the planet after graduation.

ESFP is a warm type of personality and well-matched to the **Caribbean Studies** concentration within Africana and Latin American Studies. It is unusual and draws the undergraduate to visit Caribbean nations where untraditional and simple health care systems still have a presence in the culture. This type's curiosity about people might prompt them to carve out a career in providing practical health services to impoverished nations of the middle and South American continent.

ENFP is drawn to the abstract and the major in **Philosophy and Religion**. The coursework in this major is very expansive in its review of human thought and meaning. Within the extraordinary Political Science curriculum, ENFP can fly from one intriguing course to the next. Colgate's Center for Conservative Political Thought was renamed as the Center for Freedom and Western Civilization in early 2000, but the focus remains the same. The center is quite active with intriguing speakers not often heard on America's liberal arts campuses. Topics in 2014 included Lincoln's Statesmanship, the role of religion in a free society and the US involvement in Afghanistan. ENFP, always independent, might enjoy perspectives outside of politically correct paradigms, but it will have to be fun.

ENTP in the **Natural Science** major will find a strong data-based curriculum with freedom to focus in an area to satisfy their scientific curiosity. Surely the emerging discipline of neuroscience which combines biology, chemistry and psychology is sufficiently wide enough to capture and retain the wide ranging observations of this type.

ESFJ who likes math is going to heartily approve of the **Applied Mathematics** minor at Colgate. This type lives well in orderly environments and what can be more orderly than math. As a minor, Colgate allows the interested student to bypass some of the extreme abstraction of theoretical numbers. Instead, the ESFJ is going to like using the numbers to bring reason into disorderly data dumps they may find upon graduating into the world of work.

ENFJ who is ordinarily drawn to the field of communication is going to like the **Writing and Rhetoric** minor at Colgate University. Their gift of intuition will be in the spotlight during discussion in the unique course titled Visual Rhetorics. Our society is moving away from the written communications, while at the same time relying more on visuals and sound bites and ENFJ is good at the interface of all three of these.

ENTJ might decide to concentrate in **Astrogeophysics** if they spent a lot of time star gazing as a child. Drawn to the sciences and new ideas, this type will also appreciate the high use of logic in math, physics, geology and chemistry required by this major. ENTJ has the willingness to long-range plan and is comfortable with complexity. That is perfect for upcoming scientific exploration if NASA's Ares rocket or a commercial spacecraft takes America back to the moon in the first half of this century.

COLLEGE OF CHARLESTON

66 George Street
Charleston, SC 29424-0001
Website: www.cofc.edu
Admissions Telephone: 843-953-5670
Undergraduates: 9,760; 3,581 Men, 6,179 Women

Physical Environment

The College of Charleston is located in the historic district of downtown Charleston. It's within walking distance of palatial southern homes such as the well-known historic row of houses called "the Battery," which overlook the sea and Fort Sumter in the distance. The College of Charleston is the oldest institution of higher education in South Carolina; formerly independent, it is now a public college with all the **charm** of campuses in similar historic locations. The physical center of campus is Randolph Hall and the grass-covered cistern in front of it. The Cato Center for the Arts is an expansive facility by any standard with floors devoted individually to dance/theater, photography, visual art, music and exhibiting space. The School of Sciences and Mathematics facility wraps around a courtyard, so typical of historic Charleston. This urban campus is intertwined with city streets and it is difficult to know if you are on or off campus. The facilities also include historic **Dixie Plantation,** a national archeological treasure continuously occupied for centuries prior to and including European settlements. It is a biological wildlife center for the Departments of Biology and Geology just 17 miles distant from main campus. In 2014 it will receive a new rice trunk gate, the type used in its early 1800's history to control brackish water ponds. The college has a commitment to **historical preservation**, but in this case it is also economically feasible to use the old style gate instead of the modern aluminum version that deteriorates in 10 years.

A **state of the art library** offers many areas in which to study quietly or with others. The nearby Medical University of South Carolina attracts many students who are thinking of graduate school and are interested in science, research or medical school. Even though admission requirements are higher for out-of-state students, students flock to College of Charleston, charmed by the physical environment and attracted to the **strong sciences, business and performing arts**. The nearby open air market has basket weavers and ethnic Gullah stringing sweet-grass into pleasing patterns. Students enjoy this historic cultural environment that still speaks of the 1860s post-revolutionary period.

Social Environment

The college serves mostly South Carolinians along with those heavily recruited from across the southeastern United States. It has a strong adult division and graduate school. The college also attracts international students with the international port lending credibility to their interdisciplinary programs and international logistics programs. Defined by its proximity to the Atlantic seaboard, they compete in the Colonial Athletic Association primarily with other mid-sized universities. The coed and women's sailing teams won best overall collegiate team in the nation in

2012. Campus dress is best defined as summer casual, taking advantage of the seasonable weather most of the year. The social life is light-hearted and leans toward the arts. **Volunteer efforts** mirror student hometown extracurricular activities. Habitat for Humanity and fundraising for medically at-risk children in nearby Medical University of South Carolina are well supported by undergraduates. The college has over 200 extracurricular clubs. They range from the campus democrats and republicans to crew and fencing plus the **always rockin, never stoppin Dance Marathon**.

Students who like to socialize and study with others are well-suited to this campus. Successful students summon the discipline to minimize the call of Charleston's social attraction. **Imaginative** students who are future-oriented will enjoy the grounding in history, tradition and architecture. The college's forward-looking philosophy ensures excellent undergraduate liberal arts study. Undergraduates here are very welcomed by the city's artistic and professional leaders who utilize their talents in the several city-wide performing arts venues. Facilities such as the recently projected Grice Marine Laboratory in the campus master plan strongly hint at the innovation and commitment of this public institution of learning so informed of our past.

Compatibility with Personality Types and Preferences

College of Charleston is remarkable for its emphasis on the cultural arts and location. The impact of the port and the city's historic origination in the 1600s has seeped into the philosophy of the administration and faculty. The curriculum offers an element of practicality (S) that reflects the needs of today's specialized careers and the college's location on the Atlantic coast. Students attend courses taught by faculty that is knowledgeable of the American economic environment. The performing arts curriculum is solid and mirrors the city's international reputation for beauty, charm and entertainments. The Arts department predictably connects the educational studies in the arts with the city's own strong artistic legacy. At College of Charleston undergraduate students in the arts support and participate in the city's well known festivals like Spoleto as performers and stage managers. It provides that realistic thread that undergraduates here prefer. The port of Charleston is the background for the unusual and very practical study in global logistics. Incoming freighters, offloading goods that must travel to America's heartland, bring the subject of logistics alive. The international port has also influenced the solid business school that has been teaching upperclass business courses in Spanish, French and German for many years. The college archives proudly possess rare Jewish documents from the pre-colonial period. They serve as a beacon for our Judeo-Christian heritage so often shunted to the side for trendy political reporting offered by the national media. This campus wisely reaches into its past for academic and cultural excellence. Yet with a little research it becomes apparent that this faculty is weaving academic boundaries with original, creative, risk taking.

PERSONALITY MATCH

ISTJ	ISFJ	INFJ	INTJ
ISTP	ISFP	INFP	INTP
ESTP	ESFP	ENFP	ENTP
ESTJ	ESFJ	ENFJ	ENTJ

In the following listing of college majors it is important to remember that students can fit into any college and can be successful in any major. We have found that the Personality Types below fit very well at this college. The course-of-study chosen for each Personality Type corresponds to MBTI® research and is presented as one of many examples favorable for that type.

INFJ will be at the top of their game in the business field when it involves serving the public directly. The **Arts Management** major at College of Charleston really offers this possibility. INFJs who are often artistically sensitive souls will enjoy indulging their need for personal expression through the medium of organizing and presenting arts for the community. Their independent, innovative thinking will be an asset in this field that demands flexible planning. COC offers a practical thread of required financial coursework within this major.

INTJ enjoys the responsibility and demands that come with leadership. As a result, this type often gravitates to professional positions of authority. The major in **Geology and Environmental Geosciences** at College of Charleston is representative of a discipline that is becoming critical to our country and the world community. The opportunities for specialization within this field are surprising. The department maintains research projects that undergraduate students support through field experiences around the globe, most recently in India, and especially in the field of oceanography. Now that makes sense.

ISTJ will approve of the specific curriculum in the business school for undergraduates in the **Accounting** major. Graduates in this major often pursue further training and certifications. Undergraduate students at the College of Charleston will be in a good position to apply for the Master of Accountancy at COC. ISTJs love it all: accuracy, precision and diligence. The dynamic internships off shore, for instance the Cayman Islands, may stretch ISTJ comfort levels though.

ISFP is caring all of the time and cautious some of the time. This type prefers to be out and about, performing work that requires attention to detail. ISFPs will thrive in technical professions with a cause such as ecological work that leans in green directions. The major in **Marine Biology** here takes advantage of state and federal resources at the Grice Marine laboratory. The proximity of the ocean and the inland waters in the low sections of the coast makes for ideal laboratory research found at just a very few educational campuses on America's coastlines.

ESTP is often excellent at seeing what needs to get done to competently finish a project on time. With these characteristics, ESTPs are a good bet for the **Global Logistics and Transportation** minor at College of Charleston. ESTPs can elect to declare this concentration or a minor within the business degree. High stakes decisions involving movement of company products around the globe are agreeable for this type who prefers a little action to spice up their day. The port of Charleston lends a fine opportunity to gain knowledge about intermodal transport, where commodities must transfer from ship to rail or ship to truck.

ESFP is good at occupations in the service industry. The major in **Hospitality and Tourism Management** is particularly appropriate in Charleston and for the ESFPs. This major is rather uncommon at liberal arts colleges and universities. It is also in growing demand with societies' increasing emphasis on leisure and entertainment. This type is a natural at hosting events, often making others feel appreciated and welcome. ESFP's good communication skills will come in handy as they work with municipalities and corporate leaders to win approval of their novel and fun recreational proposals. The department participates in the Walt Disney World internship programs.

ENTP must have the opportunity to think about the future during the day. This creative type will like the futuristic work involved with restoration in the major **Historic Preservation and Community Planning.** The College of Charleston is unique in combining these two specializations in such a strong, credible curriculum. ENTPs are adept at strategic planning as they utilize their vision and their willingness to take risks. This type is also pretty good at persuasion which will be needed to secure funds for cultural projects when in competition with nuts and bolts budgets. The downtown historic district of Charleston serves as a dream-come-true internship location for this type and this major. The city and the college have a unique synergy.

ESTJ is an ideal personality to pursue the concentration in **Discovery Informatics**. This original combination of courses is oriented toward data mining and its application to a range of disciplines across the sciences and humanities. ESTJs are just the type to focus on the details and organization needed to interface data with business enterprises or perhaps a career with national defense. After all, the Citadel is just next door.

COLLEGE OF WOOSTER

Office of Admission
Wooster, OH 44691
Website: www.wooster.edu
Admissions Telephone: 330-263-2322
Undergraduates: 2,116; 931 Men, 1,185 Women

Physical Environment

The College of Wooster is adjacent to lovely Victorian homes and also a small strip of convenience stores occasionally used by the students. Downtown Wooster, with its 1970s mix of storefronts and businesses, provides a contrast to the exquisite, carefully designed campus upgrades of the last ten years. The Wooster college landscape, close and enveloping, features dramatic trees and green expanses surrounded by **comfortable 1900s collegiate architecture**. The centerpiece of COW is the newly renovated Kauke building with modern and comfortable classrooms, lounges and inviting seating areas. Since Wooster students typically continue **discussions** after class, Kauke is a favorite **intellectual meeting place**. The new Scott Center for recreation is all three, clever, cheery and classy. Opened in 2012, its wall architecture of glass and light blends naturally with the heavier stone foundations of this campus. Students are very involved with campus-centric activity and the new facilities seem to retain this center of gravity. Although the cafeteria has abandoned trays, these undergrads find sled substitutes for barreling down the short hill near Bornhuetter Hall after a welcome snow dump.

Northeasterners find COW familiar and strategic planning calls for a new science facility that emulates recently built science complexes at liberal arts universities in New England. The Underground is the ever popular dance club and bar that offers a venue for the wry humor found on this campus with comedy night. The Wooster chapel is also an underground structure. Its mid-century concrete architecture sports an angular roof jutting up out of the ground. Sometimes it is used as a vantage point to find family in the crowd below during convocation and other events. The Office of Interfaith Campus Ministries defines spirituality as a 'balance of stretching and settling.' Humor indeed does accompany irony here. Historically, this campus has maintained an even balance of men and women within the student body. Now within two years, enrollment has skewed toward the unfavorable national trend of having a larger female population often observed at smaller liberal arts colleges.

Social Environment

The College of Wooster is for **individualistic** thinkers who are academically motivated to expand and explore the understanding of themselves and the world. Students at Wooster are contributors, socially and academically, on teams and in their personal way. Competition in class is infrequent and collaboration is common in the first years. Wooster's signature program, the **Independent Study Program**, brings in students who are enterprising and **heartfelt**. By the fourth year, students know how to **write confidently** and select their career paths with confidence whether it is graduate study or work. Notable numbers of graduates in the physical sciences, political science and history go on to PhD studies. Notable numbers of foreign nationals bring a worldly focus to the cultural arts because of COW's decades long established alumni networks overseas in third world countries.

Undergraduates here tend to gather and socialize by their interests. **Music** is a popular excuse for socializing. The Department of Music has exceptional resources and professional connections. Undergraduate music majors are typically bound for professional performance venues. There are several distinguishing characteristics common to Wooster students, often they each march to their own drum and many of them engage with ironic humor. They are also **resolute** in their observations, honed in conjunction with their IS advisor over three semesters. The nature of the Independent Study program on this campus propelled the university to its excellent position within college rankings. Although it is already a much admired creative experience, the new APEX campus wide program appears to insert an administrative, oversight presence. Hopefully, this decades-long faculty student collaboration will not be in jeopardy with a "third party on the date."

Compatibility with Personality Types and Preferences

College freshman line up on the steps of Kauke Hall on the first day as curious students, unusually independent folks who may have preferred anonymity in high school. At Wooster, these students often discard that anonymity and move into the educational limelight. After graduation, they move onto the national scene seeking to bring transition to the present and future. Wooster practices that successful educational mix of tremendous latitude (P) and exacting standards. It's a delicate balance that faculty have fine-tuned with much perfection. Students find the advising in the first years to be an open, light and exploratory experience. During the last two years, expectations and academic output become precisely and narrowly defined (J) in the form of Wooster's well known independent study requirements.

Faculty, programs and policies are threaded with a continuous, speculating exploration (N) of the trends in our society. Students here are not particularly counter culture, but a good number find the status quo comes up wanting. The faculty look to new avenues of knowledge in international settings. There is limited prompting for undergrads to explore and experience Americana in the town and Ohio's immediate surroundings. Rather, Wooster students get much encouragement to study outside of the national perspectives and apply their findings to our own cultural institutions. The educational climate here runs on solid optimism combined with accountability toward the world community (F). Faculty place great faith in the individual and society to solve these problems. Within the physical sciences

PERSONALITY MATCH			
ISTJ	ISFJ	INFJ	INTJ
ISTP	ISFP	INFP	INTP
ESTP	ESFP	ENFP	ENTP
ESTJ	ESFJ	ENFJ	ENTJ

the departments are assertive through research, defining the college mission as contributing to and growing the body of scientific discovery.

In the following listing of college majors it is important to remember that students can fit into any college and can be successful in any major. We have found that the Personality Types below fit very well at this college. The course-of-study chosen for each Personality Type corresponds to MBTI® research and is presented as one of many examples favorable for that type.

ENFP could find it hard to declare a major because of their wide-ranging and sincere interest in so many subjects. The field of **Geology** for that very reason is a good one for this type. From physics to policy, ENFPs can decide where they want to work—in the field collecting dirt samples or in Congress advocating for the environment. The major at Wooster is wonderfully open and laid back in that students are given great freedom to find their passion within the discipline. Once found however, it is time to step up their game and Wooster has the mechanisms in place to rein in freewheeling ENFPs. On the academic move, graduates might end up on the Brooks McCall gathering samples at the epicenter of the Gulf oil spill or coring mud tubes in the Bering Sea.

ISFP is another freewheeling type and their desire to be autonomous is honored in the **Theatre and Dance** track at College of Wooster. At this formative college, communication quickly translates to the written text in playwriting and performance. Since the department is organized around examining the human experience through art, ISFP can indulge in their favorite activity—defining living by their personal values. It's also not surprising that Wooster took regional honors in 2007 and was selected to perform "Nocturne" by Adam Rapp at the Kennedy Center in DC. The physical nature of this major is perfect and keeps ISFP's need for action deeply satisfied.

ESFP loves to entertain and the major in **Music** at COW is right for this type with prior musical experience. The Bachelor of Music offers concentrations in performance, theory/composition or history/literature for those interested in graduate study. The music therapy and music education majors offer career tracks for ESFPs who want to bring lighthearted fun into their world of work. For the ESFP who needs music for their soul, the minor will be a wonderful experience while interacting with the passionate music majors.

ISFJ wants to directly support others, one on one, in a caring way. The **Biology** major promotes creativity by expecting students to conduct early and frequent investigation in laboratories set up for this purpose. This teaches ISFJ, not always comfortable with the unknown, to be confident in their creative endeavors.

ESFJ has an ease and way with people, especially if the people are in traditional settings like a hospital or school. Wooster's degree in **Music Therapy** is a brilliant point of light as few colleges offer this study. It is nicely suited for this caring type. ESFJ will especially appreciate the Cleveland Music Therapy Consortium and American Music Therapy Association. These national organizations provide the guidelines for service delivery that ESFJ will want and need to be comfortable in providing therapeutic services.

ISTJ will fit into the **Business Economics** major here quite nicely because of the department's thorough read on complex financial environments. The major is designed for direct entry into the workforce and this makes good sense to ISTJ. The department offers undergrads the opportunity to substitute two math courses within the economics curriculum. This can focus study of financial decision through the lens of quantitative analysis, a particular strength of this type.

INTP who is enamored with computers in high school will surely be attracted to the **Computer Science** major or minor. This type loves to analyze problems and apply solutions from a distance. Software applications that embed planning and development for business or government organizations are right up their alley. At Wooster, the computer science major is located within the math department which makes it a particularly robust academic environment for this powerhouse concentrator—INTP.

ENTP can utilize the minor in **Film Studies** to support their chosen major in another discipline. At Wooster there is a wide range of film study across international cultures and subjects. The curriculum seeks to connect the dots between the visual and auditory output of films. ENTP excels at ingeniously analyzing information with an eye toward original synthesis. You can bet their independent study will draw the major and minor uniquely together because ENTP thrives on originality.

INFP can marshal their characteristic commitment studying **English** here. There is an impressive list of courses by English, American and Anglophone writers. Students at Wooster can delve into Faulkner's The Sound and The Fury which must necessarily deal with the trauma and experiences of mental retardation. In this department, undergrads can find reflections and awareness from American perspectives. Adaptable, curious INFP can search out interdisciplinary perspectives in other academic departments also since American Studies is not offered at this small liberal arts college.

ENFJ is likely to be comfortable moving into the world of speech and language pathology. The degree in **Communication Sciences and Disorders** prepares students for the graduate level study needed to practice in the field. The department emphasizes the linguistic evolution, human development, the cause of disorders and the options for service in the community. This type will naturally look to the emotional causes of speech disorders also.

INFJ likes to develop new approaches to help people out. The field of alternative health practitioner may have appeal to the INFJ. Wooster offers an exceptionally strong grounding for careers in the health field with its degree in **Chemistry**. The curriculum supports follow on degrees in research disciplines and direct entry into the work force. In whatever field the INFJ wanders toward with the major in chemistry, whether the physical sciences, medicine or business, this type is likely to want their work to promote and benefit society.

COLUMBIA UNIVERSITY

212 Hamilton Hall MC 2807
1130 Amsterdam Avenue
New York, NY 10027
Website: www.columbia.edu
Admission Telephone: 212-854-2521
Undergraduates: 8,365: 4,400 Men, 3,965 Women
Graduate Students: 13,496

Physical Environment

Founded in 1754, Columbia University is located in **Upper Manhattan**, a very lively and desirable area of this world class city. Despite the dynamic energy and heavy traffic just on the other side of their classroom windows, students tend to acclimate to the pace and drumbeat of the "Big Apple." They develop **city-smarts** while walking the streets with a buddy at night. They enjoy the outdoor cafés, the ethnic restaurants, the bookshops and the art that blankets the city neighborhoods. The students who come to Colombia usually appreciate theater and can't wait to visit Broadway productions.

The university has 22 schools most of which offer only graduate level degrees. Columbia College offers the liberal arts curriculum for coed undergraduates and the Fu Engineering and Applied Science School provides coed undergraduate degrees as well. Barnard College, the liberal arts college for undergraduate women, offers joint degrees, open courses and cross registration to all the undergraduate students at this university.

Prospective students may hear of the university's Manhattanville Project, in the first stages of development. It is projected for mixed academic and residential use on 17 acres in the west Harlem neighborhood. It is reflective of Columbia's master growth initiatives which expect to grow and spread out across the city rather than in place of refitting the main campus which is bound by commercial real estate.

Housing is guaranteed for all freshman and those students who accept the dorm assignment each undergraduate year thereafter. Approximately 95 percent of students live in school-sponsored housing. The Greek brownstones with interesting architectural details house sororities and fraternities on this campus. Some of the living and learning communities include residence for faculty families giving students accessibility to their professors for after-hours discussion and late evening imagination. Undergraduates who like the **relentless intensity** of the city thrive on this campus. Most are also attracted by the depth of resources within the university itself. The Northwest Corner building has **21 national research laboratories** and approximately 250 faculty and students find themselves daily in its **academic hub**.

Social Environment

New York City attracts people from all over the world and Columbia College reflects this pluralism. All undergraduates learn to socialize with others very different from themselves. Students here want to competently influence environments across the global economy and the world of emerging ideas. These undergraduates are busy, motivated and already have their next goal lined up. They are **incredibly focused and ambitious**. However, despite the competition, students here are still friendly and willing to collaborate which enhances the educational process.

Each student arrives with a resume already marked by accomplishment and curiosity. It makes for **searching conversation** on campus. Many of these conversations happen on the steps in front of Low Library. Social life is active during freshmen first days because each of the extracurricular clubs, fraternities and sororities are trying to encourage awareness and gain new members. After these initial weeks, many students socialize off campus in the city forming a tight group of a few friends. Social life here usually involves **intellectual endeavors**. With just the call of a cab, undergrads can haunt art galleries, music and theater performances offering the best of contemporary American culture. Humor wedges into campus life thru Varsity show. It is a Columbia tradition that makes fun of the administration in a campus satire. Most student clubs are primarily academic in orientation on this campus, although anime and culinary clubs found their way into the mix.

Columbia students are creative, **idea-driven**, searching for possibilities. They tend to come from very well-educated families with successful backgrounds. They have high expectations. All, including the want-to-be engineers, receive an exceptionally fine liberal arts exposure in the Core curriculum. Students work with non-profit centers, design intranets for inner city public schools, learn about playground engineering and come to know some of the ethnic population needs of the city.

Compatibility with Personality Types and Preferences

Columbia University is the place for educational study (P) without limits. Undergraduate students are expected and expect to conduct research in the national labs. This approach to education goes hand in hand with teaching laboratories where students are privileged to observe (S) and learn in an environment rarely constrained by budgets. Yet Columbia adds another element to this learning paradigm. The university expects and confidently predicts that during their four years on campus the undergraduates will be generating discovery in their respective fields. It is a tall order and students are carefully and precisely (J) taught to develop their reasoning (T) patterns of analysis.

The faculty and administration is equally concerned with developing the moral standard (F) and aggressively inserts that perspective within their curriculum. The Core is a series of required studies for entering students that delves into the great books and texts of western civilization as well as fundamental scientific laws. There is an expectation that students will develop a coherent belief system on the human condition and carry that forward in their educational studies and future careers (N). Columbia's remarkable storehouse of knowledge and resources awaits the undergraduate freshman. Together with the intensive academic mentoring, undergraduates are submerged in a culture that bears slight resemblance to the hometowns and metropolitan areas from which they came. Columbia University actively defines and completes part of the puzzle that is New York City.

In the following listing of college majors it is important to remember that students can fit into any college and can be successful in any major. We have found that the Personality

Types below fit very well at this college. The course-of-study chosen for each Personality Type corresponds to MBTI® research and is presented as one of many examples favorable for that type.

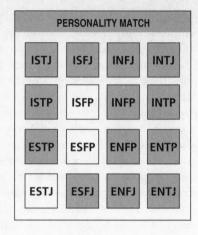

PERSONALITY MATCH

ISTJ	ISFJ	INFJ	INTJ
ISTP	ISFP	INFP	INTP
ESTP	ESFP	ENFP	ENTP
ESTJ	ESFJ	ENFJ	ENTJ

INFP will find the **Drama and Theater Arts** at Columbia sufficiently abstract and analytic. The department offers expansive coursework in the crafts of acting, directing, play writing and staging. Yet the study of theater across cultures and time periods is equally expansive. It is empathic INFP who identifies with colonial peoples when studying for the course, Early American Drama and Performance: Staging a Nation. Additional layers in the curriculum are drawn from impressions of the city's canvas and historical theaters.

INFJ and imagination go together. The program in **Linguistics** is well resourced with the multiple language offerings and New York City itself. City internships, service learning and social entertainment all brim with exposure to the 300+ foreign languages spoken in the city. The course in Language Documentation and Field Methods certainly has unequalled access to native speakers and languages for undergraduates to study. Three study components comprise the major: spoken word, cognitive processing and cultural medium.

INTJ is going to find much that suits their learning style at Columbia. This type is very energized by flexible ideas, far out concepts and the freedom to mix and match with intensity. The rather unusual discipline of **Financial Engineering** is a good example of this kind of innovation. INTJ's originality will be enthusiastically encouraged in this discipline. New quantitative methodologies are emerging in this field that requires courses in calculus, differential equations, probability and statistics. INTJs who are private and skeptical by nature may benefit from the four-year advising system at Columbia.

ISTP will find plenty of facts to noodle with the **Chemical Engineering** degree. This type loves to observe and develop their own conceptual understanding of factual data. The technologies and research subjects under study in the Columbia labs will intrigue ISTPs. Once they find practical purpose in their coursework, ISTP will become an unrelenting student likely staying overnight in Northwest Building, surprised to see the sun pop through the windows and their consciousness. Whether it will be future chemical sensors or agricultural products, they will be all eyes and ears while mastering their technical skills at the university.

ISTJ relates well to the direct nature of electricity, it is either on or off. The degree in **Electrical Engineering** at Columbia encompasses the alpha and omega of electrical transmission and this suits ISTJ just fine. This type prefers to live in the world of predictability and practicality. Nevertheless, this engineering degree has its twists and surprises that would be found the research labs. The sustained mentoring through four years at Columbia will help ISTJ to settle on their focus within the degree. They will approach and complete the Core liberal arts curriculum at Columbia with some suspicion, yet likely approve when it is completed. This type takes time to synthesize knowledge coming in from all disciplines and it will always be available for recall.

ISFJ likes to immerse themselves in the facts and master the subject at hand. The major in **Ecology, Evolution and Environmental Biology** offers this opportunity. The Saga of Life synthesizes evolution through the physical sciences, social sciences and humanities. In 2004, the International Theological Commission, headed by Pope Benedict, held that science, not theology, must resolve the debate on evolution. Columbia College faculty would heartily approve.

INTP will likely have their interest alerted by reading about the **Jazz** concentration. The nature of jazz music has random structure within its lilting sound. It could appeal to INTP who actually is attracted to random data. This power thinker would delight in homework that required analysis of jazz sounds at the clubs in NYC. Leave it to the INTP to find some patterns in the freewheeling instrumental play. The study of jazz is interdisciplinary and happily interfaces with all majors. It mirrors the musicians of this art form—intellectual, original, marching to their own drummer. This is the INTP.

ESTP will find the lively action they seek in New York City and the **Urban Studies** program. This type is a master at collaboration and they will scavenge the city for data supporting their research inquiries. It will be the ESTP who can establish near immediate rapport with the shopkeepers, finance gurus and ethnic personalities of the city. It will be the ESTP who pulls fellow students together to get a project off dead center. ESTPs like the survey nature of this major, jumping with ease from one filter such as economics to another like architecture.

ENFP is such a creative soul. Of course, the **Creative Writing** major is likely to attract simply because it has one of their favorite words in it. This well-developed major draws on literary masterpieces as well as the New York City experience. ENFPs will gladly incorporate human emotions on display in the city throughout their essays. The advisor will be important for this type. Personal relationships are highly valued by ENFPs. They look to their advisor to be an anchor for the chaotic energy of the city, as well as their own.

ENTP will like the **Information Science** major since it allows students to select a focus for the upper division courses. With the focus determined, students then learn and perfect information modeling systems. Hmmm… What will ENTP select for the focus: contemporary science, science/economy, health sciences, computer science or another discipline? This adaptable, creative type searches for value and meaning in many disciplines. Sampling the variety, ENTP will finally be willing to make that choice.

ESFJ will recognize and accept the lure of Barnard College's **Urban Teaching** track in the **Education** major. The problems of urban schools and public education await ESFJ's patient commitment and sincere attention to daily life events. ESFJs will carefully prepare for student teaching in New York City's urban schools. With the support of an experienced teacher, their warmth will shine through in the city's charged classrooms filled with emotion, expectation, optimism and anxiety. It will be ESFJs who can confidently and credibly point the way into the future for their young charges. This education program combines with the undergraduate student's declared major.

ENFJ is exceptionally compelling when armed with knowledge while speaking to audiences. The major in **Business Management** is definitely going to provide ENFJ with considerable acumen. Undergraduates interface with the professional graduate school of business at the university, as well. The abstract principles found in psychology and sociology are regularly studied in this curriculum as they influence the disciplines of finance, marketing and management. This approach will appeal to fine tuned ENFJs. This type also wants their advisor to help with the tough work of defining career goals.

ENTJ is a leader. They simply can't avoid providing direction to others. ENTJs are likely to be quite active in student-led organizations pushing for accomplishment, goals and service work. The degree in **Engineering Management Systems** also lends itself to this type of authoritative leadership. The curriculum exposes the budding engineer to many methodologies that assess risk. As such, the graduates are armed with a foundation to make tough decisions in chaotic construction and manufacturing environments. The ENTJ who likes math could immediately jump on board for this major that leads to action-filled careers.

CONNECTICUT COLLEGE

270 Mohegan Avenue
New London, CT 06320-4196
Website: www.conncoll.edu
Admissions Telephone: 860-439-2200
Undergraduates: 1,884; 763 Men, 1,121 Women

Physical Environment

Connecticut College is located on a hill that overlooks the Thames River in Connecticut. The river serves a natural boundary, rich biological study resource and one of the focal points for sciences in the curriculum. Highways, mixed residential neighborhoods and the United States Coast Guard Academy form the perimeter boundary. Undergrads get off campus with rented Zip cars or the weekly shuttle to nearby big box stores, but for the most part stay on campus. The classic architecture of formal **gray-stone buildings** appeals to **traditional, studious** students who are drawn to this charming, Harry Potter-like environment.

The **Arboretum on campus** is utilized for teaching and research. Along with river estuaries, it serves to rivet undergraduate studies toward nature. The college has an established plant collections and rotates featured plants on its main webpage. The **Science Center** is a state of the art facility that takes advantage of the surrounding **marine ecology**. Of course, it has a well-provisioned greenhouse to support the Arboretum mission.

The administration and faculty interface the outside world with five special centers and related programs. The Ammerman Center sponsors certificates, internships and colloquia intertwining the arts and technology. The Study Away program is well structured within the departmental academic goals and individually approved by advisors. Each activity and program on this campus is carefully managed for the advantage and quality it can offer.

Social Environment

Conn College has many students that come from "just outside Boston," and if not that, then from Fairfield County, Manhattan or New Jersey. They are smart **thinkers**, outgoing and come from similar backgrounds. Undergrads take advantage of the rich programming within 23 residential halls. Each provides interaction with faculty and students through the **Residential Education Fellows** program. There is considerable energy devoted to developing the cultural environment within each house. Student planning and leadership, centered within this extracurricular sphere, is a key feature of the overall four-year experience for undergraduates.

Academic study is directed toward goal-oriented knowledge. Some students gain research skills as assistants to professors in the sciences. They aspire to become **accomplished** professionals and return to the metropolitan and urban mix of the dense New York metropolitan area and northeastern seaboard. Athletics and fitness are closely tied, reflecting the administration's belief that both are an important part of the liberal arts education. Division III basketball is well attended by alumni, fellow students and faculty. There are fourteen club sport teams and 75 percent of the undergraduates participate in some form of athletics at Connecticut College. It is a great fit for those who plan ahead, are willing to step up to **demanding classes** and interface educational studies with their chosen career paths.

Compatibility with Personality Types and Preferences

Connecticut College very much delivers an atmosphere that appreciates and utilizes a student's logical thinking (T). On this campus, academic success is encouraged and appreciated. By exploring the use of emerging technologies, the college honors those who bring a futuristic, intuitive (N) approach to their learning. Anticipation and application combine well here and, together, they pull students toward problem solving perspectives. Five Interdisciplinary Centers offer certificates that expand and enrich students' knowledge of their major discipline. These certificates are an extension of the educational philosophy that promotes specialized, focused, (J) in-depth learning. Connecticut College well interfaces and supports research addressing social issues that students and faculty find compelling. Four of the centers, public policy, environment, international study and art/technology, are comprehensive collections of resources with staff and budget to further awareness and knowledge. Graduates find themselves quite prepared to enter society's business and academic institutions that draw energy from multiple platforms and operating systems. They have been advantaged by the exceptional residential fellows programs on this campus and the five interdisciplinary centers.

In the following listing of college majors it is important to remember that students can fit into any college and can be successful in any major. We have found that the Personality Types below fit very well at this college. The course-of-study chosen for each Personality Type corresponds to MBTI® research and is presented as one of many examples favorable for that type.

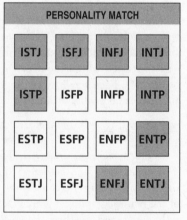

PERSONALITY MATCH

ISTJ	ISFJ	INFJ	INTJ
ISTP	ISFP	INFP	INTP
ESTP	ESFP	ENFP	ENTP
ESTJ	ESFJ	ENFJ	ENTJ

INTJ will thrive on this campus and could select the **Environmental Studies** certificate. This certificate, one of four at the college, could reward their drive to find a larger purpose in life. It could become the underlying principal with which to pull their college studies together. INTJ's inner vision will come to the forefront in the senior integrative project that presents research findings and plans for sustainability.

ENTP can transcend boundaries here in wide-ranging dynamic discussions, but they better be prepared to logically defend their intuitive leaps. The major in Environmental Studies with the **Social Science** track will introduce this talkative type to others outside of the physical sciences. Although all may not share passion for the environment, they can certainly help ENTP hone intuitive thoughts so that others can understand or disagree with reason.

INFJ can dwell on their development of personal values here at Conn College. The **Religious Studies** department broadly opens the doors of the world's spiritual practices. Analysis, problem solving and intercultural views come to the forefront of this major as it is presented at Conn College. A few undergraduates may be preparing for ordination in their own faiths. All will graduate with a humanistic perspective of religion and its expression across the globe.

INTP has a skeptical nature that is careful about making premature commitments. They might find the study of **Economics** at Conn College nicely accommodates their need to reserve judgment. This type can usually manipulate several conceptual theories at once. The impossible-sounding mathematical formulas like heteroskedasticity and stochastic trends don't necessarily scare them off.

ISTP will love Conn College's extensive research equipment and commitment to undergraduate research that is complemented with the science division's full machine shop staffed by professionals. What a dream for this tinkering type to observe and demonstrate mechanical force in freshmen level general physics. ISTPs might also tinker with the visualization of sound while pursuing the interdisciplinary certificate in **Arts and Technology** at the Ammerman Center.

ENFJ with their strong communication, empathy and idealistic vision for others could easily be attracted to the certificate in **Community Action and Public Policy**. Within the crowded metropolis in and near Hartford, there are homeless individuals that receive support and encouragement from students and faculty in this program. Undergrads pursuing this certificate come from over 20 different academic departments on campus. The banter will be honest in the student lounges while addressing social cause and effect in a pluralistic society.

ISTJ brings a mastery of the facts and complete recall that will anchor many a free-roving classroom discussion at Connecticut College. The ISTJ would probably have the perseverance to uncover complex layers in Russian society. The major in **Slavic Studies**, not frequently offered at liberal arts colleges, could be a good preparation for law school should ISTJ secure an international career track. This small department encourages close mentoring between student and faculty that extends to personalized study abroad semesters.

ISFJ is a natural for appreciating aesthetically pleasing living spaces. Their commitment and sensitivity toward others will naturally complement the **Architectural Studies** program at Connecticut College. This major will take advantage of their rich personalized memories in connecting human purpose and habitation with physical environments. It is a foundational stepping stone into graduate studies in design.

ENTJ can be direct, challenging and decisive, just the characteristics needed to pursue the unusual major in **Botany**. The science research on campus is bolstered by extensive natural laboratories in the coastal estuaries. ENTJ would likely enjoy crafting a major in the pure sciences because it would be rooted in reality, and yet have potential for research study in medicinal pharmacy. Graduate study of insects and world agricultural crops is also calling out for young scientists to step into the numerous vacancies in this much-needed discipline.

DARTMOUTH COLLEGE

7 Lebanon Street # 35
Hanover, NH 03755
Website: www.dartmouth.edu
Admission Telephone: 603-646-2875
Undergraduates: 4,200; 2,140 Men, 2,060 Women
Graduate Students: 1,168

Physical Environment

Dartmouth College was founded during the colonial period by Reverend Eleazar Wheelock who wanted to educate the Native Americans and introduce Christian belief. For over 200 years Dartmouth was a college for males. Many of the historic buildings are in use today for student housing. The 265-acre campus in Hanover is tailor-made for those who can tolerate cold weather and enjoy the outdoors.

Dartmouth is located far from any urban center, which tends to keep students focused on what's happening on campus. They may step outside campus for a Sunday breakfast at Lou's or Molly's but many have not crossed the nearby bridge to Lebanon, Vermont. In wintertime the campus is like a cocoon, an intimate and safe world for the undergrads. The new Life Sciences Center appears fortress-like, minus the expanse of glass and open spaces of current day collegiate architecture. The Black Family Visual Arts Center opened in 2012 looks to interface the digital arts and studio arts through creative collaborations in this new facility.

The "D" Plan places academic study on a quarter system which means that classes start four times a year (fall, winter, spring, summer). Each quarter lasts ten weeks so the content is intense and fast-moving. There is no time to procrastinate and digest at leisure, though students read, write and comprehend at **lightning speed** here and take only three classes per quarter, as opposed to five as at other colleges. The D-plan requires that every student who has completed sophomore year remain on campus for sophomore summer. An advantage is that **off-campus** internships are filled throughout the year lending flexibility to scheduling. If it seems that students are always coming and going it's because of the D-plan. It can be disruptive for some students to be leaving one quarter and returning when their friends are leaving. Yet **sophomore summer** on campus turns out to be a prized bonding experience for the students.

Room assignments are mixed and matched to accommodate the D plan coming and going of students by semesters. However, first year students live together in residential communities in designated residence halls or on floors within other dormitories. Housing assignments are given out in random fashion. The philosophy here is that better learning takes place in co-ed, multi-age environments that are not constricted by the residents of the same characteristics or interests.

Social Environment

Students tend to embrace tradition at this college with a strong history of scholarship. While undergrads appreciate the benefits that an exceptional education can give them throughout life, many are understated and not overly impressed with themselves. Much value within the Dartmouth degrees comes from out of class interface with other students and alumni. This campus attracts students who like to take many **challenging courses** in the liberal arts and humanities. They appreciate the opportunity to pick and choose classes around a number of distribution requirements. Engineering is also taught within the context of the liberal arts with an orientation to benefiting humanity.

Dartmouth students are "**athletic intellectuals**" with a common denominator: they work hard and play hard. Greek life is alive and well here. Students visit each Greek house to socialize and catch up with their friends, Greek and non-Greek. The President's house, on the same lane, and these social hubs serve to anchor the comings and goings of Dartmouth's student body. Two-thirds of eligible students are involved in fraternities and sororities and much social life revolves around them. Across campus, there are myriad activities students can choose and many combine socializing with them. There are special weekends every quarter, such as homecoming, winter carnival, green-key weekend in the spring and summer-fest. These are well attended and enjoyed since there are no nearby large cities to pull students off campus.

The history of **presidential campaign kickoff** speeches seeps undergraduate awareness. While Dartmouth is not a hotbed of politics, there is increasing interest in student clubs centered on political perspectives. The location in rural New Hampshire doesn't lend itself to fruitful rallies and demonstrations. Yet the spirit of individuality thrives here and conservative and libertarian political views find a place and hearing in the public square at Dartmouth. Energetic, enthusiastic, highly social and **observant**, the dysfunction in our governmental bodies will not slide under the radar here. Faculty and staff at this campus are vigilant about taking off politically correct eyewear, once in a while.

Compatibility with Personality Types and Preferences

Dartmouth College graduates are exquisitely educated in world awareness. They are bright citizens quite savvy in the nature of human society and its numerous conflicting currents. They are mobile, adept and accustomed to working with others (E) and successfully move in academic, political and business environments. This personal prowess likely grows out of the Dartmouth educational philosophy of encouraging many types of off-campus study. The Dartmouth Plan prompts learning away from campus during the four-quarter school calendar. Students are leaving and returning throughout the year while accommodating their individual interests with internships, service learning and courses at international universities. It is a calculated (J) learning strategy that allows for acquisition of information and internalizing that knowledge in a very practical and accessible way. The administration expects their graduates to quickly and aptly transition to regional, national or global organizations and graduate school.

Variety, change and new information (P) are good words for the typical Dartmouth student. Many of the academic departments clearly outline and encourage options for their students to take courses in other disciplines. Undergraduates arrive usually comfortable and confident with their ability to acquire knowledge and judiciously use that knowledge (T). The typical Dartmouth student will sign up for five courses in another discipline, identified as a modified major, just to explore for curiosity's sake. The engineering department offers the modified major which is reason enough for any aspiring engineer to select Dartmouth College, not to mention the over the top research facilities. These students seek to become effective and productive citizens in the public square. Their goal and Dartmouth's educational philosophy fit together quite nicely.

In the following listing of college majors it is important to remember that students can fit into any college and can be successful in any major. We have found that the Personality Types below fit very well at this college. The course-of-study chosen for each Personality Type corresponds to MBTI® research and is presented as one of many examples favorable for that type.

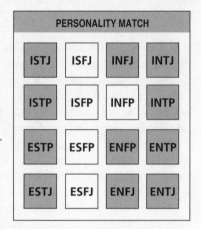

INFJ will find Dartmouth's degree in **Geography** just right for their interest in planning and emerging patterns or possibilities. Few colleges offer this degree with its interface between the social sciences and hard sciences. It is practiced at pretty abstract levels, and graduates can consult at international and national organizations on complex resource decisions. Which crop to plant, when? How will the ruling governments support or not support successful crop growth? How much acreage to plant? These are just queries about agriculture. There are many more questions posed by professional geographers in relation to space, scale, location and culture. INFJ has the imagination and insight to tackle these complexities.

INTJ will find the **Material Science** minor to be an ideal option. It is offered as an option in chemistry, physics and engineering. This type likes to quietly arrive at their positions and often with a singular idea, a seed starter, for their ultimately large vision. The material science minor could easily provide that starter concept. Dartmouth flexibility then allows for this type to follow with further studies in any of the three departments best supporting INTJ's original plan.

ISTP is a natural at learning in the labs with equipment that can be seen or handled. They move at their own pace with what interests them. They are likely to choose a research project if they elect the **Biophysical Chemistry** major at Dartmouth College. This type will be comfortable with facts and logic in the required chemistry, math, physics and biology courses for this major. They will seek out research that takes advantage of their technical acumen. Regardless of the direction their studies move toward, they will gravitate to orderly, sequenced physical properties which can be observed and documented for practical application. Very little will go unnoticed by their penetrating approach to seeing what is there.

ISTJ could find the **Linguistics Modified Major** nicely interfaces with their elected major. The five required courses will creatively complement the major elected by ISTJ. This type prefers the road ahead to be clearly mapped out. They excel at majors which avoid social theory. However, the combination of the modified major with the departments of math and linguistics could be quite appealing to this type. ISTJs will have to advocate for this, however, since there seems to be a limited selection of interdisciplinary coursework that is approved and math is apparently not on the list.

INTP will find the abstractions in the **Earth Sciences** calling out to them from the course description. Should there be a hint of mystery in the course summary, INTP is likely to sign right up for it. Give them an enigma to solve and they are happy. Dartmouth's Department of Earth Science is quite active in geological research and the undergraduate INTP is likely to find the options in this discipline fascinating. This type commonly pursues graduate study in one of the abstract sciences such as geophysics, earth magnetics, planetary sciences or geochemistry. There will be a few problems to keep them busy in each of these.

ESTP heartily will approve of the fast, productive learning pace at Dartmouth College. Off-campus programs will appeal to this type who prefers action when learning. The interdisciplinary degree in **Asian and Middle Eastern Studies** is quite flexible for service learning options. Highly social ESTP may easily move into American neighborhoods that host Asian ethnic minorities to offer an amiable ear while documenting oral history. Also the study of film and video portraying Asian cultures over the past century will be a favorite learning tool within the Black Family Visual Arts Center. ESTP often brings natural networking skills and will likely acquire a multicultural network throughout their four years of study in this program.

ENFP is highly curious and motivated by new experiences, especially those involving other people. The film and video industry could offer ENFP a moving platform of projects in which to explore many fresh subjects. The major in **Film and Media Studies** at Dartmouth College includes a course in documentary films. This is likely to delight ENFP because most work in this category includes perspectives on humanity. It will be easy for this type to become inspired and the action required in film production keeps antsy ENFP on the move. This imaginative type will have to summon caution and Dartmouth Thinking when producing Hollywood documentaries.

ENTP wants new experiences plus intellectual freedom, and **Classical Archeology** at Dartmouth has a little of both. Absorbed in the learning of the moment, time spent looking at artifacts in labs will generate a few of their original questions. Intuition serves this type well as long as they speculate with solid, appropriate information. The department's ancient holdings will push ENTP into the past, a place they rarely visit. Yet future graduate studies in archeology could allow this type to speculate in their favorite time mode: the future.

ESTJ will find the minor at Dartmouth College in **Mathematical Finance** appealing. This type is likely to go into business or manufacturing production after graduation where they can accomplish tangible goals. The combination of math and finance will open doors across the entrepreneurial spectrum of dynamic companies. Action, opportunity for leadership and management is what many ESTJs want in their careers.

ENFJ could appreciate the study of **Psychology.** The department approaches this discipline with an eye to present day issues and strong foundation in research and research methodologies. ENFJ will bring their penchant for harmony and cooperation to the discipline possibly moving toward a career in health well being. The course in Health Psychology might be the entry point for graduate studies and a career in health administration. This type often excels in leadership through personal passion and rhetorical ability.

ENTJ might start out with a minor in **Russian Area Studies** and decide to take it as a major if the study abroad term in Russia morphed into an opportunity to return and be productive in business or politics. This type makes rational and very logical decisions in league with their drive for leadership. The Sochi Olympics certainly bring up visions of emergent, entrepreneurial Russia. ENTJ is indeed going to envision and move toward their goal whether it is a new branch office in Moscow for an international business or a staff position with an international diplomatic mission. These would be typical first steps for this hard charger just out of college.

DAVIDSON COLLEGE

Office of Admission
209 Ridge Road
Davidson, NC 28035
Website: www.davidson.edu
Admission Telephone: 800-768-0380
Undergraduates: 1,790; 898 Men, 892 Women

Physical Environment

Davidson College is located in the small village of Davidson, about 20 minutes northwest of Charlotte. The self-enclosed campus sits in the center of this town. It feels cozy and protected. It provides an ideal setting for the development of a **close-knit college community**. Study abroad is well supported through the academic lens of research. Significant grant money is awarded to students who apply with self-designed research projects. About 70 percent of the students leave campus for service or international academic study. Davidson College maintains six of its own overseas study campuses.

The 450-acre, park-like landscape has impressive academic buildings, sports facilities such as a golf course, stadium and tennis courts and a choice of residence halls. The year-round temperate weather makes it possible to play outdoors throughout much of the academic year. The Knoblock Campus Center is a popular meeting place for students here. Also Patterson Court, with small residential homes for fraternities and eating houses, is a social magnet for all on campus. Fraternity houses are owned by the college and rented to students. They are popular and even encouraged here with 40 percent participation. Women don't live in sororities but rather in "eating houses" which also are rented from the college. Some houses are open and accept all who would like to join; others operate in the traditional rush. Almost all students live on campus, whether in a house or residence hall.

Social Environment

Most Davidson students were overachievers in high school and continue this pattern as undergraduates. At Davidson they stretch their minds, putting forth their best **analytical thinking and academic effort**. The entire campus is finely tuned to honor diligent learning. It speaks of the quiet relaxation you find in your favorite corner of the library on the fifth floor with the five o'clock afternoon sun pouring in. Davidson undergrads structure their days with study, homework, clubs, sports, friends and enjoyment.

This college has a distinct Christian orientation with an **international presence** even though the majority of students come from outside North Carolina. This stems from the **Presbyterian founders** who strongly envisioned a religious and ethical education. Some students form an alternate perspective and would prefer a more secular approach at Davidson. This sometimes makes for **lively discussions** on campus. Students who value service and leadership appreciate a Davidson preparation for life. Students find ways to invite underprivileged children to campus or travel with their professor to an inner city area. Adopt a Grandparent is a volunteer service club that reaches into the town pairing undergrads and senior citizens.

The **honor code** is a strong value within the student body and incoming students are quickly oriented to code policies. Undergraduate students complete tests and exams without a proctor. Undergraduates really appreciate Davidson's practice of admitting many international students to the college. The **exchange of social customs** and traditions between international students and traditional American students provides an exposure to alternative perspectives similar to off-campus study.

Students who were shy about risk taking in high school will enjoy the personal attention they receive and the **family atmosphere** on this campus. Students enjoy chatting with the President of the college often on campus. They like the fact that professors are very approachable and available for academic discussions. When life gets too quiet here, students may drive to Charlotte for a shopping spree or go sailing on the nearby lake. Athletics are popular at this NCAA Division I college, as is their basketball team.

Compatibility with Personality Types and Preferences

Davidson is an intensely academic college with bright students who really want their studies to be the primary focus of their undergraduate years. There is less emphasis on learning through social avenues. However, they make good use of innocent pranks and jokes using this lighthearted approach to relieve the academic pressures. Students here are very fond of introspection (I) as a way to acquire knowledge. Individually or in small focus groups, they ponder concepts and information gained in class and from their readings. Their personal observations and thoughts instigate dialogues across campus and in non-class settings. Moral reasoning (F) underlies pretty much all of their conjecture and purpose in learning. Undergraduates here view the ideals of service and leadership through the lens of faith and also through non-spiritual humanistic philosophies. This willingness to explore the sources of ethical behavior attracts students who are tolerant, yet strong in their personal beliefs. Refining order and structure (J) within purpose is the common process that most successful students at Davidson possess. It can provide answers and questions, equally valuable on this campus. Graduates set the bar high to achieve their individual ideals of competence and expect to bring this into their careers for a lifetime of rewarding work and caring for the larger social community.

In the following listing of college majors it is important to remember that students can fit into any college and can be successful in any major. We have found that the Personality Types below fit very well at this college. The course-of-study chosen for each Personality Type corresponds to MBTI® research and is presented as one of many examples favorable for that type.

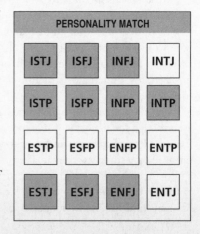

PERSONALITY MATCH			
ISTJ	ISFJ	INFJ	INTJ
ISTP	ISFP	INFP	INTP
ESTP	ESFP	ENFP	ENTP
ESTJ	ESFJ	ENFJ	ENTJ

INFP will appreciate the frontiers opening up in the field of **Neuroscience**. At Davidson, this concentration would likely be very appealing to INFP whose personal mandate is to keep life's work in synchronization with their values. Davidson funds a considerable amount of its own research proposed by faculty and students. INFP is very comfortable in this territory.

INFJ is a natural for the major in **Art** at Davidson because of their inclination for person-centered leadership. They are persuasive folks and move successfully into professional positions that interface with the public. At Davidson, the department is well-resourced with a substantial studio facility and a curriculum that emphasizes conceptualization, collection, curatorship as well as the obvious studies in art production and theory. This intellectual approach helps quietly passionate INFJ prepare for graduate studies or immediate employment.

ISTP could pair the analytical tools of the **Applied Mathematics** concentration with the natural sciences. This type is curious and objective. They don't mind a puzzle and are drawn to figuring things out. More often than not, they also prefer to tinker with hands-on instrumentation or with subject matter that involves researching with high-powered equipment. They are a natural for physics because of the elements and the observable reactions. With the Davidson Research Initiative, ISTP is likely to be stretching the frontiers of space exploration, medical instrumentation or environmental modeling.

ISTJ is exactly the type of educator many students admire and respect. This type is very knowledgeable, controlled and prefers a clear set of rules. They can be excellent classroom managers. The minor in **Education Studies** at Davidson leads naturally to graduate study in psychology, education and other social sciences. ISTJ is inclined to management and administrative positions in the social sciences.

ISFJ will find the perspectives of the **Economics** department in tune with their own idea of gathering information that can be used in a practical way. The Comparative Advantage mentor program develops cooperative interaction between professor, student and off-campus internships in Charlotte. The Davidson Research Initiative provides funds for off-campus student trips that can enliven and personalize this major with visits to stock exchanges and other financial institutions. ISFJ is intensely practical, yet also reflective. It so nicely fits in with the study of Economics here.

ISFP likes wiggle room to find their direction in life. They want a studious environment in which to examine moral issues. The study in **Religion** as a major or minor at Davidson is going to deliver. It will offer a close examination of the many facets of spiritual beliefs. At the core of these studies is the existential question about the meaning of human life. Although ISFP is not one to tarry with abstract questions, this one is rather familiar to them. Personal values are critical for this type and the overall emphasis on moral and ethical behavior at Davidson is in tandem with their own wish for a life guided by inner values.

INTP will be impressed with the facilities and the research in the Davidson **Physics** department, recognized nationally. This very abstract type does not need a course of study that is directly connected to reality. Even better is a challenge that they can work on for a couple decades starting right in the Davidson physics labs. How about generating oxygen on Mars if microbes are ultimately discovered within the soil? Keep the lab open late if you pose this question, INTP is already tuning up the instruments.

ESFJ can find themselves moving toward the health fields because of their friendly nature. They are excellent at taking in facts and pretty darn good at utilizing those facts in real terms. The study of **Chemistry** at Davidson allows students to comprehend the abstract and practical applications of this discipline. This type will prefer the research that most directly connects the chemical world with the real world. ESFJ wants to study chemistry for the purpose of moving into a helping career like nursing or teaching. Not one to likely delve into Davidson's explorations of moral reasoning, ESFJ finds comfort in traditional Judeo-Christian values as found in the U.S. Constitution.

ESTJ will like the idea of combining the **Medical Humanities** concentration with their intended major. Whether they intend to move toward the health administration with a major in economics or toward medical school this concentration has much to impress efficient ESTJ. It pulls together legal, economic and political factors that explain the patterns and practice of medicine in our society. Davidson offers this concentration within the background of its own ongoing examination of moral purpose in life and society. It is an ideal academic atmosphere and helps ESTJ, sometimes impersonal, sort out emotional perspectives.

ENFJ can be quite objective and analytical. They also possess charisma and the ability to engage immediately with a group of people. Their desire to be of service for others makes good use of each of these characteristics. The major in **Sociology** at Davidson is a broad analytical exercise in defining social life. This type is ready to sign up for the research and field work that can support change and offer solutions to underserved populations. They are excellent at painting their vision and creative in applying solutions. At Davidson, they will find the faculty very open to their projects which involve service learning especially if they gather data that can be objectively filtered through research methodology.

DENISON UNIVERSITY

Office of Admission
Granville, OH 43023
Website: www.denison.edu
Admissions Telephone: 740-587-6276
Undergraduates: 2,185; 917 Men, 1,268 Women

Physical Environment

Denison University is built on a **steep hill**, like a castle, above the town of Granville. The town itself has the feel of a New England village, with its attractive colonial houses, a quaint downtown, specialty shops and golf courses nearby. The airport is a half-hour away in Columbus and makes for an easy trip for nearly half of the students who will need to use this transportation option.

Once you've arrived at Denison, you feel completely surrounded by peaks and valleys, hosting large stands of trees on the 1,000-acre campus. Students find that they have to walk a good deal, up and down, to get to and from class. At the same time, Denison has taken great care to create many spaces that are conducive to learning. These spaces function for the students and faculty, appealing to those with an appreciation for well-designed environments.

There are places for the student who gets distracted occasionally or those who prefer to study alone in complete silence, such as in the Doane Library. There are spaces for the highly social students who learn best through discussion with peers, such as in the computer center. Residential life is geared to promote learning. The expansive renovation of Ebaugh Science Center echoes the academic philosophy consistently in place across the campus environment. In this renovation, undergraduates benefit with six teaching laboratories. The hands-on method of learning is highest priority at Denison and their graduates are well-grounded in practical skills needed for those entering our workforce.

The **Slayter Union student center** is designed for students to socialize on campus during the evenings and weekends with its dance and DJ spot, pub and coffeehouse. Lots of planning and effort went into designing the physical campus and forming this **community**. Students who choose to spend their four undergraduate years at Denison appreciate the beauty of the campus and the nice classrooms, the dorms and these study spaces.

Social Environment

A good number of students come from suburban areas and the **North East**, both from independent and academically strong public schools. The campus can be described as a safe, **supportive environment** in which undergrads look to stretch and mature. Here students develop their views about the emerging issues through their educational studies and discussions. There are students who lean toward nontraditional perspectives and exercise their elbow room in the demanding academics. In the classroom, they can assert their original thoughts with professors who are exceptionally receptive.

At Denison students range from casual, easy going to very artsy. Some are drawn to fashions taking advantage of vintage clothing stores. Denison residential staff forms **an overarching community** with all of these types since there are few, if any options, for students to live off campus. Undergraduates here tend to be less counter cultural, more accepting of hometown values and family. They look to expand their lifestyle beyond who they were in high school. Much about the residential policies will support the tentative students who arrive as First Years. Yet, much of the carefully crafted social environment also feels a bit tight for the upper school students. Greek organizations, recently deactivated and missed by a good number of undergraduates, formerly provided a 'home away from the collegiate bubble' environment on campus. Characterized by excellent **professors sharing their expertise**, this university is a solid choice for students looking for a **mentored learning environment** and **structured social activity**.

Compatibility with Personality Types and Preferences

Denison University is dedicated, in the purest sense, to educating the youth who arrive on their campus each year. This commitment directly infuses the curriculum and residential life. The proverbial phrase, No Stone is Left Unturned, applies here. The campus is carefully organized for the undergraduate experience. In a similar sense, Denison also hovers over their students with exceptional care (F) that is instilled throughout the academic programs and courses of study. The mission of the university calls administration and faculty to inspire the students who come to them. In fact, the professional educators on this campus are well able to role model inspiration. The faculty forms around a single-minded conjecture that education has an immediate utility. The annual Summer Science Symposium prompts selected undergrads to present their work to the campus community and it is open to the public. This last feature is not often the case at liberal arts colleges. Yet Denison faculty recognize the value of off campus input whether it be a retired physician or a Granville small business owner in conversation with undergraduates. Taken as a whole, this philosophy forms a campus community that reaches out to many types of learners and recognizes knowledge emanating from outside academia. Denison provides learning options for the open-ended, wondering student (N) and the one expecting to find the knowledge in an observable, structured format (S). Denison undergraduate students are likely to be smart and savvy about forthcoming careers and employment, graduating with a strong academic foundation and clear direction.

In the following listing of college majors it is important to remember that students can fit into any college and can be successful in any major. We have found that the Personality Types below fit very well at this college. The course-of-study chosen for each Personality Type corresponds to MBTI® research and is presented as one of many examples favorable for that type.

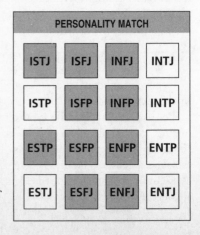

PERSONALITY MATCH

ISTJ	ISFJ	INFJ	INTJ
ISTP	ISFP	INFP	INTP
ESTP	ESFP	ENFP	ENTP
ESTJ	ESFJ	ENFJ	ENTJ

ESFJ will appreciate the concentration in **Organizational Studies** not often found at small liberal arts colleges. This type is good at communication and has a strong propensity for follow through with attention to detail. They are at home in traditional organizations that serve the public. The ESFJ might enter banking or real estate because of the exacting financial exchanges and comfort with personal relationships. Examination of problems, imagination and decisions are prompted by the faculty in this concentration.

ISFJ is very likely to think about the health services field as they head off to college. This reflective type is very much at home helping others. The degree in **Psychology** at Denison University has a nice range of options within the coursework of this developing field. Courses in Adult Development and Aging, Organizational Psychology and Social Psychology offer much to ISFJ who is considering careers in health. Combined with courses in the **Organizational Studies** concentration, this type will be well-suited to provide personal support to patients dealing with hospital financial systems and the insurance systems, not to mention the messy, backtracking health care mandates in 2014.

ESTP often has a strong sense of spatial and personal awareness wherever they happen to be. They often are attracted to and excel at sports and other movement activities. **Dance** at Denison University is available as a minor or major. The department approaches dance through three constructs: mind, spirit and body. This type could move easily into the entertainment field with their gregarious personality. Think Disney World, Las Vegas and a host of concert tours that use choreographed performances. ESTP thrives on pressure and can pull rabbits out of hats when needed.

ESFP has a lot of enthusiasm and adaptability. Those are ideal characteristics for artists. The major in **Studio Art** is a good option. The courses cover foundational design and introductions to some specialties like fiber arts and animation. An independent study at Cleveland Institute of Arts can introduce ESFP to multiple career options. An internship with a construction firm in Columbus might be a two-way win for a small business that offers pleasant, affordable facility design plans to large markets such as the Motel 6 or Fairfield chains.

ISFP can excel at hands-on activities and the major in **Chemistry** offers plenty of them. ISFP is also fond of teaching young children and Denison offers advising on completing the teacher licensure immediately upon graduation with the BA in Chemistry. For the student who may be unsure of their commitment to education, the chemistry major qualifies graduates for immediate employment in many industries. This too may appeal to ISFP who might enter the health care industry in sales or technical positions.

ISTJ has the discipline to tackle a complex language. Denison University offers basic courses in Arabic. The close attention to the details of this visually challenging set of written characters is something that ISTJ could have the patience to conquer. If combined with economics or political science majors, the **Arabic Language** would likely open doors for business or government careers that focus on the Middle East. The need for this expertise is ongoing within Western governments and businesses. ISTJ can provide the glue that holds a consulting project together in this dynamic environment.

INFJ likes to pull things together from start to finish. The major in **Theater** at Denison University takes advantage of this type's ability to understand complex viewpoints presented in contemporary theater usually offered with little resemblance to the everyday world. This type can interpret those abstract themes in theater for the audience to more easily understand. The course titled Acting: Realism 1 may challenge their reserved nature. Yet a career in this field lets , INFJ can further hone their creative visions of how things should be.

ENFJ should find the rich resources in Denison's Department of **Modern Language** ideal for foreign language study. The ears, eyes and rhetorical skills are integral to the educational methods here. ENFJ will like the modern language virtual lounge in Fellows 103. Large flatscreen TVs receive direct foreign programming and students are immersed in the sounds of the language by contemporary native speakers. The modern language association map, utilized within the curriculum, identifies locations of native-speaking neighborhoods within the United States. It supports a foreign language minor as doable with demanding, time consuming academic studies in math and physical sciences.

ENFP will find the complex systems with the **Geosciences** more than sufficient to remain interested. The department takes excellent advantage of the land surfaces in the Ohio Valley, left behind by the melting glaciers. The course in geomorphology emphasizes deposits of the late Quaternary period. There is that complex enough?

INFP can be an insightful personality. The field of education is attractive to them since they enjoy both teaching and learning where insight comes in pretty handy. At Denison University, the major in **Educational Studies** can lead to a teaching license with an additional year of study after graduation. The curriculum addresses the relationship between the teacher and the learner in childhood and adolescence. This is a difficult discipline and yet more difficult in practice across American public school classrooms. Denison offers limited opportunities to observe in public schools. Discerning INFP will likely be attracted to the policy levels within American public education. Graduate studies in education will ferret out where this type may contribute best.

DUKE UNIVERSITY

Office of Admission
2138 Campus Drive
Durham, NC 27708
Website: www.duke.edu
Admissions Telephone: 919-684-3214
Undergraduates: 6,631; 3,302 Men, 3,229 Women
Graduate Students: 5,146

Physical Environment

Duke University continues to grow leaps and bounds with new facilities and additional tenured faculty within the schools. The Pratt School of Engineering is a perfect example. By 2017, they intend to increase tenure track faculty by over 20 percent. There will also be a new science center, impressive by any standards and designed to increase **national research capabilities** and advance engineering knowledge.

Duke University is comprised of three separate areas identified as Campuses with Quads. All first-year students live on **East Campus** about a mile distant from the academic quad where most classes are held. Buses take students back and forth. The **West Campus** is the center of the university's academic facilities and houses sophomores, junior and seniors in its residential quads. **Central Campus** including the extensive **Sarah P. Duke Gardens**, houses juniors and seniors. New Campus, envisioned for the far future, is presently on hold as a result of the recession. When completed it is likely to advance the university's return to the house-based residential system.

Pretty much all of Duke's architecture trends to **clean lines and functional** style. The residence halls for upper classmen on West Campus are arranged like peas in a pod with each pod overlooking its own courtyard. It's cozy and private inside the pod, so students run into their friends often. Fraternities and sororities post banners on the public side of the pods—as do other political or environmental clubs.

Duke University along with other academic institutions in North Carolina came into being through generous endowments of the extended William Duke family. Founders of the American Tobacco Company and Methodist in Christian denomination, the family sought to advance the university, then named Trinity College with its motto "Knowledge and Religion". Today, you must travel many clicks into the webpages to find this founding spiritual influence or information about William Duke. Universities are examining and in some cases, downplaying their founders whose lives and histories did not evolve in the pluralistic culture of America today.

Social Environment

Duke students are very bright and **precise.** Their **inquisitiveness** and **reasoning** power are to the point, as is their focus on solutions rather than complaints. Many of the entering students want to major in medicine. However, far fewer enter med school upon graduation. Often, organic chemistry can be the obstacle. These students, rational and goal-driven, naturally move on to other career fields. Many are

competitive and fondly remember being on the top rung in high school, hoping to repeat that achievement at Duke.

Social life at Duke is often curtailed by the amount of study involved during weekends. If there's not a sports game to attend, many students like to go to Chapel Hill to have fun. Much social life at Duke revolves around the **Greek system**. One-third of male students join a fraternity whereas a larger number of women join a sorority. All are invited to their parties. Students who are attracted to this campus tend to have respect and love for conventional traditions, as well as a yearning for the innovative academics, even if risk is involved. They will find fertile soil here where **research possibilities** for undergraduates abound. Team projects and understanding connections between dissimilar problems are big here. In effect, students examine situations that often occur in business and industry. As Duke continues to forge more initiatives in research, it attracts investigative types who rely on facts, logic and analysis. This approach to learning tends to fall in line with the Germanic university model that emphasizes undergraduate research over the more traditional lecture and writing formats.

Duke students like their **sports** and really come out for their Blue Devils. Starting in December, a favorite and fun tradition is to camp outside the Krzyzewski Athletic Complex for tickets to the February games. Students take turns keeping their place in line while studying and socializing around the clock. Living in **Krzyzewskiville village** has become a bonding experience for many Duke students. These experiences and memories build loyalty to the university and to each other.

Compatibility with Personality Types and Preferences

Duke University replicates a thinking pattern akin to an aircraft circling to land. In this case, the plane doesn't land–Duke undergraduates always circle in a thinking pattern. The philosophy of Duke University is to engage rigorous logical thought throughout the curriculum. Free inquiry, deductive reasoning and interdisciplinary thinking pop up as the foundation in this educational environment. Students here are perpetually reasoning (T). They seek purpose in their educational studies. They apply knowledge upon graduation to benefit mankind in a determined, impactful way. For most Duke undergraduates, science and research is the chosen vehicle to ride into a future (N) of productive accomplishment (J) and discovery. The university devotedly supports this expectation of their graduates. Both collaboration and competition are valued as learning tools on campus. Duke lore, history and traditions often serve to soften the logical edges of reason. The residential life programs are designed to promote maturation and community. The typical Duke graduate is well-connected to the world and very able to both socially network and generate major contributions for the advancement of the larger community.

PERSONALITY MATCH			
ISTJ	ISFJ	INFJ	INTJ
ISTP	ISFP	INFP	INTP
ESTP	ESFP	ENFP	ENTP
ESTJ	ESFJ	ENFJ	ENTJ

In the following listing of college majors it is important to remember that students can fit into any college and can be successful in any major. We have found that the Personality Types below fit very well at this college. The course-of-study chosen for each Personality Type corresponds to MBTI® research and is presented as one of many examples favorable for that type.

ENFJ prefers to learn and study with creative peers in fields where helping others is a high priority. The health sciences are quite attractive for this reason. Duke University offers the concentration in **Plant Biology** that easily leads to advanced study. The extraordinary research labs will provide ample opportunities for this type. ENFJs will be attracted to the healing properties found in the botanical world. Foundational work at Duke in plant physiology is the spring board for passionate ENFJs to move into an exciting, rewarding research career.

INTJ likes to be original and how about **Linguistics** for originality. The major in linguistics requires the willingness to discern pattern and system in languages. It is both abstract and precise. It is the forensic linguist who comes to the forefront with translation help when archeologists unearth manuscripts of ancient languages. Duke's limitless access to journals includes the intriguing Journal of Linguistic Anthropology. INTJs will uncover all available sources for their study of linguistics and in the process develop the competence that is their Number One priority.

INFJ takes pride and ownership in their expressive work. For this type, it speaks to their inner soul and must be authentic. The degree in **Visual Arts** is offered by Duke faculty with international perspectives. An upcoming faculty book promotes the concept that state controlled Soviet culture of the 1920s was tolerant with artists of the era. An independent study of Alexander Solzhenitsyn, author of the Gulag Archipelago, would make for an interesting read by discerning INFJ as well as a few more paragraphs on Marc Chagall who chose to flee the Soviet country in 1922. This compassionate Type, double majoring in **Political Science**, might take the opportunity to research the topic.

INTP will find the nature of the **Evolutionary Biology** concentration suits their personality well. This major requires quiet contemplation of biological modeling and systems mechanics. Although titles in this discipline change from year to year, the underlying exploration of genetics, cell and molecular, organismal and ecology remain distinct categories from which concentrations are drawn. If you add in a can of Coke with a few bags of microwave popcorn, this type is set for hours of power studying and socializing INTP-style.

ISTJ who is handy with numbers probably couldn't go wrong with Duke's major in **Statistical Sciences**. This degree will be in demand at financial institutions. ISTJ naturally brings fierce attention to the exacting nature of the statistical discipline. Since this type prefers the real world, they will be in demand to predict and explain trends in the marketplace or complex social research.

INFP brings compassion and insight to the helping professions. In order to be content, they must select majors and coursework that allow them to develop their own values, so the field of **Psychology** calls out to this type. In guiding others through personal difficulty, this type simultaneously defines their own life expectations and meaning. The department offers a broad-based analytic and foundational knowledge. It prepares students for graduate studies as well as entry level positions in research institutions. INFPs are likely to opt for the first and only stay for a few years in a direct entry research job.

ESTJ is often an efficient personality who could be attracted to the degree in **Computer Science** at Duke University. The very powerful computing resources here allow for levels of programming that can be applied to ginormous data problems. Here ESTJ can be productive, take charge and reason their way into advanced computing with Duke encouragement all the way.

ENTJ could easily adapt to a favored role in consulting as a **Biomedical Engineer**. The work environment needed for development of advanced medical devices is just right for this type. They enjoy perfecting operating systems. Once envisioned, the system is brought to the market by the ambitious ENTJ. Throw in Duke's competitive, motivating educational environment and this type will likely be quite content with their undergraduate experience.

ENTP is willing to tackle the tough problems. No shrinking violet, this type has the determination to succeed at any major that piques their interest. The advantage of a certificate in **Information Sciences and Information Studies** is that it is specifically designed to be applicable to a variety of academic disciplines for research purposes. Original ENTPs don't mind studying technology as long as it can lead to creating new information technology.

ELON UNIVERSITY

Office of Admissions and Financial Planning
2700 Campus Box
400 N. O'Kelly Avenue
Elon, NC 27244-2010
Website: www.elon.edu
Admissions Telephone: 800-334-8448
Undergraduates: 5,599; 2,294 Men, 3,305 Women

Physical Environment

Elon University is located in the very small and quiet town of Elon near the "triangle," within a 30-minute drive of Greensborough, Raleigh-Durham and Chapel Hill. The campus is very attractive with many new red-brick buildings amidst two lakes, trees, flower beds and circular open areas. With fewer than 10,000 people, the new Elon Town Center across the street from the campus houses the Elon Bookstore and specialty foods.

Approximately three-quarters of students will live on campus by 2015. The **Global Neighborhood** will house 600 students in individual houses. Each residential house will be complete with high tech classrooms, recording studio, black box theater and dance studio. With the feeling of a village in part, it will also provide for live-in faculty and international cafes. Some units will be heated with geothermal energy. Language learning communities, themed houses, Greek houses, all female and all male dorms, singles and apartments represent just some of the residential options on this campus. They are grouped by differing locations on campus and referred to collectively as Neighborhoods. The **Colonnades Neighborhood** has thematic and service learning that connects the academic majors in business and the sciences in interdisciplinary study.

Many new academic buildings dot this active campus, the latest of which is the Francis Center, housing the facilities for the physical therapy and exercise science programs. Strategic plans call for ongoing construction over the next decade. Much planning is developed in reference to the several **academic neighborhoods**. Elon is unique in this ambitious plan which is remarkable for its efforts to synthesize non-traditional interfaces like business with science.

Mosley's student center is popular on this **social campus**. Fonville Fountain is another meeting place, especially on Tuesday morning when students and faculty connect over coffee to chat and visit. No classes are held during this time. On Thursdays there is an optional interfaith service in the historic Whitley Auditorium, another way for this community to come together.

Social Environment

Elon students come from all over the United States. A small minority of students are residents of North Carolina. At least half of the student body comes from the New England states. Elon bolsters the ethnic diversity on campus by bringing in many international students from all corners of the world. **Fraternities and sororities** play a large role here, often generating leadership initiatives that impact across many organizations on campus as well as parties and social events. Students are active in their club memberships, many of which are oriented toward career fields. When students want to leave the "Elon bubble," they drive nearby to Chapel Hill or Greensboro. The overall tone of the campus is **upbeat** and vibrant.

As high school students they demonstrated considerable academic and **extra-curricular skills**. Undergrads here are intellectually curious and prefer experiential learning with a practical application of knowledge. Students are required to complete an **internship** before they graduate, so they are **well prepared** for the workplace. They graduate with an **experience resume** that describes their extra-curricular accomplishments as well as academic study in college. They engage in initiatives to help society at large, such as raising funds or organizing food drives to stock the local food pantries. Elon is a great fit for academically strong students who enjoy an active social life and expect to garner an education that prepares for dynamic careers.

Compatibility with Personality Types and Preferences

Elon University is future-oriented and leads the individual undergraduate through a strong understanding of today's best practices and technologies. The university is committed to community in the familiar, traditional Christian ethic. Elon is a very supportive and affirming campus (F). The professor-student relationship takes on a personal nature while advising graduates for careers to come on graduation. Much administration thought and effort is devoted to programs and activities that encourage leadership acumen throughout the campus community.

Undergraduates are happy at Elon who want to be active doing important work in the world (E) and on the campus during their four year sojourn. They could be active in service learning, participation in research labs, contributing to theater productions, participating in social recreation or selecting internships that offer double the value for the student and the community. There is also a significant international component which is supported by the assertive and nontraditional study abroad options, as well as new initiatives like the Global Neighborhood. At Elon University, study abroad tends to move in the direction of well planned, substantial works for the benefit of those who need help. Study abroad locations require students to be open and OK with the unknown (P) as well as physical discomfort. Elon graduates maintain involvement and the do-it-well ethic toward life and upon graduation.

In the following listing of college majors it is important to remember that students can fit into any college and can be successful in any major. We have found that the Personality Types below fit very well at this college. The course-of-study chosen for each Personality Type corresponds to MBTI® research and is presented as one of many examples favorable for that type.

INFP is definitely motivated by working for causes that meet their approval. The major in **Human Service Studies** at Elon University is ideal for INFPs. This type naturally settles

PERSONALITY MATCH			
ISTJ	ISFJ	INFJ	INTJ
ISTP	ISFP	INFP	INTP
ESTP	ESFP	ENFP	ENTP
ESTJ	ESFJ	ENFJ	ENTJ

into the health, education and counseling fields. INFPs are just fine with complexity and they enjoy the opportunity to develop well thought out responses to those challenges. Once their career choice is identified, this major will give excellent access to immediate employment. The experiential approach in this major provides a solid background for application to immediate employment in the helping professions.

ISFJ is inclined to be reflective without much fanfare or publicity about their thoughts. At the same time, they are outstanding with the details and minutiae. It is an unusual combination of skills. ISFJ is somewhere between the proverbial ivory tower and monitoring the moat filled with water below. The major in **Computer Science** with a minor in **Geography** at Elon University fits nicely into this paradigm. The minor in geography looks closely at how space is used through human impact. With computing skills and knowledge of human land use patterns, ISFJs will be at the ready to provide valuable data and modeling systems for corporations and research institutions.

ISFP excels at attention to detail that helps real people in need. Elon University's bachelor of science degree in **Medical Technology** can lead to two different career paths. One would be the technical side of health services, diagnostic systems and medical equipment software systems. The other is the ecological side with work/research in environmental sciences. Elon is well positioned to support environmental studies with their curriculum and coursework in the fields of geography and geographical information systems. ISFPs could select either direction.

ESTP has the smooth moves to calm down ruffled feathers with a plan that works. In the fast-paced field of media production, it helps to be spontaneous and capable of solving a problematic feature story line. The concentration in **Broadcast and New Media** pretty much falls into this description of career fields that require folks who think on their feet. Elon's courses in the journalism and strategic communications within the very strong School of Communication really add the beef to the program. Graduates of this university are likely to aspire to media outlets that present absolute truths rather than political trends.

ESFP goes for the active, hands-on learning. Elon University will not disappoint them. The **Exercise Science** major is a strong understudy for professional graduate study in occupational or physical therapy or wellness positions with corporate and athletic organizations. ESFPs are realistic and can handle change with ease. They enjoy solving problems by combining their typical common sense with the known information at hand. Their friendly, easy-going personality is an asset in this field.

ENFP is a creative type and loves to collaborate with others in the process. The major in **Journalism** is excellent for these reasons. ENFP gathers new information while expertly collaborating with those who have that information. It is all on behalf of the reader who they want to involve in their own excitement about the subject with news articles or radio/TV broadcasts. Elon University has very robust programs in the School of Communications and the minor in **Multimedia Authoring** would be a natural course of study for ENFPs who intend to move toward the visual arts and marketing.

ESFJ can be counted on to cooperate and give a personal touch to their work. The bachelor of science degree in **Physical Education and Health** fits this Personality

Type quite well. ESFJs direction with students in the classroom and gymnasium can be counted on to be pleasant and productive. The major leads to qualification for positions in K-12th grades. However, a good number of undergraduates pursue advanced training for specific fields such as Athletic Trainer. ESFJs enjoy solid advising and encouragement within the **Department of Health and Human Performance.**

ESTJ is all about organizing themselves and other people and they like to have fun too. The major in **Sport and Event Management** at Elon University is not commonly available at undergraduate liberal arts institutions and is indicative of this campus' commitment to rewarding follow-on careers and work. This major develops planning and management skills across several venues: tourism, cultural arts, sports stadiums, national parks plus more. The no-nonsense list of courses will definitely meet with ESTJ approval.

ENFJ likes to think analytically while in conversation. They will enjoy the typically close professor/student relationships on the Elon campus. Research projects, service learning projects and internships are frequent options at Elon that really speak to ENFJs. The **Leadership Studies** minor is a perfect complement to any major idealistic ENFJ might pursue. They often follow their hearts into teaching or counseling. The field of education is calling out for empathic leaders with a solid moral grounding. Elon University and ENFJ can certainly do their part with this minor in Leadership.

ENTJ likes variety and independence in their educational studies. The major in **Economics** at Elon University offers both through their focus on undergraduate research. It suits ENTJs especially because they typically are opportunists ready to move forward into individualized study within the economics discipline. Their desire to long range plan is also usually pretty strong and they look after their own career track as well as their employer's business objectives with ingenuity. The major in economics at Elon requires an original research project that ENTJs will view as an opportunity to learn, network and develop their business acumen.

EMORY UNIVERSITY

1380 Oxford Road
Atlanta, GA 30322
Website: www.emory.edu
Admissions Telephone: 404-727-6036, 800-727-6036
Undergraduates: 7,655; 3,368 Men, 4,287 Women
Graduate Students: 6,677

Physical Environment

Emory University is located in vibrant, thriving Atlanta, Georgia. Atlanta's Hartsfield International Airport and the public subway and bus system make it easy to reach this campus. As soon as you walk on campus, the pink granite buildings call out with their modern, striking architecture. One of these buildings is the Cannon Chapel Worship Center that supports students who see no contradiction between academics and spirituality. Adjacent to the campus is the Center for Disease Control and Prevention and Emory Hospital that calls to students who are focused on careers in the **health sciences**. Dedicated in 2013, the **New Sciences Health Research** building is devoted to pediatric research.

Students here are likely to engage this unique location and many actively use the large park on the far side of the campus for concerts and walkathons. Emory University is **deceptively large**, as one walks from one small space to another without expansive, interposing lawns. Buildings on campus are typically three to four stories and designed in several styles with the newer adjacent to those of earlier decades. The campus itself gives one the feel of Atlanta that surrounds it. The students here are often **astute**, **independent** and can function in a demanding environment. The contemporary library with much light promotes study. The Roberto Goizueta Business School, named after the former CEO of Coca-Cola, is located on the Emory campus and pulls in students who have an interest in entrepreneurship. True efficiency is a strong undercurrent on this campus surrounded by the city. For those who prefer a gentler touch, **Oxford College—a satellite campus** 45 minutes east of Atlanta—draws students who want a more relaxed setting socially and in the classroom. It is open to first and second year undergraduate students and offers a unique and distinguishing feature at this university.

Moderate southern weather and Emory University attract **cosmopolitan students** from all over the U.S. and the world. The numerous Fortune 1,000 companies headquartered in Atlanta add to the superb choices for internships and off-campus learning. The Whitehead Biomedical Research building, among several health-oriented research centers near or on campus, is an award-winning, environmentally sustainable laboratory that offers numerous research directions.

Social Environment

At times reflective and reserved, many students expect their activities and connections will lead to power and success in their future careers and personal goals. Emory is a **rigorous** and **structured academic powerhouse**. Students here meet high academic and intellectual demands. They are **driven**, hard-working and inclined to set and meet their expectations. Many value tradition, honesty and being responsible in their academic work. Here, the students started and maintain the honor code. This environment is also supported by the **spiritual programs** and the college's relationship with Candler School of Theology on campus which reaffirms the moral, ethical value system.

Socializing occurs around structured academic group projects, service learning and sports. Emory's intramural motto is "Athletics for All." As a Division III university, more than half of the students are active in intramurals. There is also traditional socializing within the many Greek organizations. The Greek life is well-supported and approved by the university in part because they are providing connections and service with the surrounding neighborhoods. The leadership and friendships within the Greek houses also help to unify the overall campus environment. **Service initiatives** organized by students are common. Since bustling Atlanta is right outside the campus, they often go to a new restaurant, a baseball game at the Brave's stadium (although it is slated to move to the suburbs in the immediate future), shopping in eclectic stores or to volunteer in the community. The substantial northeastern student population is right at home in the big city.

Emory works for **bright, resolute** individuals willing to tackle issues that cut across regional and national borders. They can assign fun to second place in order to reach a larger purpose.

Compatibility with Personality Types and Preferences

"Students who explore and expand upon the current body of knowledge with world class professors" is a good way to think of Emory's broad educational philosophy. Emory students are obliged to learn and to apply that knowledge while improving the world during college and after graduation. Self-sufficient students thrive here. A healthy appreciation and comfort level (S) with the facts is a necessity and a given. At the same time, Emory demands interpretation and synthesis of all within the curriculum. Logical, sequential thought (T) is expected to lead somewhere—be it an end point or a beginning point. At a minimum, one's study would travel the route of previous brilliant minds in their endeavors. Intuitive leaps (N) are routinely accepted and expected in the classroom, although not as the primary learning tool. The administration and faculty at Emory are exceptionally open to creative students who may want to propose a new line of study or a new location for an off-campus experience. The energy here is purposeful and directed toward accomplishment as well as accrual of knowledge. The business school, mirroring preeminently successful Coca-Cola, has an overarching steady influence within the administration academic philosophy. The School of Theology has an equal if not greater influence with the university in that ethical standards and ethical practices must stand up to critical review. In its own way, Emory is a very affirming, optimistic environment for undergraduate students coming of age within a recession and American bipolarization. This campus is judicious, wise and successfully promotes pluralistic concepts within their community and their outreach. At graduation, students are well-positioned for continuing professional studies and are likely to serve as ethical anchors in their communities.

In the following listing of college majors it is important to remember that students can fit into any college and can be successful in any major. We have found that the Personality Types below fit very well at this college. The course-of-study chosen for each Personality Type corresponds to MBTI® research and is presented as one of many examples favorable for that type.

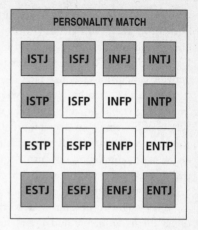

ISTJ will find the campus environment to their liking since it focuses on learning first and residential life activities after that. Learning makes sense when the very best mastery of the subject is the goal. The minor in **Computer Informatics** is a great choice for this type who wants to bring utility to uncorrelated data. ISTJ can be data mining and completing their major in any number of related disciplines. The Emory campus has the clean lines and functional organization that ISTJs approve of.

INTP is the curious, global type who understands quickly and gets intensely absorbed in their studies. They are an excellent fit for intellectual Emory. The joint major in **Economics/Math** allows this type to solve equations and/or puzzles, favorite pastimes. At the same time they can be quite successful in management positions within complex environments. Leadership is an unknown quantity to the young INTP, but the Goizueta School of Business provides the exposure and introduces INTP to executive level careers in business.

ENTJ will appreciate Emory's joint degree in **Psychology and Linguistics**. This latter field is becoming well entwined with brain development. The ENTJ who has a passion for this field will also gain much from Emory's comprehensive graduate programs in psychology. In fact, undergrads will often conduct research in Emory's exceptional medical laboratories for the physical sciences. ENTJ is all about energy and enthusiasm, just like Emory.

ESTJ likes the familiar educational model i.e. the teacher as the giver of knowledge and students as the eager recipient. With the BA in **Physics,** this type can be ready to enter medicine, law, teaching or business. ESTJs, however, will want to narrow down the focus early in the freshman or sophomore year to make sure they satisfy their requirements for a planned degree. They will look to the faculty for input in reaching this decision and faculty builds strong relationships with undergraduates here through the research studies.

INTJ, ever the original, independent and skeptical student, will find that Emory applauds their style. There is enough wiggle room in the curriculum to explore emerging interests. INTJs penchant to directly challenge the wisdom presented in class may not get an eager welcome in Emory's model of education. However, the depth in curriculum offerings overcomes any self doubts and this type's internal vision will develop and mature in four years. The minor in **Science, Culture and Society** is just the ticket to stretch that vision with its self proclaimed "intense discussion of research issues."

ISTP who is detached and seemingly "laid back" could draw some arched eyebrows from their hard-charging peers. Fortunately ISTPs pay close attention to the process and will be appreciated in the **Biology** major. If field work with the Yerkes Regional Primate Research Center is available, all the better. Observing primates and drawing conclusions through facts comes naturally for ISTP.

ISFJ is the careful individual who wants to serve mankind and absorb facts delivered in a stable environment. The department of **Nursing** at Emory's Woodruff School of Nursing considers it a privilege to care for the ill. ISFJ would agree. With attention to the details, Emory efficiently offers graduation with this professional degree after completion of four calendar, academic years. This type might find extracurricular programs offered by the school of theology for undergraduate students definitely worth exploring.

INFJ might relate quite well to the **Religion** major at Emory which is exceptional for its academic and moral foundation thanks to the Chandler School of Theology. The School, while remaining solid with its historical Christian heritage, offers a plethora of extraordinary courses to the undergraduate. The curriculum addresses religious questions that we are familiar with, minus contemporary political agendas. INFJs will salute the complex nuances this department is willing to take on. Emory University has multiple foundations of strength, to counter contemporary political agendas, such as the prestigious Transforming Community Project, funded by the Ford Foundation.

ENFJ likes to start with the people approach before acknowledging the hard facts. The interesting joint major in **Classics/History** gives this determined type flexibility to sort out a career track. Emory undergrads wrestle regularly with abstract thought, infused by moral reasoning. At the same time, the campus environment is covered up with reality through the School of Nursing and the Goizueta Business School. Within the dorms, the extracurriculars and the social scene, ENFJs will interface their abstractions with peers who prefer employment on graduation. This type can handle the juxtaposition and move forward confidently after graduation to employment or grad school.

ESFJ could easily be attracted to the hands-on **Business** undergraduate degree at Goizueta School of Emory University. The undergraduate degree calls for courage, knowledge and an ability to spontaneously make informed decisions. With a favorable view toward entrepreneurship, this type is resourceful and motivated in salesmanship. They can be invaluable, loyal business partners, especially when the enterprise is offering services to the public.

FLORIDA SOUTHERN COLLEGE

111 Lake Hollingsworth Drive
Lakeland, FL 33801-5689
Website: www.flsouthern.edu
Admissions Telephone: 863-680-4131
Undergraduates: 2,257; 902 Men, 1,553 Women

Physical Environment

Located half-way between Orlando and Tampa, Florida Southern College sits on the edge of a small lake and adjacent to the town of Lakeland. The most striking features are the many buildings designed by the American architect, Frank Lloyd Wright. The chapel has long rectangular windows that shoot rays of light throughout the day, creating a mood and feel that encourages **spirituality.** Newer buildings such as the library blend in with **Wright's classic architecture** and call to students interested in **America's architectural heritage**. The Becker Business building, designed by architect Robert Stern of New York, will complement the Wright architecture and house a simulated trading floor, classroom, labs and cafe. Florida Southern's connection with the **business community** and the state are strong and there is ongoing philanthropy for the college.

The Rinker Technology Center includes a cyber lounge and the latest technology for seminars and work spaces. The modern Christoverson Humanities building features the deep red colors of the college and compliments the Wright architectural perspectives. The performing arts facility does an outstanding job by drawing in students who are serious about **music and dramatic performance**. The planetarium offers students and the community a way to come together as they explore the heavens and appeals to prospective students who like a **family feel**. A wellness building and athletic center provide students with many activities that foster fitness and health. The religious center accommodates students who want to continue their worship experience in college.

The pool and lake offer a **fun-in-the-sun** lifestyle and competitive water sports. Campus traditions like Steak and Shrimp night speak for themselves. Students who want more diversion drive to Orlando or Tampa and the gulf coast beaches. Orange trees are part of the campus landscape, a practical reminder and laboratory for those interested in studying citrus **horticulture** and turf grass management. These niche degrees are well supported by the Florida climate and this particular campus. Florida Southern College draws students who want that residential, private college feel.

Social Environment

The majority of students come from Florida and prefer an established community with **small town ambiance**. The successful Florida Southern student graduated high school with solid credentials and several extracurricular activities on their resumes. Professors are attuned to students with differing learning levels, interests and abilities. This campus is drawing those who look to weave traditional liberal arts studies with employment and career options.

Undergraduates at Florida Southern are **cooperative**, casual and friendly. Relaxing in the fall sunshine while peering into iPads or quietly talking over energy drinks, they settle in quickly on this well-designed campus. **Fraternities and sororities** receive good support here from the administration and the student body.

The college administration has a lengthy, cooperative relationship with the town of Lakeland. Since the 1970s, students and community leaders have pooled their efforts through a non-profit organization in order to benefit both town and college. Students participate in the many **service projects** for Lakeland families and seniors who are representative of solid **Middle America**. Enactus, a nonprofit student-led organization, just recently connected the Central Florida Speech and Hearing Center with technology that improves hearing aids. Students here focus on their studies with daily attention, energy and a mind to service. They are proud of their academic and artistic work and expect to be successful and productive throughout their careers.

Compatibility with Personality Types and Preferences

Florida Southern College has a solid tradition of easily recognizable American social values which evolved on this campus community through decades of membership and affiliation with the Methodist Church. Florida Southern's ethical belief system is easily understood in the Cornerstone Concept that outlines the standard of behavior expected of all students who enroll at the college. The honor code is considered a personal obligation of each student and care is taken by the administration to communicate it to prospective students. The standards identified in procedures and policy are written to apply equally to faculty, staff and students. Academic philosophy leans heavily toward practical knowledge and skills. Much of the faculty in business has had entrepreneurial experience in the private sector.

The helpful website is loaded with considerable detail (S) that is designed to be supportive. Care is taken to spell out any impact college policies may have on the students. The Second Year Experience focuses attention on returning sophomores akin to that given to the first year students on campus. The entire community honors friendliness and contribution to others through service learning (F). From this foundation of strong values and helping others, the college promotes educational excellence. The Junior Journey is an overseas or domestic off campus learning program that is individually tailored and organized at the department level. The nature of Junior Journey assures each undergraduate student travels with faculty in their department. The sites visited directly correlate the major with the world beyond the campus boundaries. At Florida Southern, there is much to be appreciated in traditional American perspectives.

In the following listing of college majors it is important to remember that students can fit into any college and can be successful in any major. We have found that the Personality Types

PERSONALITY MATCH			
ISTJ	ISFJ	INFJ	INTJ
ISTP	ISFP	INFP	INTP
ESTP	ESFP	ENFP	ENTP
ESTJ	ESFJ	ENFJ	ENTJ

below fit very well at this college. The course-of-study chosen for each Personality Type corresponds to MBTI® research and is presented as one of many examples favorable for that type.

ISTJ will get solid coursework with the **Business** degree and Finance track that emphasizes skills and management tools. The latter offers an emphasis which familiarizes ISTJs with risk management who are not ordinarily comfortable with chance. Often meticulous in their approach, ISTJ will respect and thrive with the excellent student-professor collaboration at Florida Southern.

ISFJ would rally to the call for help from juveniles in our youth detention facilities. On this campus, the degree in **Criminology** is well supported by the overall educational philosophy of service to others. Their reflective nature and ability to clearly see reality will be an asset in the career field. There is also an option for a double major, **Sociology and Criminology**, that would position this type to serve both the individual and the community at large.

INFJ has a mind full of impressions best understood by non-INFJs as "artistic impressions" straight out of the art history books cataloging calm landscapes in nature. The major in **Youth Ministry** here is traditional in spiritual foundation. INFJs will find commitment to bring relevant and supportive programming into our teen communities. This passionate type will naturally help adolescents sort through social media influences.

ISFP and art is a natural and likely combination. Artistic expression on this warm campus is also a natural. This type might look into the **Studio Art** major with flexibility for concentration in sculpture, painting, ceramics, printing or photography. The department seeks to explore the relationship between art and emotion. This type, both sensitive and astute, will also appreciate other majors offered by the department in art education, art history and graphic design.

INFP seeks to find meaning in human existence and it's a tall order, even for them. The **Religion** major at Florida Southern is a good starting point for their inquiry. The department has a well developed Judeo-Christian course of study. The McKay Archives Center is a treasure trove for American spiritual and cultural research. Well-documented historic collegiate traditions, dating back decades, help students search for lost cultural experiences which may inform current day meaning and human purpose for twenty-somethings.

ESTP is lucky to have the unusual **Landscape Horticulture** major at Florida Southern. The courses emphasize the high risks in the horticultural business and this suits the action-oriented and trouble-shooting ESTP. Dare we say, it is a hands-on discipline? This department has other desirable options in citrus farming and turf grass management which also allow this type to be outside and on the go.

ESFP interested in sports, whether participating or as a fan, might look into the new **Sports Communication Marketing** major at Florida Southern. This campus with its strong business and communication faculty is ideal for this unusual major. Florida spring training camps in baseball, college football teams and Disney's nearby ESPN center have good options for sports reporting and internships.

ENFP is going to find that the **Graphic Design** studies here offer a wide scope within the discipline. First there is a print emphasis or web emphasis to choose from within the minors. This choice in minor pairs with the advertising major in communications. On this campus there is no shortage of coursework that ENFP is likely to want to take.

ESTJ will smooth into the **Accounting** major or minor with comparative ease. This very exacting discipline allows the student with this type to bring their impersonal powers of judgment into the arena of objective numbers. Combine this activity with the need for taking charge while auditing a client's firm and it's an awfully enticing major for take-charge ESTJs.

ESFJ is a natural conversationalist as well as news reporter. Their innate interest in the well-being of others is a distinct advantage when interviewing eye witnesses to traumatic events in our communities for the nightly news. The News Media I, II, III coursework provide the primer for both anchor and news reporter positions. The major in **Broadcast, Print and Online Media** takes advantage of their memory for details and steady approach in critical situations. This type would enjoy utilizing the archived documents in college reporting at the McKay Center and perhaps bring some of the innocence of those 20th midcentury decades forward.

ENFJ will find a warm, personal faculty in the department of **Psychology**. The curriculum emphasizes human behavior and interpersonal relationships which suits this type just fine. ENFJs will thrive on the personal mentoring within this department. Their extraordinary communication skills will be amplified with new insights secured in this degree.

FURMAN UNIVERSITY

Office of Admissions
Greenville, SC 29613
Website: www.furman.edu
Admissions Telephone: 864-294-2034
Undergraduates: 2,753; 1,183 Men, 1,570 Women

Physical Environment

Located on 750 acres at the base of the Blue Ridge Mountains, this academically rigorous liberal arts university mixes colonial Williamsburg architectural style and red-brick walkways that crisscross in a Jeffersonian way. The **landscape** with the trees, flowers, fountains, lake, softball fields and an 18-hole golf course is nothing less than breathtaking. The classroom buildings are modern. Many of these buildings are environmentally certified and designed with recycled materials for energy efficiency. Furman led the way among its college peers with the first environmental awards for new college construction in the south. The **technology** classrooms are designed to pipe in fresh air and oxygen. The geothermal project completed in 2013 provides all cooling and heat for the campus apartments. The university PAC solar project completed in 2011 is sending electricity to the grid. The business office assertively monitors commodities like natural gas and ties down advantageous prices. Energy and facility planning on this campus is a study in **beauty and efficiency**.

Pretty much all of the campus has undergone renovation in the last ten years. The Bell Tower, a **60-bell carillon**, overlooks the small lake, flanked by an amphitheater used for **outdoor concerts**. All of it reminds the passerby of the Furman music conservatory. New apartment-style residence halls and the conference center take full advantage of the views. The architecture here appeals to students who are lively, active and caring of the environment.

Social Environment

Furman students value their family and hometown traditions that reflect Christian values, being well-groomed and mindful of personal presence. About one-third of the students are actively involved in a religious organization with the university becoming independent of its formal Baptist association in 1992. A Furman education is a family affair. During family weekend, everyone is invited, including cousins, uncles and grandparents.

Undergraduates form a strong community that is civic-minded. The local area is the prime beneficiary of **undergraduate volunteer hours** and all are involved. Furman students are also environmentally conscious and politically interested. Well known speakers are often on campus, scheduled by the university's non-partisan political think-tank which also funds student research. About half of the student body belong to Greek organizations and initiate volunteer activities like Relay for Life and Special Olympics. The university reflects conservative tradition that focuses on moral, prosocial community.

Students like the liberal arts and like to dig deeply into a major. They gain that depth while participating in internships, study abroad and other experiential education. The Furman academic **calendar is nontraditional** and it adds length and **rigor** to the collegiate workload. The great majority of students come from out of the state. The **social scene** is lively at Furman. The Trone Student Center, undergoing renovation in 2014, maintains its own Facebook account and puts out weekly invites. Students must guard against becoming over-involved with so many activities.

Compatibility with Personality Types and Preferences

Furman University purposely combines traditional religious values of the 20th Century with a trendy educational outlook. Faculty and administration set a vibrant foundation of social and academic experiences for undergrads. There is a strong attraction to technology in use by today's generation. Furman embraces and uses it. Students are familiar with class collaborative projects that are supplemented by text messaging. This experiential learning is a hallmark of the university's attraction to the future. Students who have mastered the scientific method are encouraged to join faculty in research where they are closely mentored during research activities.

Research opportunities are plentiful. Faculty are tuned to the future and well connected to today's American practices in the public and business square. It would not be surprising if the university already has a budget line for bitcoins. Faculty actively encourage students to integrate their new-found knowledge gained through this research with off campus travel. Each department frequently offers small, quick trips overseas and domestically by taking advantage of budgetary support at the university level.

Service to others (F) is a common theme and most students participate in volunteer events that are organized and developed by national collegiate service organizations. There is also a strong ethic for productivity. The pathways (J) are in place for undergraduates to double major and take additional coursework. Furman provides a creative environment through hands-on research and direct learning. Students who appreciate getting the facts and details (S) in place first and then moving toward a general understanding of their subject will do well here.

In the following listing of college majors it is important to remember that students can fit into any college and can be successful in any major. We have found that the Personality Types below fit very well at this college. The course-of-study chosen for each Personality Type corresponds to MBTI® research and is presented as one of many examples favorable for that type.

INFJ will find the **Theater Arts** curriculum at Furman University really quite thorough. Each undergraduate will be practiced in stage management, technical crew, publicity and acting. Introspective INFJ brings imagery and symbolism to this discipline. The theater department is ideal for its smaller size, mentoring and three annual performances. In fall 2013 Furman theater presented the world premiere of Pomp and Circumstance. The play-

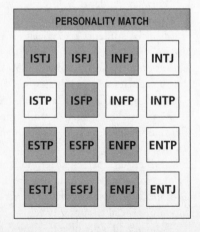

PERSONALITY MATCH			
ISTJ	ISFJ	INFJ	INTJ
ISTP	ISFP	INFP	INTP
ESTP	ESFP	ENFP	ENTP
ESTJ	ESFJ	ENFJ	ENTJ

wright, Resident Artist and Furman '91 grad, David Randall Cook, writes for the Gotham Stage Company, New York City, and is a member of Dramatist Guild.

ISTJ might take a close look at the **Economics** degree at Furman University. It has much that appeals to ISFJs, specifically the step-by-step survey of the economic discipline. This sequential approach is their preferred way to master the abstract discipline. The required capstone course in senior year has several prerequisites that include the course Empirical Methods in Economics. This type of direct observational study leads to the best understanding for ISTJs.

ISFJ with a good ear for music will want to take advantage of the impressive music department at Furman. The major in **Music Theory** rotates emphasizing performance in the choral, vocal, solo, ensembles and string quartet. The ISFJ is a sensitive person and quite aware of how others are feeling during any given activity. This type will bring a personal meaning to their musical composition and performance along with a precise, possibly understated performance.

ISFP just might move toward a career in pharmaceuticals. The **Chemistry** major at Furman offers further specialization. The track in biochemistry has the action and practicality that they want. ISFP appreciates the utility of hands-on research in the labs along with the detailed observations of chemical reactions. This major prepares ISFPs for pharmacy school or fundamental research for industrial applications. ISFPs prefer to see a light at the end of the tunnel. The department shines forth through student faculty collaboration in research and numerous other learning experiences.

ESTP could sign right up after scanning the courses at Furman for the **Information Technology** major. It is their practice to quickly jump in with a practical, expeditious goal in mind. This major offers graduates a broad and solid understanding of business practice and application of software and programming. ESTP will benefit from the nuts and bolts in the course titled Project Management. With this practical collection of skills ESTP is quite ready for technology-intensive business environments.

ESFP is a natural at public relations. The major in **Communication Studies** will prepare this type for several dynamic, fast-paced career options. Above all, ESFP needs to be with other people in an environment charged with purpose and fun. Their social acumen is ideal when combined with grounding in communication theory. Undergrads formulate their message via topical analysis as well as social, moral implications. ESFP's infomercials, produced at WFTV, would be chocked with useful, factual information. The Furman student-run TV News has got to be a place to find a little fun too.

ENFP will start off the freshmen year at Furman sampling most if not all of the fun cultural events and activities. This campus is ideal for ENFP since Furman enthusiasm and optimism runs high. The major in **Business Administration** gives good exposure to the wide entrepreneurial field. This works well for ENFP who likes to take in all the possibilities before selecting a career track. The investment club is pretty successful and active on campus and another good bet for ENFP.

ESFJ should find the friendly, harmonious environment they prefer within the Department of **Biology** at Furman University. Academic work tends to comprise two avenues of learning favorable to the ESFJs. First there is the read-study-memorize of most first-year courses. This is followed by the application in the laboratories and exceptional field experiences such as in the course, African Ecology. It is one of the 'traveling' courses in the department. Students can bring 10 pounds of clothes to give to the local community clothes bank, that leaves eight pounds in the carry-on for them. Social ethics will travel at this university.

ESTJ is often a go-getter. This type sees their goal and efficiently pursues it. The major in **Accounting** prepares graduates for the gate-keeping function in fast-paced financial economies. It will be the ESTJ who can guide organizations with firmness while identifying errors with resolve. The department offers a broad education that could lead to graduate study or employment on graduation. This practical approach, tied to the reality of facts and numbers, is desired by ESTJ.

ENFJ is going to be fine with the major in **Health Sciences**. The curriculum essentially requires graduates to become strong advocates for a healthy life style. ENFJ is interested in the individual as a whole person—their emotional health, spiritual health and physical health. The department functions almost as a center that advocates for well-being. There is a well-equipped laboratory for studying performance in running and anatomy. Since this type is exceptionally talented at speaking to large audiences, the message of well-being could easily become their prime career focus.

GEORGE WASHINGTON UNIVERSITY

212 I Street, NW
Washington, DC 20052
Website: www.gwu.edu
Admissions Telephone: 202-994-6040
Undergraduates: 10,464; 4,604 Men, 5,860 Women
Graduate Students: 15,189

Physical Environment

George Washington University's downtown campus, fondly known as the Foggy Bottom campus, is within blocks of the White House. Visitors may walk the city streets E to J or 20th to 24th and admire the **tall buildings and Federal style houses** without immediately realizing they are on the campus of GW. The architecture lends credibility to the university image of being well connected to the power circles in the district. Most of the campus buildings occupy the area formed by the Avenues of Pennsylvania, New Hampshire and Virginia. Students walk to **DC museums and monuments**, from the Smithsonian to the Vietnam Veterans Memorial and the Korean War Veterans Memorial. Prospective visiting high schoolers are wowed by the history here.

The university master plan for development was completed in 2007. It calls for redevelopment of several blocks of its current real estate holdings. Square 54, up and running in 2011, includes residential, retail and commercial business. It is a mixed-use property that functions as a town center for students, faculty and DC residents. Square 55, opening in 2015, will house the School of Engineering and the Physical Sciences. Square 77 projected to be ready for Fall 2016 will expand residential housing and include live-in-faculty residences. Each of the squares generate tenant income which is quickly budgeted into the university academic programs and research facilitates.

The **city hustle and bustle** is amplified by a multitude of ethnic shops and restaurants. Students who are attracted to power and important venues find this university very appealing. Here the physical environment combines the nation's capital with classroom education and recreational city experiences. The housing options at GW are many, ranging from living and learning to residences for fraternities and sororities. The university tries to keep students busy on campus, although the city itself remains a huge draw. Each day there are dozens of on campus events ranging from debates to athletics to concerts to comedy. GW also offers a quieter location at its Mount Vernon Campus, fenced in with mature trees and red-brick buildings contrasting dramatically with Foggy Bottom sidewalks and vertical architecture. Students can take classes at either campus.

Social Environment

Students come from a considerable **variety of socio-economic** backgrounds. Some have parents in the diplomatic core. Others may be referred to GW by their country's embassy in Washington DC. Home-grown U.S. students from across the nation regularly enroll for this unique collegiate experience. The worldly international students provide an open door to other cultures for the American undergraduates. US students expect to secure **internships in federal offices**, political lobbies, corporate business headquarters and nonprofits. **International students** expect to enlarge their knowledge of American society and practices.

GW is a large university and students gain bureaucratic skills simply by negotiating their own educational study and presence on campus within the first year. They learn to expertly navigate the somewhat tight rules of the university. To counter the impersonal impact of the city and largeness of the student body, the residential life is bolstered with **homey, fun activities** that remind undergraduates of the calmer lives in their hometowns. **Volunteer initiatives**, very familiar with the millennial generation, are well supported. Collegiate activities help to bolster and resupply student energy reserves to deal with the city and remain positive, self-directed. DC political, corporate and governmental soirees create a privileged setting very much unlike most of lower and middle class America.

Compatibility with Personality Types and Preferences

George Washington University takes much of its persona from DC, the nation's capital. GW echoes the nature of bureaucratic DC with practicality. On this campus questions within all academic disciplines are: What works? What is of value that we all agree on? (T) The university is a good neighbor, mindful of adjacent businesses, residences and corporations, including them regularly in university expansions that may impact neighborhood activity. Students drawn to George Washington University want to experience it all, so their friends on campus and the student body in general must serve as a stable anchor.

Prospective students appreciate that the campus offers a secure, predictable collegiate atmosphere within its buildings. The environment is fast-paced energy outside of campus and students want a safe place at the end of the day. They are expecting to build and advance their academic skills. They want to learn how to negotiate the administrative environments of lobbies, regulatory bodies, executive offices and national government. GW's curriculum is magnified several times over through its faculty and access to contemporary speakers. Collaboration between the university and other influential partners, such as Ford Motor Company, add to the allure of real time problems and solutions. Professors can be careerists who function as high level civil service employees, policy makers, party officials, lobbyists and think tankers among the legions of administrative types who work in DC. Above all else, students who are successful at GW are drawn outside of themselves, outside of their dormitory and outside of their campus (E), drawn into the movement of the city and happy to catch a last minute ride (P) for a wide-eyed day of learning.

In the following listing of college majors it is important to remember that students can fit

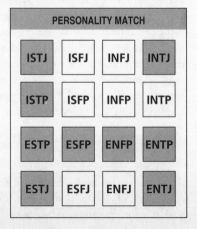

PERSONALITY MATCH			
ISTJ	ISFJ	INFJ	INTJ
ISTP	ISFP	INFP	INTP
ESTP	ESFP	ENFP	ENTP
ESTJ	ESFJ	ENFJ	ENTJ

into any college and can be successful in any major. We have found that the Personality Types below fit very well at this college. The course-of-study chosen for each Personality Type corresponds to MBTI® research and is presented as one of many examples favorable for that type.

INTJ has the intellectual objectivity, the vision and the determination to deal with the most abstract ideas. The degree in **Geography** has the potential to give INTJs all they require to be content. The discipline has evolved as a result of the multiple demands on the land and the spaces that we occupy. Geographers highlight and predict land usage with their mathematical methods and ethical perspectives. In fact, there is a wide focus within the field itself: political geography, historical geography, social geography, urban geography or economic geography. INTJ will fit right into the all-encompassing discipline that has many philosophical aspects to it. At GW, the department focuses on spatial patterns of human impact.

ISTP would respond, "I don't think so" to a degree in **Sonography**, after all who even knows what it is? However, on closer examination ISTPs understand they will be operating complex medical equipment/procedures for diagnostic purposes. This type enjoys technical fields and is normally quite adept with complicated, sensitive equipment. They have patience to find and understand conflicted data and information. GW is one of the first universities to offer this degree. Undergraduates are permitted to take examination for national certification in junior year and this is desirable for immediate employment on graduation.

ISTJ is going to like the looks of the degree in **Accountancy** at George Washington University. The business school provides programs to assure GW undergraduates will be prepared for the national certification. Research with well-connected faculty benefits ISTJ who gains a lot from observing successful professionals. This type avoids risky activity, sticking with the tried and approved. They would likely join a research project currently underway where the professor was soliciting student help in a paid position. ISTJs thrive on the structure and preplanning needed for this degree. They are exacting and precise by nature, ideal for businesses who must respond to regulatory agencies.

ESTP is often coordinated and excels in physical activities. At the same time they are quick thinkers who respond very well in crisis situations. The degree in **Exercise Science** with a concentration in **Pre-Athletic Training** leads to entry positions in several career fields including rehabilitation, professional athletics and college or high school athletics. Ever social and often sophisticated, ESTPs are gregarious and function well in the athletic environments. At GW, the undergraduates will be interning in an excellent variety of locations: NCAA universities and colleges, independent and public high schools, medical clinics and other health settings. These opportunities will not be lost on ESTP who will build a personal network for job opportunities after graduation.

ESFP is excellent at conversing with staff and patients in the health field. This type is practical and gregarious so they naturally draw others to them. The emerging discipline in **Pharmacogenomics** has a lot that ESFPs will find desirable. GW is one of the few universities offering this degree that focuses on the interaction between an individual's inherited gene pool and prescribed medication. Think personalized medicine. This type can easily solicit information from reticent patients. They also have an affinity for facts and excellent recall. It could be ESFP who best determines which medications are potentially harmful due to genetic inheritance.

ENFP has a tender heart and really enjoys supportive relationships with others. The **Speech and Hearing Sciences** major offers four concentrations, one of which is Hearing and Deafness. GW offers a solid experience in clinical exposure through its own Speech and Hearing Clinic. The department also conducts research and curious ENFP would easily be drawn into research designs that interface with children. Speech pathologists interact with many different people and ENFP likes the diversity and cultural experiences.

ENTP plus the unpredictable politics in the nation's capital form a great combination. The government generates thousands of information drops daily, each with a political underpinning. These messages always impact some group of citizens, PAC, lobbyist, elected representative, nonprofit or corporate entity. ENTP reads between the lines of this released information and is drawn to political reporting on behalf of interested citizens and clients. The degree in **Political Communication** prompts undergraduates to ask questions: Who, What, Where, Why. ENTPs spend their waking hours posing these types of questions anyway so they will have a head start in this major.

ESTJ is especially good at discerning cause and effect relationships. This type is systematic, organized and efficient. The specific world of languages could very well appeal to ESTJ who may enjoy translating professional documents, specializing in fields such as international law, health or technology. The degree in **German Language and Literature** could introduce and launch ESTJs into a career that places them in pivotal work discerning the translation and transfer of knowledge between advanced technological cultures, Germany and Australia. GW maintains a well-provisioned language center downloading television programming from around the world in native languages. This large department with over 50 faculty members provides familiar access to global cultures through selected internships.

ENTJ will find that the **Japanese Language and Literature** lives in two academic centers at GW: The Elliott School of International Affairs and the Columbian College of Arts and Sciences. Straddling two different perspectives in East Asian studies, the undergraduate at GW gets both worlds: arts and politics. Ultimately, this assertive, goal-oriented type will be able to craft a unique direction for their undergraduate study. Options for ENTJ after graduation with this background would include diplomacy, government, higher education, law and business. The important nature of the Pacific Rim nations will not be lost on ENTJ who is a strategic type that prefers to move in power circles. Exposure to Asian culture in the nation's capital adds another layer of competence for creative ENTJ.

GEORGETOWN UNIVERSITY

Office of Admission
37th and P Streets, NW
Washington, DC 20057
Website: www.georgetown.edu
Admissions Telephone: 202-687-5084
Undergraduates: 7,552; 3,322 Men, 4,230 Women
Graduate Students: 9,805

Physical Environment

The two tall steeples of Georgetown University soar above the Potomac River as they did in much earlier times, before **Washington, DC** became the capital of the United States. In the early 1800s the nation's capital moved from Philadelphia to Washington, to a strip of land between Maryland and Virginia, and established an independent district named after Columbus. Today Georgetown University occupies 110 acres of this very strategic property. The city subway and buses make transportation to and from the airport and into town a streamlined trip. The university is intrinsically part and parcel of the nation's capital with its many resources and opportunities.

The historic architecture portrays the original religious philosophy of Georgetown founders, the **Catholic Jesuits**. Dahlgren Chapel of the Sacred Heart, located right in the center of campus, offers daily religious services. The campus buildings have many inclusive spaces for celebrating the spiritual life of students, regardless of their religion. Residence Halls at Georgetown call up the **familiar dormitory style floor plans**. Each floor has two bathrooms for common use and floors may be single gender for freshmen, but coed for upper classroom. This type of traditional living prompts community and friendship within the larger numbers on each floor verses the apartment style suites that segment undergraduates from each other. Each dormitory has a chaplain in addition to resident assistants. The university has a vigilant security presence on the campus to help undergraduates negotiate the unpredictable nature of the city.

Regents Hall houses biology, chemistry and physics. Chock full of the latest technological labs and equipment the facility bears a resemblance to historic architecture prevalent on the campus. It also hosts the Institute for Soft Matter, research in nonsolid matter. The Georgetown campus is not only a stone's throw from the **White House** but also a stone's throw from the nation's most important monuments and museums. When students need a diversion from the intense academics, Washington, DC offers many options.

Social Environment

Georgetown students are particularly adept at **abstract reasoning**. They enjoy ethical and religious discussion on the human condition and what it means to be

Catholic in 21st Century America. Georgetown students tend to come from worldly, influential families. It also has a multi-ethnic student body from across the globe. True to its Jesuit tradition, GU embraces people of other religions and respects their ideas and customs. The campus has a **pluralistic spiritual presence** with all faiths as well as atheism welcomed. The university supports over 100 off campus initiatives involving undergraduates serving the needy population in the nation's capital. Many students speak **more than one language.** The student body is as diverse as the city itself.

A number of majors in the undergraduate curriculum, such as in the **School of Foreign Service**, cover **unique disciplines** that are offered as graduate study in other universities. The undergraduate educational studies tend to be compartmentalized. It is usually difficult to take courses outside of your major in other schools and departments on this campus. Undergraduates can, however, consider an interdisciplinary major which must be designed and approved within departmental guidelines. Excellence in academic disciplines seems to be the philosophical glue that holds this academically wide-ranging university together. Students who fit in here value the contemporary concepts of peace and justice. It's for those who want to secure policy positions within government, diplomatic corps and international organizations. At Georgetown and in the capital, students **observe power and policy** at work. They see the government up close.

Georgetown students work hard and play hard. This demanding academic environment finds students partying on the weekends. Other stress busters include rooting for the Hoyas, often nationally ranked in several sports, especially basketball. Students also join religious and other ethnic fellowship clubs. With over 150 years of continuous performances, student-led theater at Georgetown University takes on a life of its own. It must call audiences to pause as they occupy seats taken by others through decades of American history. Georgetown Athletics boasts **Jack the Bulldog,** Hoyas mascot, available for private engagements as well as antics at the basketball games since circa 1964.

Compatibility with Personality Types and Preferences

Georgetown University could be thought of as a successful experiment in strategic engagement. This influential university is in a privileged position from which it develops educational content, now through international, global perspectives. This university, predating the Revolutionary period, has an exceptional history of its own in reference to a time when America struggled to become a viable nation. Looking over to the Capitol, two blocks from undergraduate housing lofts, provides a visual cue as to the university's familiar coexistence (E) with power and leadership in our national government.

Much like the government itself, this university is organized by departments and colleges similar to a wiring diagram (J). The undergraduate schools and colleges are quite separate from each other. One can imagine the State Department with its own culture and mission as quite separate from the Treasury Department. In this way, Georgetown's School of Foreign Policy and the School of Business can be envisioned as existing quite independently of each other, yet part of the same university.

Students who see decision and policy making very clearly in their career path are well served at Georgetown. Undergraduates are exposed to a full academic fire hosing of abstraction (N). An excellent example is the unusual Entrepreneurship Fellows Program. It helps students gauge their own aptitude for success. Factual knowledge (S) is equally honored on this campus with emphasis across the curriculum on analysis, methodology, systems and technologies.

In the following listing of college majors it is important to remember that students can fit into any college and can be successful in any major. We have found that the Personality Types below fit very well at this college. The course-of-study chosen for each Personality Type corresponds to MBTI® research and is presented as one of many examples favorable for that type.

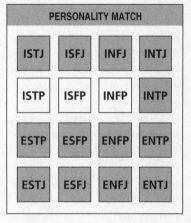

PERSONALITY MATCH

ISTJ	ISFJ	INFJ	INTJ
ISTP	ISFP	INFP	INTP
ESTP	ESFP	ENFP	ENTP
ESTJ	ESFJ	ENFJ	ENTJ

INFJ desires an understanding of other peoples and their cultural values. They apply their insight to ethnic cultures with ease because of their natural empathy. In the School of Foreign Service the major in **Culture and Politics** looks to understand how societal outlooks, perceptions and beliefs are translated in power and action. It is pretty abstract and the INFJ is particularly suited for it. With this degree, INFJs will be valuable consultants for many international and national organizations.

INTJ often has a strategic plan after sufficient study of a particular problem. However, they are not inclined to speak up about that plan since it usually contains a few unorthodox ideas. They analyze rapidly and with ease. A field with fast-moving factors and data points is attractive to INTJs. The study of **Finance** at Georgetown University would seem to provide this. The department focuses on financial models, techniques and methods as applied to business problems. The domestic and global financial markets serve up plenty of problems for application of these tools. Disciplined and objective, INTJ happily would don a suit for a day at that office.

ISTJ likes to correct infractions of rules that we all should have followed in the first place. This type is dedicated to accuracy and doesn't mind studying the fine details for total understanding. The major in **Operations and Information Management** could appeal to ISTJ for these reasons. It explores the nature of businesses that 'run smoothly' from production and procurement on to delivery. The curriculum focuses on systems and application of technologies.

ISFJ often has a technical side or at least an affinity with technology. Drawn to the fields of health and medicine, the major in **Human Science** at Georgetown holds out good options for ISFJ. Undergraduates get a firm grounding in biological and chemical principles in the state-of-the-art teaching laboratory. Faculty regularly focus on current research and its applicability to current problems in health. ISFJs equipped with analytical skills are just the type to introduce new concepts in established organizations such as government bureaucracies.

INTP can find the right amount of complexity in the **International Health** major at the School of Nursing and Health Studies on the Georgetown campus. The course descriptions and overview by the department call attention to the nature of disease as it travels across regional and political boundaries. The issues in this field are truly sobering. INTPs, with their objective analysis, can develop potential solutions for discussion. INTP is happiest bringing order and purpose out of seeming intellectual chaos. Global Health will offer them many opportunities, as well as America's own changed up health initiative introduced in 2014.

ESTP at times will be drawn into the field of trade, especially if there is dynamic action and a little risk. This type is skilled at identifying the unspoken goals in negotiation between buyers and sellers. The major in **International Business** at Georgetown University focuses on the business trends and practices. This foundational knowledge supports ESTP managers as they smoothly enter the environments of negotiation. The international qualifications can be gained in several ways. It meets the plug-and-play personal style of ESTPs.

ESFP has the common sense to go into tough management environments like health care and survive with flair, helping others to cheer up also. The major in **Healthcare Management and Policy** in the School of Nursing and Health Studies can prepare ESFP for the demands of the nationalized health care system rolled out with confusion in 2014. At Georgetown, the undergraduates will focus on management competencies as well as the various bureaucratic environments within hospitals and nursing facilities. ESFP, tolerant and adaptable by nature, will bring enthusiasm and cooperation to the policy discussions.

ENFP likes to be around a group of self-directed peers who are enthusiastically tuned to the task at hand, preferably several tasks at once. This type has a way with persuasion. The concentration in **Marketing** at Georgetown explores several marketing focuses. One of them, brand management, includes the life cycle of products studying the alpha to omega that represent the big picture so favored by ENFPs.

ENTP may not immediately jump at the concept of getting a degree in **International History.** However, it could make sense because it follows themes throughout history and roams across national and cultural boundaries. Following the thread of a topic, like labor relations through the centuries and across continents, could easily attract ENTP. The curriculum requires each student identify their desired theme and develop a foreign language proficiency. This is ideal for ENTP who can lose interest in assignments that are too familiar or do not hold out a tantalizing discovery.

ESFJ might look into the degree **Biology of Global Health** at Georgetown. As is found on this campus across the curriculum, methodology and analysis will be applied to health issues crossing continents. ESFJ will not be lost in policy discussion that involves regional, national or international perspectives. Their strong organizational skills will be valuable in personalizing the policy nature of work in public health settings. The demanding science courses in this major will prepare them for the complexity of transnational diseases.

ESTJ marches down the road of life as a very determined and practical traveler. The Bachelor of Arts in **Government** provides grounding in both theory and causal, logical analysis. Not typical, this approach looks at the subject from the greater picture, seeking to find systems that may explain the behavior of government. Both national and international governing bodies will be under the lens. This type has the personal determination to push through to their goals, securing a foundational understanding of the nature of governance. The advantage of studying this subject in the nation's capital will not be lost on this results-oriented, practical type.

ENFJ will take leadership positions in the right circumstances. Supportive, harmonious relationships with an organization would likely draw them forward to those positions. The degree at Georgetown University in **American Musical Culture** is unusual yet prepares graduates for careers in journalism, arts management and/or entertainment law. In each field, ENFJs would bring their creativity to the workplace along with their distinct desire to include all players in the decision making. This major requires a senior capstone project. The options for musical internships in the nation's capital are considerable and varied. Poised ENFJ will find fascinating internships in DC museums, the Library of Congress and other national sites that are housing musical treasures.

ENTJ is happy to step out and conduct the orchestra. The certificate in **Eurasian, Russian and East European Studies** would be seen as another instrument in the band. This entrepreneurial type will see the value when paired with a major in the School of Business. These emerging markets just a few decades into the capitalistic markets are intriguing. ENTJ has the resilience and strategic thinking skills to survive and prosper in the dynamic businesses. Georgetown has the financial savvy to educate in reference to these intricate global markets.

GEORGIA INSTITUTE OF TECHNOLOGY

22 North Avenue, NW
Atlanta, GA 30332-0320
Website: www.gatech.edu
Admissions Telephone: 404-894-4154
Undergraduates: 14,527; 9,734 Men, 4,793 Women
Graduate Students: 7,030

Physical Environment

Georgia Tech is a premiere public state university located in **downtown Atlanta** where I-75 and I-85 merge. The Georgia Tech campus has an **enclosed, angular** appeal with its many new buildings and architecturally bold design. 'Enclosed' may be why this large university also manages to feel comfortably hometown and small as contrasted to Atlanta just across the street. The sports complex and natatorium attract athletes loath to give up their HS track records and winning team statistics. These sports-minded students like to exercise, swim and play on the intramural teams. Creative techies are right at home in the state of the art **laboratories** inside the dramatic modern architecture. The **concrete, aluminum and glass** structures on this campus are similar to the manufacturing and technical environments that most will enter as they start their careers.

Students attracted to innovative solutions come to study environmental science and technology at the top research complex donated by the Ford Motor Company. Ford and Georgia Tech developed the **first solar hybrid car** premiered at the Las Vegas Computer Electronic show in early 2014. Georgia Tech School of Architecture and School of Engineering combined to write the book on designing green buildings. Called the Georgia Tech Yellow Book, it is a blueprint for architects and planners for new buildings and additions to achieve efficiency with sustainable utilities and infrastructure. The Georgia Tech undergrads placed sixth in the **Solar Decathlon,** an international competition to build and operate an 800-square foot solar-powered house. There are PhD programs in the physical and engineering sciences pushing the sciences into the future along with a handful other universities in the states. Undergraduates are in the laboratories **pushing the state of knowledge** in multiple disciplines, and the solar sun is just one of hundreds of research strands here.

Social Environment

The majority of students come from the state of Georgia. Many come from familiar towns and countryside across the state, lending a cohesive feel to the social life. They are not turned away by the **study and work demands** of this unique, public institution. Students keep good balance between **fun** and the books, yet academic study is intense. Many join Greek life because of their sponsored social activities on campus. Some form networks through friends at the nearby colleges for other social outlets. The Braves and Falcons, as well as the Atlanta Symphony, add to the social calendar. This campus draws those who like **traditional school spirit** and strong competitive teams to cheer. Students retreat from the hectic city pace on the tree-lined campus. Many students walk to Ponce de Leon Avenue over the connector to well known local restaurants, clubs, galleries and shops.

Undergraduate students have an **intense affinity** and aptitude for the sciences and math. The pervasive research on campus is underpinned by the collegiate imperative to solve **mankind's problems.** It is within the air on this campus. These students form a strong can-do attitude. They see the future through the lens of **current technology** and emerging possibilities. Those who like practical, hands-on research are thriving. A fair number of students branch out from the physical sciences. The Ivan Allen College of Liberal Arts interfaces the application of emerging manufactured systems, computing and technological services. **Initiative** and creativity are typical of these undergraduates. On this campus, students approve of the clear expectations, **accountability and progress**.

Compatibility with Personality Types and Preferences

On many Saturday mornings, a surprising number of students are out and exuberant in the morning. Students are likely to go through their day actively, with physical vigor and a twinkle of humor. This campus is for the folks who like to see, touch, feel or listen to materials (S). They seek to understand the environment and its properties; they are comfortable with themselves, metal, the circuits, the temperature, the physicality which is always present on this campus. At the same time they are fairly logical (T) folks who analyze and put stuff together for a purpose. The GA Techie likes to dissect the step-by-step presentation of what actually exists: whether in a theorem or in a piece of metal. The learning experience expects to move undergraduates into the future through the foundations of each discipline and experimentation.

Educational philosophy is strongly centered on benefiting society at the macro level. Sustainability concepts have long been featured at Georgia Tech. Faculty and students support living in an environment that shepherds natural resources while being efficient but yet comfortable. Graduates have a strong grounding in the benefits and reality of technology. Academic philosophy well incorporates multidisciplinary approaches within the Institute's several schools. Foundational and advanced knowledge within the individual disciplines is current, practical and reflective of reality. Alert to the societal costs of emerging technologies, they become capable of making the tough calls between reality, ideals and politically correct agendas. Georgia Tech undergrads do not own a pair of rose-colored glasses, nor the faculty either.

In the following listing of college majors it is important to remember that students can fit into any college and can be successful in any major. We have found that the Personality Types below fit very well at this college. The course-of-study chosen for each Personality Type corresponds to MBTI® research and is presented as one of many examples favorable for that type.

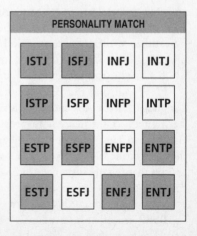

PERSONALITY MATCH

ISTJ	ISFJ	INFJ	INTJ
ISTP	ISFP	INFP	INTP
ESTP	ESFP	ENFP	ENTP
ESTJ	ESFJ	ENFJ	ENTJ

ESTJ is an outstanding fit at Georgia Tech. The Institute's course catalog is exceptionally clear in setting out information about what a student will need to graduate. Course credit is awarded at Georgia Tech for top scores on the SAT Subject Tests taken in high school. The degree in **Building Construction** is a good choice here for this type. The department emphasizes the management skills needed to monitor large construction sites. ESTJ is a natural administrator and has the no-nonsense personality to reason profitably with the construction trades, also no-nonsense folks.

ENTJ wants to take the practical material that abounds on this campus and reshape it into something new, futuristic and maybe just a little beyond the truly practical. ENTJ has the driving force to open their vision up in the classroom discussions and in the labs. Aeroelasticity should appeal to a person of this preference who has a penchant for math and calculated risk. It's possible that the Navy or Air Force will need engineers with courses like this in the **Aerospace Engineering** degree, to repair and monitor the aging American military aircraft fleets.

ENTP could easily be attracted to the Bachelor of Science in **History, Technology and Society**. The breadth of this curriculum appeals to the type's desire for the big picture and originality. Inclined to be avid readers, albeit later in life, the ENTPs like the variety and survey approach of this degree. The courses offered are compelling to the ENTP. They promise to reveal emerging concepts in application and technology. The graduates in this major have excellent analytical skills that are applicable to developing countries planning to upgrade their industrial capacities.

ISTP is quite observant but likely to be one of the less vocal students at outgoing Georgia Tech. Outside of the classroom however, ISTP will be on a mission if it comes to collegiate robotics competitions. This type would know if the robot will work before other team members push the start button. ISTP is a good partner on collaborative student teams making friends along with the metallic parts. The degree in **Materials Science and Engineering** is an excellent choice here for ISTP. Upperclassman work in teams to design, build and operate a process, component or material studied in the first years on campus.

ESTP would find the **Civil Engineering** degree at Georgia Tech a good bet for their inclinations. The course work includes projects which require students to lead and collaborate. They prefer hands-on experimentation since they are typically very accurate in their observations. At the same time, their natural skills in smoothing over ruffled feathers between the skills and trades that come together on construction projects is ideal. ESTP will be first in line when it comes to fun at Georgia Tech to let off academic steam built up throughout the week.

ENFJ will find the Bachelor of Science in **Global Economics and Modern Language** searches for creative solutions to really big problems in society. Georgia Tech interfaces the many human issues confronting world populations with financial mechanisms and economic theory. Courses like Health Economics will warm the heart of the ENFJ. Their desire is to care for others. This type is comfortable in courses that require sustained reading like economic theory. The choice of language concentration of German, French, Japanese or Spanish allows them to take economic expertise to other locations on planet earth.

ESFP can often have a good eye for design. This type is naturally curious and prefers to learn with others in study groups or with people in collaboration. ESFPs might like the program in **City and Regional Planning** with its certificate in Land Development. Visits to observe and record patterns of urban activity will please this type while studying the social and economic impact of design and location. The projected move of the Atlanta Falcons stadium from downtown Atlanta to the northern suburbs will be an excellent study in politics and societal impact. The program resides in the College of Architecture which also offers a degree in industrial design. It would not be unusual to find ESFPs in any of the artistically-tuned careers that require good communication with clients.

ISTJ has a dynamite combination of strengths that fit well on this campus. The Bachelor of Science in **Applied Math** with a business option is likely to appeal to their sense of utility and tradition. The degree in Discrete Mathematics might be another good choice. The ISTJ is not likely to be fatigued by the intensity of these degrees as long as learning follows the step-by-step process of accumulated knowledge.

ISFJ often believes learning is a serious business and will likely be loyal to projects, classmates and assignments throughout lengthy, even tedious research. The **Biomedical Engineering** degree that requires mastering both life sciences and engineering demands the perseverance and willingness to live in these two distinct worlds. Demonstration, faculty guidance and feedback in the labs will help this student conquer the mechanics of living tissues, such as the heart, ligaments and muscle.

GUILFORD COLLEGE

5800 West Friendly Avenue
Greensboro, NC 27410
Website: www.guilford.edu
Admissions Telephone: 336-316-2100,
Undergraduates: 2,462; 1,034 Men, 1,428 Women

Physical Environment

Guilford College is located in the university-rich area of the city of Greensboro. Guilford College, with its own distinct flavor of education, was founded during the Civil War by the **Quakers** who took in wounded from both sides. Founders Hall, completely renovated in 2012, functions as the student center with a neat aquarium, dining hall and atrium. Buildings face inward to enclose a very large wooded garden where students walk and bike. The city of Greensboro has numerous bike paths and greenways to easily visit the lively downtown area. The Guildford College **Bike Shop** maintains a fleet of bikes and cycle services for the undergraduates. The city provides buses for college students in Greensboro to **cross-register** for classes. There are two nearby historically black colleges adding to the cultural richness of the area.

Guildford College has a fascinating greenhouse, **The Farm,** that uses passive solar and tunnels to raise crops that, starting in 2012, were sufficient in quantity to sell to the campus dining services. Without electricity but with **commitment and ingenuity**, the students on this campus are pushing into food production with very little beyond what the weather, soil and sun have to offer. The **Green Kitchen** is also unique. The campus dining hall operation is a study in efficiency, wasting little, using less and fully supported by students on this campus.

Social Environment

Students who like Guilford College tend to be **passionate** and willing to discuss their ideas inside and outside the classroom. The philosophy of **inclusion** foundational to the Society of Friends is a consistent campus theme. It attracts students from many ethnicities. **Reflection with observation** is on the lunch menu pretty much every day. When different views collide, the values of peace and inclusion are ever present and hold out in the long term. The seven percent of students on campus who are Quaker remind all of the inherent value of peace and **conflict resolution**. There is a significant, ongoing research in conflict resolution and mediation. On this campus, activist methods reflect civility toward others and reality.

This college is standardized-test optional and students can substitute a portfolio of writing samples in lieu of test scores. Intellectually inclined, some students with B averages may have under-performed in high school. They bloom on this campus totally fitted out with that fine Greenhouse. WQFS is the campus radio station run by students and community volunteers. Featuring primarily independent labels with much variety, it has won national awards. It speaks to the excellent partnerships between college and community.

At Guilford, the liberal arts curriculum is moving toward **applied and practical knowledge**. Non-traditional students live off campus and take classes in the evening and weekend. The college is committed to the First Year Experience with the three-story addition to Founders Hall. Residential living within this expansion promotes first years to take classes together and live on the same residential floors. This is an ideal place for those who would like to learn in a community admiring of Quaker values.

Compatibility with Personality Types and Preferences

Guilford College fits uniquely among small liberal arts colleges with its Quaker vision of education that incorporates equality. Surrounded by southern cultural roots, it is a meeting place for varied perspectives. The administration and faculty bring a profound sense of tolerance that translates into caring (F). The curriculum and the many activities outside of the classroom capture the quality of life students here hope to generate in their work and living environments. Service and volunteer initiatives are considerable and support the nearby neighborhoods in creative and long-lasting programs. Undergraduates have the full support of the campus resources and administration when they initiate projects and improved practices for nearby residents. Students here are going to be comfortable expressing multiple views (P). You could say that there is a common theme in questioning the status quo in a manner that accepts both quiet indifference and steady potential for change. The undercurrents of Quaker philosophies promote sustained inquiry. It is the sensitive, individualistic student who is likely to find his way to and remain at the Guildford campus. The college educational philosophy strongly encourages experiential learning in off-campus experiences, internships, field studies and research, often in the local area. Graduates, regardless of their major, will be acutely knowledgeable of pluralistic currents within America and the impact each has in shaping and forming the larger nation.

In the following listing of college majors it is important to remember that students can fit into any college and can be successful in any major. We have found that the Personality Types below fit very well at this college. The course-of-study chosen for each Personality Type corresponds to MBTI® research and is presented as one of many examples favorable for that type.

ENTP is just the type to cope well with rapid change. The dynamic **Computing Technology and Information Systems** major at Guilford might attract this type. Operating systems, networking systems and computer software provide the foundational coursework. Students will select one of two tracks, Information Systems Track or Information Technology Track. Students will be expected to take a position on the ethical uses of technology, and ENTP is more than willing to take a position.

PERSONALITY MATCH			
ISTJ	ISFJ	INFJ	INTJ
ISTP	ISFP	INFP	INTP
ESTP	ESFP	ENFP	ENTP
ESTJ	ESFJ	ENFJ	ENTJ

ENFJ might find value in the **Health and Fitness** track within the Sport Studies major at Guilford. Improving health through diligence in exercise and activity makes good sense to ENFJs who prefer diagnostics and therapies that holistically support the clients. The overall cultural environment at Guilford is likely to be exceptionally satisfying and energizing for this type who diligently seeks harmony.

ISFP would rather show you with action rather than tell you with a college test, essays or discussion. The solid Theater Arts Department offers this type an alternate expressive form in theater stage productions. At the Guilford campus, **Theater** is especially oriented to serving others. This type is adept at creating pleasing visual interiors and will enjoy expressing their deeply held values in stage art. The course Filmmaking Capstone will let them shine forth.

ENFP likes the complexity that is found in the unique **Peace and Conflict Studies** interdisciplinary major at Guilford College. The subject is directly supported by the Quaker philosophy of nonviolence. ENFP has the ability to inspire and finds the creativity required for conflict resolution. The interrelation between individual, local and global levels of conflict is a focus of the major. As protest movements grow within our nation and the world, this background gives ENFPs access to employment with organizations that are being forced to deal with aggressive behaviors, short of physical violence.

ISFJ is one to prize accuracy, notice the details and stick with a demanding job. These characteristics match up quite well with the strong **Forensic Biology** major at Guilford College. The course in Forensic Chemistry is focused strictly on examining physical evidence at a crime scene. This makes good sense to ISFJ who seeks to partner productively with others in the community. This type, occasionally in need of a little cheerleading, is inclined to underestimate their contributions. At Guilford, faculty and student reflection is likely to bolster the ISFJ's confidence.

ESFP will like taking several introductory science courses in the **Earth Studies** minor here. It is very suitable for this curious type because it relies on considerable hands-on field work—a preferred way of learning for ESFP. This degree is complimentary to majors in physics, chemistry and biology. At the same time, the optional course in Images of the Earth: GIS and Remote Sensing can be invaluable for professions in law, science and journalism. ESFPs will find firm agreement on campus for their disinclination to form critical judgments about others.

ESFJ has what it takes to be an excellent translator and the **German** major at Guilford has much to commend it. As the European debt crisis develops and lingers, the linchpin strong economy of Germany has much influence within the governmental bodies seeking resolution. ESFJ with elective courses in conflict studies and a solid knowledge of this language will be well-situated as an international translator within these power circles.

INFJ tackles studies with a passion and the Bachelor of Arts in **Biology** at Guilford College could be just the right ticket. This type prefers to ruminate on their relationships, values and possibilities refining and defining each of these with precise thinking. Guilford is an ideal environment for those wanting to go into environmental law, science writing or illustration.

INFP has a good helping of insight and ability to self-direct. In fact, they are excellent researchers. The major in **Forensic Accounting** might be attractive since this type likes complex systems. The white collar crime and accounting fraud is often deeply layered. Along with their strong penchant for communication through the written word, INFPs could become crackerjack investigators. Their humanistic vision would necessarily drive an interest in cleaning up financial enterprises preying upon the unsuspecting public.

HAMILTON COLLEGE

198 College Hill Road
Clinton, NY 13323
www.Hamilton.edu
Admissions Telephone: 315-859-4421
Undergraduates: 1,884; 923 Men, 961 Women

Physical Environment

Hamilton College is a bright, **educational laser light** in the landscape of liberal arts colleges. Namesake and Founding Father, Alexander Hamilton, would approve of its legacy and stable relevance in undergraduate education today. Looking at the way the buildings are huddled together on a hill, the college may seem like a farming community or an Indian settlement. It overlooks the village of Clinton and owns 1,300 acres near the Adirondacks. Of different historical periods and assembled like a hamlet, the campus well accommodates the life and activities of the student body. Founded by Samuel Kirkland, a missionary to the Oneida Indians in the 1700s, this frontier school educated the children of white settlers and Indians. The Sadove Student Center has the fun architecture expected of this campus. It pulls together Southern Appalachian extended porches, with New England Salt Box design and multiple gables for shedding ice dams. In 2014, the new studio arts building will open with a unique program of studies in the discipline.

Much of the Hamilton design permits students to remain indoors and walk from one end of the campus to the other in 15 minutes. The remarkable architecture of the Beinecke Student-Activities-Village, a **yellow rambling structure**, also includes the Filius Barn. Here many events such as concerts, lectures and parties take place. The connecting bridge, Martin's Way, brings students to McEwen dining hall and other impressive residential and academic buildings on the south side of campus.

The **outdoor education center** satisfies many students who want to leave behind their urban residences and experience life without red lights and traffic jams. The cooperation between the campus and the small town of Clinton is enviable. Students select lengthy internships that function to interface community programs with successful initiatives across struggling small towns across America. The university has a **Town to Gown** grants program that annually provides thousands of dollars to city departments. The food is fresh in the dining halls and much hails from the Farm to Fork initiative which supports local farmers and their products. Ahead of the curve, the college built a glass, ultra-modern and "**ultra-green**" science building, heated through geothermal methods, in 2005. Students are actively drawn to the science majors which coincide with a strong **environmental stewardship** perspective and ongoing Antarctic and Artic research.

Social Environment

Students desiring complete **academic freedom** will appreciate being able to take classes they select, without having to satisfy a set core of requirements. In 2002 the decision go without a core curriculum was made. With the help of **close advising**, students sign up for challenging classes. The college provides a strong safety net via the academic advisors and the professors who become mentors. The academic advising is very strong and in sophomore year **students defend** their course selections to satisfy their academic plan which is similar to an independent study. The only required courses are three **writing-intensive** classes reminiscent of this college's past emphasis on rhetoric and elocution. Writing and public speaking are at the core of a Hamilton experience. Many choose an internship in Washington, DC and complete a thesis in senior year. Every year the college has nearly 50 graduates in the government major. Other popular majors are psychology, mathematics, public policy and world politics.

These students are **bright, ambitious**, motivated and **intellectually curious** enough to risk getting a lower grade to learn outside of their major course of studies. The college curriculum is bulging with research internships off campus, both for credit and with financial support. At Hamilton, the **internship as a teaching methodology** is evident across the curriculum. Here the physical environment is prized and infuses subtle prompts for healthy community. It is a distinct advantage for undergrads who travel frequently off campus and can observe differing community behaviors within the American landscapes.

Compatibility with Personality Types and Preferences

This college is quite interesting because of its long history and evolution with educational practices for students who like analysis (T) and thrive in an atmosphere that relentlessly seeks answers for problems. At Hamilton, these students can run with their ideas and innovations (N) and are not likely to experience much interference. The Hamilton undergraduate would not be satisfied with a midterm and final exam approach to grades. Speaking and writing, which allow for eloquence and intellectual rigor, are king on this campus. The intellectual work on this campus moves toward order and productivity. Alexander Hamilton, revolutionary proponent of the national banking system, is both the namesake of this college and the guiding philosophical light for educational studies.

Not particularly doting or focused on their feelings, the Hamilton student is committed to intellectual exercise. Departmental philosophies exhibit and approve of intellectual courage among the students. Learning often centers on solving problems and collaborating with peers for the solutions. It can be a humbling experience with the bright undergraduate student body on this campus. In this way, students move forward with their personal beliefs while refining their ability to analyze and honor accountability. Tender-hearted sensibilities are reserved for socializing at Hamilton. Collaboration and cooperation in the curriculum enhance interpersonal skills that will be used in power positions many on campus aspire to in government and industry.

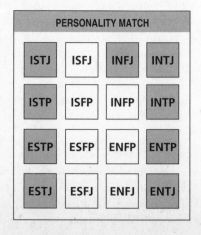

PERSONALITY MATCH			
ISTJ	ISFJ	INFJ	INTJ
ISTP	ISFP	INFP	INTP
ESTP	ESFP	ENFP	ENTP
ESTJ	ESFJ	ENFJ	ENTJ

In the following listing of college majors it is important to remember that students can fit into any college and can be successful in any major. We have found that the Personality Types below fit very well at this college. The course-of-study chosen for each Personality Type corresponds to MBTI® research and is presented as one of many examples favorable for that type.

ISTJ will use their intellectual storehouse to collect, maintain and retrieve all the geologic formations that are spelled with 10+ letters. In the unusual **Geoarcheology** studies on this campus, they will can work quietly and hone skills with this exacting science. The discipline is growing as it uses geological methods to interpret the ancient sites. Much work in this discipline seeks to further ground the biblical story. ISTJ will excel at the two semester capstone.

ISTP is going to fit right into the forward thinking **Computer Science** department here. This type will relish the independence of developing their own course of study and it may easily be connected to technical application. ISTPs with their wry sense of humor will sign right up for the course Secrets, Lies and Digital Threats. Focus within this discipline is sorely needed as civilization becomes more dependent on computers for everyday safety and basic needs.

ESTP fast-paced trouble-shooting skill will be well used and grounded through the **Environmental Studies** concentration at Hamilton. The senior project gives ESTP a chance to employ newfound research skills with their natural bent for bringing competitors together. For example, this type would get a productive dialog going between Save the Guppie's Club and the employees of Bulldoze Construction Company. Don't you wish you could sit in on this meeting? This is an educational activity that makes sense to this type who isn't all that impressed with traditional approaches to learning.

ESTJ will like the concentration **Economics** because of its overview of financial mechanisms in advanced economies. This is followed by the required flexible Senior Project. This type is a strong administrator who understands rules. Their senior project is likely to highlight foundational understanding of advanced accounting methods rather than an issues-oriented subjects. It's about accountably for ESTJ, abstract explanations and policy-laden practices will be given an arched, skeptical eye by this natural leader.

INFJ is ideal for the major in **Neuroscience** at Hamilton. This type has an inner vision that calls out and demands attention. This particular major is focused on the biological basis of human behavior. INFJ will love peering through the microscope to study the brain's operation at cellular levels but also approve of this interdisciplinary curriculum tapping into psychology and philosophy here at Hamilton.

INTJ will not be daunted by the string of impossible sounding courses in the **Biochemistry/Molecular Biology** major. Their incise, intense reasoning will come in handy as they plow their way through organic chemistry, vertebrate physiology, cellular neurobiology and perhaps, geomicrobiology. This last is a newly emerging discipline and this type wants to be at the head of these emergent boundaries.

INTP enjoys working individually. The **Philosophy** department at Hamilton College pushes undergrads to develop original inquiries into fairly common human experiences, like telling lies or collaborating to agree that zebras are gray. These are human behaviors that are becoming too familiar on the American scene. INTPs are curious and dispassionate enough to understand gullibility in America today. Here at Hamilton, there will be an opportunity to explore this phenomena, as long as INTP brings their powerful thinking to the table. This degree exemplifies why Hamilton College is a laser light in education. The department curriculum is remarkable, honest and references the word Moral often.

ENTP has to try everything, more or less. Shakespeare's quote "all the world is a stage" is one that this type can live by. At Hamilton, the **Theatre** student has several options for their Senior Program: research paper, writing a play, performing an acting showcase, directing a play or designing a production. This variety gives ENTP the elbow room to freewheel their way into the Senior Program decision.

ENTJ on this campus is going to relate to the power and accomplishments that seem to flow in and around the exceptional Hamilton graduates. Perhaps this type might like to reach for influential positions addressing American society and governance. ENTJ will be very well served in the **Government** major at Hamilton College. This department is well on top of relevant study and seeks to graduate students who can dispassionately address our problems. The course in The Politics of the Supreme Court likely address their shaping of American culture over the past 100 years. ENTJ will study the political realism, as well as idealistic governance.

HAMPSHIRE COLLEGE

893 West Street
Amherst, MA 01002
www.hampshire.edu
Admissions Telephone: 413-559-5471
Undergraduates: 1,492; 646 Men, 846 Women

Physical Environment

The idea for Hampshire College was put into practice with the purchase of 800 acres of orchard and farm land in the 1960s. Prospective students get a close look at the Red Barn and sense firsthand that this isn't your regular college. The wide-open farm land and country setting creates a sense that students can experiment with new ideas. The dormitories that are environmentally-friendly draw **eco-minded** students. The Longsworth Arts Center hosts a Solar Canopy of photovoltaic panels used for both research and generating electricity. A large yurt, of Native American heritage, blends nicely with the collegiate environment and houses the campus radio station.

There are **eclectic students** on this campus, possibly former wallflowers, who want to experiment with new activities. For some, developing kayaking skills in the pool naturally translates into white-water rafting in the nearby hills. The Hampshire setting becomes a working farm and a living laboratory for others who want to test out their "**earth and animal friendly**" philosophies. Students often use their bikes on the nearby dirt trails and to cycle over to the other campuses in the **Five College Consortium** for cross-registered classes. Vegan and vegetarian students plant organic gardens, and some conduct research on the campus farm. Other students like quiet, private living arrangements and find the campus is well-suited for this also.

Social Environment

Hampshire students are creative and quirky. Their curiosity plumbs the depths as they study the past, seek out the new and follow their intuition. More than half the entering students say they are going to study in a particular area but end up changing. It's part of the **Hampshire experience** to share ideas and be open to many perspectives. They evaluate and re-evaluate their point of view. Students become very good at connecting seemingly unrelated information to their course work.

Hampshire students are comfortable with the unusual academic assessment and grading policy. They don't receive grades, rather they receive **personalized narrative evaluations** from their professors. This qualitative grading system encourages the generation of ideas and refinement of those ideas in discussion and papers. Core academic courses are identified at the departmental level with faculty and student working together to individually tailor those learning objectives.

Activism is an element of the social activity on campus. Frequently, it is directed into their educational coursework and social life. The faculty and administration support questioning, alternative undergraduates. The campus sports a large list of activist clubs, some familiar such as Amnesty International and others of local concern like Re-Rad which is the re-radicalization of Hampshire College. This college was established as a direct response to the 1960s feminist movements. During that short period of radical change many collegiate academic policies were dropped and social policies were changed, some innocent like required skirt lengths and others not so benign, like sexual experimentation. Over the years, these freedoms in study and social life were open to question themselves at Hampshire College. It is this tension between liberty and accountability that the Re-Rad club addresses its energies to. Today, Hampshire College has typical residential life policies and academic rigor found in liberal arts colleges. The portfolio assessment stands out as the salute to the founding principles.

Compatibility with Personality Types and Preferences

Always looking out to the world, past the campus boundaries of the college, Hampshire students are drawn to the optimism of their own creativity (N). Their academic focus is not on the student body or the college town of Amherst. They are oriented toward their discipline and see potential. Students are often drawn to the expressive forms of literature, art and performance. Faculty are equally devoted to creativity and support reinterpretation of current knowledge within their disciplines. At this academically unorthodox campus, research in the social sciences springs up from current reality and is pursued through the committed lens of undergraduate individual study.

Policy protests are not first choice solutions for this student body, rather internships and service learning are often selected to explore options for change. This gives Hampshire the appearance of being radical at times. It keeps them exploring (P) and open to solutions of their own devise. The faculty acknowledge this approach to learning by offering areas of study, rather than majors or minors. In fact, students spend the first year in Division I, exploring four of five content areas. The middle two years, Division II, are oriented to defining and securing knowledge in the chosen concentration. Division III, the last stage, is reserved for a two semester project and internships. With this approach, undergraduates hold a trust in emerging knowledge and they strive to transfer those benefits into their chosen career paths. The ongoing practice of observation and analysis drives the faith in human kind (F) that lies at the core of Hampshire College.

In the following listing of college majors it is important to remember that students can fit into any college and can be successful in any major. We have found that the Personality Types below fit very well at this college. The course-of-study chosen for each Personality Type corresponds to MBTI® research and is presented as one of many examples favorable for that type.

ENFP can be quite expressive as well as creative. The **Music** area of study at Hampshire encourages both through their emphasis on composition and improvisation. This type will be comfortable with the Divisional studies and the nature of personal

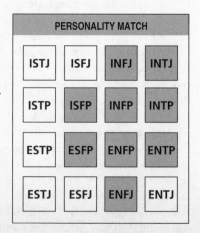

PERSONALITY MATCH			
ISTJ	ISFJ	INFJ	INTJ
ISTP	ISFP	INFP	INTP
ESTP	ESFP	ENFP	ENTP
ESTJ	ESFJ	ENFJ	ENTJ

input and development of their course work. ENFP's Division III project will benefit from the close faculty attention as follow through can be tedious for this imaginative type.

ENTP is often drawn to computers and their capacity to theorize problems. This is darned perfect for the study of **Astronomy.** At Hampshire College, undergrads will take advantage of the excellent labs and research within the Five College Consortium. Bold ENTP will thrive at the other campuses in analytical coursework.

ENFJ enjoys suggesting change and often does so with compelling communication. Here at Hampshire, ENFJs will practice their inclination to change the status quo. The faculty would encourage studying the unintended effects of do-good improvement projects. ENFJs would get a realistic grounding in what is actually possible vs. what seems to be possible. **Architecture and Environmental Design** could be the intellectual foundation for ENFJ's career.

ISFP will love studying **Agriculture** at Hampshire which focuses on the challenges of small farmers competing with US agricultural conglomerates. In the last ten years, increasing patents were granted on agricultural seed. The government is regulating the price and quantity of seed allowed to be purchased that was formerly available to the public at large in a competitive marketplace, as recently as 2008. This runs directly counter to the individual farmer's enterprise, ingenuity and cash flow. Students at Hampshire College, and the other four Consortium Colleges, are likely to investigate powerful individuals and the government offices, who are out to "help us" from remote locations in the nation's capital and banking centers. Undergraduates at Hampshire just might also look into the purchases of thousands of acres by Bill Gates in mid-2000, as well as his recent purchases of independent biomedical institutions researching genetics.

INFP is often committed and compassionate. The area of study in **Marine Science** provides for the study of food production along the coastal regions. Much of the course work is offered through the Five College Consortium. It includes the emerging study of coastal engineering. INFP might easily seek to research practices that sustain fish populations for harvest in small coastal villages across the globe.

INFJ will find **Middle Eastern Studies** on this campus pursue a holistic and foundational understanding of the region. With this knowledge in place, undergraduates then concentrate within the lens of their favored discipline, be it art, religion ethnicity or perhaps health practices. Regardless of the lens, Hampshire faculty can accommodate.

INTJ with a scientific interest will like the intellectual wrestling with dilemmas in the health sciences. This type will take part in the discussion and research with original perspectives. The **Biological/Life Sciences** will be ideal for graduate school or med school and this type is likely to bring along that same originality to the first years in med school.

INTP could be inspired by the Kinetic and Animated Objects course. Sometimes retiring in social conversation, INTPs are attracted to puzzles and challenges. The title of this course seems to include a little of both and could open the door to the world of **Applied Design**. At Hampshire College this area of study is focused on designing universal industrial products and alternative transportation.

ESFP arrives on campus with impulsive energy and a willingness to try alternatives. The area of study in **Animal Behavior** certainly offers a unique approach to studying cognition and awareness. The Hampshire Farm Center has flocks of sheep, goats and llamas enhancing the study of animal behavior, cognition and communication. ESFP will delight in reviewing primate research by Dr. Penny Patterson with gorilla, KoKo. Starting her studies in 1972, she has interfaced communication, gorillas and cognition. Her work is very applicable to linguistic studies also.

HARVARD COLLEGE

5 James Street
Cambridge, MA 02138
Website: www.fas.harvard.edu
Admissions Telephone: 617-495-1551
Undergraduates: 6,6,652; 3,333 Men, 3,319 Women
Graduate Students: 13,867

Physical Environment

Imagine living in the same residence as Ralph Waldo Emerson and David Henry Thoreau. The **historic significance** permeates the academic experience at Harvard College. First-year students will live in 15 residential dormitories reserved for their class. These buildings are located in the historic center of the university. Some Georgian-style residences were built in the 1700s while others are more contemporary, built in the 1970s. Each building has a distinct floor-plan and feel, which exerts a certain influence on the students who room there. First-year students stick together and eat at Annenberg dining hall. These common experiences bind incoming undergrads together and help them comprehend this **complex university**. It helped when the Campus Service Center opened in 2011, since it houses many offices needed by undergraduates.

In this setting, first-years meet with people very different than themselves. They become accustomed to the city just outside their dorm room. They can guess whether the people they run into on campus are prospective students or individuals observing the passing scene. Upon completion of their first year, students know one another well and have formed solid relationships. Freshmen quickly realize that Harvard assigns the upper class dormitories, identified as houses, to students so as to form **well-balanced student communities**. They will be placed into one of the 12 upper-class houses, where they will likely stay for the following three years. Some students may form groups and put in a request to live together in the same house, but the remainder go through the lottery system as individuals.

Each house forms a small community with its own flavor and identity. The housemaster, proctors and tutors come from a variety of backgrounds. House masters often are professors who live on a floor with their family, lending guidance to students in a **family-like setting**. They mingle with students and help them evaluate their academic selections and possible areas of concentration. In some departments, sophomores taking tutorials are assigned to course sections based loosely on their houses. Thus houses become an extended classroom as well as a playground for fine tuning artistic talents, from music to dance to sports. With so much to do and learn there is no uncommitted down time. Students learn firsthand of new cultures, divergent political views, **international perspectives**, as well as the talents and skills of those in their house. The house residences are in rotation for a much-needed remodeling. Students assigned to these two houses reside in other buildings nearby for the academic year and return to a pleasant, updated residence the following year. Each of the remaining houses will go through a similar cycle.

Typically students become extremely **loyal to their house** and Harvard guarantees housing for all four years. This tends to be more economical since rents in Cambridge, a suburb of Boston, are quite expensive. Accessibility to Boston city life is by subway, the T, and students travel into the city as their time permits.

Social Environment

Students who are admitted to Harvard College have the **intellectual curiosity** and emotional resilience to pursue much of what Harvard has to offer. Students have achieved well beyond that expected of their 18 years of age. Not only have they completed high school with top honors, but they have honed out a particular skill or two in music or dance or sports. Some **artists and well known professionals** compose another category of students, taking a break from their career to complete an undergraduate education. Regardless of their achievements, they all arrive at Harvard ready to soak up the knowledge that both the professors and other students bring to the table.

Intellectual intensity in the classroom is expected, as students set extraordinarily high standards for themselves. They rarely power down—rather each waking moment is interfaced with intellectual inquiry. For those who want to study another field in addition to their primary concentration, there is the program called Secondary Field. Undergraduates at Harvard may select one secondary field from a predetermined list. Limits like this are rarely put on academic study. In the first years, they begin to see the **relativism** of their own ideas. Thus the campus environment promotes students who soak up knowledge and search for their own clarity and belief. The collegiate academic environment selectively presents absolute truths and relative truths. It animates an environment where everything can be honored for some kind of 'truth.'

During Harvard's "shopping week" students test-drive classes by attending any they might like. Some are interested in so many areas that they enroll in courses outside of their favorite departments or create their own major. Academic curiosity outweighs **academic risk**. Passion for knowledge is strong among first year students. This translates into highly-focused individuals who intend to become masters at their craft. Students form values that accommodate their career goals and they intend to benefit society. Graduates may enter Harvard with conventional success in mind, but others may look to redefine that phrase.

At Harvard, **social clubs** are officially recognized. There are also unofficial organizations that students seek to join as a popular forum for social interaction. Some social clubs are more exclusive than others. They leave their gate more or less open. In a way, these clubs can be compared to **Greek life** which requires that students rush to be admitted. Some of these social organizations form individual **social networks** spanning the decades of graduating classes with their loyal alumni. Harvard administrators have developed an extensive policy and practice for reporting hazing, including anonymity of the person reporting an act or action perceived as hazing. The university is very active in monitoring the Harvard College social environment on campus with a descriptive website of both acceptable and unacceptable behaviors by undergraduates. Both Scavenger Hunt and Tug of War are offered as acceptable undergraduate entertainment on this website. Reported hazing incidents at other universities are posted on the Harvard College website to help undergraduates recognize hazing by example.

Compatibility with Personality Types and Preferences

Harvard is all things to bright students. Simply put, there is not a personality preference that cannot be accommodated quite well at Harvard College. The educational philosophy is both deep and wide in scope. The structured students (J) who like to plan with defined objectives, practical rules and clear regulations will find them in Harvard's concentrations, tutorials and general exams. The curriculum reflects faculty belief that knowledge is approached from a variety of avenues. A concentration in biology includes courses in all the physical sciences as well as anthropology and psychology.

The core course requirement at Harvard is fulfilled by choosing from among hundreds of entry level courses in the 40 available concentrations. These 40 are further expanded by options within each. This all really suits the flexible, free-flowing (P) students who will want, and maybe try, to sample most of the disciplines that Harvard has to offer. For folks who like their facts and details straight up (S), observable, verifiable knowledge rules over the world class research venues in the physical and applied sciences. The faculty and student body are constantly reasoning with logical analyses (T). Undergraduates expect to expand the universal body of knowledge through exploration, discovery and novel investigation.

Students preferring other ways of knowing, often intuitive or instinctual (N), will really enjoy the residential house system where Harvard College expects students to learn from each other. In fact, this house system is ideal for the undergraduates who want frequent, close communication with others (F). Those students who are outgoing and expressive (E) will find the social contact they want outside of the classroom with club participation and house participation that is expected and extensive. Those folks who are quieter (I) will actually find some anonymity in the academic world which is very individualized and can be tailored as to feel like a solo educational experience. Upon graduation, students hold a world view that prompts them to move aggressively and competently through their career work that should, indeed, increase the body of knowledge.

In the following listing of college majors it is important to remember that students can fit into any college and can be successful in any major. We have found that the Personality Types below fit very well at this college. The course-of-study chosen for each Personality Type corresponds to MBTI® research and is presented as one of many examples favorable for that type.

INTP is a good bet for the concentration in **Earth and Planetary Sciences**. This field is developing as fast as the NASA exploration of Mars is sending back new images. The department has purposely fashioned the studies

PERSONALITY MATCH			
ISTJ	ISFJ	INFJ	INTJ
ISTP	ISFP	INFP	INTP
ESTP	ESFP	ENFP	ENTP
ESTJ	ESFJ	ENFJ	ENTJ

across physics/chemistry/biology and engineering. The INTP will love to find patterns and solve riddles about earth's oceans, atmosphere and solid core. Within the concentration, emergent knowledge is pursued thru geobiological and geochemical research. At Harvard's house, they are likely to be easy and casual on the social scene when they appear. In fact, they may miss more than a few events hanging back, trying to solve the latest complex riddle in physical space. Activities and intramurals may serve to bring reality into their week and give their minds a much needed time out.

ESTP is quick to sum up a problem and gifted with the ability to offer a workable solution. The concentration in **Environmental Science and Public Policy** offers the possibility of indefinite troubleshooting within the public arena after graduation. They excel at what can be done with efficiency. They have less enthusiasm for theory and abstraction; it interferes with real action. Students may specialize in natural or social science within the concentration. However, the foundational courses are clearly in the hard sciences. In the house, ESTP will be first in line for the party, the fun and the social learning. They are likely to initiate house social activities. This type is often well-coordinated, physically athletic and may lead and participate in sports activity. This type may also be attracted to seeking entrance into one of the selective social clubs.

ISTJ is very accepting with the high academic structure in the first two years of engineering sciences at Harvard. In fact, this type will be just fine with signing up for the suggested basic course Math 1. Their need for accuracy requires a step-by-step, comprehensive mathematical understanding. The **Engineering Sciences** curriculum allows new concentrators to take the four introductory courses that preview the five types of engineering degrees. It allows ISTJ to judiciously sample the disciplines of engineering and ultimately select the one right for them. This synchs with their motto—"Do it right the first time." Most often humor is one of their underlying traits. It is a wry humor reserved for their close friends. In the House system they will likely find and add humor in the social programs, or perhaps the college website on how to behave. In the social activities they can express their penchant for accuracy. This could give them satisfaction as they set and reach their personal goals.

INTJ will find the **Mind, Brain and Behavior** initiative just original enough for their liking. They will not shrink away from seeking and gaining permission to be admitted to this initiative. They have the confidence to enter the process. This type has powerful inner vision and the ability to transfer those original thoughts into the real world. The interdisciplinary work of tying together cognition, neuroscience and computers is ideal for this type. They can look for patterns in the data bits to their mind's content. Then they can follow a hunch to search out similar patterns in the brain's chemical pathways. In the house they will review and pass judgment on the various social offerings. They are likely to more fully participate if it exposes them to novel activities.

ENFJ absolutely enjoys an audience. They can beguile and guide listeners to a different viewpoint or novel interpretation. They are masters of the use of language. The **Romance Languages and Literatures** program allows ENFJ to double their fun and charm audiences with a second or third language. A personal connection between student and professor works well for ENFJ. The mentor/advisor relationship is defined in tutorials and is a feature of this concentration. ENFJ is likely to find ways to please their advisor in the process. They will join in house social learning and activities with ease. They may be prompted into leadership of the house because of their genuine interest in others and great communication skills.

INFP absolutely must have time and emotional space to search out their personal understanding of life and its meaning. Once this is completed they extend the vision to the larger community expecting to make a worthy contribution. This type sees value in the **Comparative Study of Religion.** INFP is just fine with abstract speculation like the moral development of civilization. Even the study of differing methods used to understand religions is up their alley. This area of study could quickly lead to a joint concentration in religion and another field. In the residential house, this type is likely to be a quiet participant who carefully considers their options before joining in with the faculty and other students. Their perfectionist tendencies might easily come out when participating in social activities where they would strive to be the best.

ESFP is often quite entertaining and a career in the entertainment field brings spontaneity and emphasis on enjoyment. ESFP could look favorably at the **Visual and Environmental Studies** which embrace film, photography, video art and environmental studies. Yes, environmental studies. It is common in liberal arts colleges this decade to insert environmental studies and sustainability into just about any major. The ESFP is likely to go for the filmmaking because film, of all the arts, can contain and express enthusiasm, enjoyment and be visually appealing. The actual production of film and the study of theory behind it suffice for ESFP who may elect not to write a thesis. In the House system this type will be front and center with most if not all of the social programs and social activities. ESFP lives to socialize and socializes in order to live. They would join any of the activities involving participation with others and would likely show interest in joining one of the selective clubs.

ENTP can take advantage of their intuition in any of the disciplines studying human behavior. It is a complex arena since it attempts to understand the basis of the human personality. As a concentrator in **Psychology**, ENTP would excel at impersonal analysis while researching perception, memory or motivation. These basic processes are likely to be of more interest to the ENTP than counseling or rehabilitation. Harvard's Psychology Department can accommodate the wide and evolving nature of this discipline. Without a required thesis, ENTP has more time to participate in undergrad research. This type will likely try a succession of activities at Harvard; their curiosity draws them into many possibilities and ENTP might be bored with the repetition. ENTP will try to sample all of the social activities in their house. They must be careful to avoid burn out on this campus.

ISTP will be in high heaven in Harvard's **Mechanical and Material Science Engineering** concentration. State of the art equipment will entice them as they build robots and design experimental parts. In these labs, the ISTP will absorb the theories and engineering knowledge with much enjoyment while observing the physical properties with accuracy. This concentration also suits ISTP because a written thesis is not required in the engineering sciences. They will likely select an activity or club to join that allows a lot of room for spontaneity and being laid back. In the house system, they will scout out a few good friends whom they respect. Once they have that small circle of similar-minded friends they will pick and choose social opportunities that suit their interests and are less personal in nature.

ISFP devotes much thinking time to clarifying their personal values. They are likely to want to focus in an area that is contributing to the welfare of the community. The concentration in **Chemical and Physical Biology** has the right stuff for ISFP if they have a tolerance or liking for math. Although not necessarily an innovator, this type will be extremely happy with the action of dissecting and reconstructing cellular networks. Their penchant for careful observation and meticulous accuracy is ideal for this discipline. Their sometimes fragile sense of self will get much recognition and approval from others in this pioneering field that is advancing knowledge through genetic research and discovery. This type will thrive and develop in conjunction with the spontaneous and planned social learning within their house. They are joiners. To ISFP the house could become as intimate as a home environment. Their quick adaptability to change will find ISFP always present and ready from day one of the sophomore year.

INFJ will thrive with Harvard's philosophy of clubs and activities supported with professional equipment and resources. INFJ only has to decide which of the student activities to join. They are very good at comprehending complex subjects such as liberty, a basic human right when defined as an Absolute Truth. The relativist definition of liberty opens doors for restriction and governmental tyranny. Liberty is also defined under the guise of intellectual philosophers such as Machiavelli who capture society with arresting logic. Harvard's **Social Studies** concentration examines these basic philosophical principles. INFJ has the resolve and grounding to analyze primary texts in this chimerical discipline. Progression through the study is culminated with the tutorial where the topic is mutually selected by advisor and INFJ, followed by a senior thesis. This mutual process is important to INFJ because they must be passionate about their work to do it well. It will give them a notch up in the petition and application required to be selected for this concentration.

ISFJ will like the detailed and sequential nature of **Human Evolutionary Biology**. ISFJ's excellent memory and love for facts nicely combine with their inclination for reflection. If you add in their typical thoroughness you see how the learning style of ISFJ fits this concentration so well. Research is encouraged and follows either a laboratory or field-based study approach. On graduation this type could pursue researching disease through individual medical trials. Or they might go into the work force directly to apply their knowledge through wellness programs. They will enjoy Harvard's exceptional attention to student programming. Within their house they will be loyal contributors to the learning and living experience.

ENFP will gladly consider all the options and possibilities on the Harvard campus. With 40 available concentrations and 300 clubs to consider for participation, this type is all smiles during freshman year. Aggression by despotic leaders across the globe is accelerating along with United States diminished credibility in foreign policy. This points to needed global competencies in the Pacific Rim, Middle East and East European Russian border conflicts. Within the **South Asian Studies** secondary field, there is the option to focus on Sanskrit and Indian studies. The cultural overview is complete with a language citation in Hindu-Urdu. This suits ENFP who can be indifferent to what they consider mundane details. The optional thesis, if they decide to write one, will be a first-class read.

ESFJ will be very comfortable in their house at Harvard which will quickly become their home. They will really like the academic and social programs that promote friendships within the house. In fact, they will be encouraging others to participate. They value loyalty and it allows them to really benefit from Harvard's residential living. As dependable members, they are likely to accept leadership positions on occasion. The **Physics** concentration with a teaching option could be a good choice for this type. Their strong need for order and sense of responsibility are very desirable traits for K-12 teachers. ESFJ's persuasive skills adapted for the classroom will be well appreciated by school administrators. ESFJ will also like the department's practical approach to this concentration. Down to earth ESFJ sees that the general exam, tutorial or thesis would take away time and effort they would rather use in developing classroom skills and gaining experience.

ENTJ is usually attracted to complex, very large systems. The Harvard concentration in **Neurobiology** definitely fits this description. ENTJs are goal-oriented, but capable of opening up their visual lenses to catch otherwise unnoticed patterns in volumes of data. The human nervous system, as the focus of this concentration, presents this type of gigantic perspective from molecule to human body. It may be over the top and unappealing to some other personality types but certainly not to this type. Ambitious ENTJ might just join the scientists who are emulating the nervous system via software. Imagine the diagnostics and profit. Socializing and social choices are likely to revolve around ideas, action and projects. Harvard will not fail in providing near endless opportunities that meet this demand by the ENTJ.

ESTJ will very likely approve of the **Applied Mathematics** concentration at Harvard College. The department has excellent flexibility within the first two years for undergraduates to explore areas of interest while getting good exposure to the interdisciplinary nature of applied math via neighboring concentrations in the physical and social sciences. Undergrads tailor their own curriculum and degree in consultation with an advisor. This is a rather intensive effort and ESTJs are definitely up to the challenge. However, they will be anxious during the departmental meetings and quite relieved when their educational focus is settled upon with the advisor. Within their house and during the first year on campus, this type is likely to enjoy and interact with the many different types of students on this campus. The endless action at Harvard College, only slowing down while most are asleep in the wee hours, calls out to ESTJs to participate and take on administrative and organizational roles within the clubs they choose to join.

HAVERFORD COLLEGE

370 Lancaster Avenue
Haverford, PA 19041-1392
Website: www.haverford.edu
Admissions Telephone: 610-896-1350
Undergraduates: 1,205; 567 Men, 638 Women

Physical Environment

Located 10 miles outside of Philadelphia, Haverford College has a suburban campus with all the charm and mystery of a Thomas Kinkaid painting. The college belongs to the **Quaker Consortium** affording cross-registration at three other nearby colleges. The Haverford campus reveals itself slowly, allowing the visitor to enjoy the paths through the woods with reflection. Students who feel comfortable here probably looked for smaller, less imposing environments. Centuries-old trees surround these Quaker buildings and add to a spiritual feeling of safety, both physical and emotional.

This 19th century campus is one that encourages students to explore through discussion and **close knit social fabric**. It all makes a great canvas and counterpoint for the 'Fords Dungeons and Dragons Guild whose outrageous costume and make-believe mirrors reality and experimentation. The Magill Library has a comprehensive collection of original Quaker books and students have access to rich historical documents. The Koshland Science Center includes advanced research options such as nanofabrication which act as a modern counterpoint to the historical presence on this campus. Students who like the sciences and wish for strong pre-med advising are attracted by this exceptional science center. The Center for **Peace and Justice** arranges for field trips throughout the world, such as Africa and Guatemala, for these students who are typically focused on social justice in the world. The Gardner Athletic Center offers everything a student athlete or non-athlete would desire in order to keep in shape during college. The favorite walking trail is called the "Trust Trail" which is part of the first year orientation experience.

Social Environment

Students come from New England and the Mid-Atlantic regions; they are typically excited and thoughtful at the same time. The essence of this college community is to understand what **tolerance and non–sectarianism** means. Incoming freshmen became 'Fords for this very reason. As First Years, they are assigned to **Customs Groups** of 8-16. They live and socialize as a unit with upperclass mentors. Throughout the first year, they discuss and explore the nature of their diverse backgrounds and the meaning of tolerance. Formerly as students woven into a high school social tapestry, they appreciate the non-competitive experience in the classroom and the extracurricular scene at Haverford. They will learn to become precise **observers**, starting with their own Customs Group. This is a characteristic of the historic Quaker meetings and will ultimately radiate through their four years of studies.

Within the paradigm of tolerance, Fords' enjoy crossing conventional boundaries with each other's support and the administration honors this experimentation.

Co-ed assignments to individual rooms were initiated in early 2000, yet, the majority of students live in single rooms with common spaces for bathrooms and gathering space. The new Kim Tritton dormitories were designed with input from the students, i.e. cubbies in the hall bathrooms. It all affords both privacy and prompted togetherness for **tentative souls**. The Cannabis Law Reform Club invites activist speakers and its website posts legitimacy by NORMl - the national organization to reform marijuana legalization. This extra support for the club mirrors the student body that is cautious of unraveling community standards without consent. FAB, 'Fords Against Boredom, is a much larger presence on the campus and sponsors free social events without alcohol.

Students here almost hold a paternal world view as they incorporate and examine the many evils evident around the globe. Professors focus on the moral, ethical education of the individual student. This **value-driven education** attracts students who may have attended a Quaker high school who add depth to the discussions about social justice. Students without the Friends background are likely to have heard similar discussion at the family dinner table centering on community, politics and education. Graduates will move forward into their careers with great openness and considerable awareness of the positive and negative inclinations of society. They are resilient through their knowledge because of this **talk-discuss-argue education**. The Haverford education might be thought of as active listening whose purpose is to build a literate community ensuring peace and prosperity.

Compatibility with Personality Types and Preferences

Haverford College offers an education that intensely seeks to understand other peoples (F) of the world. It is a high purpose and very true to the founding Quaker principles of the college. Undergrads are typically analytical with a humanistic perspective. They come to the campus eager to learn and expect to debate and master written expression with articulate, commanding thought. They study humankind looking for positive qualities (N). Their internships take them to areas in the world where much of the population is destitute. They are courageous in their choices since their idealistic observations of human nature must be accommodated with the reality of poverty and cruelty. They commonly bring back knowledge or plans for improved living conditions overseas and a fair number remain in touch with their study abroad locations, expecting to return.

Students at Haverford ask very difficult questions and quickly discern the endemic nature of misery in large segments of the earth's population. Undergraduates look within themselves and to the faculty for explanations and solutions. Yet the educational philosophy is to mentor students in examining their own roots and personal experiences for answers. Overall, resignation is not an answer and the campus culture defiantly stands up to the ills and errors in human society. In partial answer, there is an ever-present overlay of values and ideals for the human condition expressed in the curriculum through conventional courses and majors. Also in answer to the dilemma of societal ills, the campus itself models a community populated by rational people. During four years of undergraduate education at Haverford College, students are going to discuss, search for, argue and practice living a life congruent with their well-defined ideals. The Cannabis Law Reform Club may even invite speakers with research pointing to the lifetime short term memory deficits associated with marijuana.

In the following listing of college majors it is important to remember that students can fit into any college and can be successful in any major. We have found that the Personality Types below fit very well at this college. The course-of-study chosen for each Personality Type corresponds to MBTI® research and is presented as one of many examples favorable for that type.

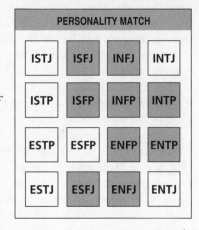

INFJ is persistent and penetrating, just the qualities needed to study and practice **Economics.** This type is caring and yet very private. The field of economics offers them a complex and intriguing subject of study. INFJ will be very interested in theories of economic practice that contradict each other. As graduates, this type will bring passionate energy to analyses of production, distribution and consumption of goods in society. Haverford will refine their ability to develop a penetrating approach to this discipline that will also provide them access to jobs and grad studies after commencement.

ISFJ has a memory that won't quit. This type can take in facts and store them for retrieval like a researcher in the congressional library. The major in **Computer Science** at Haverford College asks this intriguing question: Are there algorithms not presently known that can solve intractable problems? In reality, the coursework also is somewhat straightforward compared to the other highly abstract curriculum offerings. After all, computers are simply tools and ISFJ is comfortable mastering skills and bringing them to the community. ISFJ can get the ideal preparation to design and operate data systems utilized by nonprofits and international aid organizations.

ISFP and **Classical and Near Eastern Archeology** are a quick, natural fit. The curriculum takes advantage of cross-registration in the Consortium. ISFP's sense of design and proportion will be an advantage on digs of ancient city states around the Mediterranean Sea. The focus of this degree is to collect wisdom from the classical age and bring those positive social constructs into the light of modern day. This type is ideal for learning by sight, sound and touch, basically being active. It is a direct, real, here and now activity that offers freedom to reflect – a favorite ISFP pastime.

INTP will like the **Chemistry** major at Haverford College because there is an opportunity to complete required core chemistry courses at foreign universities. This type is always looking for clarity in their thoughts and is quite curious. The field of chemistry offers the complexity they seek and the ability to cross-check their intuition by predicting outcomes of lab experiments. This is just swell stuff for an INTP. Haverford takes an interdisciplinary approach to this science and INTP can quickly synthesize seemingly unrelated topics. This independent type will take advantage of both overseas study and interdisciplinary courses for the freedom and rewards gained via their logical analysis.

INFP might find personal meaning in something simple like an ice cream cone on a hot day. Indeed they are searchers of meaning. The major in **Fine Arts** has courses in the third year identified as "experimental." The faculty expects undergraduates to take artistic risks and bring forth ideas cussed and discussed during their first years on campus. The fine arts majors must develop personal themes and communicate those ideas through their art. Studio work produced by INFP might reflect the dilemmas of the human psyche. INFP will be up to the challenge and has loads of peers across campus ready, willing and able to imagine.

ENFP will find a welcome place for their enthusiasm and persuasive skills in **Education**. This major is well-supported by cross-registration, faculty and resources at nearby Consortium campuses. This philosophy of teaching encourages awareness and use of multiple intelligences. It resonates well with ENFP who is often a cheerleader supporting improvement in others. This major also has the level of complexity needed by ENFP to keep them engaged and fulfill their own creative instincts.

ENTP at Haverford College might like the major in **Growth and Structure of Cities.** It is unusual because planning for urban communities is studied as a process that travels through other disciplines, such as law, communications, the arts, medicine and social justice. The course Analysis of Geospatial Data Using GIS could fascinate this type. Through cross-registration, the major presents opportunities galore to make sense of geographic and social constructs as viewed by the satellites with software interface. It might just be the ENTP who decides to look for evidence of peace and serenity in communities around the globe via satellite data feeds.

ESFJ is all about the community and the people in it. They want their studies to directly benefit humankind. They also have a fine ability to collect, remember and use facts. The Haverford Biology department offers a core program in **Biology** which is focused at the molecular and cellular level. It is an extraordinary curriculum that offers a taste of over-the-top cellular research at the introductory level. Traditional ESFJ may find it a bit too large, but the warm nature of this campus, with its calming Quaker heritage, will help tame the impersonal nature of the discipline and maintain the personal, human perspective.

ENFJ will find that the **Peace, Conflict and Social Justice Studies** echoes back to the founding principles of the Quakers who were practicing non-conflict when the founding fathers were meeting to declare the Revolutionary War. Two centuries later, liberal arts colleges across America have the freedom to strongly endorse this concept. At Haverford College, there is no shrinking from the ills of collective human society. Students here are intellectually prepared to travel and return from geographic locations with little human hope. ENFJs who take these journeys will have the perspective to compare and contrast the American neighborhood with personal knowledge of human conditions across the globe. Graduate studies for this type might then focus on American Studies. Perhaps their dissertation topic would be: Why People from Across the Globe Seek Entry to the United States of America.

HENDRIX COLLEGE

Office of Admissions
1600 Washington Avenue
Conway, AR 72032-3080
Website: www.hendrix.edu
Admissions Telephone: 800-277-9017
Undergraduates: 1,416; 636 Men; 780 Females

Physical Environment

Hendrix College is located in central Arkansas, about a half hour from Little Rock. The campus is in a **park-like setting** and has a mix of traditional and modern buildings, such as the library with its semi-circular entrance and bright skylight. The new Student Life and Technology Center is described as the "living room" of the campus and well deserves that name for its function and comfort on this forward-thinking campus. The large, rotating Hendrix theatre stage presents five annual productions. In 2010, the college and city of Conway opened a mixed use residential and business setting across from campus. Containing the Hendrix Bookstore, it houses 130 upperclass students in multistory apartment units aside private residential units. There is a strong two-way commitment to regional community between the town of Conway and the college. In the campus park-like setting there are other interesting nooks and crannies. "Pecan Court" is another location to chill out.

Social Environment

Hendrix undergraduates were **studious** in high school and achieved positions at the top of their class. At Hendrix they gain clarity through similar attention to study. They are open to areas within our communities that truly are forgotten. Hendrix is one of the growing number of liberal arts campuses that has a student organization devoted to mental health issues, called Active Minds. The trauma of schizophrenia, rarely mentioned in trendy media and political circles today, just could become an Odyssey service project.

Undergraduates are imaginative thinkers, often with a good sense of humor that combines with **self-drive**. First year classes are **comprehensive**, demanding and require the undergraduates' attention and ability to synthesize large amounts of information quickly. Academic expectations remain high and increase with intensity as graduates are expected to synthesize and form personal perspectives in reference to the global nature of learning at Hendrix. Students here are quite interested in cultural activities and discussions are richly supplemented by visiting speakers and foreign documentaries. There is noticeable absence of conservative political views within student organizations and antipathy toward Greek life. However, the student body generates a solid list of student organizations devoted to the arts, sciences, service and good fun with intellectual underpinnings like Hendrix College Quidditch.

The award-winning **Odyssey Research Program** is the foundational learning experience at Hendrix. All students participate in three Odyssey projects prior to graduation. They involve petition and approval by the departmental faculty and presentation to the public on completion. Frequently supported with grant monies, they often include **travel** to foreign cultures combined with service. Closer to home in Seattle, a 2013 Odyssey project documented the effects of music with dementia patients when hearing music from decades gone by. He summed up the empirical result in one concise statement - "People can progress from utter confusion to incredible clarity within the course of one song."

Compatibility with Personality Types and Preferences

Hendrix College and studying social cultures is almost synonymous. Faculty and administration see huge value in learning through the perspective of others. This education follows several paths and most definitely includes development of personal character, ethical inquiry and sensitivity to contemporary issues involving other cultures as well as service (F) travel within the United States and foreign countries. Students are encouraged to submit detailed service and research plans for individual learning. Their development of the proposal is quite sophisticated. Undergraduates are mentored by professors who support these undergraduate one-of-a-kind research strands. The overriding purpose of student research on this campus harkens back to student learning and imaginative plans (N). The frequent and encompassing nature of these projects prompt campus-wide attention and enhance undergraduate anticipation (P) of contributing toward the greater community after graduation. There is regular attention and deep interest in current world problems and defining the needs of the greater global community.

In the following listing of college majors it is important to remember that students can fit into any college and can be successful in any major. We have found that the Personality Types below fit very well at this college. The course-of-study chosen for each Personality Type corresponds to MBTI® research and is presented as one of many examples favorable for that type.

INFP approaches learning by gleaning large intuitive hunches as they survey text or subject. The discipline of **Psychology** nicely lends itself to this initial approach. INFPs live in the larger world of idealism and psychological research holds out the potential to benefit mankind. The department nicely introduces the undergraduates to the major subfields in psychology and focuses on the methods of scientific research that advance those specialties. The mapping of DNA has generated hundreds of genetic studies associated with human behavior and the human nervous system. It all fits for INFP who is likely to move on to graduate school.

INFJ likes variety in the work place and the major in **Allied Health** at Hendrix College is created for entry into several career paths. Courses examine the human body from head to toe and all in between. Students select a concentration from physical/occupational therapy, physician assistant or nursing. INFJ refines their personal

PERSONALITY MATCH			
ISTJ	ISFJ	INFJ	INTJ
ISTP	ISFP	INFP	INTP
ESTP	ESFP	ENFP	ENTP
ESTJ	ESFJ	ENFJ	ENTJ

belief system with precision and will select one of these, while assertively preparing for admission to graduate schools.

INTJ is focused on turning insight into reality. Their careers often turn to research. The major in **Chemical Physics** focuses on molecular interactions that lead to behavior and certain properties. Who knew that molecules had behaviors? In 2014 student research topics included laser physics, molecular cluster ions and chemical process in high pressure water. There has to be an idea for more than one research career field in that list.

ISFP really enjoys working with their hands while creating useful products. The **Biology** major is presented by faculty with a wide range of expertise. From paleobotany to genetics to marine ecology, the department is focused on advising students with practical options on graduation. The Odyssey program, so amenable to research proposals, could well support an enterprising concept in either marine ecology or botany in combination for feeding small village populations around the globe.

INTP will like the flexibility of the **Computer Science** major at Hendrix College. It is quite possible that a few select friends will team up with INTP and generate novel computer applications in one of the social or natural sciences. In many of the courses, projects allow INTPs to apply their innovative concepts in software programs. INTPs are always ready to learn in depth and will appreciate the final phase of study as each student selects a focus for specialization.

ENFP should really check out **Theater Arts** at Hendrix College. With its practical and vocational curriculum, the department prepares students for community or professional theater. ENFP could also excel as the high school drama coach. Students will write original plays and senior seminar productions are performed on campus. The department is well-supported with curriculum in dance, choreography and costume design. Faculty has depth in Shakespearian productions with an interesting side bar in Irish Theater.

ENTP is going to like the idea of studying political science at Hendrix College. The major in **Politics** starts out with the basic freshman course in Issues in Politics. This course directs students to study a single, topical issue through the lens of political theory, comparative politics, American politics and international relations. With a strong leaning toward impersonal analysis, ENTPs will be introduced to multiple approaches and the advantage of dispassionate inquiry. Hendrix College will expect confident ENTPs to reach their positions utilizing scientific inquiry first and passion second. ENTP could not agree more.

ENFJ who enters the business world often prefers a small enterprise. They enjoy the personal relationships that come with single product financial organizations. The degree in **Economics and Business** at Hendrix College is a good bet for ENFJ. It includes the complex subjects of fiscal policy, trade and interest rates plus others, yet it also includes the reality-based subjects of accounting and business law. This type of preparation lets ENFJ discover financial institutions that thrive on connections between employees, consumers and the product such as that found in fair trade markets.

JOHNS HOPKINS UNIVERSITY

3400 North Charles Street/140 Garland
Baltimore, MD 21218
Website: www.jhu.edu
Admissions Telephone: 410-516-8171
Undergraduates: 5,156; 2,696 Men, 2,460 Women
Graduate Students: 2,029

Physical Environment

Johns Hopkins University is located in northern Baltimore on 140 acres punctuated by trees and handsome brick buildings. The university and hospital were founded by Johns Hopkins in early 1800s. The university adopted the German educational model around 1880-1910s and proceeded to build large physics and science laboratories. They would go on to anchor undergraduate and graduate learning, supplying vibrant, industrializing America with Doctoral scholars. Thus, the long-established emphasis on medical research and graduate education at Johns Hopkins. In the process, Johns Hopkins laid out the template for the public higher education across America. It is hard to overestimate the depth and continuing relevance of this university's outreach.

The flagship building on campus is Gilman Hall, easily recognizable by its **huge ionic columns, stained glass windows** and indoor circular staircases. Named after Daniel Coit Gilman, the first Hopkins president, it's a 24-hour student-study area. Reopened after a major renovation in 2010, it sports an atrium that houses the university archeological collection. Those artifacts are reimagined by an artistic rendering suspended mid air in the multistoried space. Alumni Memorial Residence, "AMR," has single rooms and is coed by floor. The majority of first year students live in the freshmen quad. The campus also expanded on the other side of North Charles Street, where newer residences and a bookstore offer upperclass students more amenities right in the city. The new undergraduate laboratories were opened in 2013 also with a dramatic atrium and comfort spaces for the mind and body. Johns Hopkins, always ahead of the scientific bow wave, has placed the departments of **Chemistry, Biology, Biophysics, Psychological and Brain Sciences** within this new space. The field of Psychology is coming out from under the aegis of social sciences and getting a welcome into the physical sciences and it is more than appropriate. The Brody Learning Commons, opened in summer 2012, enhances the library study experience where undergraduate students especially spend considerable time. This is an intense university, and students benefit from calming, comfortable design while wrestling with concepts most of us cannot spell or recognize.

Social Environment

Students themselves shape the essence of the Hopkins undergraduate experience. They create a peer culture that values intellect and collaboration. It's the highly **self-directed** and self-motivated student who takes well to JHU. The JHU millennium T-shirt reads: *academics... social life... sleep* on the front, on the back *pick any two*.

Undoubtedly, life at Hopkins is about prioritizing and finding time for all that there is to do.

Undergraduates learn in the lecture halls and after hours by exchanging their views, discussing the **challenging material** presented in the curriculum. Research opportunity is quite competitive and students must independently petition for grants. The enterprising undergraduate, given the nod for research, will join professors in **emergent research** within the prestigious Johns Hopkins labs. Many who come to this university for pre-med quickly realize they can take fascinating classes in other subjects that they want to explore. Hopkins has a strong reputation for pre-medical studies, yet many in the student body do not go on to major in the sciences. In fact, less than half go on to medical school. Undergraduates here secure **competency** in other fields, such as creative writing or international politics. Students say their professors are simply amazing since they direct state-of-the-art research and undergraduate teaching at the same time.

Successful students at Johns Hopkins developed leadership skills and were committed to a select few extracurriculars while in high school. Is there a social life on campus? Yes and no. It depends upon the student. Those who seek it out will find it through participation in organized sports. The Division III football team went into conference playoffs in 2013. Lacrosse is played at Division I level and generates much campus enthusiasm. The many student organizations tend to combine service, fundraising and fun. Orientation for freshmen is a week-long affair that packs in JHU **talent and performance** like the a cappella and drama groups showcasing their enthusiasm. Others will join fraternities or sororities for leadership opportunities, philanthropy and friendship as well as social events. The premier tradition on campus is the **Spring Fair** which is the largest student-run fair in the collegiate country. Thousands come from off campus to attend. Undergraduate students participate, plan and direct it. They enjoy face-painting the little kids who attend with their parents, often professors at Hopkins. The Spring Fair offers light entertainment after two semesters of pounding the test tubes. Undergraduate **commitment to discovery** and collaborative spirit works well within the student body.

Compatibility with Personality Types and Preferences

Johns Hopkins University is a research center in scope and application that infuses our national economy. The administration and faculty consistently center academic study on invention and innovation (N) in the classic sense. Activity in the research labs is driven to pursue, invent or discover new applications through current scientific (S) properties. This university aggressively pursues generating knowledge. Their discovery radiates through our governmental agencies and society. The academic philosophy is nicely understood as JHU finds learning and research to be codependent as well as all-inclusive when it comes to teaching undergraduate students.

Faculty builds research designs that are reflective of current problems in our society. The head of NASA at the turn of this century was a former Johns Hopkins faculty member. He exemplified the very real and extraordinary research interests of Johns Hopkins University as applied to national space exploration goals. Now, with NASA's insignificant national budget, this university will turn its attentions toward other nations pursuing space exploration along with independent corporations.

All undergraduates spend the first years coming up to speed in the highly technical scientific, behavioral sciences and social sciences (J). Upper-class coursework draws widely from expansive (P) current day societal problems in need of realistic solutions. JHU graduates are steeled in the art of 'what is and what could you make of it' (T).

PERSONALITY MATCH			
ISTJ	ISFJ	INFJ	INTJ
ISTP	ISFP	INFP	INTP
ESTP	ESFP	ENFP	ENTP
ESTJ	ESFJ	ENFJ	ENTJ

In the following listing of college majors it is important to remember that students can fit into any college and can be successful in any major. We have found that the Personality Types below fit very well at this college. The course-of-study chosen for each Personality Type corresponds to MBTI® research and is presented as one of many examples favorable for that type.

INTJ will find the major in **Earth and Planetary Sciences** is well-designed for turning their ideas into research inquiry. Johns Hopkins' department presents basic concepts in the undergraduate years, specifically geared toward further research at graduate levels. This wide-ranging discipline includes the processes that shape the Earth as well as those planets in our solar system and beyond. The labs on campus and strong scientific orientation of faculty will allow INTJ to dream of designing research projects for the moon landing, hopefully mid-century.

ISTP will want to look into the **Materials Science and Engineering** degree at Johns Hopkins. Without a doubt this type will appreciate Johns Hopkins' focus on utilization and practical application. In fact, ISTPs can specialize with advanced courses in their last two undergraduate years. Energy research is currently looking at phase transformations during self-propagating reactions in multilayer foils. How about that for intense? ISTPs heartily approve of the self-propagating words since they are all about efficiency. This type of advanced study can lead to industrial positions in research or application to graduate engineering programs.

ISTJ is one for knowing the rules and keeping track of the reasons behind the rules. A BA degree at Johns Hopkins in **General Engineering** could be the perfect preparation for law school and a career in intellectual property or patent law. The several JHU programs and centers focused on the social sciences and humanities will offer appropriate elective courses in combination with solid grounding in the engineering sciences. ISTJ is up for courses in engineering technology as a comprehensive foundation for intellectual property law.

ISFJ has a wonderful ability to revisit the day from an hour-to-hour perspective. They do not miss much as the passing scene unfolds before them. As a result, they are particularly good at understanding and preserving the meaning of cultural practices. The minor in **Museum and Society** at Johns Hopkins supports practicum options in working with museum artifacts and archival collections. This type is thorough and values much about the traditions of society which are both excellent characteristics for a museum curator.

ESTP often has a personality with pizzazz and, combined with their skill at negotiating, they might enter the health policy career field. The major in **Public Health Studies** offers preparation for the masters program in Public Health at JHU. The coursework crosses many other disciplines and offers numerous opportunities for specialization. ESTP prefers the real world and all of its messy, problem-generating practices rather than theories. The Affordable Health Care Act has provided a wealth of messy administrative requirements and ESTP is ready for this type of action.

ENFP will like the flexibility of the minor in **Psychological and Brain Sciences**. The department specifically designed the minor to easily combine with a major in the social or behavioral sciences. Cause-related and passion-prone, this type will benefit from the sampling of topics through introductory courses. It will likely help them settle on a major.

ENTP will want to check into the new minor **Marketing and Communications** at JHU. The curriculum is in planning stages in early 2014. The Center for Leadership Education is sponsoring this new minor. A career in marketing is often alluring to this entrepreneurial type. They are all about competency too, so this is the ideal university for studies that combine promotion with leadership.

ESTJ often moves toward professions which require administration or other functions of leadership. The major in **Civil Engineering** at JHU is a perfect fit. Here there is an emphasis on problem solving, teamwork. Making critical decisions with their impersonal objectivity comes naturally. It is so important in the construction phases of our multistoried, multiuse modern structures composed of glass and metal frame. The Johns Hopkins dynamic environment, so closely related to advanced research, will also help tradition bound ESTJ learn to appreciate the utility of evolving metals for strength.

ENTJ is not likely to regret signing up for the **Entrepreneurship and Management** minor in combination with any of the engineering degrees at Johns Hopkins University. JHU even allows students to take just three basic courses in this area or complete the seven courses for the minor. The three-course option is ideal for enterprising ENTJs in the engineering curriculum that is already packed with research and requirements.

KALAMAZOO COLLEGE

1200 Academy Street
Kalamazoo, MI 49006
Website: www.kzoo.edu
Admissions Telephone: 269-337-7166
Undergraduates: 1,446; 631 Men, 815 Women

Physical Environment

There really is a Kalamazoo College in Michigan! It's been in existence for 181 years, making it one of the oldest liberal arts colleges in the country. Students walk together in **small groups** down the college hill to get to the shops in town. The college takes advantage of its location in this working community by focusing on service within the immediate neighborhoods. In 2013, undergrads in Psych 460 completed the **service learning component** which administration encourages within the curriculum. After the 'Playground Crew' finished the course, they developed materials and a website now used across the nation to address the troubling trend of bullying on American school playgrounds. Kalamazoo College also has one of the highest participation rates in **study abroad and internships**. The energy often flows in and out of the campus by semesters as many are coming or going. Kzoo excels in learning by doing, experience (S) and integration.

Very typically, students took an interest in the construction costs of the Hicks Student center. Some objected to the extra cost of certification as a green building. True to the colleges' reflective philosophies, undergraduates here discerned there are extra costs in government-directed mandates which necessarily represent politics far removed. Undergrads here bring an **ethos** of not being wasteful, reminiscent of the Dutch Reformists who settled along the southern Lake Michigan region. This **efficient,** (J) few-frills approach characterizes the students who find congruence between their values and conservation of resources.

The campus buildings hug a steep hill encircling a cozy quad forming the campus center. The quad projects a **calm**, smallish space where students gather on steps in twos and threes. In early fall and late spring, it becomes the student center for this **reflective student body.** The commanding mural in the dining room reminds one of the magnificent Diego Rivera murals at the Detroit Institute of Art. It is an arresting mural of American historical significance and human productivity (F). 1930s era rural Michigan farmers, Detroit's industrial workers, their leaders in the manufacturing era and academic Kzoo students and faculty take their positions across the large canvas.

Social Environment

Students who enroll at Kalamazoo may have approached their high school studies stoically. At Kalamazoo, they branch out with confidence and **intellectual exploration**. Many were admitted to other selective colleges. They enroll at Kzoo because they want to build strong relationships with their professors and pursue a values-driven education. Students have **free rein** to explore what they want to study before they commit to the college's signature **K-Plan**. It is an educational tool that outlines the four-year course of studies clearly and results in a professional, experience-based resume. Students will work on developing a plan for their **career** and complete an extensive thesis-like research. They will study abroad for the most part in third-world countries in conjunction with objectives of their K-Plan. Kzoo is ideal for rational, hard-working students who care about exploring and getting to know the world. They visit India or Botswana to learn the local dialects, live with a family and integrate with that particular culture. Perhaps upon their return they continue with individualized instruction in that dialect as part of the Neglected Languages Program offered on this campus.

Kalamazoo College students often go beyond the required study in order to earn an above average grade. Students are **down-to-earth** and dress for comfort more than style. Many of the quieter students really get animated when they engage in a conversation about their beliefs or observations from out-of-country studies. They return with a strong **cultural knowledge** base which they meld with their K-Plan resume. These students follow an intellectual approach to their careers and their future. Fun takes on characteristic collegiate activity and loves to pun the Zoo. Dances with light names like Haunted Hicks, Crystal Ball and Monte Carlo exist within the Zoo After Dark rubric, run by the student-led activities board.

Compatibility with Personality Types and Preferences

Kalamazoo College adopted experiential ways of learning decades ago when few other colleges pursued this type of education. The concept of learning by doing (S) forms the foundation of the academic curriculum here. Kzoo very much encourages students to select a variety of off-campus experiences. These real world environments in profit and nonprofit research laboratories, businesses and communities within and outside of America are honored as primary avenues of knowledge. The next level of learning is the hallmark of Kzoo faculty, foundational knowledge. Here, interdisciplinary study is not a major but rather expertly woven into the undergraduate majors. Professors guide undergraduates to supplement their discipline's foundational knowledge with experiential learning. As a result, undergraduates encounter vibrant classroom discussion and considerable written requirements that forge individual passion with analytic skill. Structure and order (J) is critical to this process as well as intensity. The experiential activities purposely reach for the outer edges of the familiar world as well as the practical, everyday world. Kzoo students mix it up as they define their cause-related perspectives. They are returning from studying abroad in unusual locations or within the U.S. that are less traveled or overlooked. Those attracted to Kzoo come seeking a precisely intellectual and utilitarian education. Kalamazoo College delivers exactly this.

In the following listing of college majors it is important to remember that students can fit into any college and can be successful in any major.

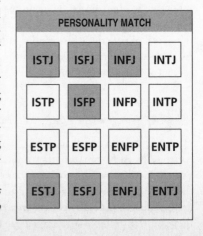

PERSONALITY MATCH

ISTJ	ISFJ	INFJ	INTJ
ISTP	ISFP	INFP	INTP
ESTP	ESFP	ENFP	ENTP
ESTJ	ESFJ	ENFJ	ENTJ

We have found that the Personality Types below fit very well at this college. The course-of-study chosen for each Personality Type corresponds to MBTI® research and is presented as one of many examples favorable for that type.

ISTJ will probably like the Kzoo approach to **Computer Science**. Not surprisingly, the department approaches this evolving science with a practical bent. Students will first learn about emerging trends in computing technology that seem to be serving, or is it shaping, humankind. Software modeling, think hurricane predictions, and algorithms, think your flight cancelled without seeming reason, is the guts of the expanding computer sciences. Here at this college, ISTJ will get a good dose of the practical applications that help them accept and incorporate new ideas in this rapidly evolving field.

ESFJ could select a concentration in **African Studies** to accompany their major in the social sciences. This type is a strong cheerleader for organizations. Much of the service work in Africa is delivered through international agencies within currently functioning programs. This avenue is appealing to ESFJs who like to work within traditional organizations. However, to stay content with a career path ESFJ must provide services or products to needy populations. Kzoo has extensive study abroad options on the continent.

ISFJ might go into the major of **Psychology** through the field of education. This type is responsible, loyal and supportive of fellow workers. Combined with a strong foundation in human personality theory, ISFJ could become a dynamite educational administrator or school psychologist. The department prepares undergraduate students to select from three broad options for graduate school as scientists in research, practitioners in counseling or consultants in professions such as business and law.

ISFP fits in nicely on this campus with their enjoyment of active, supportive environments. The degree in **Math** at Kzoo lends itself to practical applications and ISFP can look forward to good internships whereby this abstract discipline can be put to hands-on use. ISFP could easily seek internships in industry and government. Kzoo is actively building discipline area Guilds with alumni through LinkedIn. ISFP, quite adaptable to change, may start the math guild. Future employment guaranteed!

ESTJ may just like the **American Studies** concentration here at Kalamazoo College. The program offers an interesting set of courses in American literature from the colonial period to present. As a concentration it will supplement the major selection of ESTJ, who may elect the interdisciplinary study of Public Policy and Urban Affairs. Both of these studies might open avenues for a career in management or executive positions. ESTJ is a natural leader in traditional environments.

INFJ is OK with the **Environmental Studies** concentration that includes both the physical sciences and social sciences. At Kalamazoo College, the concentration is interdisciplinary and the senior individualized project is advised from INFJ's major department. This type is especially adept at initiating their ideas within traditional organization such as a nonprofit, commercial business or governmental office. They understand the mechanisms of power within and expertly plan to set about their goals.

ENTJ gets interested in complex material and the major in **Biological Physics** will offer that up for sure. The newly emerging science resulted from much of the DNA research completed in the last 20 years. After freshman level courses in physics, chemistry and calculus, ENTJ will start the search for upper level curriculum and the options for careers after graduation. Ever practical Kalamazoo College and the K-Plan will guide the search and likely provide the realistic career paths this efficient type prefers.

ENFJ is excellent at training professionals in business and corporate environments because of their persuasive and polished personality. The Kalamazoo major in **Business** with foundational courses like Theory of the Firm and National Income and Business Cycles is both overarching and real. The studies give ENFJ needed exposure to the tough problems in this sector. The practical, signature approach to education at Kalamazoo prepares this creative, compassionate type to confidently enter professional enterprises such as Apple, Verizon, Citibank, Macy's, etc. They bring harmony and cooperation to the team as they take on tough managerial issues.

KENYON COLLEGE

Gambier, OH 43022-9623
Website: www.kenyon.edu
Admissions Telephone: 800-848-2468
Undergraduates: 1,705; 786 Men, 909 Women

Physical Environment

Walk onto the Kenyon College campus and be reminded of an **English rural landscape**. They have much in common. Kenyon's Quarry Chapel is on the National Register of Historic Places. The mature oak trees cast shadows on the heavily **Gothic** stone buildings, creating a surreal feel, especially under an overcast sky. Ascension Hall was built in 1859 and casts a mysterious visual impression with a time-worn front door and original leaded glass windows. Students really identify with **haunting tales and ghostly traditions** associated with the campus. The fall colors and temperatures keep students outside in the evenings speculating about old campus rumors. The centuries-old cemetery on one corner of campus is fodder for Kenyon legends. It's not surprising that Halloween is a favorite holiday. The modernization of this campus has not taken away the **renaissance fair** aura. It definitely draws students who are OK with trying out fun social traditions from earlier times.

The new Gund Art Gallery and athletic center stand in stark contrast to Gothic architecture. The **Kenyon Athletic Center** is over the top for avid athletes who come from all over the U.S. and international locations. Kenyon students support their teams. They also use the Olympic-size swimming pool, the indoor and outdoor tracks and the Fitness Center with 200+ pieces of equipment. Athletes on Kenyon's Division III teams review their performance in last week's games and hold team meetings in the Athletic Center theater. Add in multiple ball courts with a spectacular arching glass wall and its easy to see how accomplished high school athletes would be attracted to this campus.

Social Environment

Kenyon College recruits predominantly suburban students from across the country, as well as the major cities of the middle states. Out-of-state students far outnumber those who come from Ohio. Students attracted to Kenyon often have a full resume of extracurriculars. They look to continue those interests and try out others, including student leadership positions, on this campus. They are familiar with a active pace of life and seasonal extracurriculars whether sports or arts. The small, enclosed feeling of the campus promises an opportunity to **further refine their personal skills**. There are three levels of club sports on the campus. They accommodate the serious sportster with skills who wants to continue competitive intercollegiate games, the sportster who wants to improve skills and get qualified instruction and the good old hoops gamer with practices and clinics on occasion.

Students read, review and practice their writing skills on this campus in a structured progression. They graduate with **clarity of thinking** and clarity of **written expression**. The underlying philosophy holds little value in acquired knowledge if one can't express it. The nature of the student professor relationship is intense on this campus. Students have freedom to follow their interests. They may sign up to do an independent study or blend several majors and finish up with an interdisciplinary degree. Yet they must interface that passion with academic structures and requirements within the departments. Across the campus, the faculty goal promotes competent graduates with foundational knowledge and the ability to communicate it.

The **social scene** is lively, full and generates **sentimental loyalty** to Kenyon. Traditions like First Sing and Senior Sing historically mark the beginning and end of the four collegiate years. In between, there is constant activity, Greek Life, Homecoming, Late Night Breakfast, etc. Without a nearby metropolitan center, students finish each academic week with collaboration as a byword, at Friday Cafe. It is all comfortable and familiar. They form a **close-knit** community together with the professors who live nearby.

Compatibility with Personality Types and Preferences

Kenyon College is very straight forward (S) in its dedication to teaching students. The faculty and staff provide an environment that is totally centered on individual student progress during their four years of undergraduate studies. Kenyon students, in turn, passionately connect with the social and learning atmosphere at Kenyon. Undergraduates here enjoy and actively participate in building and maintaining the intellectual community through collaboration. There is agreement between student and professor to acquire and solidify personal knowledge (T). Learning at Kenyon College is greatly characterized by specifics, analyses and principles - in that order. There is a guided curriculum for each major which assures graduates enter professional studies or the world of work with specific skills. Students who find Kenyon attractive also very much appreciate the numerous programs supplementing residential life. Faculty and students devote much energy to the advising and learning process with collaboration is a byword, whether its faculty/student or student/student.

In the following listing of college majors it is important to remember that students can fit into any college and can be successful in any major. We have found that the Personality Types below fit very well at this college. The course-of-study chosen for each Personality Type corresponds to MBTI® research and is presented as one of many examples favorable for that type.

ISTP will find the major in **Physics** takes a broad survey approach in the first year courses. Since ISTP likes to collect, organize and retain facts this characteristic will come in handy. Next they will like the course in Experimental Physics I because students experiment and demonstrate classic mechanics of motion, rotation, electrical circuits and momentum. This is simply the best for ISTP who likes to tinker with stuff that can be observed.

ISFJ has a terrific, almost sponge-like memory for people and places. It works well

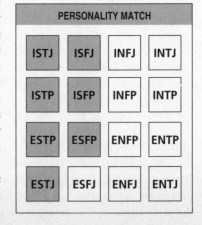

PERSONALITY MATCH			
ISTJ	ISFJ	INFJ	INTJ
ISTP	ISFP	INFP	INTP
ESTP	ESFP	ENFP	ENTP
ESTJ	ESFJ	ENFJ	ENTJ

for the **Asian Studies** concentration at Kenyon College. This reflective type will find a well-planned series of courses and study abroad options. The year of foreign language in Japanese, Chinese or Sanskrit can be fulfilled in the traditional semesters of language on campus or by an approved immersion summer program. Asian Studies becomes a very attractive addition to any other major that ISFJs might choose, perhaps art history or anthropology.

ISTJ will not shrink from the Senior Exercise in Kenyon's **Economics** degree. It is just right for this type. Kenyon emphasizes economic models as a way of understanding the behavior of society. So ISTJs who are people-oriented, yet not all that touchy-feely, can participate in building community with economic models that analyze and predict behavior. This type is very much attracted to facts and data, so the precise nature of the course work will be fine with them.

ISFP needs openness and flexibility to sort out what will be their life's work. This type prefers to be doing things that are related to helping other folks. The interdisciplinary program in **Neuroscience** at Kenyon College offers a track in biopsychological courses that will take advantage of ISFP's astuteness in observing people. With a few years of additional training, ISFPs with this degree can move into any of the specialized health services like physical therapy. It would also be ideal preparation for technical positions whereby kind-hearted ISFPs could 'gentle' patients through the medical procedures.

ESTP is quick to size up a social environment. Gregarious and socially smooth, ESTPs will be in and out of the action at Kenyon with ease. The concentration in **Public Policy** is easily paired with a major in economics or political science. ESTPs like variety so taking courses in several areas is fine. They will be drawn to off-campus experiences to supplement the Kenyon bubble. The efficiency and one-stop shopping of Kenyon's Center for Global Engagement makes it more likely that ESTP can find that experience that is packed with active learning and perhaps a little risk taking.

ESFP loves to socialize and Kenyon College offers multiple ways to become attached in the college community. This campus will work very well for ESFPs. The major in **Studio Art** will also provide a fine foundation for careers which involve offering pleasing design services to clients. With limited income and fall out from the ongoing recession, Millenials are looking to improve their living spaces with affordable improvements. Enticing courses like Painting Redefined have a large component of fun and interest within. Since these art forms draw the viewer into sensory experience through sound, sight and smell, ESFP will be delighted to create it and may market it also as Affordable Art.

ESTJ will be very approving of the concentration in **Law and Society**. It seeks to provide a wide, solid study of legal institutions and laws. As a foundational body of knowledge, this allows graduates to competently frame the tough legal issues of our day. Whether ESTJs go on to medicine, law or government, this concentration prepares them to deal with the conundrums that seem to regularly pop up in these fields. ESTJ is just the impersonal, practical leader to become a fine administrator, rarely allowing confusion to overcome the day.

LAWRENCE UNIVERSITY

Office of Admissions
115 S. Drew Street
Appleton, WI 54911
Website: www.lawrence.edu
Admissions Telephone: 920-832-6500
Undergraduates: 1,518; 668 Men, 850 Women

Physical Environment

Lawrence University is a liberal arts college located in downtown Appleton, Wisconsin. It overlooks the bank of the **Fox River**, before it empties into Lake Winnebago. Built during the Industrial Revolution by the mill owners, opulent mansions that now form "millionaire's row" line the banks of this river. Undergraduate Lawrence students like to shop or walk **together in groups** to downtown Appleton, adjacent to the campus center.

Lawrence University is the major attraction in Appleton, with its beautiful art galleries and theaters that bring in students and citizens for **musical and theatrical performances**. The **Wriston Art Center** on campus hosts permanent collections of paintings and exhibits the art work of graduating students. Often, students gather together and sit on the steps of Wriston to chat or play an instrument, except in the winter when everything is snowed under. The campus architecture is a medley of modern and traditional. The buildings are laid out with pleasing regularity on **horizontal and perpendicular streets**, like a Monopoly game. Most students live on campus, and the residence halls are arranged according to specific themes, such as "opera appreciation house" or "swing dancing club." The Warch Campus Center generates much energy with its multiple use spaces and amazing glass portals to view the sky and landscape. It was made possible by an anonymous donation, quite rare nowadays.

Social Environment

Students are very creative here and **artistically inclined**, whether or not they are part of the **music conservatory.** They sing and play the many pianos found throughout the campus, and enjoy the blend of liberal arts with the performing arts. Pluralism is an undercurrent within the curriculum at Lawrence University. Knowledge is sought to be individualized and internalized. In the Freshman Studies program, students read a selection of **original texts from ancient to modern times. It is a huge body of knowledge** as it seeks to cover multiple humanistic concepts on the meaning of man. The program draws materials representing all divisions of the college's curriculum with a somewhat thin representation of Judeo-Christian thought. It prompts the students to search out their personal perspectives on these critical questions normally reserved for doctorate level studies. It also prepares the freshmen for the college's signature **individualized learning** as upperclassmen.

The coffee bar in the student center stays open every night. All the better to practice up for the annual Lawrence University Trivia Contest, celebrating its 50th anniversary in 2015. Teams compete from across the country with a good number of Lawrence teams and local Appleton teams. It is iconic now with Google search expanding the arcane. Some Lawrence students look a bit like the 1960s groupies, yet they fit in within current alternative norms. This is in contrast to students who are in the **music conservatory** comfortable in formal wear and dress attire. One-third of the student population comes from the state of Wisconsin. Greek life comprises about a fifth of the students. Together, these groups form a cohesive, **diligent** student body and yet each student is quite individualistic.

Although the weather is brutally cold here it is mitigated by the genuine warmth of people. Students boast they are "real" and are not interested in trends. Perhaps it's the study of human nature in ancient texts or it's something in the water that develops the internal compass of students at Lawrence University.

Compatibility with Personality Types and Preferences

Lawrence University pretty much defines educational cohesion. Intellectual ideas come to the campus and freely float around for students to snag and incorporate for their own use. Conversation is continuous and debate, argument and agreement (T) is a regular extracurricular activity. Those concepts that are retained by students, faculty or administration find their way into the curriculum and the independent learning projects of the students. Lawrence University offers students the option of tutorials in many majors which further expands the vehicles by which ideas are generated. Over half of the course listings are essentially tutorials. These one-on-one tutorials tend to radiate out, combining and recombining with other disciplines for the purpose of forming future knowledge (N).

The residential life, extracurricular programs, the study abroad and the service learning all support the academic goals of student and faculty. There is a collegial atmosphere of respect and admiration. All the aspects of residential life come together and form an intellectual spirit on campus, yet it is not a sober or quiet place. On the contrary, it is quite an active, chatty campus (E). Undergraduates enjoy and expect to be in dialog with each other. Their academic interests can become political passions over the course of the four undergraduate years. Their focus is on the future and contributing to their disciplines. Students who want to become competent through the vehicle of precise thinking will find the campus ideal. Most look to graduate studies as an extension of the undergraduate studies. All this, to position themselves as unobtrusive decision makers and leaders in society.

In the following listing of college majors it is important to remember that students can fit into any college and can be successful in any major. We have found that the Personality Types below fit very well at this college. The course-of-study chosen for each Personality Type corresponds to MBTI® research and is presented as one of many examples favorable for that type.

INFP wants to get their studies in agreement with their values. They prefer to study

PERSONALITY MATCH			
ISTJ	ISFJ	INFJ	INTJ
ISTP	ISFP	INFP	INTP
ESTP	ESFP	ENFP	ENTP
ESTJ	ESFJ	ENFJ	ENTJ

a topic in depth and to keep it organized, preferably by themselves. The major in **Biochemistry** definitely will require their typical commitment and curiosity. This discipline came into being as scientists started to study the connection between nutrition, metabolism and human disease. We must thank these biochemists for putting us onto yummy blueberries and blackberries. The field promises to give INFP a lifetime of opportunities to improve human nutrition.

INFJ might like the **Chemistry** major on this campus. The small department and one-on-one tutorials will really speak to intense INFJ. The faculty prepares students to move into a number of areas on graduation from research to medicine, law, business or public service. It will be an ideal springboard for this creative thinker to move forward with a passion identified in the undergraduate years. Perhaps INFJ will be a Lawrence professor in this very department in some future decade.

INTJ with their bent for originality and an interest in computers will like the **Mathematics-Computer Science** interdisciplinary major specifically designed for post-baccalaureate study. It allows the viewing of large data constructs through methodological manipulation. Once INTJ defines the problem in a quantitative sense, any number of algorithms will be researched for the solution. This challenging type of work is very much desired by INTJ who naturally jumps between these two disciplines for the methods and solutions.

INTP can indulge their curiosity in the study of the nervous system at Lawrence University. This field is a frontier with lots of challenges and discoveries yet to be made. INTP is attracted to fields with challenges and the major in **Neuroscience** is just such a one. It lends itself to research at the undergraduate level through collaboration with faculty. This is a favored way of learning for this type. They like to see how one factor or piece of data fits into a larger system. They enjoy speculating about potential outcomes. They like the What-If Game. This focused discipline with its numerous unknowns is right up their proverbial alley.

ENFP likes to speculate about the future. Studying foreign countries during times of national transition has appeal. The major in **Russian Studies** offers focus on a rapidly changing, yet pivotal and historic nation. The department encourages students to study for a term in Russia. Independent and energetic ENFP just may do this. This background could prove valuable across corporations and state governments seeking business contracts with Russian enterprises, especially after the Sochi Olympics shortly followed by the sudden, foreboding military movement into the Ukraine.

ENTP often finds their way into the sciences. Analytical and clever, they enjoy going into the **Physics** laboratories just to see what is going to happen during a trial. The major on this campus weaves together theory and experiments in the undergraduate study. In this way, graduates are well-grounded in this sought after discipline. It especially appeals to ENTP because at its boldest the discipline of physics seeks to explain the nature of the universe. ENTP wouldn't mind being involved with finding the answer. It would keep boredom at bay, of which they have no tolerance.

ESFJ will find that the interdisciplinary major in **Natural Sciences** with an **Education** certificate really meets their career inclinations. The natural science majors at Lawrence University include course work in biology, chemistry, physics and geology. This is ideal for the ESFJ interested in becoming a science teacher in high school. Their expertise with these disciplines will be desired in the secondary schools by the students who sign up for AP Chemistry or Physics. ESFJ will be very much appreciated by these 'show me' AP high school students. Lawrence University has a solid program of internships in the local schools. This meets practical ESFJ's expectations and desire to be supporting community.

ENFJ will make good use of the **Biomedical Ethics** minor. This type's interest in resolution and harmony often pushes them into consulting careers. ENFJs like the independence but want to be connected with others. Their inclination to make improvements while remaining open is an ideal set of characteristics for mediation and negotiation. They are competent public speakers and will wade into thorny social situations utilizing this vehicle to establish their credibility. This will likely be a sought after skill set with the passage of the troubled Affordable Health Care Act.

ENTJ would find an interdisciplinary major to their liking in the **Mathematics-Economics** major at Lawrence University. The Senior Experience is a great exercise in guided creativity and demonstration of mathematical prowess. ENTJs will take the option to shine here, stepping out into an assertive, logical, orderly research design. Lawrence University administration expects that graduates will become influential in large policy venues. The option to combine economics with math bolsters ENTJ's application for prestigious graduate study in economics. This type is also very practical and just may move straight into the world of business which delivers the action and leadership opportunities that they seek.

LYNCHBURG COLLEGE

1501 Lakeside Drive
Lynchburg, VA 24501
Website: www.lynchburg.edu
Admissions Telephone: 800-426-8101
Undergraduates: 2,089; 842 Men, 1,247 Women

Physical Environment

Lynchburg College is located in the center of Virginia nestled on a hill with views of the surrounding Blue Ridge Mountains. The campus architecture of red-brick buildings features prominent white columns on the porticos of the Georgian style. Schewel Hall, among the newest on campus, sports huge walls of glass behind the columns and adds the feel of contemporary 21st design. Inside it houses state-of-the-art communications equipment to support that curriculum, as well as the School of Business and Economics. Major buildings are arranged in circular fashion and encircle a large expanse of green lawn with crisscrossing sidewalks. Those sidewalks comprise the **Friendship Circle** and call to students seeking traditional, mid-20th century atmosphere. The campus gives off a sense of physical safety because of its familiar, predictable and cohesive architectural design.

Lynchburg College was established as a **Christian**, liberal arts college by **the Disciples of Christ in** 1903. The college seal symbolizes the commitment to **faith and reason**. The Spiritual Life Center is well used and staffed by Chaplaincy honoring spiritual worship of Disciples, Jewish, Catholic and most Protestant denominations. The Chaplain's webpage recently featured a Jewish undergrad from New Jersey who participated in a Taglit trip to Israel.

The collegiate administration and faculty strongly interface their mission with central and western Virginia culture of the Blue Ridge Mountains. The **Claytor Nature Study Center** provides an environmental laboratory of upland forests and wetlands. Education majors focus on lesson development for K-12 at the center. Heated with geothermal energy and recently enlarged, it is proof positive of Lynchburg commitment to extend biological research through observation. The center houses the Herbarium that stores botanical specimens of Virginia. Established in 1927, it has over 60,000 specimen plants. In 2014, the entire campus transferred over to 100 percent electricity generated by landfill methane gas. Now that is sustainability, reason and faith!

The Hobbs Science Center provides special labs for pre-professional studies in physical and occupational therapy, pre-dentistry, pre-optometry, pharmacy and veterinary science. Shellenberger Field, refurbished in 2011, calls to the excellent athletes who enroll and continue their sport in the Old Dominion Athletic Conference. Lynchburg is a **Division III athletic powerhouse**, just clinching the NCAA's women's soccer award for most goals per game in 2013. Shellenberger Track field is also the location for serious **flag football** competition in the annual November Turkey Bowl.

Social Environment

Students who like sports and the outdoors will enjoy this college where physical fitness is both walked and talked. Most students find a place on a sports team of their choice and get to play often. The academic majors in athletic training and exercise physiology support the **fitness and sports** programs on campus. It follows that Lynchburg College boasts many athletic awards. Those looking for that classic college experience will enjoy the Greek **fraternities and sororities** that are accepted on campus with opportunities for leadership and service. For those who marched in the high school band, the campus offers jazz, brass and percussion ensembles, hand bells, musical theater, orchestra, concert band and choral groups. They add to the traditional nature of fun at Lynchburg College.

Academic classes are taught in an **interactive,** discussion-style manner. Students become hands and minds-on learners as they pursue their major studies with **supportive professors** and **apply** what they learn. The incoming students' profile is representative of average to well above average scholarship. Primary source readings are interfaced throughout the curriculum to develop students' speaking, writing and reasoning skills. The academic philosophy embraces experiential learning with internships and service learning common throughout the departmental curriculum.

Compatibility with Personality Types and Preferences

Lynchburg College has a solid understanding of the American Appalachian culture and landscape. Echoing Protestant work ethic, they have interfaced their business curriculum with service for decades. Founded on religious and ethical perspectives, the administration reached out to these communities and established an historical and ongoing appreciation from its founding to the present. This inclusive perspective, many decades later, provides the student body with a optimistic educational environment that is based on realism. As such, the curriculum is a cross between human rights and moral principles (F) and today's careers and occupations (S). The college is focused on helping students learn skills and develop their talents that are useful in today's society. Complementing this appreciation for traditional American community, the college has always turned to experiential learning. Collaboration with local public and private enterprises plus regional organizations has a significant presence in the undergraduate degrees. Off-campus (E) study is comfortably incorporated into the curriculum by Lynchburg's faculty, most with experience in their field of expertise outside of academia. In fact, the educational philosophy seems to embrace whole person, integrated learning concepts like the strongly amplified program in physical and spiritual wellness. Undergraduates who appreciate a warm yet realistic approach in the classroom will find success here. Prospective students who seek entry into career tracks after graduation will

PERSONALITY MATCH			
ISTJ	ISFJ	INFJ	INTJ
ISTP	ISFP	INFP	INTP
ESTP	ESFP	ENFP	ENTP
ESTJ	ESFJ	ENFJ	ENTJ

find their preparation to be above and beyond. Lynchburg College is connected in many senses.

In the following listing of college majors it is important to remember that students can fit into any college and can be successful in any major. We have found that the Personality Types below fit very well at this college. The course-of-study chosen for each Personality Type corresponds to MBTI® research and is presented as one of many examples favorable for that type.

ISTJ might find the **Exercise Physiology** major at Lynchburg College falls in line with meticulous procedures that they prefer for their own lifestyle. ISTJs are superb, dependable workers in these precise occupations. The department maintains a strong network of area facilities that offer internships for the students. With this major ISTJs will be helping folks experiencing difficulty in fitness, health or performance. It is also a strong background for graduate study in many of the health-related careers. This type's appreciation of common sense nicely combines with physiology theory and its application to physical fitness.

ISFJ will find the **Business Administration** degree is focused on competency with a capital C. The faculty in the School of Business emphasizes this attribute through a solid curriculum heavy on foundational knowledge. It equips this hard-working type with the skill set to pursue the accuracy they favor. ISFJs very much enjoy one-on-one time with their professors and the department requires undergrads to select a second major. At Lynchburg College it will be easy to select the second major in the helping professions. This personal approach to the business workplace, combined with their desired competence, comes naturally.

ISFP will find that Lynchburg College honors fitness and spiritual, emotional health in the minor **Outdoor Recreation.** It combines with any major and this type is likely to select a major in the health sciences providing direct service to patients. The college curriculum is ideally set up for transition into these careers. Outdoor activity and rehabilitative services often are intertwined in locations with moderate climates as found in the southern states. A career such as this would be ideal for ISFP, a gentle and observant soul.

ESTP likes to operate by the proverbial 'seat of their pants', yet their pragmatic awareness and preference for facts and what is real can be an asset in following the trail of activity within organizations or individuals. The major in **Economic Crime Prevention and Investigation** at Lynchburg College is unusual and requires knowledge from several traditional academic fields. ESTPs might relish the thought of investigating white collar fraud and corruption, especially if risk or mediation is involved. This type also likes the survey approach to building a body of knowledge. Faculty in this department have law enforcement and fraud investigative experience. Their credentials are the sad result of today's cultural, relativistic, compartmentalized reasoning. Without moral conviction, the slope gets slippery.

ESFP very often likes to be with other people and in the middle of the action, often times outdoors. The minor available at Lynchburg College in **Outdoor Recreation** will be an excellent companion to the other careers which appeal to this type: Education, Health Care, Entertainment, Social Services and Business. A second minor and another appealing choice for this type would be **Coaching**, especially if

ESFP intends to go into education. It is unusual for a liberal arts institution to offer these two minors. Both of these minors add very desirable skill sets for the graduates.

ESFJ typically has the inclination to be of service and support to others. In the world of business, this can translate to sales representative. ESFJs with their pleasant, affirming personality can bring this asset to the **Sport Management** major or minor at Lynchburg College. Organization and dependability are bywords for this type and well interface with the highly scheduled, seasonal world of sports. Lynchburg College actively updates this curriculum to reflect the increasing presence of sports entertainment, sports leisure and sports commerce in today's society. Internship offerings are exceptional from the Baltimore Orioles to Special Olympics Virginia to U.S. Marine Corps – Quantico. Wow.

ESTJ hangs on to their no-nonsense approach in emotionally charged environments. This type is often pulled toward the traditional professions such as law, medicine and engineering. The investment in additional graduate school training comes naturally to ESTJs. This type is masterful at putting together cause and effect lines of reason which allow them to excel in high stakes careers. Lynchburg College developed a system of advising for its **Pre-Professional Program** that provides direct, timely advice in each of the dental, medical, optometry, pharmacy, physical therapy and veterinary fields. Advisors are selected to mirror the professional interests of the undergraduate ESTJ. Advising takes on the dual role of foundational undergraduate studies and admission to professional school

ENFJ often wants to be personally productive for the benefit of others. ENFJs also love to be mentored and advised in a one-on-one relationship with their advisor. This type interfaces passion/cause with their education and seeks to personalize their knowledge and its application to the community. Lynchburg's minor in **Museum Studies** carried this quote in October 2011: "Curators piece together the puzzle of times we didn't see. It's a puzzle that will never be completed." So well said. ENFJ is superb at "well said."

ENTJ has the inclination to compete for one of the desired openings in the **Athletic Training** major at Lynchburg College. The entry level, professional positions secured by ENTJs on graduation with this degree will lead to the stature and levels of influence sought by this type. This independent type likes the challenge and wants to be accountable for their own organizational plans. Athletic trainers are key to athletes and professional or semi-professional sports teams. ENTJ does not mind stepping into this dynamic, powerful environment.

MARQUETTE UNIVERSITY

Office of Admission
Marquette Hall, 106
Milwaukee, WI 53201-1881
Website: www.marquette.edu
Admissions Telephone: 414-288-7302, 800-222-6544
Undergraduates; 8,046, 3,841 Men, 4,205 Women
Graduate Students: 3,218

Physical Environment

The city of Milwaukee is a **vibrant** place to visit and attend college. It was settled by Eastern European immigrants who came down from Canada, probably via the Saint Lawrence Seaway and the Great Lakes. The streets are clean and not jammed with traffic. The **downtown skyline** reveals sharp new buildings alongside old-world neighborhoods built in the 1900s. Marquette's campus blends in quite well with the city architecture in that it is also a tall, perpendicular campus with an inviting skyline of its own. Marquette University encourages students to become familiar with the cultural and social opportunities of the city, literally across the street. Yet "when the gales of November come hauling," to borrow the words from Canadian singer Gordon Lightfoot, students are inclined to stay indoors on campus. Those comfortable with the nature of American cities are attracted to this university. They bring their **city smarts** and openness to explore the city culture.

Approximately half of the student body lives on campus in the **tall rectangular** residence halls referred to as towers. Some upper class students move off campus to limited university-owned apartments. These desirable residences adjacent to the campus, with an easy walk to and from classes, generate a waiting list each calendar year. The Discovery Learning Complex opened in 2011 is a spectacular engineering and science facility that promotes student-generated research projects to explore fundamental science concepts.

Social Environment

Marquette University appeals to students who are used to working hard and producing results. This strong **work ethic** binds the city together as it does the university. In addition to a very **rigorous course of study**, students get involved in serving the community. This campus is most remarkable for the intensity of service and leadership activity within the undergraduate student body. The city with many nearby neighborhoods offers students additional options to serve.

About half of the students at Marquette come from traditional **Catholic** families. It would be a bit difficult to be an out-and-out atheist here. **Service learning** on this campus reflects Catholic doctrine in work productivity and spiritual centering. Students commonly respect rules and have a deep respect for **social convention**. They may not be leaders when they arrive on campus but they will almost certainly develop **leadership** acumen here because of many prompts to transfer new knowledge into benefiting the larger community.

Fraternities and sororities have been an institution at Marquette for more than 100 years. They offer multiple ways to engage in **volunteer activities** and leadership. Student leadership was instrumental in developing **Late Night Marquette** which mirrors contemporary twenty-something culture in entertainment on and off campus. **Sports** are also very popular and games are well attended in the Bradley Center, especially their Division I basketball team. No matter which tower students choose or which organizations to join, they will develop a **wide circle of friends** from all over campus. Social life and parties are always at the ready here. Marquette graduates do indeed have a wide network of peers and the student body greatly benefits from strong **alumni support.** Pride in the city and the university is very evident.

Compatibility with Personality Types and Preferences

Marquette University is quite orderly (J) and reasoned (T) in its educational philosophy stemming from Catholic tenets. The mission of the university infuses values of truth, excellence and faith throughout the collegiate environment. Analysis of ethical responsibility throughout the curriculum is pervasive. Along with development of resolute personal character, students are offered a series of programs and opportunities that build leadership skills. All this is to encourage harmonious (F) values of community, the community within the city of Milwaukee and the American community.

The undergraduates here are discouraged from remaining in a small, familiar circle of friends found during the freshman year. Many programmatic and informal mechanisms are in effect to encourage undergraduates to enlarge their circle of acquaintances (E) on this campus. The underlying advantage of this social prompting allows students to become familiar with the many current organizations and enterprises on campus and in Milwaukee. The university, with its realistically (S) oriented curriculum, graduates young adults likely to secure immediate employment in career tracks that are needed by society. Students who are drawn to this university, beyond comfort with religious spirituality, are conventional in the sense of their expectations. They intend to have one heck of a good time in college and then settle down after graduation or post-graduate study, raise a family and make lifelong contributions within their selected discipline while actively supporting America, their state and city of residence.

In the following listing of college majors it is important to remember that students can fit into any college and can be successful in any major. We have found that the Personality Types below fit very well at this college. The course-of-study chosen for each Personality Type corresponds to MBTI® research and is presented as one of many examples favorable for that type.

ISTP is a maverick on occasion but in a quiet way, often with a wry smile. The major in **Business Economics** with a minor in **Air Force and Aerospace Studies** just might suit their sense of the efficiency. Very realistic edu-

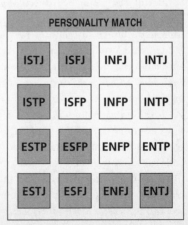

PERSONALITY MATCH

ISTJ	ISFJ	INFJ	INTJ
ISTP	ISFP	INFP	INTP
ESTP	ESFP	ENFP	ENTP
ESTJ	ESFJ	ENFJ	ENTJ

cation taught by faculty active in independent business consulting passes the ISTP reality test. The hands-on orientation for selecting internships and the mentor program junior year will open up options for multiple career tracks. The minor in Air Force and Aerospace will certainly move ISTPs toward the large military industrial complex for a career. That career is likely to be satisfying for this very mechanical type that enjoys being around metal and moving parts.

ISTJ is excellent at covering all the bases as does the natural science major in **Biochemistry and Molecular Biology** at Marquette University. It allows ISTJs to acquire, explore and analyze life-regulating mechanisms from the traditional world of biology and chemistry. This persevering type will not become discouraged with the precise and intense studies or the effort needed to retain and apply it. Naturally, these qualifications will be well received at research institutes across the nation. Yet, common sense ISTJs like having both of the options: work and/or advanced degrees in the field.

ISFJ with their strong work ethic fits in perfectly at Marquette University. The major in **Biomedical Sciences** will serve this type well. The hands-on nature of health care specialties, such as dental hygienist and respiratory therapist, are very rewarding for ISFJs. This type is intensely private, but also gentle with people and very sincere while helping others. This major provides an excellent foundation for entry, with additional graduate training, to many of the medical professions or research institutions in the health sciences. The department is well-resourced and quite up to date with advising for career options in this dynamic field.

ESTP is brilliant at pulling a team together with workable, impromptu redirection. This skill will come in handy as they manage construction projects, nationally or internationally. The school of engineering at Marquette University has this much needed degree in **Construction Engineering and Management** for this restless, action-oriented type. Smooth ESTPs won't pause for reflection, but maybe lunch, as they work with electricians and plumbers. The required co-op helps this type recognize the best way to leverage their skills and knowledge. Dinner with the investors at the end of the day, no problem. At Marquette, graduates will have the financial acumen as well as the engineering credentials.

ESFP will find that Marquette University is one of a small handful of colleges offering the major in **Advertising.** This type is excellent at conveying messages. ESFPs with an artistic talent will enjoy this productive, opportunistic curriculum. Marquette University alumni networks generate extensive listings for internships. Students may well arrive at the office ready to go having generated ad copy in the Mac labs on campus. Milwaukee's fine urban design and visual spaces sitting on the western edge of clear, turquoise Lake Michigan provide plenty of visually-pleasing inspiration.

ESFJ occasionally will consider a career in business. To keep ESFJ's interest it must combine the interests of customers or employees within the entrepreneurial goal. The major in **Human Resource Management** is an excellent choice for solicitous, supportive ESFJs. Their strong loyalty and appreciation of organizational structure will be advantageous in this position at large corporations. At Marquette University, there is a solid integration of human values and community responsibility, and the business school is assertively pro-profit.

ESTJ is a solid bet for a career in **Real Estate** with their predisposition for standard operating procedure. At Marquette, students will gain skills and ability with transactions of current properties, but equally important the development of future properties. Commercial real estate transactions are well understood on this campus. ESTJ only has to communicate with peers in the construction management major for realistic valuation. The College of Business also expertly interfaces the studies with ethical frames of reference for graduates who will necessarily be involved in community changes and development. It's very close to an interdisciplinary degree.

ENFJ is frequently caring and sensitive of others, quite capable of promoting the well-being of those they meet on the job or in the community. The major in **Social Welfare and Justice** at Marquette University is a natural course of study for this type. The curriculum at Marquette offers a concentration in **Victim Services.** There is clearly a growing need for this expertise as ethical behavior is often snarled and devalued in legalistic renderings by bureaucracies and the courts.

ENTJ is cool under pressure more often than not. This characteristic is ideal for a career in **Public Relations.** Not particularly well known among members of the Millennial generation, this degree gives entry to powerful positions within large business enterprises. First years study public relations principles, sophomores study media writing and advertising. Upper-class students take interdisciplinary electives. All of this prepares dynamic ENTJs to refine their analytic skills and move confidently to front and center on the public stage.

MASSACHUSETTS INSTITUTE OF TECHNOLOGY

77 Massachusetts Avenue
Cambridge. MA 02139-4307
Website: www.mit.edu
Admissions Telephone: 617-253-4791
Undergraduates: 4,252; 2,449 Men, 2,031 Women
Graduate Students: 6,937

Physical Environment

Massachusetts Institute of Technology is located on the bank of the **Charles River** in Cambridge. The river is like a window to the most happening parts of crowded Boston. It provides a mental break for MIT students who like to jog along the banks or set sail on the waters. Sailing and crew are well-developed sports here since they tend to rest the mind while watching the Boston traffic jams along the banks on Storrow Drive. The **Division III** designation of athletics encourages MIT students to be athletes and go out for the teams, as they play at a less demanding level.

This 155-acre **urban** campus has an eclectic mix of buildings, from neoclassic to I.M. Pei design to slab and limestone. Some were put together like a Lego construction, giving the campus a **utilitarian feel**. These buildings don't have names and are referred to by numbers. The "infinite corridor" connects buildings 7, 3, 10, 4 and 8, so that students don't have to walk outside. The "infinite corridor" has lots of student traffic and it's a metaphor for the pursuit of knowledge, which is **endless** here.

Some of the dormitories are unadorned and simple as are the lawns and grounds. The newly renovated Maseeh Hall is an exception with trendy yet simple design. It is representative of the major building boom in early 2000 that opened many new attractive glass and metal buildings, including undergraduate residence, Simmons Hall, which is a delight to contemplate visually. The front lawn of the "dome" is where students traditionally hold their **"infinite buffet,"** which consists of long lines of tables filled with yummy food. All in all, bright students who like MIT also favor clean cut, angular design and practical spaces.

Social Environment

Students enjoy themselves here if they can balance the intense study schedule with a social life. Students must get used to taking in knowledge as if drinking water from a fire hose. Competitive students are the exception rather than the rule. Yet many perfectionists strive for all A's. Most students like to **collaborate** and work well in research teams. With high intelligence as the common denominator, MIT students are creative in many ways. They are over the top with their conversations full of far-out, theoretical ideas. They are the musicians who played instruments in and out of school. They are **innovative** in math and science and appreciate delving into the liberal arts and humanities. Most were the acknowledged **math and science wizards** of their high schools.

Their questions are perceptive and logical creating a **dynamic learning environment** where it's fascinating to speculate on cellphone programming possibilities with one another. Maybe Linux's new Zorin? They are likely to linger over lunch and get wrapped up in a discussion about the chemical composition of copper. Each will wrestle with reaching for the A's, accepting mostly B's or tolerating an occasional C. Undergraduates here learn by doing research. The work ethic at MIT is intense and students are set in two frames of mind: **work hard and work harder**. They quickly realize that there is a lot they don't know. This causes them to behave academically **like grad students**, jumping right into research when the opportunity regularly presents itself.

With such academic rigor, students find **humor** to be paramount in relieving stress. They enjoy clever practical jokes and love pranks. Who can forget about the Boston police car that was hoisted on top of the Dome? MIT undergraduate students bond over their love for the sciences and possibly other things, like food. **Food** is nurturing for undergraduates who are learning to socialize across many diverse cultures and ways of thinking. Parties at MIT form around food, often times with the students striving to become chef-like. **Eating together** also includes socializing at some of the finest restaurants in Boston. Most MIT students are down-to-earth and easy to please in social venues with food.

MIT students dress for comfort and not trends. Undergrads fit socializing into their schedule when it makes sense with their academic goals. They might select two or three organizations to look into from the 450 on campus. About one-third of the students join **Greek Life** for yet another social outlet. Yet friendships often start out as a common interest in an academic subject or class. Conversation may roam over to the realm of politics but it is not a dominant topic on this campus. MIT is a unique university with extraordinary national implications coming out of its technological efforts. Alumni are powerful and tend to observe, with a critical eye and doubting mind, many of the expansive pluralistic philosophies of the Institute's peer intellectual institutions.

Compatibility with Personality Types and Preferences

Massachusetts Institute of Technology is a powerhouse of technical invention. No surprise there. There are few universities of this caliber in the world. MIT remains true to their technical roots, decade after decade. That being said, MIT's School of Humanities, Arts and Social Sciences has broad courses of instruction. An undergraduate can declare a social science major and still be immersed in technology simply by living on this campus. The student body is powerful in intellect, commitment and energy. Both social science and science degrees lean toward objective, technical applications. On graduation students are likely to promote this technology at regional or national levels and, of course, use innovation (N) in their work places. There are few universities that educate well in the humanities and provide their graduates interface to the most advanced technical applications available for their discipline. MIT is one of them. Here there is little that goes unnoticed (S) in independent research or student collaboration. Those admitted are competent, objective observers (T) of their environment. Students come with a strong inclination to improve life's experience for themselves and society (F). They are only constrained by the physical laws of nature and common sense which actually find a home on this campus. All technical discoveries get a thumb's up (P); the new knowledge will be quickly interfaced.

In the following listing of college majors it is important to remember that students can fit into any college and can be successful in any major. We have found that the Personality Types below fit very well at this college. The course-of-study chosen for each Personality Type corresponds to MBTI® research and is presented as one of many examples favorable for that type.

PERSONALITY MATCH

ISTJ	ISFJ	INFJ	INTJ
ISTP	ISFP	INFP	INTP
ESTP	ESFP	ENFP	ENTP
ESTJ	ESFJ	ENFJ	ENTJ

INTJ reigns supreme when it comes to original thinking. It is often difficult for them to clearly express their never-before-heard-of ideas, yet given time, this type will conceptualize plans that will be awesome when revealed. In the **History** major at MIT, their opportunity will come with the two required theses. The department's scope is necessarily broad and seeks to bring the lives of those who walked in our shoes in decades past forward for today's history major at MIT. INTJ will bring coherent perspective to theme, geographic area or historical period. INTJ may need to do an independent study if they want to study the Founding Fathers as the curriculum seems to offer no courses in this area.

ISTP will be surprised and impressed with a look at the **Middle Eastern Studies** at MIT. This interdisciplinary minor is designed to familiarize the student with culture, history and politics of the Arab world. Quite naturally, it is an introductory level of knowledge but highly valuable given the extraordinary conflicts that have erupted in this region since America's withdrawal from Southeast Asia in the mid 1970s. ISTP will search through the electives for an applied, useful perspective such as Issues in Islamic Urbanism.

ISTJ is just the type you would want to manage our national nuclear infrastructure. Their penchant for accuracy and perseverance meets up nicely with this precise discipline. The national demand for expanding energy sources puts MIT's **Nuclear Science and Engineering** major in the spotlight. Although ISTJs don't seek the political spotlight that accompanies this field, they are drawn to the detail of operating nuclear reactions. Floating nuclear plants are in the research spotlight currently and undergrad internships are open for the taking.

INTP would be studying the past and the future with the **Earth, Atmosphere and Planetary Sciences** at MIT. This curious type will delight in formulaic rabbit holes sloping into global climate, tectonics, deformation and the solar system. INTP is intrigued by the impossible. In fact they are not sure it is impossible. They will devote all their energy to the solution. Sign them up for planetary missions. They have the patience to work decades toward that sought after human Mars landing in the latter part of this century.

INFP could find their ideal course of studies at the ideal location with the double major in **Science, Technology and Society** at MIT. The purpose of this study is likely to warm the heart of idealistic INFP. It addresses questions many have asked: what is technology doing to help humanity? The MIT Initiative on Technology and Self is researching questions like: How is 24 hour social media advancing their agendas? What are their agendas'? It will be INFP who cannot walk away from these difficult queries. The curriculum is complimentary, i.e. abstract/technical, to most MIT majors. It offers the newly minted MIT graduate an uncharacteristic depth of knowledge in the world of social media.

ESTP is a great troubleshooter when it comes to stalled projects involving people and processes. The **Civil and Environmental Engineering** degree also emphasizes another of this type's talents, getting the most bang for the buck. Satisfaction for ESTP means carefully using resources, working with folks in a pleasant manner and solving problems. The Department's direction focuses on applied technology and avoiding resource depletion. This type's gifts synch perfectly with unstable environments, both political and geographic. Their easygoing personality and passion for a solution find a home at MIT in this degree.

ESFP will elect to perform in the arts on occasion. Their unerring sense of beauty comes in handy in this very visual medium of communication. The flexible major in **Theater Arts** at MIT is the result of student/advisor collaboration. The department seeks to connect theater with the world of science and has plenty of resources at their disposal. ESFP, always up for novelty and fun, will likely take elective courses in MIT's media and arts lab. The entire engineering acumen is at the disposal of this creative laboratory focused on the visual and moving image.

ENFP might at first think the **Urban Studies and Planning** degree nice for other people, but generally dry and potentially a bit boring. At MIT, however, the department has interfaced plenty of abstraction. The curriculum cuts across subjects in sociology, business, geography, engineering, education and transportation. Of course applied technology is readily apparent in the daily undergrad experience at MIT. Enthusiastic, inventive ENFP will love the idea of enhancing urban living with technology. They have the empathy and innovation to short circuit development sprawl with solid alternatives in city planning.

ENTP may find the details in the foundation courses for the **Economics** degree at MIT to be less than exciting. In fact, their enthusiasm may peak before they reap the rewards of putting their instinctive hunches into action. For those who stay on, the dynamic financial markets will be theirs to observe and learn about during the independent research phase of the curriculum. ENTP will then step forward to solidify their foundational knowledge in preparation for an MBA or off to work at graduation.

ESTJ will be able to put their precise ways to good use in the **Aeronautics and Astronautics** degree. ESTJs require prove-it-to-me logic that is ideal for space exploration. Their penchant for thinking and learning in steps is also very desirable in the unforgiving space environments. ESTJ understands the goal: get it right. This degree has numerous departure points within it. The process of getting man into space involves application of the most advanced knowledge across many systems. ESTJ must decide which system to focus on: will it be propulsion or computing in the spacecraft? This degree has ESTJ written all over it.

ENTJ will not shy away from the **Management Science** degree at the Sloan School of Management. Faculty inundates this undergraduate curriculum with studies in optimization, math modeling and other formulaic approaches to efficiency. The productive, quick ENTJ sees the reasoning behind this approach and will stay on top of the daily inundation of systems science. They are motivated by competition and move toward taking charge. Upon graduation, this type will confidently enter the risk and reward side of enterprise armed with quantitative skills.

INFJ will find that the degree in **Biology** at MIT heavily interfaces mathematical formulas. There is great research interface between the live organisms and the chemical codes dictated through DNA. The major has considerable flexibility and undergrads can find themselves in courses with grad students if the topic interests them. The variety of research is over the top, but the 70 major research groups throughout the campus hint at where the top stops. INFJs are self-directed for sure and can shuttle between the test tubes and electronic data banks with ease. During the go-betweens, this type is looking to push out of the amorphous box.

MIDDLEBURY COLLEGE

Office of Admissions
Middlebury, VT 05753
Website: www.middlebury.edu
Admissions Telephone: 802-443-3000
Undergraduates: 2,516; 1,233 Men, 1,283 Women

Physical Environment

Middlebury College is located in the north-central part of Vermont, about an hour from Burlington and three hours from Montreal, Canada. Although the location is isolated, the town has about 8,000 people. The average winter temperatures fall below the **freezing mark**. The weather plays a large influence here across the campus community. Ross Commons dining hall and dormitories are connected so students can walk the interior hallways. Students who make friends with the **ice and snow** head for the skating ponds, hockey rink and nearby **ski** slopes.

This beautiful campus, established in the 1800s, is a large expanse to negotiate. With Adirondack mountain slopes to the west, it seems as if the campus structures gently rolled off, came to a stop and established their stone foundations, each preferring not to be too close to the other. **Interior space** becomes familiar and the center point of the undergraduate student daily experience. The literary connections to Robert Frost and other poets serve to prompt meaningful questions about purpose and life. Taken together, the literary focus and the interior feel of the intellectual spaces make for a **Romantic landscape** in several senses.

The **academic quad** is surrounded by the Mead Memorial Chapel, the McCullough student center, the main library and several academic halls. On the other side of College Street, the Freeman International Center and Atwater dining hall function as summertime hubs for students from across the country. They are focused on learning a foreign language through this college's excellent programs developed in association with its literary focus.

Middlebury's residence halls are referred to as **The Commons** and this is where first-year seminars are held. There are five buildings in the Commons and freshmen identify with the community of their particular residence. This physical housing arrangement facilitates interaction with professional residential staff, the Commons Head, Commons Dean and Commons Coordinator who live in the residences with their families. Together with the students, they coordinate events such as field trips, speakers and socials.

All juniors and seniors on campus are required to rotate out of their Commons to other housing options across campus. However, students, often elect to move with their Commons hall mates in small groups to other residences.

Social Environment

Middlebury College attracts **super-achiever** students, **serious** and determined to study and get the most out of college. Over 90 percent of the student body comes from out of state. They abide by rules, respect convention and look to their **residential staff to provide the foundation** for friend-making when they arrive. They tend to be disparate in their backgrounds and through discussion and common activities learn to become a member of this new whole called Middlebury. A good number have international residences or lived overseas at some point in their lives. It is not uncommon for undergrads to have experienced a lifestyle other than suburban. As a result, risk taking within the undergraduate student population tends to be of a conservative sort: intellectual exploration and **pushing the edge athletically** with winter sports like snowboarding.

Sports are a way for students to get out of their heads. When they take a break from ongoing academic speculation, '**Safe Silly**' works. With assistance and support from the college, several recent graduates developed the first Muggle Quidditch competition. Now over 200 collegiate teams compete internationally in New York City. The campus has two new, over-the-top athletic facilities open in 2014, for indoor squash and intramural field house.

Did we mention Middlebury students are **cerebral**? Undergraduates gain an exposure to foreign cultures and civilizations through the exceptionally strong emphasis on **foreign language study**. Through off-campus study in other countries, they synthesize multicultural perspectives with their academic disciplines. Many become aware of social issues, such as poverty and immigrant laborers, that are present in northern Vermont. Blessed with high intellectual ability, these students combine careers with research and service to the community. They take their place in quiet leadership positions after graduation.

Compatibility with Personality Types and Preferences

Middlebury College is rooted in historical literature. The academic environment honors the works of the early American poets with a philosophical thread. The developing American psyche of the 1800s combined with the poetic observations on life's meaning painted an ethical and responsible citizen in this literature. That ethic is studied at Middlebury College. It prompts the undergraduate to let go of self-oriented perspectives that could be considered intellectually inhibiting. Individual goals of the undergraduate student are likely to be interfaced with responsibility toward the world. This is a strong overarching theme at Middlebury College.

By using multiple viewpoints, questions are posed and faculty ask students to find shades of meaning (N) within the several answers offered by the undergraduates. The academic studies are all about anticipation and inspiration. Students must be comfortable with ambiguity at some level. However, there is optimism in the student body that ambiguity will retreat and clear purpose will emerge. Middlebury students are inwardly (I) confident. They are expectant of serious and even tedious study to achieve their goals. Their resultant expertise is not comprised of facts or skills, but it is an overall intellectual view of the world through the lens of their

PERSONALITY MATCH			
ISTJ	ISFJ	INFJ	INTJ
ISTP	ISFP	INFP	INTP
ESTP	ESFP	ENFP	ENTP
ESTJ	ESFJ	ENFJ	ENTJ

academic discipline. That viewpoint is abstract and graduates are often cause-and passion-related upon graduation (J).

In the following listing of college majors it is important to remember that students can fit into any college and can be successful in any major. We have found that the Personality Types below fit very well at this college. The course-of-study chosen for each Personality Type corresponds to MBTI® research and is presented as one of many examples favorable for that type.

INFJ absolutely must look at the **Biology** major at Middlebury College. The department has state of the art technical equipment and imagination to keep vision-prone INFJs happy. These individuals are always dreaming about what could be—given the current state of things. They do not live in an ivory tower. Rather this type starts with reality and typically develops a darned good grounding. This completed, INFJs strap on all kinds of wonderful goals that could improve the current state of things. Independent research is a strong thread within this curriculum. Students are expected/encouraged to develop their own strands of investigation. Additionally, Middlebury's extraordinary programs in the language can give this type access to research in their choice of geographic areas around the globe. How about a minor in **Chinese**?

INTJ will find that the **Geography** major at Middlebury explores the abstraction of space coming together with human utilization. The department website elegantly describes the nature of this long-standing discipline. It is an excellent choice for INTJ who is original and digs deeply. The faculty is innovative and bold. With the course in Geographic Terrorism, INTJ may find answers for the relentless attacks on western civilization which have marred this century to date. The major may be nicely paired with the well-balanced **American Studies** major at this campus. You go for it INTJ, society needs a lot of bright young adults to enter this field. Fairly resistant to current political trends, the geography major has the long legs for applicability to intractable problems.

ISTJ is one for knowing the facts and keeping them quite straight. This type could easily become an archivist or librarian cataloging and retrieving precious documents and everyday useful knowledge. The major in **Literary Studies** would provide this type with an uncommonly fine understanding of literary works. Thorough ISTJ will precisely capture the author's literary meaning. This type can find the building blocks of perspective within each of the world's masterpieces. The many world authors included in this major will not deter ISTJ, rather they will attract.

INTP wants to create and develop complicated plans. The goal is important, yet the process is the prize. The major in **Theater** at Middlebury offers much in the way of process. The department approaches theater through analysis. INTPs excel at analysis. Drama interpretation will absorb this type. There are multiple major tracks and specializations within this major. INTPs are likely to look for dilemma as an inherent part of the arts they pursue. After graduation, they might move toward performance or administration of the arts. Clever, ingenious INTPs may also secure the business acumen through appropriate internships to act as an agent.

ENTP might get intrigued by the major in **International Politics and Economics** at Middlebury College because of the complexity. Second majors and minors are not approved because of the sheer volume of content in this major. ENTPs may overcome hesitation though because they are attracted to power, typically optimistic and confident. This interdisciplinary major is well-supported across the collegiate curriculum. ENTP will enjoy jumping from one perspective to another through the variety in study abroad, foreign language and regional specialization.

ENFJ could be ideal in a career associated with higher education. The major in **American Studies** at Middlebury College offers a smorgasbord of subjects on the list of courses approved for the curriculum. The department approaches the discipline utilizing primary sources which may help undergrads interpret our society without the influence of today's pervasive national media outlets. The curriculum has a course in Immigrant America which focuses on the extraordinary European influx of the 20th century, rarely found at liberal arts colleges today.

ENTJ likes complexity with a little challenge and pursuing a foreign language at this campus is well advised. Most students who declare **Japanese Studies** take their first course in the language at Middlebury College. This type likes a challenge and with their entrepreneurial spirit guiding them, they are likely to move on to an international career in business with an MBA in immediate vision on graduation from Middlebury College.

MUHLENBERG COLLEGE

2400 Crew Street
Allentown, PA 18104-5586
Website: www.muhlenberg.edu
Admissions Telephone: 484-664-3200
Undergraduates: 2,422; 1,018 Men, 1,404 Women

Physical Environment

Located in the Lehigh Valley, Muhlenberg College feels like the geographical and philosophical middle ground between **Pennsylvania Dutch** country and the city of **Philadelphia.** Founded in 1848, the college is an Evangelical **Lutheran** campus. Critical **interfaith initiatives** like the Institute for Jewish-Christian Understanding seek to bring the human rights values of the founding fathers into the public square again. Not a campus to shrink back from today's unhealthy trends, The Center for Ethics has selected the theme of Sex, Ethics and Pleasure Politics for the undergraduate student body and general public in 2013-2014. The Institute for Public Opinion similarly **examines contemporary trends** that impact the collegiate community, regional and national stages.

The campus has a landscape that entrances a viewer with its picturesque rolling countryside and **doors painted in Amish red**. Seegers Union has inviting spaces for student collaboration. The newer **Trexler Theatre** encourages some to cross over and participate in the Broadway-quality productions offered by the drama department. The science building with its superb facilities draws in students who are interested in pre-med and pre-vet programs. The Life Sports Center is a combination of newer glass, winding architecture and the homey older brick and mortar left in place. It encourages the widespread **athleticism** on campus.

Students' input was essential in the construction of the newest residence halls which foster student involvement and a sense of community. Upcoming renovation of East Hall will retain its historical presence during modernization. Their expectation of graduating intellectually agile, reasoned young adults capable of civil debate is just what the doctor ordered for the increasing polarization of American society.

Social Environment

Students who want to grow in their spiritual beliefs will find open dialog and encouragement on this campus. They value work that helps humanity, whether through research or active volunteerism in the Lehigh Valley or abroad. They appreciate the orderliness on this campus and seek to interface that with future careers. In some ways it reflects their hometown values. They often enjoy getting to know their professors and are usually confident in those **mentoring relationships**. Muhlenberg students are **very active** and vocal in the classroom and socially. They thrive on academic assignment, friendly competition and a challenge. They have a conventional sense of risk-taking, like pulling harmless pranks.

The majority of students played **sports** in high school and enjoyed it, so they continue in college. They like taking the one semester of required physical education. Through these activities many become confident and find their academic niche on campus. Since 95 percent of students live in college housing, they form a loyal, tight-knit community. They are **high-achieving** and rank at or near the top quarter of their class. Many Jewish students and ethnic minorities feel quite comfortable here because there is a sizeable number of each at Muhlenberg. Students graduate with a solid moral perspective of responsibility and citizenship. While mindful of the recession and the extra time it will take to land that first step on the career ladder, graduates have the resilience to attain personal and career success.

Compatibility with Personality Types and Preferences

A Muhlenberg education is sanely traditional, solid and moral. A student will find academic guidance very clear and spelled out with detail in the course catalog. Here, friendly and frequent (E) conversation is welcome and one would likely find students conversing around the campus pretty much anytime. This carries over to the classroom where discussion is guided and amplified by faculty. In this manner, students acquire content and knowledge. This educational philosophy prompts the individual student to accept responsibility, become productive and offer humane service (F) to others. The Lutheran religious tradition comes forward in this way. You can also find a simple efficiency in the academic course of studies and the campus recreation options. Excess or wastefulness of human energy and Earth's bounty is dimly viewed. Departments are well interfaced with the economy and job markets that the graduates will soon enter. Academic experience outside of the classroom is highlighted throughout the curriculum. Students expecting to transfer to professional schools find the same care and advising for this next step as those starting employment immediately on graduation. At Muhlenberg, undergraduates seek balance and use of their personal talents. It is a moral imperative.

In the following listing of college majors it is important to remember that students can fit into any college and can be successful in any major. We have found that the Personality Types below fit very well at this college. The course-of-study chosen for each Personality Type corresponds to MBTI® research and is presented as one of many examples favorable for that type.

PERSONALITY MATCH

ISTJ	ISFJ	INFJ	INTJ
ISTP	ISFP	INFP	INTP
ESTP	ESFP	ENFP	ENTP
ESTJ	ESFJ	ENFJ	ENTJ

ENFJ will find one of the eight **Foreign Languages** a desirable course of study with any choice of major. Typically astute with languages, a second or third language magnifies the power of this articulate type. The Language Learning Center offers lessons for undergraduate students. ENFJs will be well positioned with this major to pursue graduate work in disciplines that typically interest them: communication, education and counseling.

ENTJ is going to like the practical idea of combining the **Asian Traditions** minor with their declared major. Both courses in Modern China and Modern Japan will position this student for 21st century careers in emerging markets. The five required courses are interdisciplinary and chosen from five academic fields. It all makes sense for this type who wants to make things happen. ENTJs are likely to appreciate the sound practicality here.

ESFJ will readily approve of lifetime fitness through physical exercise and activity. Muhlenberg requires all students to take the **Principles of Fitness and Wellness** course. It connects the dots between exercise and achieving "the highest potential of personal well being." The excellent athletic facilities are equally matched by students' enthusiasm for their athletes, club sports and NCAA competitive teams. Travel and service are preferred activities for ESFJs. The major in **Italian Language and Literature** could be ideal for career tracks in international tourism, language translation and the arts. Being sound and fit, ESFJs can handle the rigors of air travel.

ESTJ with a mind for numbers will totally like the Accounting Department. With an eye to the international nature of finances, the department encourages a study abroad at University of Maastricht in the Netherlands in approved business courses. **Accounting** majors can seek the certified public accounting credential by completing extra credits in the department on campus or transfer into a Master of Science in Accounting degree at a nearby university.

ENFP will be able to take advantage of their warm persona in the **Media and Communication** major. This major introduces students to the pervasive presence of media messaging in our culture today. Media theories and application compose the second focus in the major with courses like Audience Analysis. Students will also produce media in film, radio, television and/or advertising.

ESFP finds the **Dance** major on this campus congruent with the college's philosophy that athletics and wellness are foundational building blocks in life. This type's energy and enthusiasm would be welcome in the strong dance and theater programs on campus. ESFPs are natural entertainers and will find it easy to connect dance and drama. Double majoring is an option with biology and ESFP may elect **dance therapy** for a career focus.

ISFJ will be comfortable with the minor in **Public Health**. The coursework in the minor prepares ISFJs to enter the helping professions with administrative acumen. The **Education Certificate** at this college is one of the few that purposefully addresses the political realities impacting public education today. The faculty presents the perspective that graduates with this certification have a moral responsibility. Graduates are charged to understand the implications of their work in the classrooms and to advocate for the needs of their students, perhaps as a school nurse.

ESTP is going to take advantage of the undergraduate Muhlenberg Investment Society and the **Finance** major. ESTPs like to acquire skills through experience. Faculty provide undergraduates with a sound understanding of complex financial mechanisms. The department seems to avoid the practice of linking foundational courses with trendy cultural paradigms. The curriculum is without electives that can dilute skills and understanding in this discipline – a discipline which can be punishing in cyclical and bear markets.

NEW YORK UNIVERSITY

22 Washington Square North
New York, NY 10011
Website: www.nyu.edu
Admissions Telephone: 212-998-4500
Undergraduates: 22,498; 9,000 Men, 13,498 Women
Graduates: 22,018

Physical Environment

The physical environment of New York City is part and parcel of the NYU experience. The 22,000 undergraduates at this university place it in a category that can be described as urban education. Urban University could be a second name for NYU. Yet, the university is subject to the troubling national trend of significant male under-representation in its student body. On the way to class students walk in, through and around tall skyscrapers, **negotiating the jamboree** of streets, traffic and people outside the many NYU buildings. There is no traditional, self-enclosed campus and the **14 schools in six different buildings** are accessed by the university bus system and good old fashioned foot work. Students negotiate a **complex physical landscape**. The campus stretches from lower Manhattan to Midtown, with Greenwich Village functioning as the unofficial campus center for students and faculty who use the retail shops and relax at the restaurants.

There are over 400 student clubs on campus and naturally, the city has an equal number of venues within blocks of the dormitories. It attracts **bright, independent, physically and emotionally resilient** students. Some like to take in operas at the Met or legendary plays and musicals on Broadway. Some who are already "citified" become even smarter at navigating urban environs. The city is a research laboratory for the social science majors with its **over-the-top internship** opportunities. The administration and faculty seek to benefit undergrads with limited access to the amazing research labs and research faculty. Undergraduate students showcase their studies in the annual Undergraduate Research Conference, much like students at smaller liberal arts colleges.

Many visiting high school students react to the university and the city together. They either love it or hate it, with nothing in-between. Those who enroll at this **cosmopolitan** university settle in with basic support in one of the first year residential halls. Some will explore the immenseness of NYC for the first time and may like the anonymity of being in a wave of people entering the subway. Yet even the livelier NYU student will find that needed quiet nook in one of the numerous NYU libraries. Successful students engage the city, carve out their places and excitedly tour visiting parents and siblings as upperclassmen.

Social Environment

The name recognition and **excellence** of the academic education attracts students with many different personalities. Each incoming student searches out like-minded friends to form a stable place from which to live in the city and pursue their academic studies. For some people it can be a month's long task to find that close-knit sense of community. Very often the social life and emotional connection to NYU is through the particular department or school a student attends. This is supported by the fact that about a quarter of the students do not live in university housing and disappear into their city apartments after classes. Students in the College of Arts and Sciences come across the greatest variety of individuals in their courses. Tisch School of Art has a very cohesive social scene with the fewest traditional-minded students. Stern School of Business students are likely to take more conservative views. Advising at the university is a process that starts with website instructions on how to find an academic advisor. Remember, this university mirrors the city. There are hundreds of byways.

Like the city, NYU is distinguished by its enrollment of undergraduate students from many ethnicities and **cultural backgrounds**. Approximately one-half of the student body identify themselves as a member of a minority group. On the whole, undergrads are fairly **assertive** individuals able to take advantage of the university's extensive academic offerings. They form a student body of very bright, preppy, funky, funny, actively involved individuals. Aside from the sidewalks connecting the NYU facilities, the extensive physical fitness facility is a magnet and meeting place for all. For some students the social scene revolves around intramural and club sports, for others private parties and the local club scene keeps them so busy that they may need an extra semester to graduate. A few will engage the newly completed Center for Spiritual Life where religious faiths are identified as organizations or clubs. Facebook spirituality and Yoga spirituality are listed as clubs here too.

Compatibility with Personality Types and Preferences

New York University may seem like an enigma. On a first visit the university can seem cold, distant and indifferent. The next visit changes your mind as you see the careful wrap-around services and academic attention given to the students by the administration and faculty. It is indicative of how the university grew as the city's namesake and was always tuned to the city population and city needs. As expected, the resources of this world-class city extend into and throughout the university which offers 2,500 courses of instruction. NYU accommodates most personality preferences with an exceptional selection of learning options and degrees. The student who comes to NYU already is, or wants to become, swanky in the current and classic sense.

The required list of core courses, as outlined in the Morse Academic Plan, guides students in the classics during the first two years. The faculty utilize statistical data to objectively view social issues as presented in the classics and ancient thought. The curriculum goes to considerable length to reveal what the limits of that objective approach can be (T). The graduate of NYU is also going to explore how the written word in historical texts creates society (N). Both this study of objectivity and the creation of society are highly abstract and not often featured in required core courses at universities. Similarly, the NYU website featured a compelling video on the use of mathematics. That portrait of the math discipline, as it applied to future America, could entice a student to declare the math major. The student who is most successful here will find those exceptional professors and enroll in their majors. All must cope with the demands of the city however (S) and must glide across the millions of steps on city sidewalks seeking out those exceptional cultural offerings hidden within.

In the following listing of college majors it is important to remember that students can fit into any college and can be successful in any major. We have found that the Personality Types below fit very well at this college. The course-of-study chosen for each Personality Type corresponds to MBTI® research and is presented as one of many examples favorable for that type.

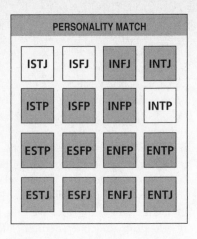

INFJ can bring their insights to **Medieval and Renaissance Studies**. This major will occupy INFJs as they ponder the decades of time between these two distinct periods. Their careful expertise in the discipline will be in demand if they pursue internships in archival work places, likely right in New York City.

ENTJ may pursue **European and Mediterranean Studies.** The department offers a five-year BA/MA and a political science focus. High powered ENTJs can secure internships with international organizations in the city, possibly the United Nations. Diplomacy may be an area of interest because of the inherent power and need for decisive leadership in the career field. ENTJ may select the European language of greatest utility for their intended career track, or perhaps add a second.

ENFP has the big picture and abstract perspectives that it takes for the curriculum in **Metropolitan Studies** at NYU. For those who pursue this interdisciplinary major, careers materialize in the not-for-profit, public administration and government planning sectors. This is fortunate because ENFPs like to solve problems and consider a variety of solutions and may just pursue each of these career tracks.

ENFJ likes to be independent and yet in close empathy with others. The degree in **Sociology** at NYU is so credible because of the hundreds of ethnic languages. ENFJs will combine their interests with societal needs and pursue research topics in this underappreciated discipline. Much of the curriculum is focused on American culture and its shortcomings. ENFJ pursuing an international career track may have to propose a strand of research that identifies social inequalities in other cultures or nations of interest to them.

INTJ and NYU are a delightful combination of letters. This type will jump right into questioning the historical texts and the art forms that are studied in the core courses. Beyond that, the field of **Economics** offers limitless speculation with hard, factual data to power INTJ innovations. This all works for these private, power house thinkers. The department offers two tracks, the more practical policy concentration and the more abstract theory concentration which INTJs will likely explore first.

ENTP absolutely enjoys the idea of the Mind. Powerful thinkers in their own right but not particularly verbally savvy; others sometimes miss ENTP's penetrating, original perspectives. There is a very good interdisciplinary major for this type, titled **Language of the Mind**. It crisscrosses through linguistics, philosophy and psychology. ENTPs will puzzle at night, quietly, to interface these disparate disciplines. With much practice, they will capture the dreamy ideas the next morning for class.

Language is precise at its basic, but linguistics interfaces meaning through the philosophy and psychology courses grounded in this major.

ESTJ can bring their quick, crisp decision making to the health field with a degree in **Neural Science.** This degree focuses on one of the new frontiers: the brain. NYU has the resources and the medium to grow both ideas and biological cells as this science moves forward. Large, expansive, roaming NYU will sometimes challenge this type, but this major will provide refuge with its science base.

ESFJ will be the lucky child who studies **Psychology** at NYU. The department is exceptionally focused yet intentional in its excellent survey of this evolving field for the undergraduate students. Courses in the natural sciences, social sciences and lab research really round out the foundational studies. Research seeking to understand human personality abounds at NYU. This type likes to deliver personal services in schools, hospitals or community health centers. NYU has a fine observatory for studying individuals within the larger community: New York City.

ESTP just might decide the BS in **Computer Science** at NYU offers the efficiency they like. The degree is tailor-made for ESTP who might meet the requirements for the degree in three undergraduate years. This would leave a couple semesters to enjoy the Morse plan academic options and have fun in the city. ESTPs with 4 or 5 on their AP language exam may opt out of the foreign language requirement.

ESFP could select a minor in **Biology** at NYU since it will allow them to explore career tracks that interface human health and preventative medicine. ESFPs might respond to the growing need for specialists in addiction research. The NYU national research laboratories in genetics inform the entire department with evolving knowledge. ESFP can find that firsthand experience they prefer with summer undergraduate studies in this department with successful application for the available positions.

ISFP could bring their special talents to the curriculum in **Urban Design and Architecture Studies.** The course work at the elective level will delight thoughtful ISFPs who prefer to work with real services/products for real people. These titles bring smiles to the face: Parks, Plants and People, Reading the City and Architecture in New York: Field (Fun) Study. Careers that come to mind in museums, conservation, city and metropolitan planning and historical preservation would appeal to ISFPs.

ISTP understands the value of a minor in **Physics**. In fact, it probably appeals to this type so handy with physical and mechanical properties. The minor complements many other concentrations in the sciences, math and engineering. Independent and objective, ISTP can sit back for the first two years filling the core courses while picking up the physics minor. Junior and senior years can be reserved for completing the major concentration.

INFP with the love of books may decide to pursue a minor in **Irish Studies** at NYU. In addition to the mythic Irish qualities, the poetry and drama often laced throughout their history will very much appeal to this type. Perhaps INFP will move toward the career of librarian or research specialist. This potential focus will definitely take great advantage of NYU's unusual archival collection in Irish Americana. The distinguished professors on faculty, specialists in Irish studies, will come to know and warm up to the INFP.

NORTHEASTERN UNIVERSITY

360 Huntington Avenue
Boston, MA 02115
Website: www.nnortheastern.edu
Admissions Telephone: 617-373-8780
Undergraduates: 16,685; 8,305 Men, 8,380 Women
Graduates: 7,855

Physical Environment

Northeastern University is located in that part of Boston defined by the Huntington and Mass Ave intersection. It's extremely **accessible** by both the MBTA subway trains, which stop right on campus, and the trolley that runs on a continuous loop on Huntington Avenue. Distinction between the city and the university is thin with approximately 17,000 undergraduate students on campus alone. The main campus looks a bit like a business park with modern buildings, cobble-stoned walkways and high rise elevations. The campus perimeter is **asymmetrical, like Boston,** because it borders other colleges and is divided by a busy avenue. Northeastern's new Science and Engineering research facility opening in Fall 2016 will expand the physical science curriculum and opportunities for undergraduate internships in the city. The effect of this physical environment for undergraduate students is to subliminally remind them that they are preparing for the real **world of employment**. On Northeastern's campus they will become comfortable **navigating the crowded cityscape** and the buildings in the financial districts. Co-ops and internship programs in Boston also blur the line between university and city.

A favorite for all students is the Curry Student Center, renovated in 2012, which stays open in late evening for students who are together absorbed with iPhones, iPads and hanging out. As Northeastern grew, more residential complexes were added around its perimeter including the Marino Athletic center. Undergrads readily embrace the **urban lifestyle** of Boston, retreating to recharge in the evenings in comfortable college facilities that mirror the city just on the other side of the avenue. Some develop business and individual personas that match the offices of their co-op experience.

Social Environment

Northeastern started out as the first American branch of the YMCA in the very late 1800s. Young men attended YMCA talks and used its library. The university has re-invented itself many times over since then. Present day NU is all about productivity and **emerging entrepreneurial phenomena**. The College of Arts Media and Design sponsors an annual Global Game Jam where undergrads from international campuses compete at developing digital games with one common theme. Most undergrads come from suburban areas of New England and find the expected ethnic representation within the student body that most large, international cities draw. Some continue service through the campus clearing house which is a lengthy list of opportunities to volunteer within the city.

Socially, they get involved in clubs, activities and sports. Some really jump into student government and leadership activities, honing their skills for similar positions after graduation. The college plays at the Division I level and students like to watch the Huskies basketball games. **Personal fitness, intramurals** and **club sports** have a good presence on the campus with four separate facilities and multiple classes and groups to join.

On this campus all undergraduates will explore their personal expectations in relationship to work and career. Students and parents are attracted by the robust co-op program. It offers **excellent job experience** and occasionally a paid position, often during the summer. These field experiences start early in the sophomore year and are frequent to the point that most Northeastern students graduate in five years, instead of four. Yet, students must be motivated to find such work during the co-op terms. Most students secure enough real work experience to successfully enter the job market on graduation. Although with the extended weak economy, they may be underemployed like many in the Millennial generation.

Compatibility with Personality Types and Preferences

Northeastern University is true to its history of preparing students for employment and careers. The modern urban setting of this campus adds credibility to the college promise. Students and faculty are in agreement that emerging skills and capabilities are desired. These are acquired through a sequential learning (S) process, typically involving direct work experience. As Bostonians, and Americans for that matter, become absorbed with smart phones for information and entertainment, the lines blur. Not lost to NU, this entrepreneurial campus expanded its digital arts with six separate majors in the field and several more interdisciplinary studies involving digital arts. The mentoring and advising relationship between the faculty and students (F) is carefully conducted. Students at Northeastern enroll to acquire expertise and professors have this knowledge to provide. The faculty-student advising is reciprocal and dynamic. It generates its own information set which reflects Boston's economy. The university is very much in tune with the city's financial fortunes. Energy flows between the students, faculty and city giving the student's day an outward feel (E) of productive, purposeful activity. Students are drawn to this energy and learn to manage studies, city internships, personal health and fitness with the persistent call of the vibrant Boston social scene.

Undergraduate student leadership is adept at sizing up opportunities for service learning in nearby communities. Volunteer service to the community is encouraged by scholarship grants for those who apply. Boston's mega building boom this past decade found thousands of NU undergrads in the middle of the mix through their internships and co-ops. Productivity, productivity, productivity as they say.

In the following listing of college majors it is important to remember that students can fit into any college and can be successful in any major.

PERSONALITY MATCH			
ISTJ	ISFJ	INFJ	INTJ
ISTP	ISFP	INFP	INTP
ESTP	ESFP	ENFP	ENTP
ESTJ	ESFJ	ENFJ	ENTJ

We have found that the Personality Types below fit very well at this college. The course-of-study chosen for each Personality Type corresponds to MBTI® research and is presented as one of many examples favorable for that type.

ISTP will be intrigued by the **Music Composition and Technology** program at Northeastern. It connects the aural tones of music with the logic of computers and sound equipment. ISTP takes in information through their senses and thinks with it logically. In this case, musical patterns, tones and rhythms are interfaced with software. The degree requires music composition and this type could compose a kaleidoscope of notes into a pleasing musical track.

ISTJ often has the attraction for details in the business world. The degree in Business Administration at Northeastern has seven robust concentrations. In fact, the college encourages undergraduates to select two concentrations or add a minor from other disciplines. ISTJs could declare **Finance** which explores accounting principles, economic theory and quantitative methods in tracking money as it is acquired and distributed. On this campus there will be a course in Bitcoin and possibly a few more courses added after the first. This suits ISTJ who is thorough and knowledgeable.

ISFJ likes research combined with structure and some level of predictability. The concentration in **Criminology and Public Policy** very much orients itself to prevention through structure and predictability. Students find the curriculum centering on the criminals and the institutions, organizations and communities that unknowingly enable crime. The major requires knowledge of current social research. Establishing personal connections with others in this humanely-oriented career track is much preferred by this type.

ISFP is an active soul that enjoys the outdoors for the most part. The combined major in **Environmental Studies** and **Environmental Geology** can certainly accommodate. It all appeals to ISFP's boots-on approach to learning. They are good at discerning the impact of human activity on the physical environment. They have the technical predisposition to excel in the geology courses and labs which utilize a fair amount of equipment.

ESTP has a fine memory for details and they miss very few if it interests them. The business degree with a concentration in **Accounting** may seem a little dry on first pass. However, that is misleading, especially at Northeastern University where ongoing interface with the career field reveals the increasing responsibility and power that is conferred on accountants. This suits ESTP who also likes to be where the action level is high. As an accountant or chief operating officer, ESTPs bring commitment to getting past problems with an acute awareness of the issue at hand. There are internships available just a few T stops away on the subway in the financial district.

ESFP is a creative soul and this might easily be channeled into music. The major in **Music Industry** at Northeastern is ideal for this type. The department takes advantage of the social network between Northeastern and the city of Boston. The city offers much entertainment for the 20-something crowd and ESFPs excel at entertainment. In the process, they will gain the skills and network to secure a position within this major industry, perhaps in Nashville, Orlando or maybe with Apple iTunes.

ESFJ will really approve of Northeastern's emphasis on community service and awareness of urban needs just outside the multi-storied dormitories of this tall, compact campus. This type enjoys bringing information and coordination to the work environment. They are very social and often combine this ease with their attention to detail. The major in **Organizational Communication** is a discipline that would interest and make sense to them. The degree easily prepares ESFJs for public relations positions in large organizations, business, government, teaching, etc.

ESTJ is usually comfortable in positions of authority. They tend to be natural administrators. ESTJs could declare the business major with a concentration in **Supply Chain Management**. This type will analyze objective data with ease in relation to critical resource allocation. Advanced study and certification can lead to powerful positions within manufacturing enterprises. Northeastern University is ideal for helping ESTJs orient to differing perspectives on productivity.

ENFJ is most enthusiastic when working on behalf of others in friendly supportive work places. This type also likes to generate creative solutions with the big picture in mind. The major in **Human Services** at Northeastern offers it all. The major is also paired in a dual degree with **American Sign Language**. Obviously this would move ENFJ into the world of hearing-impaired. At the same time, it could take advantage of the type's natural language ability and skill in communicating causes they believe in.

ENTJ will thrive in active Boston and on the Northeastern campus. This type would do well to merge the concentration in **Management Information Systems** with coursework in entrepreneurship also offered at the university. The major provides study of databases, integration and design with digital media and electronic business. In conjunction with the extensive offerings in the College of Arts and Media at Northwestern, this is an ideal major at the ideal college for this type. The entrepreneurial side of information technology comes naturally to ENTJ.

NORTHWESTERN UNIVERSITY

633 Clark Street
Evanston, IL 60208
Website: www.northwestern.edu
Admissions Telephone: 847-491-7271
Undergraduates: 8,406; 4,121 Men, 4,285 Women
Graduate Students: 8,648

Physical Environment

Northwestern University is located 12 miles **north of Chicago**, on the banks of Lake Michigan. Construction since 2000 has emphasized horizontal design, open atriums and of course, sweeping inside and outside lake views. The latest structure about to open in Fall 2015 is a delightful building set on the edge of the lake. From ground level it calls up the image of a cruise ship. Fun and inviting just looking at, it will provide 140 practice rooms for music majors. Each with a window, perhaps they are the cruise ship cabins? A second huge structure just in the ground breaking stage is the Global Hub, a multipurpose space for international conferences and undergraduate classrooms. As the campus expands, students take to their bikes and the hardy may still use them in winter weather, when the walkways are scrupulously snow plowed.

Northwestern offers popular majors in **business** and **journalism**. Significantly expanded in Fall 2012, the **Technological Institute Infill** now offers students analytic labs for **biomedical research** and a clean room. The Institute is perched on the edge of a foot path for passersby to view inside. The casual glance showcases the potential for rich learning experiences within. The "**Rock**" is near and dear to the students' hearts and gets painted pretty much every night with promotional slogans or to announce an upcoming event. This tradition of 100+ years is now enhanced with a webcam view that is refreshed each five minutes. How about that for getting the word out?

Social Environment

Students accepted to Northwestern are attracted to the **well-resourced schools** within the university. The vibrant, outgoing faculty also calls out to prospective students. There are **fascinating research designs** within all of the departments. In many ways the words **best, biggest and bold** apply here. Not affiliated with any religious faith at its founding, the university adopted the motto "Whatsoever Things Are True." In search of the Whatsoever, individual faculty members may be in the national news for research discoveries, and occasionally for pushing at the edges of society. It is not out of the ordinary for Northwestern administration to explain just exactly what their professors were doing. Early 2014 found their football team quarterback requesting union representation. This became national news as a **radical approach** to undergraduate collegiate sports. Presently the university is examining the life of one of the Northwestern founding father's, John Evans. A civic leader in his time, the namesake of Evanston IL, he also founded the University of Denver, the Illinois Medical Society and was instrumental in founding Lakeside Hospital. He served as governor of the Colorado territories.

Northwestern attracts students who relate to best, biggest and bold in all they do. The student body is active, energetic and optimistic. They want **the full college experience**. Along with the Division I athletics, the performing arts are a big part of the culture here. The **Greek life** is vibrant and Greek chapter houses are involved in scholarship, fundraising and civic initiatives. In 1975, ATO men's fraternity and the student government founded the **Dance Marathon** to raise funds for local charities. Since that start, they have raised 14 million dollars. Equally impressive, there are about 30 student-led Christian groups of **faith** at Northwestern including the Korean Christian Fellowship, Chinese Christian Fellowship, Adventist Student Association and Asian American Intervarsity Christian fellowship. There are also student groups for each of the world's major religions. **Spirituality and optimism** have a solid presence among the students at Northwestern University.

Compatibility with Personality Types and Preferences

Northwestern University has an expectant feel to it. A walk through the campus reveals a very large physical facility. The open spaces between buildings are filled with energetic, purposeful students moving toward their next destination. That might be a class, research lab, social club or internship since rest and relaxation is probably allocated to the middle of the night and weekend mornings. These students are engaged (E) and interested in connecting with each other. There is a sense of expectancy.

Educational study, casual conversation and academic discussion with other like-minded movers and shakers is common. The purpose is to gather up and digest (T) knowledge. This is to prepare the graduate for a professional position, preferably as a leader within their career field. Political passion within the school and department faculties at Northwestern University is very strong. It translates into firm positions on the emerging cultural topics. Traditional perspectives are not noticeable, but rather there is an undercurrent of change for present day American society.

Students who are successful at Northwestern select their major with certainty. The schools of engineering, journalism, communication, education and music are very visible and accessible to the whole undergraduate student body through introductory and elective courses. Undergraduate academic policies within each of these specialized schools reaches out and encourages the undecided student to identify and align toward their department or major. Students typically bring intensity to their major once identified. Northwestern University is mindful of their ability to inform the public square and they do so regularly.

In the following listing of college majors it is important to remember that students can fit into any college and can be successful in any major. We have found that the Personality Types below fit very well at this college. The course-of-study chosen for each Personality Type corresponds to MBTI® research and is presented as one of many examples favorable for that type.

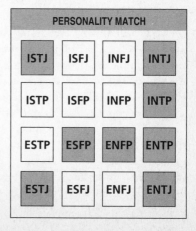

PERSONALITY MATCH

ISTJ	ISFJ	INFJ	INTJ
ISTP	ISFP	INFP	INTP
ESTP	ESFP	ENFP	ENTP
ESTJ	ESFJ	ENFJ	ENTJ

INTJ would find a strong element of design in the school of engineering. They might enjoy the **Manufacturing and Design Engineering** program because it expects and requires innovation. Product design interfaces with many of the engineering projects and the Segal Institute of Design is often in the mix. Yet their recent penguin shoe that made the cover of the Chicago Tribune would not require much in the way of manufacture.

ISTJ will find the **Civil Engineering** degree at Northwestern ideal for their duty-bound personality. The department focuses on the pervasive problems of mega metropolitan centers like safe drinking water, dependable energy, efficient transportation and waste disposal systems. You go ISTJ, we need your talents, your leadership and your duty bound personalities in charge of our growing cities.

INTP will find the degree in **Chemical and Biological Engineering** filled with the underlying principles of physical properties in matter. Wow. This is just what this intense thinker is liable to take on during undergraduate studies. Fortunately, the entire campus, including this department, is going to facilitate an easy, gentle introduction to this difficult discipline. Only in the upperclass studies will INTP get into research involving polymer science and nano technology.

ESFP and the **Certificate in Design** is a happenin' combination. Yes, this type is excellent at interpreting comfortable interior spaces. Social ESFP will find enthusiastic, adaptable faculty. Their penchant for movement and activity could translate into a degree in transportation engineering possibly. The Segal Institute of Design takes its rightful place in Chicago's extraordinary history of architecture and design.

ENFP will enjoy the solid foundation in the **Art Theory and Practice** major. Talent and Type are separate to be sure, but the ENFP with talent will do well finding their way into this degree. ENFP will have to stand in line with those who show up for the introductory courses. Once a place is secured in the course, they will appreciate the fine foundational courses offered in this department. How about a couple of electives over in the Segal Institute of Design?

ENTP is attracted to the sciences and the program in **Integrated Sciences** offers the big, overarching picture they look for when taking in volumes of knowledge. It offers a swell foundation for the next step in graduate studies. ENTP is attracted to power and comfortable in those positions. How about a Churchill fellowship after graduation? This type can find a connection between Winston's values of freedom and fear of tyranny and foundational science.

ESTJ will like the orderly way the Department of **Biology** presents this wide-ranging, evolving discipline. Students are first grounded in foundational knowledge, then emerging knowledge through exposure to current research studies. Undergrads then concentrate in one of five subspecialties. ESTJ may elect the Plant Biology track. Currently, few Millennials are entering Ph.D. graduate study of crop invasion by insects. With eminent baby boomers retiring the field is wide open.

ENTJ could select the minor in **Transportation and Logistics**. This type is often successful in complex manufacturing environments. ENTJs would like their efforts to bring order to the disorganized world they perceive. The nature of this career field requires analytic thinking and a willingness to take calculated risks. Both of these are characteristic of ENTJs who will use this minor study profitably in the long term.

NOTRE DAME UNIVERSITY

South Bend, IN 46556
Website: www.nd.edu
Admissions Telephone: 574-631-7505
Undergraduates: 8,462; 4,523 Men, 3,939 Women
Graduate Students: 3,478

Physical Environment

The Notre Dame campus opens up to velvet lawns, tall trees and a straight path to the **gold-domed** administration building that can't be missed. It's a mystical sight, flanked by the **Basilica**, with pealing bells that ring throughout the day. The statue of the founder, Father Edward Sorin, in friar's garb, stands facing the gold dome. No wonder Notre Dame students call themselves "Domers." Students are attracted to the grandeur of the architecture that appears to be devoted to the power of God more than the power of humanity. This campus has age and character with 1,250 acres and main entrances punctuating stone walls that define the campus perimeter.

Large numbers of influential **alumni** groups come into town for football weekends, staying in the newly developed south side of town. Prospective students take notice and appreciate this renovated section of the city. Undergraduates remain on campus for the most part because the **Notre Dame campus facilities** are over the top. The Compton Family Ice Arena follows in this over the top tradition. The bookstore is the extra large version of Barnes & Noble in your local neighborhood, well stocked with philosophical tomes to read at leisure.

Notre Dame football has a life of its own. The football stadium is another signature facility that preserves tradition at this university. Its stadium, renovated in the 90s, seats 80,000 fans and showcases the Notre Dame marching band, with its bagpipes and fiddles, featured on national TV during televised games. They even beat the 2014 Rose Bowl champs.

Social Environment

Compared to their peers at other liberal arts universities across the nation, "Domers" here are in the middle of the road with their political views. They are traditional, endorsing their **Catholic faith**, but there are also some liberal Catholic views on this campus. Students might find the familiar religious practices and teachings of their home parishes or might not. Regardless, these undergraduates are **confident** in their abilities and work very hard. On the weekend they play hard. Students are comfortable joining this proud, vibrant and **well-established community** and find fun traditions within the single-sex undergraduate dormitories and the restaurants on the campus. The university is successful at countering the troubling national trend of male under-representation in college over the past 20 years.

The majority of students come from public high school and one-quarter are ethnic minorities and first-generation. There are hundreds of student clubs which communicate with a blizzard of notices posted just inside the halls on the way to the dining rooms. Friendships are formed and grow in the 29 residence halls. Most live on campus for four years. The residences become part of a student's identity on campus which is fostered by the 'stay hall' system. If a student lives in North quad he's loyal to the North environs and activities. However, there are also hundreds of well-supported student groups, and one of our favorites is the Big Yellow Taxi. Another focused on childhood cancer, the Bald and Beautiful Club is representative of the social concern prevalent in the student body.

The ethos of Notre Dame revolves around **strong academics**, mighty athletics, thoughtful religious and service initiatives. There is a clear representation of the whole in the Notre Dame collegiate family: students, fans, parents, alumnae, the priests and the administration. Well-connected and well-known alumni in entertainment and media secure access to celebrity speakers for campus events. The clear expectation of graduates is for success and service to others, in part by leveraging the powerful Notre Dame network.

Compatibility with Personality Types and Preferences

Notre Dame is a reflection in reason (T) and community. The community takes on many layers of meaning at Notre Dame. At the most reflective level, it relates to the larger community of mankind as evolved in the Bible from Adam and Eve through Jesus Christ. That is pretty reflective. At the most obvious level, community means the present day campus environment. At its core, education at Notre Dame means service to the community, and the purpose of the service is to bring justice to the community. Social justice is approached via contemporary American political trends. President Obama spoke at the university shortly after his first inauguration. His strong support for abortion became an immediate subject of controversy within the larger Notre Dame community as briefly reported in the press. The Orestes Brownson Council on Catholicism and American Politics, a student group, focuses on these turbulent political currents so prevalent in the nation now. Legal challenges to this administration's policies are continually in front of the Supreme Court and likely in discussion at the Orestes Brownson council.

In respect to the daily educational experience at Notre Dame, faculty and departments are very much connected to the present day world of careers and vocations (S). Undergraduates find much academic depth and familiarity in the structure (J) of the curriculum. The First Year of Studies ensures comprehensive knowledge of Notre Dame's educational options as well as professional advising for all incoming freshmen. At the completion of the first year, students move into upper level programs and courses with confidence as a result of this professional advising experience. "Domers" are both academically and socially gregarious in the Notre Dame community (E) and beyond.

In the following listing of college majors it is important to remember that students can fit into any college and can be successful in any major.

PERSONALITY MATCH			
ISTJ	ISFJ	INFJ	INTJ
ISTP	ISFP	INFP	INTP
ESTP	ESFP	ENFP	ENTP
ESTJ	ESFJ	ENFJ	ENTJ

We have found that the Personality Types below fit very well at this college. The course-of-study chosen for each Personality Type corresponds to MBTI® research and is presented as one of many examples favorable for that type.

ENFJ with the big picture perspective fits in nicely within health science career tracks. The program here in **Preprofessional Studies** allows ENFJs to study and research their interests in biology in preparation for follow on graduate studies. The program further offers three sequences, science-business, science-computing or science-education. It suits this type to be improving the quality of life for others which nicely pairs with Notre Dame's sense of community.

ENTJ is OK being the center of attention, especially if leadership is involved. **Theatre** at Notre Dame gives this type the opportunity to be innovative. Access to the business side of the entertainment industry, after graduation through an MBA, would also appeal to this type's appreciation for power positions. The major offers three concentrations: film, TV or theater.

ENTP will like Notre Dame's interdisciplinary minor in **Journalism, Ethics and Democracy** because it combines politics and communication. This type will be at ease in the world of ideas and could easily gravitate to the concept of promoting those concepts. Through 2012, the Red Smith lecture series featured mostly well-known journalists of similar liberal views in this department. ENTP is an original and can supplement this curriculum with their willingness to listen to news sources across the political spectrum out of curiosity.

ESTJ often relates to cause-and-effect reasoning. The degree in **Electrical Engineering** is ideal for ESTJs because electricity is predictable. Even though this degree requires very complex math acumen, ESTJs will not retreat as long as they also have the ability in math. At Notre Dame, there are optional concentrations in semiconductors and nanotechnology, biosystems, multimedia and communications. This degree offers ESTJ a structured set of courses to more specifically explore career options within the discipline.

ISTJ likes Notre Dame's expectation that engineering graduates will become technical leaders because this type is, above everything else, accurate and precise. The **Mechanical Engineering** degree nicely translates into exacting work expectations. Moving metal parts either fit together or they don't. Critical operations on the space station are about parts in the right tolerance. This all makes perfect sense to ISTJ, who might decide to write an optional thesis.

ESFJ can enjoy the business world as long as their responsibilities directly include serving their clients and customers. The degree at Notre Dame in **Marketing** encourages second majors or minors that explore and expand the students' prospective career track. ESFJs might select the interdisciplinary minor in **Education, Schooling and Society** that explores social values while finding that interface with business practices.

ISFJ can prepare for a couple of work environments at once with the sequence in **Science-Business** at Notre Dame University. This type is often found in health care industry assisting others with technical and practical information. The background gained in this sequence could find ISFJ on the sales force servicing medical centers, home and assisted-living care locations. The degree also prepares ISFJ to move on to an MBA and enter a career track in hospital administration.

ESTP may be interested in Notre Dame's **Management Entrepreneurship** major. It places emphasis on bringing innovation to products and services within the frame work of the start up business. This is a risk environment and ESTPs are often OK with risk taking. The emphasis on skills and experience within this curriculum is ideal for this type. They can learn to gauge qualified vs. unqualified risk from the financial and legal standpoints.

ISTP usually up for a contest in the physical sciences is going to approve of **Civil Engineering** at Notre Dame. The optional course titled Big Beam Contest is a definite must-have elective. The undergrads collaborate in teams, a natural activity for this flexible, passionate type. OK, they are passionate about technology, not life's issues. ISTP is also likely to assume the leadership on the team.

OBERLIN COLLEGE

Office of Admission
101 North Professor Street
Oberlin, OH 44074
Website: www.oberlin.edu
Admissions Telephone: 440-775-8411
Undergraduates: 2,861; 1,300 Men, 1,561 Women

Physical Environment

Oberlin College has a heavy sense of history portrayed in its architecture. Facilities were designed for a purpose and with efficiency in mind well before the current sustainable movement in architecture. There is red brick, yellow brick, stone, 1950s, domes, 1990s, 1980s design, it's all here, living together comfortably on this campus Given time for reflection, the architecture speaks to an **idealism of utility.** Students seeking this will not be disappointed.

There is a strong synergy between the college and the immediate region. The **Oberlin Project** is a decades long business plan to reach 70 percent **sustainability** within the immediate geographic region. This landscape also includes generations of Amish farmers. The impressive Oberlin Project goal includes infrastructure, training, education, workforce development and entrepreneurial organization. It expects to become a **climate positive city**, essentially researching sustainable practices presently unknown. This campus draws students who are comfortable with the words radical and different.

Oberlin's president took a radical step forward in early 2014 disagreeing with a complex progressive agenda that acted out across liberal arts campuses with support in U.S. Congress. On this campus, radical speech, conservative speech and progressive speech get their allotted time on the soapbox.

The Center for Environmental Studies sports solar panels, bio-degradable materials and a natural, self-sustaining greenhouse. Administration and faculty pursue efficient utilization at considerable monetary investment such as newly installed geo-thermal wells and mechanicals operated by stringent climate controls. Solar arrays constructed on campus in 2012 are another example of investment. Covering 10 acres of land, they are providing knowledge and experience needed to successfully complete assessment objectives of Project Oberlin.

The Allen Art museum holds several rare collections in art and Greek statuary, historic treasures are in safe keeping and students enjoy classes within the renovated Art Museum. The **music conservatory** is now bolstered by the Kohl Building, opened in spring 2010 which houses the jazz department along with a priceless collection of jazz memorabilia. Conservatory students form a tight knit group reaching for superlative musical performance.

Social Environment

Oberlin students arrive with an interesting list of assets, both academic and personal. **Independence and efficiency** are highly prized living skills among these **resolute** students. The collegiate environment truly meets the expectations of the student body and the long Ohio winters do not prevent students from living their own, unique lifestyle. The phrase going off the grid comes to mind. Undergrads are **free-spirited**, rarely impacted by marketing of the materialistic lifestyle, big box stores or fashion labels. They are avant-garde types who typically remain so after graduation. They strive to be accomplished, intensely academic, yet not competitive with one another.

The most popular cause is that of service and it is intertwined with sustainability. Volunteerism and service learning in the surrounding communities seek to promote individual independence so prized on this campus. On today's campus, Oberlin students prefer to combine reality with their **alternative viewpoints**. Studying abroad coming into contact with severe poverty in other countries, brings new energy and support for the concepts behind Project Oberlin. In this intellectually-charged atmosphere, students absorb and reformulate ideas. It may lead to activist causes on graduation, guided by a **unified vision** of how society should work.

Housing options are really quite varied. Freshmen live in traditional dormitories. Upperclass students might choose the Victorian homes where undergraduates **share responsibility** for planting vegetables, planning meals, buying the food and cooking. In some houses students create a commune-like atmosphere. There are eight co-ops of this type, with a waitlist and application to become a member. True to Oberlin's ethos, these houses are independent, not affiliated with the college.

Compatibility with Personality Types and Preferences

Oberlin College brings to mind the word alternative, but not in the sense of fashion. Educational philosophy here is about shining a bright light on organizational practice that is viewed as wasteful of human potential. As a result, the range and approach to educational studies is wide open. This intense intellectual environment leans heavily toward a future orientation (N). After all, significant change requires planning for the future. Productive change is not often accomplished in the present.

Students here are very capable of dissecting a verbal argument in a precise way (T). This is certainly their inclination, and they favor learning in this manner. With background provided by their advanced high school courses, they arrive on Oberlin's campus ready to be engaged in their passions. Oberlin undergraduates carefully study the present day body of knowledge in the field of their interests. This serves two purposes, the obvious reason being pure and simple knowledge. The second reason is to discern the shortcomings in that field. Once the deficiencies are known, students are then inclined to identify systems of thought and lines of research to overcome or undo those deficiencies. Four years of undergraduate study at Oberlin serves to sharpen commitment for promoting change that translates into sustainable policy and planning for regional communities across the globe.

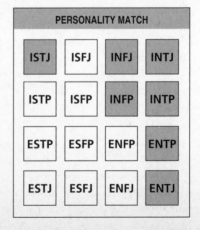

PERSONALITY MATCH

ISTJ	ISFJ	INFJ	INTJ
ISTP	ISFP	INFP	INTP
ESTP	ESFP	ENFP	ENTP
ESTJ	ESFJ	ENFJ	ENTJ

In the following listing of college majors it is important to remember that students can fit into any college and can be successful in any major. We have found that the Personality Types below fit very well at this college. The course-of-study chosen for each Personality Type corresponds to MBTI® research and is presented as one of many examples favorable for that type.

INFJ will appreciate the sophistication and desire for objectivity in Oberlin's course of instruction in **Religion**. This type is often passionate in respect to their beliefs. Integrity is also critically important for INFJs. The department credibly approaches religion in three critical areas not typical of collegiate curriculum: traditional, modern cultural and religion-based. It seems that with spirit and intellectual bravado, this department has avoided current day cultural amorphisms that dilute the nature of theology.

INFP could be fascinated by 21st century emerging knowledge about the human brain. The major in **Neuroscience** at Oberlin College is a great foundation for this type who may become a pioneer pushing the science forward in 2045. INFPs like to come up with original work that is comprehensive and penetrating. Faculty are determined to help undergrads find their niche among the many disciplines it crosses.

ENTJ can study **Physics**, a fundamentally abstract subject, at Oberlin College, yet still prepare for the practical world. The major is a gateway to numerous advanced professional degrees. ENTJs prefer to have work that is acknowledged by others as being important and needed. At Oberlin, students may also find courses in astrophysics and materials physics. Leave it to the competitive ENTJ to figure out a way to generate revenue for their cause, workplace and passion.

INTJ is a perfect fit for Oberlin College in our opinion. This precise thinker is truly capable of peering into the future and crafting a vision. Powerful and single-minded with their original projects, INTJs sometime seem like a freight train on a slow, steady roll. The concentration in **Applied Mathematics** will put them in dynamic collaboration with other students and professors of a similar persuasion at Oberlin College. The department supports using math as a stepping stone to other fields of study. The power of math and the power of the INTJ personality together make for a very astute graduate.

ENTP is interested in so many subjects. What will they be when they grow up? This type will likely try several careers, so an undergraduate degree in history with a good dose of abstract thought is ideal. **Jewish Studies** at Oberlin deliver on both and ENTP will be required to concentrate in religion or history of the Jewish nation. Regardless, awareness of this rich field of knowledge will guide this type to pursue a specific strand of knowledge in graduate study. ENTPs often identify dynamic fields in the social sciences such as economics or political science.

INTP could enjoy the **East Asian Studies** at Oberlin College, a major that attracts many students. This type likes to put patterns together. Astute INTP can find a pattern in chaos or just plain confusion for that matter. They will not shrink from the economic complications of emerging China or resource-constrained Japan. With graduate study in economics, this type could successfully consult on the differing challenges faced by these two nations.

ISTJ might take the major in **Biochemistry** right into the agricultural sciences, a traditional discipline that is becoming critically important. This type has the attention to detail that will be needed to address crop production and land efficiency. ISTJs will be pleased with the department's rigor in the field. The curriculum is noticeably absent of interface with social, trendy topics that divert energy from the difficult work in mastering this subject even at the undergraduate levels. Don't stand in ISTJ's way on the way to class in Quantum Chemistry and Kinetics unless you are sharp enough to catch some of their wry humor as they circumnavigate you.

OCCIDENTAL COLLEGE

Office of Admissions
1600 Campus Road
Los Angeles, CA 90041
Website: www.oxy.edu
Admissions Telephone: 323-259-2500
Undergraduates: 2,113; 924 Men, 1,189 Women

Physical Environment

Occidental College is located in an area called Eagle Rock which was one of the first towns to be founded around Los Angeles in the late 1800s. This area is gentrified with artists and people from various cultures who have settled in to the small houses. The campus is simply in the middle of all **that is Los Angeles**, a bus ride away from numerous internships. The campus has **Mediterranean architecture.** It was designed by Myron Hunt, well-known architect, and is nestled between the **mountains of San Gabriel**. Characterized by many steps and hills within its 120 acres, its historic buildings have received a well-appreciated renovation in the last couple years.

Students are **relaxed and playful** in the welcoming **California weather**. Yet, if the weather becomes arid and exacerbates brush fires in the mountains, the beautiful Gillman fountain at the entrance to the college is turned off, reminding all on campus of the fragile ecosystem. Students enjoy walking to the Johnson Center, a popular meeting place, renovated and reopened in 2013. Swan Hall, renovated and expanded twice its former size, holds one-third of the faculty offices on campus. Thorne Hall is the major auditorium used for the graduation ceremony and **musical** performances. Students are required to reside on campus for the first three years and are assigned to a dormitory by the first year seminar topic they select. In this way, through living-learning residence, faculty and students form familiar, comfortable relationships. There are 13 residence halls, all **governed by students**. The academic buildings and especially the extensive science labs are the settings for **experiential education**. The California Semester is an optional first semester course that brings students into the Los Angeles sprawl to study its natural history and geography over a series of multiple day trips.

Social Environment

Adventuresome students enroll at Occidental College and sign up for classes that may be very challenging, novel or exciting. Oxy students value the **relationship** that they build with their professors and the intellectual stimulation of the classroom. The ethos of this college is "equality for all," "valuing diversity" and "change." Oxy students wear many hats and have **many interests**, from playing Division III athletics to performing arts clubs. In association with the 100-year anniversary of the campus in the Eagle Rock neighborhood, there is a strong movement on campus to capture the history and experiences of students currently attending Oxy. Numerous graduates from decades past were also interviewed in 2012 to record their recollections in an oral history project

There are approximately 100 social groups on campus that **affiliate around specific interests**. Some of the most active organizations are Hillel and Inter-Varsity Christian Fellowship (IVCF). The Greek life at Occidental is well supported by the student body as the chapters actively participate in athletics and other campus causes as well as hosting open social mixers for Greek and non-Greek alike. The performing arts are a staple within the campus community. The dance ensemble is very popular. With two performances annually, it always has sellout crowds. **Dance Production** is put on by the students and features their own choreography and dance routines. Oxy students have developed the weekly campus TV show called CatAList. It features informal, impromptu talent and performance by undergrads on campus. The curriculum prompts personal growth and intentional conversations are familiar during the four-year curriculum. Graduates are preparing to enter the complexity of Los Angeles for careers and to start their adult lives. They know firsthand of the need for skills and **personal goals**.

Compatibility with Personality Types and Preferences

Occidental College focuses much energy toward integrating service learning experiences in Los Angeles' ethnic neighborhoods. Undergraduate students peer through the lens of these L.A. communities seeking world cultural and knowledge. Students sign up for service learning in the city as easily as signing up for a required course in their major. Occidental College and Los Angeles have a blurred boundary line in respect to where the campus stops and the city starts. The administration, faculty and student body are all equally devoted to learning from the metropolis which is viewed as a microcosm of other regions of the U.S.

The nature of this expansive type of learning requires the Occidental community to search out, discover or develop innovative (N) social viewpoints that lead to enterprise such as the student governed Oxy Impact Fund. It invests $3,000 each semester with third world country NGO's. The undergraduate student body and its individual members would hope to see their successful initiatives find a life in community practices throughout the nation. For this reason, the undergraduates at Occidental often translate their values-oriented perspectives into practical plans and initiatives of action (J). In certain ways, the administration pointedly develops a self-governing campus fabric that encourages introspection. Students here move toward personal goals that are accepting of the today's world, tipping their hats to what is practical and possible.

In the following listing of college majors it is important to remember that students can fit into any college and can be successful in any major. We have found that the Personality Types below fit very well at this college. The course-of-study chosen for each Personality Type corresponds to MBTI® research and is presented as one of many examples favorable for that type.

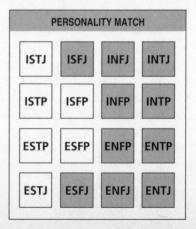

PERSONALITY MATCH

ISTJ	ISFJ	INFJ	INTJ
ISTP	ISFP	INFP	INTP
ESTP	ESFP	ENFP	ENTP
ESTJ	ESFJ	ENFJ	ENTJ

INFP likes the time and solitude to develop their ideas. Those ideas pretty much have to be in harmony with their own belief system that incorporates helping others. The major in **Sociology** at this college is quite robust with nearby multiethnic Los Angeles to serve as a classroom. This is a stepping stone degree to careers in law, social work, journalism, public health, education and, of course, graduate studies in sociology. The faculty offers a rare, yet much needed course in Masculinities, an academic subject which is absent in today's liberal arts curriculums.

INFJ occasionally enters the field of health science research. The Department of Biology here offers an emphasis in **Cell and Molecular Biology.** It is an ideal foundation for advanced graduate study. INFJ will want to peer into the DNA and cell physiology. This type prefers to study alone. The campus is chatty, yet respectful so they will be able to withdraw to quiet spaces on campus as preferred.

INTJ sees far into the unknown and enjoys creating systems that might reveal new information. The major in **Physics** at Occidental College offers further options in chemistry and mathematics. INTJs are prone to scientific research and this degree opens doors in two frontiers, that of geophysics and astrophysics. Geographic features in the LA basin just might influence the decision.

ISFJ will find the study of **Music** at Occidental College ideal because of its location. A great deal of entertainment programming originates in the city, bolstered by nearby Hollywood and broadcast studios. At this college, music is also a major form of relaxation and reason to gather socially for the weekly jazz sessions offered by Oxy students. This strong department offers a breadth of music courses and the city offers the options to observe professional musicians at work. ISFJs gain energy and build resilience with the hands-on activity of the performing musical arts.

INTP will smile at the idea of a minor in **Computer Science.** This type who is drawn to solving puzzles likely could not walk by a table with a Rubik's cube on it without giving it a twist. The skills attained with this minor will bring extra power to solution finding in INTP's major. Biology, chemistry and history each are fields that call out to them and benefit from statistical analysis. Supplemental courses can be taken at the nearby institute of technology also.

ENFP loves to be with and around a wide variety of people. They appreciate and need the various perspectives to energize plans for themselves and others. The degree in **Urban and Environmental Policy** at Occidental College is linked to public affairs and civic action. ENFPs will find this field satisfies their innate curiosity and need for an abstract challenge. Internships will abound in the city of Los Angeles. The major allows for specialization in economics, housing, health, transportation, air/water quality, etc.

ENTP can be attracted to the sciences. The major in **Biochemistry** has a solid foundation for graduate study in a number of follow on fields. As a result, ENTP can take time to explore all the options prior to graduation within the fields of biology and chemistry. Admission to the Keck Graduate Institute is a possibility with this major.

ESFJ is an ideal candidate for the major in **Kinesiology**. ESFJs enjoy and excel at utilizing skills they have learned. They are conscientious and naturally make those around them feel valued and comfortable. This is a science-based discipline that prepares graduates for further study in the health related professions. ESFJs are up for learning and memorizing the sequence of physical movements. They naturally take a personal approach to their work which will help them avoid costly and potentially dangerous errors in directing patients.

ENFJ often enjoys careers associated with counseling. The major in **Psychology** at Occidental can be nicely interfaced with internships in the Los Angeles communities of health providers. There is a senior comprehensive written examination that will draw out this type's expressive inclination. Certainly in this field, that is an important characteristic for professional service providers.

ENTJ will take advantage of careers in the discipline of **Cognitive Science** offered here. It requires coursework in the traditional fields of linguistics, philosophy, psychology, computer science and mathematics. It is an evolving scientific field that offers much challenge and opportunity. ENTJs are naturals at long-range planning, innovative thinking and leadership. This major calls out to them.

PEPPERDINE UNIVERSITY

Seaver College
24255 Pacific Coast Highway
Malibu, CA 90263-4392
Website: www.pepperdine.edu
Admissions Telephone: 310-506-4392
Undergraduates: 3,488; 1,499 Men, 1,989 Women
Graduates: 3,831

Physical Environment

Pepperdine students enjoy breathtaking **views of the Pacific Ocean** and the sunny Malibu beaches. The university is affiliated with the **Church of Christ** and the large majority of the student body seek the many spiritual offerings on campus. Approximately one-half of the students are from California, with another quarter from the western states. International students primarily from the Pacific Basin nations comprise about ten percent. The typically moderate weather and the hills on campus make for a physically active lifestyle. Although directly across from Malibu's surfing beaches, sports and campus recreation programs do not feature water sports.

The physical presence of the campus outwardly speaks to both **spirituality and stewardship of resources**. In today's parlance that is often thought of as sustainability. The university has a comprehensive, ongoing custodial plan that addresses the disposal of all unused resources. Heating, air conditioning and lighting on campus is centrally controlled. All dishware in the dining rooms and snack spots are reusable. Styrofoam is banned from campus. Dining options are not buffet style because of the waste typically encountered in help yourself venues. We outline these practices in detail because they speak to the ethos of the university. All within the realm of the campus environment belongs to God and is treated with spiritual respect.

Social Environment

Pepperdine was founded by a very successful Christian business entrepreneur. Students carry on his legacy by **serving others** through productive enterprises such as non-profit management, service and fundraising. It all mixes quite well with Pepperdine's philosophy of helping others in a contemporary way. Pepperdine is not for students who harbor doubts about religion or **Christianity**, although not everyone is necessarily intensely spiritual. Most students live on campus. Residential dormitories are staffed with a professional Resident Director. Student spiritual life advisors and student resident advisors are assigned to each hall under the mentorship of the resident director. The student advisors provide program and peer support that prompts **holistic growth** within the members of their community.

Student-led ministry is well supported by the administration with budget, facilities and communication services. Students seek to **develop personal skills** and serve others in each of these ministries. Undergraduates may accompany academic staff on service trips to serve impoverished islands in the Pacific Basin. More typically, undergraduates provide direct services to children and adolescents living in Los Angeles shelters, group homes and on the streets. They do this through the supervision of nonprofit organizations resident in the LA neighborhoods and get into the city by public bus.

In these ways students become involved with less participation in traditional social outlets. There's a strong emphasis on clean living and **healthy** eating habits. Dating might lead to marriage following traditional societal values. **Songfest** is a musical talent show put on by the students, hundreds of them, showcasing their performing arts in accompaniment with a professional orchestra. Its always sold out, even with six performances. Optimistic, healthy and caring describe the campus environment.

Compatibility with Personality Types and Preferences

Pepperdine University and Seaver College, for undergraduate students, are exceptionally clear in communicating their educational goals (J). Even the website is easy to use and well organized. A purposeful life is the outcome of education and Pepperdine students reach this goal through reflection, service to others and promoting values which are Christian-centered. The college campus environment is both consistent and caring (F). Practically all of the activities outside of the classroom are driven by humanitarian concerns. The momentum of shared beliefs and cultural campus activities builds contemporary friendships within the student body during the college years. The university predicts these relationships will be life long. Friendship and community is expected to serve as the guidepost for a turbulent American 21st century. All in all, loyal and dedicated students fit in well at the Pepperdine campus. Students who like traditions and people-centered activities in the larger community (E) are also likely to be comfortable here.

In the following listing of college majors it is important to remember that students can fit into any college and can be successful in any major. We have found that the Personality Types below fit very well at this college. The course-of-study chosen for each Personality Type corresponds to MBTI® research and is presented as one of many examples favorable for that type.

PERSONALITY MATCH

ISTJ	ISFJ	INFJ	INTJ
ISTP	ISFP	INFP	INTP
ESTP	ESFP	ENFP	ENTP
ESTJ	ESFJ	ENFJ	ENTJ

ISFJ, often times a reflective and thorough soul, could enjoy the degree in **Liberal Arts** at Pepperdine. This rather unusual degree is rich in the fields of history, culture, sciences and the arts. It is a fine course of study for a student who might want to become an archivist or librarian. It will allow the ISFJ to identify their subject specialty and be well prepared to select an appropriate graduate degree.

ISFP is good at remembering and using information that is practical and useful. This is the right attitude for a **Nutritional Science** Degree. The course titled Communication in Dietetics has a service learning requirement where students learn to counsel, program and evaluate differing dietary problems of those in the nearby community. This type of learning-by-doing is perfect for the ISFP.

INFP hopes to express their inner thoughts with a lot of personal distance between themselves and others. Art serves a wonderful channel for this purpose. If you combine art with words, you have a minor in the Fine Arts department called **Multimedia Design**. An option here at Pepperdine might be to pair a minor in multimedia with a communication major such as journalism. **Rhetoric and Leadership** is another enticing minor available. All are appealing to INFP.

ESTJ is going to get an exceptionally fine **International Business** degree at Pepperdine University. Part of the philosophical core of this campus is to reach out and learn extensively about Pacific Basin cultures. The university has access to many cross-cultural currents because of its location on the coast and proximity to Los Angeles. The exceptional list of courses includes Ethics and International Politics.

ESFJ often enjoys people and it shows through their natural ease and curiosity about others. They typically like to support other people and help them move forward. The minor in **Sports Medicine** is a good choice for this type. The Natural Science Division offers a curriculum that is anchored in personal fitness. Courses in human physiology, anatomy, neuroscience and biomechanics round out the fitness-oriented courses for a well-balanced minor.

ENFJ can jump right into the **Public Relations** degree and find an outlet for their passion and dedication. The degree has both theoretical and practical courses. This type's desire for harmony within the community nicely fits in with the public relations curriculum. Casework presented as actual business problems require students to identify the real motive as well as the most ethical solution.

ENTJ is usually quite extraverted and functions as a go-to-person. If they are gifted with artistic talent, the degree in **Advertising** could be right for this type. Located within 30 minutes of the huge Los Angeles metropolitan area with its extraordinary entertainment industry, there are more than a few exceptional places to secure an internship in advertising. Always remember, however, that talent and Personality type are not connected. Talent would be an inherited gift, while Type is a personality preference that each of us have.

PRINCETON UNIVERSITY

Admission Office
P.O. Box 430
Princeton, NJ 08544-0430
Website: www.princeton.edu
Admissions Telephone: 609-258-3060
Undergraduates: 5,234; 2,667 Men, 2,567 Women
Graduate Students: 2,691

Physical Environment

Princeton is a town that plays host to its namesake university and suburban up-scale neighborhoods with shops that ring the university perimeter. The campus is a mecca for intellectual activity that spills out onto the town through the arts, music and clubs. The town also hosts Dow Jones and Company and Educational Testing Services who offer the SAT instrument which aspiring collegians labor with during their last two years of high school. After office workers go home and the shoppers leave Nassau Street, this suburb becomes quieter and students head out to Prospect Avenue, which they refer to as "the street." The street has many Eating Clubs, where students meet and talk with their peers over dinner. Just about all of the students reside on campus or in school-sponsored houses for all four years.

It's clear to see why the campus architecture and the park-like setting are simply breathtaking with **castle-like residence halls**. There are Gothic and Georgian-style buildings, and the impressive Blair Arch. With over 500 acres, the campus transportation is by bus, foot and the much-loved Dinky train that connects campus to public New Jersey transit. Presently there are two large construction projects which somewhat mar the views on campus. The massive **Arts and Transit Project** will feature 21 acres, three **performing arts** buildings in a park setting with large expanses of green. It is projected to be complete in 2017. The Andling Center for Energy and Environment will open in Spring 2015. It will do exactly what the name infers**, research** for sustainable energy, conservation and environmental remediation. These modern steel and glass structures sit amid Princeton's old world, English Harry Potterish structures and the later buildings designed by I.M. Pei and Robert Venturi. However, the Dinky is in the construction site lines and may be discontinued without a compromising solution. When construction is done however, it will make for an impressive, **striking campus** worthy of the academics pursued behind the walls.

Social Environment

Assured, possessing **intellectual and social acumen**, these undergraduates have near endless opportunities available for activity outside of class. Weekly and monthly dinners are designed to bring students together and foster **academic community**. Bi-monthly lunches are planned to give students and faculty a chance to communicate outside the classroom. Other socials avenues without academic interface build communities within for like-minded students, like the **eating clubs**. There are 10 eating clubs, all coed, located off campus near Olden or Prospect Streets. Each eating club has a different theme and is run according to its own goals. Some houses offer elegant dinners served on china. Other eating houses function like old-fashioned frat houses, with pool table, video games and beer nearby. Membership is open to all students, however, there are a limited number of positions open annually within each.

Greek fraternities and sororities, along with the Eating Clubs, provide **leadership** opportunities and social activities such as formals, sponsorship of arts events and service. Approximately 75 percent of the undergraduates affiliate with one of these. Division I athletics is excellent with national ranking in 22 sports. More than half of the undergrads participate on one of the 38 varsity or 35 club sport teams. In addition, there are **200 clubs** that represent the arts, hobbies and causes. Students **look to clubs** primarily for exploring their social inclinations.

Although some competition in class arises from the way the grading system works, the atmosphere is one of cooperation. Academically, in first and second year, students take classes to fulfill **distribution requirements** in seven to nine different areas of study, including **epistemology** – the study of knowledge, its limits and validity. The first two years are like a warm-up that prepares them to chart their individual academic path as upper class students. Undergraduates select their major among 29 departments and while they cannot double major, they can add an independent concentration, similar to a minor. Students are required to **conduct independent research** as part of their **junior paper** and in conjunction with their **senior thesis**. This requires the approval of an advisor with whom they work one on one. This thesis could be a basis for a post-baccalaureate study or PhD program, or perhaps might become a successful addition to our American society like the program Teach for America which started out as a Princeton thesis.

Students who want to study abroad are advised to do so during their first and second year of college, because it's too difficult to do so in junior and senior years. Princeton now offers a gap year experience to admitted high school graduates who are selected and elect to volunteer service in third world countries for one year with most expenses covered by the program. Princeton undergraduates typically come from independent schools or excellent public schools. They hail primarily from the eastern seaboard. Close to half of Princeton's recent incoming classes are students of color. Sleep may be the only real down time here. In Spring 2011, campus humor jestingly advised "get clones" as an answer for not enough time in the day.

Compatibility with Personality Types and Preferences

At Princeton, students enter the freshman doorway and proceed in any of 360° directions (P). It is a precise university that can be thought of as an infinite three dimensional grid of informational cubes. During their four years, undergraduates will traverse the infinite cube, a cerebral mind puzzle. They will rearrange those cubes of information already assimilated and known from the previous week or semester. Princeton undergrads are always searching for the next (N) nugget of fact that brings meaning to their understanding of a discipline. It is exciting, intense, rewarding and cautious labor. After all, one wouldn't want to get lost in the infinite cube of knowledge. One might miss dinner at the eating club.

The Princeton undergraduates' life journey is about utilizing thought (T). Students approach their educational studies in a measured way; their pace is regulated by their interests and curiosity. The administration and faculty expect an independent search for knowledge. Academic courses and methods encourage students to research information (S) and occasionally present it as a formal lesson to others in Preceptorials. Professors listen and become observing advisors with mildly directive mentoring. Some students reach for their understanding of a discipline through collaboration that is inclusive of peers (F). The Reading Courses are a type of learning experience agreed upon by professor and student. Both of these educational tools provide information and knowledge that is not going to be covered elsewhere in the curriculum. Students can put their own educational plan together (J) and propose it to the faculty. It is yet another avenue for the curious undergraduate with a desire to enter a particular cube in the infinite grid on this campus.

The junior year brings a most intense effort, known as the Independent Work. It calls to mind the nature of how these very bright students learn—independently. Graduates of Princeton are most capable of standing resolutely, moving forward into discovery and accurately crafting new knowledge into useable information cubes for society at large.

In the following listing of college majors it is important to remember that students can fit into any college and can be successful in any major. We have found that the Personality Types below fit very well at this college. The course-of-study chosen for each Personality Type corresponds to MBTI® research and is presented as one of many examples favorable for that type.

PERSONALITY MATCH			
ISTJ	ISFJ	INFJ	INTJ
ISTP	ISFP	INFP	INTP
ESTP	ESFP	ENFP	ENTP
ESTJ	ESFJ	ENFJ	ENTJ

INFP is most satisfied when they can devote their talents to the benefit of others. The certificate in **Language and Culture** at Princeton would allow INFPs to move into the international arena. This certificate is paired with any other concentration at Princeton. Perhaps this type will concentrate in a field like sociology that also leans toward benefiting others. The coursework must remain separate in the language certificate from the sociology concentration. Passionate, committed INFPs normally have a level of perseverance necessary for this additional academic load. It follows from their continuous search for personal meaning. INFPs can be valuable members of any team that needs a little vision, perhaps expanding the service projects at Panhellenic week.

INFJ will really take to Princeton's infinite educational pathways of knowledge. They are always focused on thought and values which turn over and over within their minds. Princeton offers a curriculum that can respond to any of their insightful interests and they are likely to thrive here. This type prefers to pursue those insights independently, quietly and with a drive toward new concepts. The concentration in **Psychology** is well suited for INFJs. The department organizes itself as an explosion of ideas in studying the human personality. INFJ is also the type to tackle metaphysical questions. This topic has segued into the work of psychological theorists such as

Carl Jung and Christian apologists like Ravi Zacharias. Socially, INFJ may be too busy to devote much time or energy to theme-oriented social clubs.

INTJ is most independent and private in respect to their ideas that typically take months or years to percolate and come to full fruition. However, when the time is right, they are compelled to share those ideas. Very intense thinking is their specialty, so much so that they are sometimes unsure of how they got to the position they now command. The concentration in **Astrophysical Sciences** gratefully accepts these bold thinkers. Courses such as Extragalactic Astronomy call out to their imagination if interested in the sciences. This type will appreciate the novel performing arts and join with others who also like music with an intellectual beat. Eating clubs and social clubs that feature the arts, lectures, music and theater will appeal to this type.

ISTP goes for little machines that move around on the floor. There is a child lurking within ISTPs. Therefore, the **Robotics and Intelligent Systems** certificate is likely to bring a smile to their face. In fact, ISTP wants to get their hands on the control stick. Better yet, ISTP wants to program the data commands and make this little machine do more. They want those little machines to hip hop. This type might focus on any product, service or technical gadget that can become useful with application from pacemakers to space technology. The Princeton clubs are ideal for this type. They will enjoy finding that interest whether it is the billiards club or a club devoted to redheads. Socially, ISTPs will put a wry smile on their faces and show up for the meetings.

ISTJ can catalog huge numbers of facts and have them available for spontaneous recall. It is their specialty which is indispensable in many organizations. Princeton's certificate in **Finance** could easily take advantage of this desirable skill. It is common for ISTJs to master categorizing and assigning value to financial assets. This very precise discipline is a good bet if the ISTJ is inclined to math. Undergraduate ISTJs may elect to find a few friends together and follow their collective social interests in one of the Princeton clubs or residential college social activities.

ISFJ looks closely, sees what is there and commits it to memory. This is done with ease. They should look into the major in **Art and Archeology** at Princeton. This unique combination of disciplines mirrors educational philosophies at Princeton. It is also perfect for the ISFJ who fills their inner world with portraits of personal meaning. The department expects their graduates to be able to put linguistic meaning into visual art and artifacts. It's a tall order and rather painstaking detective work is required. ISFJs will benefit from Princeton's style of socializing. They take a unique perspective and bring their own kind of humor to a social gathering. Whatever their inclination, there will probably be a club that matches their interest. ISFJs must be gently pulled away from their studies and encouraged to drop their anxiety over taking a break.

ISFP brings to college discussions a lighthearted, practical touch which overshadows their deep-seated personal values. Many times, others are often not aware of this. Give them a problem to solve along with the space to tackle it and they are satisfied. ISFPs prefer people-oriented problems. The certificate in **Environmental Studies** offers a selection of elective coursework that provides flexibility for a people centered perspective. A course titled Disease, Ecology, Economics and Policy fits the bill because it ties together the land with its inhabitants. It also doesn't hurt that their terrific memory for people-oriented information will be at their fingertips. Princeton's social style offers a good helping of the unusual for this type who tends to march to their own drum. Here they will find others interested in the same tune and that will also be affirming to this type who can be self-conscious.

INTP will find the **Computer Science** department at Princeton University full of very interesting options like artificial intelligence, bioinformatics, digital media and computational social science. Upon meeting the major's course requirements, INTP can pursue a certificate for Applications in Computing in one of those options. That certainly works for most INTPs who are always on the lookout for the unknown. This type likes to analyze and logic is their specialty. They are most capable at putting together large conceptual schemes to generate solutions. It is an ideal characteristic for those willing to learn how to program computer software. They can also be pretty informal and messy in their work. Last minute socializers, they will temporarily stop right-clicking the mouse when a few buddies encourage them to play.

ESTP is a type that appreciates a little snazz in life. Sometimes this type will define that snazz in the form of risk-taking, so environments and ideas that include the element of risk are fine. The concentration in **Mechanical and Aerospace Engineering** will not disappoint them. The department is organized such a student could receive an engineering degree that is one or both of these two types of engineering. ESTP will quickly determine which of these two delivers the most adventurous learning. ESTPs can survey the ten broad areas of research in the department, potentially choosing the Lasers and Applied Physics or the Vehicle Sciences and Applications. They like to socialize with an interdisciplinary approach. They are likely to find several clubs, perhaps an eating club that combines excitement and physical finesse. In these they will be lively and get things going.

ENFP might just be interested in the concentration in **Sociology** at Princeton once they understand how enthusiasm seems to drive the department's approach to problem solving. In this discipline, the focus is on society and the nature of what is not working well within society. It can be a sobering study without humor and might tax some ENFPs because they need excitement and fun in their life. School violence and increasing mandates by government come into critical focus as large negative currents in America. ENFP will want to lighten it up. Their enthusiasm will carry over to the Princeton clubs. This type will enjoy the freedom to join and unjoin any clubs that capture their interest.

ENTP finds it difficult to come across an idea or a topic in politics that isn't interesting. They risk over-committing at times trying out so many things. At the end of the day, this type tends to move toward sources of power and the application of power. The concentration in **History** at Princeton with a certificate in **Contemporary European Politics and Society** is a nice combination for ENTPs. It could give them an entrance into the world of European-based world organizations. This type will likely offer up novel perspectives in the Independent Work and Senior Thesis. The ENTP must summon up the discipline to choose their topic earlier from among the interesting choices in western civilization. They are likely to have fun with clubs and social activities that engage their mind which is never at rest.

ESFJ is very interested in what makes other people tick. They are caring souls themselves and often wish that everyone else would be too. The concentration in

Religion at Princeton moves toward the study of other cultures. Spiritual authenticity is much approved by this type who supports community and tradition. The religious practices of a culture within the historical period will humanize this abstract subject for ESFJ. This warm type will also light up rooms they enter with their affirming observations. Collaborative studies and joining in a group preceptorial suggested by fellow students is just fine. They are likely to be quite active in social activities, finding several clubs and remaining with those throughout their years on campus.

ESTJ is often excellent at officiating and becoming a source of accuracy for others who do not have time to find the right answer. ESTJ is very credible in this role because of their practicality and willingness to make a decision. The certificate in **Translation and Intercultural Communication** focuses on revealing the meaning in written documents. Such documents as foreign language, poems, cultural stories, webpages and technical writings might have meaning to the author but not necessarily to all readers. This type wants to translate that meaning for others to use. As a cultural translator, the ESTJ is likely to be accurate, observing and impersonal in providing listeners with the meaning. With this major, ESTJs might bring an intercultural perspective to socializing at Princeton by translating good stories for the membership in several of the clubs.

ENFJ could select the concentration of **Comparative Literature** and then choose to express their typical charm through the **Creative Writing** certificate. In exploring these two disciplines, the ENFJ will delight in the use of the word, the turn of the phrase and the double meanings. They are more than capable of utilizing any of these masterful techniques in oratory. They are also capable of bringing humane lessons found in substantive literature to the audiences of today. They are empathetic, often with a tolerant perspective. Literature and language most commonly explore and satisfy their need to connect with others. They are likely to find social venues in the clubs or in the residential colleges that are empathetic in nature. Others in the clubs will welcome their cuddly natures.

ENTJ doesn't mind making a few considered judgments for improving the state of the art. They are often right up front with their interest to organize and innovate. Princeton's certificate in **Global Health and Health Policy** is likely to catch their attention as a worthy subject. This type wants to influence others and has the ability to support and craft plans that are frequently successful because of their considered judgments. The concept of disease patterns will certainly draw them into computational research, nicely tied with a major in Computer Science. Their instinct to be innovative and to try something new will also gain credibility in the crucial arena of worldwide diseases. Participation in Princeton's clubs is a win-win for typically confident ENTJ. Their ability to lead and to withstand anxiety could prompt them to consider application to a selective eating clubs. They will also bring their leadership talents to several other social clubs.

ROANOKE COLLEGE

221 College Lane
Salem, VA 24153-3794
Website: www.roanoke.edu
Admissions Telephone: 540-375-2500, 800 388-2276
Undergraduates: 2,060; 824 Men, 1,236 Women

Physical Environment

Roanoke College is located in downtown Salem, a small suburb of the city of Roanoke, within 20 miles of the **Blue Ridge Mountains**. Prospective students will relate to Roanoke's strong emphasis on their location in the Blue Ridge Mountains. Students see themselves as wanting to be a member of this collegiate community for the next four years. The physical landscape and buildings are very much valued for their **beauty and function** in promoting learning and social development. Older campus buildings have stately columns and six buildings are listed on the **historic register**.

There has been a building boom, no other words suffice, of construction on this campus since 2005. The university has also purchased properties in town, reaching out to enliven and support downtown renewal efforts. Newer buildings on campus are over the top functional and welcoming. Caldwell and Ritter Residence Halls, open in Fall 2012, bring definition to the Athletic Quad with stately, vertical architecture. The new Kerr Athletic Stadium was dedicated in 2013 and with eco-friendly lighting extends the hours of the beautiful Appalachian fall track meets.

Students appreciate this lovely campus as it often mirrors their home communities. The streets that surround the campus, except for Route 311, tend to be quiet. This setting appeals to undergraduates who are looking for a campus where learning and undergraduate socializing comprise all the action. It is an environment with few distractions. There are numerous intercollegiate **athletic teams** and many **intramural** and recreational programs including outdoor-adventure-type programs.

Social Environment

Roanoke College is populated by spirited students who are **socially involved** and **morally responsible**. This is not a campus where a student can be anonymous. Judeo-Christian faiths have active programs on this campus. Undergrads are fun-loving, **purposeful**, actively engaged with each other and very involved with community service. The annual **Sweet Potato Drop** adds a big dose of creativity and efficiency to service. One morning about 40,000 pounds of sweet potatoes will arrive on the lawn. Within two hours, the students will bag, then fill a truckload for distribution to shelters throughout the state.

Greek life and **RC After Dark** provide plenty of spirit while nicely balancing academic and service pursuits on this campus. Students who are politically aware express themselves on this campus. They may protest the fact that an ordinance is not environmentally-friendly. However, they are more likely to participate in causes that involve service. At night, various groups will come out and paint **The Rock**. The following morning, on the way to class, passersby read of the latest pronouncement.

Roanoke is remarkable for its academic diversity that well reflects the undergraduate student body at most public state universities. Affiliated with Evangelical **Lutheran faith**, the administration seeks to lift boot straps. A small number of incoming students participate in the undergraduate research program with stipend. Academic top scholars selected for the Honors program **start the year with Freshman Retreat** off campus. No matter their major, the Roanoke student is bound to encounter academic conversation and policies that teach social **responsibility, ethics and values.**

Compatibility with Personality Types and Preferences

The Roanoke College campus is for folks who are comfortable with reason and service. The faculty expects students to seek and apply that reason in their daily lives and upon graduation. Roanoke College naturally communicates the expectation of being responsible with the commendable goal of getting things done (J). High energy stands out on this campus and it helps build an active community (E). Balance is the byword for emotional health. The interface between faculty and students is evident and purposeful in preparation for graduation and beyond. Experiential learning in multiple off-campus settings is encouraged and supported throughout the courses and the extracurricular programs. The educational philosophy nicely supports several highly sought-after technical and vocational degrees. Academic philosophy here harkens back to the workplace and the current skill sets needed for employment. Career trends that emanate from the recession starting in 2008 are reviewed and adopted into the curriculum for currency in advising for undergraduates here. Roanoke College grows out of its Lutheran roots with both human caring (F) and a solid, realistic affection for American society.

In the following listing of college majors it is important to remember that students can fit into any college and can be successful in any major. We have found that the Personality Types below fit very well at this college. The course-of-study chosen for each Personality Type corresponds to MBTI® research and is presented as one of many examples favorable for that type.

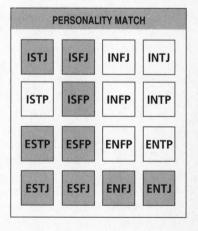

ISTJ might take a look at Roanoke's unusual **Health Care Administration** concentration. It offers a strong perspective from which to explore industry career options. Of course the concentration also offers immediate employment in hospitals, clinics and insurance companies. ISTJs, with this major, will gain an understanding of conflicting health data in the Affordable Care Act.

ISFJ has the ability to collect large quantities of information from the disciplines of biology, chemistry and physics. **The Pre Medical and Health Professions** program will open up a wealth of career options. Their precise recall of facts and perseverance will come in handy as they seek additional training at nearby hospitals. Equally attracted to the world of people, their strengths are very desirable for Physician Assistant. Their gentle, reflective ways will be more than welcome in stressful medical environments.

ISFP at Roanoke College absolutely must look into the **Health and Exercise Science** major, perhaps with the additional concentration in **Health Care Delivery**, offered in the Sociology Department. This combination of courses reflects ISFP's and Roanoke's philosophical combination of reason and service. The course Aging and Society emphasizes "an examination of the aging process, both for the individual and the nation." Roanoke is all about the belief in their graduates who will influence health perspectives in their neighborhood, community, region and nationally.

ESTP will want to consider the **Athletic Training** major. ESTPs like to get the gist of an assignment from several angles. Taking courses for the Inquiry program in chemistry, literature, statistics, physics and psychology will give them plenty of angles to consider a second major or a minor that will increase employment potential on graduation.

ESFP is quite oriented to the here and now which makes them darn good at handling a crisis. The Roanoke major in **Criminal Justice** could lead to a position as a probation officer. This college campus, focused on practical knowledge, has what it takes to introduce both caring and correction into the criminal studies coursework. Alert, sociable ESFPs would do well to consider this major at Roanoke.

ESTJ would be interested in the **Business** degrees here. The department offers a concentration in Business Information Systems. The practical nature of courses offered within the business department, along with the Roanoke educational philosophies, promote strong analytic skills. ESTJs are masterful at practical judgment and can bulk up their less preferred inclination of spontaneity in the course titled eCommerce.

ESFJ and the **Human Resource Management** concentration is a fairly good bet. Their curiosity about others often allows them to remember detailed information. This type is fair with others while patiently explaining the law of the land. ESFJs will insist on balancing the needs of the company with the needs of the employees. Their loyalty, being a strong characteristic, will be evident at their work environment.

ENFJ who is interested in teaching will do well to look at Roanoke's wealth of coursework and experience available for want-to-be-teachers. This type is likely to relate well with children. Roanoke covers the multiple issues surrounding our community schools in the course titled **Principles of Education**. ENFJs might also consider a teaching internship in the Department of Defense schools overseas or internationally accredited schools.

ENTJ is inclined to be in charge and might pursue advanced credentials in graduate school. Combine this with an inclination for business, and you have an argument for an undergraduate major in **International Relations**. Students may focus on one geographic area or take a global emphasis with historic and economic perspectives. The department taps into the Model UN program on campus offering a United Nations Security Council simulation. With terrorism on the rise and American power drawing down, this council will remain relevant for the near future.

ROLLINS COLLEGE

1000 Holt Avenue
Winter Park, FL 32789-4499
Admissions Telephone: 407-646-2161
Website: www.rollins.edu
Undergraduates: 1,884; 765 Men, 1,119 Women

Physical Environment

Rollins College was founded with the support of the Congregational Church in 1885. The church on campus stands as a reminder of this historic past, yet the **location** today calls out to speakers from around the world who don't mind the excellent fall and winter weather. A quick trip from the Orlando international airport with stops at nearby Disney World have parlayed an opportunity to bring an **international perspective** to this liberal arts college tucked away in a **quiet, residential** area of Winter Park.

Many of Rollin's buildings are soft, calming colors, pale pink and white, with terra-cotta tiled roofs. Several new buildings have brought a touch of the modern to this old world charm. The new Bush Science Center, opened in 2013, offers multiple lab spaces for student research in three fields: biology, chemistry and psychology. This trend of collocating these three disciplines is currently evolving across college and university campuses in the enviable position of building new facilities. At Rollins, the **accommodations are excellent** for undergrad researchers with same size offices adjacent to their professors' office, complete with a mini lounge. It makes for a small unit of about 4-6 to build academic community and interface the three individual disciplines.

Many students from the north are quickly taken by the warm climate, architecture and **lakes**. The Cornell Campus Center, the library and adjacent outdoor courtyards are filled with social conversation. The new Bush Center has an IT lobby complete with snack shop. It has fast become another gathering spot. Students appreciate being tanned, healthy and nattily dressed. The physical setting of this college invites a love for leisure, recreation activities and lifelong individual sports. Overall, the campus has a **compact feel**. Nearby, the downtown area has fun boutiques and great sidewalk eateries. The outdoor recreational lap pool is open year-round for students to swim and tan. The **architectural and natural beauty** of the campus is part and parcel of the Rollins attraction and college experience.

Social Environment

Classes are small and the **faculty is dedicated and attentive** to the students. Students here like their professors who communicate **clear expectations** for class requirements. Undergraduates will find this clear, sequential method of learning used throughout the curriculum including new requirements adopted in Fall 2014 identified as rFLA, Rollins Foundations in the Liberal Arts.

The college is committed to serving the **central Florida** community as well as out-of-state students. A good number of the students hail from the north and graduated from independent schools and strong suburban schools in the Midwest and

East. About half of the students are from Florida. There are also "non-traditional" students in the undergraduate Hamilton Holt School, such as adult, graduate, part-time and evening students whose presence is felt, especially in the evenings, on this small campus.

There is a strong **Greek system** where approximately one-third of the students are members of sororities or fraternities. There are three living and learning residences. Students may elect to live in these themed residences where they will take classes with their residence hall mates and attend artistic and social events for their residence. Students who are attracted to Rollins College like the extra programming in residential life. **Services for the undergraduate student body** like the Arts at Rollins College interface participation between Winter Park museums and the festivals at Rollins' own Annie Russell Theatre, now in its 82nd season.

Compatibility with Personality Types and Preferences

At Rollins College students will gain foundational knowledge in the rFLA (S) curriculum with traditional competencies clearly identified for graduation. A new feature of this curriculum includes the requirement to take five courses in one of four Neighborhoods. First term freshmen will declare their Neighborhood from one of these four: Cultures Collide, Mysteries and Marvels, Identities: Windows and Mirrors or Innovate/Create/Elevate. The Rollins College Conference courses are first year seminars that require students to analyze a particular topic. The RCC fulfills two purposes. First year students get to know a small group of fellow students. The topic studied in their assigned RCC is also the same topic studied in a separate course taken during the semester. In this way students can analyze (T) one subject from two different perspectives.

The administration has an attentive faculty which oversees the undergraduate student body on this campus. There are a number of programs and activities which include features of mentoring and guidance which are offered to the students. Undergraduates attracted to this campus appreciate the clear communication, thoughtful recreational planning and emphasis on service options that the administration offers. The international emphasis is felt through the increasing collaboration with higher education at international universities, international speakers and the Rollins student body which is diverse in make up, similar to greater metropolitan Orlando.

In the following listing of college majors it is important to remember that students can fit into any college and can be successful in any major. We have found that the Personality Types below fit very well at this college. The course-of-study chosen for each Personality Type corresponds to MBTI® research and is presented as one of many examples favorable for that type.

ESTJ is an excellent fit on this campus. They will understand and value the accountability required to earn a Rollins degree with

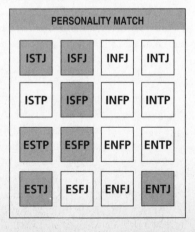

PERSONALITY MATCH

ISTJ	ISFJ	INFJ	INTJ
ISTP	ISFP	INFP	INTP
ESTP	ESFP	ENFP	ENTP
ESTJ	ESFJ	ENFJ	ENTJ

academic practices that are technologically aggressive in combining efficiency with learning on this campus. ESTJs are more than able to analyze information and reformulate organized patterns, similar to algorithms. The software principles and capstone project in the **Computer Science** major are nicely organized and likely to meet with ESTJ approval throughout the four years. The Neighborhood Innovate, Create and Elevate will help this conservative type expand in their approach to academic subjects.

ISTJ is going to be rewarded for their sustained effort and desire to unearth a large collection of pertinent fact. The **Biochemistry/Molecular Biology** major is just such a degree that will ultimately make heavy use of technology. ISTJ may find the new digs in the Bush Center a little wanting for that private space they need and retreat to the library. This type may enjoy When Cultures Collide as their Neighborhood focus for its comprehensive effort to look at global subjects.

ESTP will get appreciation from their peers for their ability to quickly solve problems in the social scene. For example, they will jump in and work through the natural tension generated in the artistic process of playwriting within the Fred Stone Theater group. The minors in **Theater Arts and Dance** at Rollins, as well as the majors, are outstanding. This type is one for the action and they enjoy performing. ESTPs could also be attracted to other Rollins clubs like the Campus Reporters because their energetic, focused style of leadership will shine with older generations.

ISFJ is also an excellent fit on this campus that is near many of the ground water lakes in central Florida. The degree in **Marine Biology** at Rollins College is quite a good fit for this type. ISFJs will find there is a demand for precise observation and manipulation of the recorded information. They are very adept at this as long as standard procedure is followed. Rollins College faculty are quite well-structured in their approach to education and ISFJs will find that very helpful. This type is likely to enjoy When Cultures Collide for its global fact-based content,

ISFP learns through hands-on participation. They seek to secure a personal inner meaning that is critical for satisfaction and fulfillment. They prefer to support and encourage others. At the same time, they are likely to add variety and change into their daily work. All in all, these characteristics support selection of the major in **Education** at Rollins College. With additional coursework, ISFPs can complete the Teacher Education Program that is outlined by the state of Florida.

ESFP might try the new minor in **Neuroscience** at Rollins College. It is designed to compliment those going on to careers in the health sciences. It must be combined with a major in biology, psychology marine biology or biochemistry. Without doubt, this will place ESFP squarely in the middle of taking classes and spending time in the new Bush Science Center and they will love all the social and academic interaction at the Center.

ENTJ will like the look of the **Environmental Studies** major at Rollins. The location is ideal with coastal estuaries, the Everglades, and numerous fresh water ponds and lakes dotting central Florida. Courses in biology will surely take advantage of the research projects in the new Bush Science Center. This type will appreciate the opportunity to connect with the extensive land programs at Disney World designed to support their complicated ecosystem of human entertainment and natural habitats.

SAINT LOUIS UNIVERSITY

Office of Admission
13 Dubourg Hall
St. Louis, MO 63103-2907
Admission Telephone: 314-977-2500
Website: www.slu.edu
Undergraduates: 8,800; 3,608 Men, 5,192 Women
Graduate Students: 5,100

Physical Environment

St. Louis University, or SLU as students say, is located in mid-town St. Louis, near the art district and medical centers. This **Catholic** university covers about a mile of the downtown area. The linear, inner city campus is connected by land-scaped lawns, pathways and architectural spaces that create a **self-enclosed and cohesive** environment. Upper class students walk downtown to the many restaurants and theatres. Students **readily volunteer** with Catholic Charities and other relief organizations and the university is well connected with local services for the needy and recent immigrants. Opened in 2013, the Center for Global Citizenship is devoted to international programs along with the robust international studies programs at this university. The Intergroup Dialogue utilizes trained peer facilitators to lead weekly discussions around the hot button topics of current day international America.

The newly renovated Pius Library is remarkable for its **historic collections** documenting this institution from 1639 to 1966. Although it is fragmentary in nature, it is uniquely rich in its ability to inform culture through this period. The **St. Louis University Hospital** is located one-and-a-half miles from main campus and the 2012 urban renovations make it very accessible by bike and foot traffic. Undergraduate internships are excellent in this beautiful facility. The hospital draws in students seeking **medical careers** in occupational and physical therapy, pediatric research, nursing and public health. The long-established Parks College of Engineering and Aviation is located on the other end of campus. It has a wind-tunnel and advanced technical instrumentation. On November 19, 2013, NASA, US Air Force and Parks College launched the first Saint Louis University spacecraft from Wallops Island, Virginia. Have we mentioned the **really remarkable research facilities** at SLU?

Social Environment

Students **strive for excellence** in academics and in life, under an umbrella of ideals. They typically have a good idea about what they want to major in when they arrive. Students here are career-oriented and **goal-driven**. They are comfortable with their spirituality and having fun at the same time. They are motivated to transform society, not in words but in deeds. Study abroad opportunities are over the top. Each year a fair is organized to introduce and inform the undergrads of all the locations and study options.

SLU offers a variety of on-campus housing options including **living-and-learning communities** which make it easy for residents to form a friend group of like minded souls. There is a significant freshmen orientation program spanning five days prior to class start. **First Year Interest Groups** are optional and well worth looking into for ongoing community building amongst a smaller group of students in the residential dormitories.

The **Billiken Club** is supported by the university's Student Life Division. It brings in loud, noisy, honkin' bands with hashtag kind of names like: No Age, Trauma Harness and Ghost Ice. Performances are in the Busch Student Center, also a hashtag, happinin' kind of place. Members of the 18 Greek sororities and fraternities engage in campus leadership, fun and initiatives that tend to be service-oriented. **Sports** have a good presence on campus. SLU is in the Atlantic 10 conference. Undergraduates support their basketball team with energy and enjoy the new Medical Center Stadium that is the home for SLU's track and field team. Others take in a Cardinals game or watch with amusement as the city begins to love the Rams again. For fun, students enjoy visiting nearby Forest Park for picnics or long walks.

Compatibility with Personality Types and Preferences

Saint Louis University calls out and welcomes prospective students on their website in the familiar text and language of high school students. The university reaches out to students in a trendy way yet the message is clearly about service to the community, Saint Louis and beyond. Students are comfortable at some level with searching for truth and competence in God's world. The central theme of this philosophy is serving (F) the poor and disadvantaged. It supplements the educational curriculum with distinct purpose and practical utility (S) in each major and minor. The university projects its deep optimism in mankind's ability through supporting the American national community.

The faculty and administration fine tune their course offerings to reflect today's occupational demands. It is adjusted when the needs of society transform and evolve. Graduates are typically in touch with and contribute to their professional career fields at many levels over a lifetime. This sensitivity also translates into personal balance and students actively seek relaxation in athletics and the latest bands coming to campus (E).

Since current majors and degrees answer the needs of America's "help wanted," students are pursuing some pretty demanding majors. Experiential and technical learning is common and available through the university's local, regional and national networks. The SLU campus in Madrid, Spain is strongly conversant with the nearby Spanish citizens and accesses the European sensibilities for those studying abroad in international majors. Graduates of Saint Louis University typically excel in graduate schools and workplaces. They move into community service and leadership that underlies their personal career goals.

In the following listing of college majors it is important to remember that students can fit into any college and can be successful in any major. We have found that the Personality Types

PERSONALITY MATCH			
ISTJ	ISFJ	INFJ	INTJ
ISTP	ISFP	INFP	INTP
ESTP	ESFP	ENFP	ENTP
ESTJ	ESFJ	ENFJ	ENTJ

below fit very well at this college. The course-of-study chosen for each Personality Type corresponds to MBTI® research and is presented as one of many examples favorable for that type.

INFP always has a couple of dreams and possibilities up their sleeve so flexibility in course studies is a prerequisite. At Saint Louis University, the degree in **Nutrition and Dietetics** exposes students to several work environments in this field and adds one more—personal nutritionist/chef. Regardless of their employer, INFP will find the freedom and autonomy they need to be creative and satisfied. Often this degree will lead to positions as a consultant. The educational philosophy at SLU is music to their ears.

ISTP has the intuition and patience to use sensitive diagnostic equipment. The degree in **Clinical Laboratory Science** at Saint Louis University is demanding of both of these inclinations. Much of the course work focuses on biological processes and so the ISTP is going to jump at the chance to intern in the hospitals. This type is fascinated with the options and potential use of technical equipment. On the job, they are likely to improve the state of the art in diagnosis.

ISTJ will relate to historical and spiritual perspectives at Saint Louis University because this type prefers stability and traditional organizations. This dependable type is a natural for the field of **Accounting.** At SLU, this is a concentration within the Business Administration degree. ISTJs can tote up a line of figures more accurately than just about any other type. This university, this degree and this type are exactly what American corporate business and government policy can use to bring account-ability back into the American political landscape. The pharmaceutical industry and the politics of the Affordable Health Care Act will provide an ideal study of "cooking the books."

ISFJ likes to be directly involved, one on one, helping others. They are often found in social service and health care careers. The degree in **Occupational Science and Occupational Therapy** is perfectly tailored for advanced graduate study in the field of occupational therapy. The university's hospital and the downtown medical centers in Saint Louis make access to clinical settings a breeze. ISFJ is thorough and the extra year will not likely be viewed as a burden. Rather, this type will appreciate the department's clear guidelines and expectations in a major that requires attentive advising and precise training. These are both SLU specialties.

ISFP is the perfect personality to be interacting with patients receiving medical treatment for illnesses. The program in **Radiation Therapy** within the Allied Health Sciences offers technical training that would be enjoyable for ISFPs to bring to the work place. They are naturals at affirming and supporting those around them. Their patients are likely to be grateful for their emotional support during treatment visits on those inevitable down days.

ESTP likes to be working with and studying how things really are. The Bachelor of Science degree in **Aviation Management** fits the bill and SLU is one of the few universities offering it. ESTPs will be in the hangar at Park's College aviation facility among the aircraft. Upper level class work includes aircraft fleet management and engineering disciplines in aviation such as reliability, life cycle and project engineer-ing. This type is a good troubleshooter and can excel at pulling together materials and people to accomplish aircraft operations.

ESFP will find that Saint Louis University offers the **Social Work** degree. This type is quite comfortable helping others. The excellent internships and experiential learning are available within a quick walk to the St Louis neighborhoods which will prepare ESFPs for the demands of social work. SLU's educational philosophy and moral emphasis will also help protect against discouragement that can accompany this helping profession occasionally.

ESFJ can tailor a business degree at Saint Louis University to secure employment that meets their strong need for a harmony in the work place. The major in **Human Resource Management** with a certificate in **Service Leadership** is ideal for managers who must monitor hiring and firing, retirement and other critical services provided to employees. Typical city municipalities and large corporations all have resource managers and internships will be forthcoming for ESFJs who are curious about and supporting of others.

ESTJ is often quite good at collecting, finding and analyzing facts. What could be better than a major in **Investigative and Medical Sciences**? The degree has a flavor of intrigue since it was added several years ago into the curriculum to meet the forensic science needs of our nation's crime labs. ESTJs will also appreciate the practicality of the degree since it is a fine option for entrance to medical school or pharmaceutical research. All in all, ESTJ's penchant for organizing facts and applying logic will be ideal for this undergraduate degree.

ENFJ likes a diverse array of people and their viewpoints. At the same time, they are excellent communicators and talented at delivering messages that are in synch with their personal ideals. The certificate in **Political Journalism** will offer this type a focused practice in all of the above. It pairs up with any major and especially fits well with a degree in communication or political science. This type has a natural inclination toward leadership with internal discipline. These skills just might keep ENFJ on the job in the rapid, swirling world of political campaigns. Certainly their moral vision will find a home at Saint Louis University.

ENTJ has the vision to work in an emerging field like **Biomedical Engineering**. There is much on the horizon for this type to look forward to while utilizing their crisp strategic planning. ENTJ is very much about business at the same time. Perhaps there will be patents in the future for this entrepreneurial type. Saint Louis University is all about applying your knowledge. The course work and department will fit this type's inclinations pretty well.

SALVE REGINA UNIVERSITY

100 Ochre Point Avenue
Newport, RI 02840
Website: www.salve.edu
Admissions Telephone: 401-847-6650
Undergraduates: 2,603; 824 Men, 1,779 Women

Physical Environment

Salve Regina University is bordered by the **opulent Victorian mansions** of Bellevue Avenue and **The Cliff Walk** towering over the Easton Bay inlet from the Atlantic Ocean. The university was founded in 1947 by the **Catholic Order of the Sisters of Mercy** who in early years utilized the **historical buildings** in **resourceful ways** to build financial reserves.

Historic Ochre Court is the first stop for visitors, the focal point of campus and the center for many ceremonies and orchestral performances by Salve ensembles. The elegant architecture draws in students who are curious about the values and ways of the Gilded Age. Sophomores are housed in these historic buildings on campus, while first years are assigned to traditional dormitory style residences that support community building. Upperclassmen usually elect modern housing options adjacent to campus.

There is a defining relationship between the campus and this geographic location. Students will descend the "40 steps" to the huge boulders by sea. At times, sections of the walk are closed off after storms, yet they reopen eventually. It is an experience to walk the ocean's edge and ponder how this beauty came into place. The three-dimensional, mathematical sport of **competition sailing** is offered at Salve Regina. In Fall 2013, the Salve Seahawks captured 3rd place in three regional competitions. **Surfing** is legendary and Salve students definitely surf on Second Beach, a few seconds from campus. Traditional sports such as football, hockey, track soccer, tennis and more round out the athletic options on campus.

Social Environment

The administration seeks to promote **inclusivity** in the freshmen programs and curriculum. Undergrads arriving on campus will enroll in English 150: What It Means to Be Human. It sets the stage for many conversations and reflections in the coming years. Immediate friendships form quickly in the first weeks. The well-documented collegiate sophomore slump is headed off on this campus with the excitement of returning students and their assignment to palatial residences. Students of all faiths are taught in the **Catholic** tradition of **harmony, justice and mercy**. During the 1990s, the long-serving president of the university and the Order generated stability and diligence. She set the university community standard which continues with **Service Plunge**. It is a year-long commitment that starts with a leadership retreat for incoming freshmen and transfer students who desire a weekly, consistent service commitment. Others participate in the Halloween Party where disadvantaged youth are invited to trick-or-treat in the safe, historical dormitories.

The male, female student population on campus reflect the unfortunate trend of reduced participation by young men in collegiate education, now too common in

American universities. The vast majority of students come from out of state. Students who may be concerned about their academic and organizational track record in high school will find **solid academic support** from the Salve faculty and staff. The curriculum is very much designed for **developing skills** to take into the workplace and to recognize human dignity in all walks of life.

Compatibility with Personality Types and Preferences

Salve Regina University is for students who like their education to be straight forward (S) in an evenly-balanced atmosphere. The entire feel of the campus has much in common with the words responsible, healthy and caring (F). The faculty and administration pay close attention to the needs of incoming freshmen. The Student Government Association is quite active in partnership with the administration on academic policy. The comparatively safe and nearby city of Newport encourages exploration and offers undergraduates the ability to acquire city sophistication. The university has taken considerable advantage in developing certain educational programs that feature the impact of the international port and the historical presence of the Navy. The Salve Regina's Pell Center for International Relations sponsored the U.S. Israeli Ambassador to speak to the student body on location at the U.S. Naval War College in 2011. Collaborating with other students in teams and projects is a common learning experience at Salve Regina. This approach to learning helps students gain leadership and social acumen as well as set realistic goals. A constant thread in the Salve Regina education is to build skills, develop a strong base of knowledge and identify personal values for the work force. Overlaying all of this is a delightful social atmosphere that supports healthy emotional growth.

In the following listing of college majors it is important to remember that students can fit into any college and can be successful in any major. We have found that the Personality Types below fit very well at this college. The course-of-study chosen for each Personality Type corresponds to MBTI® research and is presented as one of many examples favorable for that type.

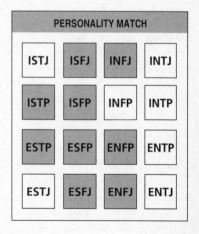

ISFJ will really appreciate the historic and elegant architecture at Salve Regina. Aside from this however, ISFJ's inclination for personal precision will point in the direction of a **Medical Technology** degree. Their meticulous observation is well matched with serving others both of which provide this type with a sense of accomplishment and satisfaction. It is a major not often offered at liberal arts universities.

ISFP may look closely at the **Social Work** degree at Salve Regina. The department has an international perspective that is well understood in Newport which served as an international port for centuries. Social work with an international perspective looks at worldwide community development. The curriculum also explores intergenerational attitudes within cultures around the world. Interaction with young children or the elderly is naturally appealing to ISFPs.

ESFP is quite attracted to work environments that require specialized skills. The major in **Early Childhood Education** certainly fits this description. The course in "Authentic Assessment" prepares the Salve Regina graduate in this field to recognize when a child's development is out of synch with the typical growth patterns. Who better to play with the kids, yet notice both the strengths and weaknesses of each child entrusted to their care, than fun-loving ESFP.

ESFJ relates to a founding philosophy at Salve Regina: relieve misery and address its cause. The **Nursing** degree is comprehensive through internships in densely populated Newport. There is a strong coursework in mental health fields. ESFJs will gain sustenance and comfort from the pervasive helping nature that permeates this campus. Moral guideposts allow ESFJs to avoid becoming overwhelmed while nursing the sick and dispirited.

ISTP is just about always comfortable with technical stuff. The major in **Theater** at Salve offers a technical theatre concentration. This skill set finds employment options along the eastern seaboard in New York, Washington DC, Disney World, etc. Salve's historic Stanford White Casino Theater is brilliantly renovated now. And ISTP will also gain from the interdisciplinary program called Vital Studies for Whole Life Design. The six courses are centered on imagination, humor, humility, intuition and ethics.

ESTP likes to work with real things. The major in **Cultural and Historic Preservation** will take advantage of both of these. Laboratory courses in this major are on location at preservation projects within the local community. On occasion, coursework will involve archeological digs and ESTP's fine observational skills will shine in the dirt. The coursework in this major is well-selected. ESTP will appreciate this rather unusual major at a small liberal arts institution.

INFJ could really enjoy the long established and unique **Administration of Justice** degree at Salve Regina. Mercy, in all its senses, is the go-by for the Salve Regina administration and faculty. The curriculum helps students explore the meanings of mercy, harmony and justice, three very different words. Practical, reality-based components are explored relating to probation, parole and juvenile justice. This educational study will keep the INFJs content pondering the values and relationship in the practical enforcement of justice.

ENFP might be drawn into the combined major in **Anthropology and Sociology** through their preference for the big picture and change. Certainly our nation is experiencing changing social patterns. There is a need for ENFPs who can readily provide constructs to decipher social issues. It is important for this type to bring enthusiasm and creativity to their workplace. ENFPs also prefer to work with a diverse group of people. This is all consistent with Salve Regina's educational philosophy.

ENFJ and the **English** degree jump into place after a review of curriculum options in this field. Students specialize in one of three areas: English Literature, Secondary Education or English Communications. Fine literature is woven throughout the three majors so that the student gains practice in writing and thinking precisely. Combined with the Christian ethical perspectives, this curriculum offers both the complexity and service perspectives which are attractive to ENFJs. Mid 19th century authors William Faulkner and John Steinbeck will bring a soft, Christian grace defined in their striking prose.

SARAH LAWRENCE COLLEGE

1 Mead Way
Bronxville, NY 10708-5999
Website: www.slc.edu
Admissions Telephone: 914-395-2510, 800-888-2858
Undergraduates: 1,374; 373 Men, 1,001 Women
Graduate Students: 255

Physical Environment

You won't find big bold signs announcing the location of Sarah Lawrence College as you exit the Hutchinson River Parkway north of New York City. The pale green signage for the college is barely noticeable as one drives onto the campus. Located 30 minutes north of the Big Apple, Sarah Lawrence welcomes the visitor with a sudden silence, tall trees, green lawns and **English Tudor-style** buildings. Modern buildings have been added to one side of the campus; they are covered by ivy. Below the tall canopies of fir trees, students can imagine the tales of Robin Hood and the **enchanted forest**. It's an inviting place, ideal if you want to set up an easel or get down to **exploratory conversations** with other students. SLC was established as a liberal arts college in 1926 and became coed in 1968.

The Tudor-style dormitories house faculty offices, classrooms and conference rooms where morning meetings with the Don (student advisors) are held. Professors' work-spaces are close to the student residences and that fosters easy interaction and ongoing communication between the two. These dorms characterize the nature of Sarah Lawrence where **learning and living** take place together in a lot of living spaces, cottages, houses and dormitories. Ninety percent of the students live on this campus that is so conducive to personal self-expression, thus there is a psychological symmetry between the park-like setting, the work of these undergraduates and SLC's invitation to discover their talents within a tutorial academic setting.

Social Environment

SLC students merge their private world with that of others on campus by actively **sharing observations, sentiments and beliefs**. They seek out conversations for the benefit of the process, not to arrive at positions, but to learn about self. They like to study what is meaningful to them. Those students who **commit to their chosen area,** be it Humanities, Social Sciences, the Arts or Natural Sciences in the first year will secure all the advantages of a Sarah Lawrence education. The hallmark student is the one who is attracted to the medium of writing and interested in the wide range of liberal arts. Written evaluations are rendered and grades recorded only for the purpose of a transcript.

The curriculum and the mentoring system keep these students on track as they enroll in **three year-long Seminars.** One of these Seminars will also have a **Conference** whereby a professor, called a "Don," becomes a tutorial mentor in the field or discipline. Students select which professor to work with. The Conference has many features of a tutorial as the undergraduate student meets one-on-one with the Don several times a week throughout the semester. Thus the Conference is the distinguishing academic feature and at times the social jewel in a SLC degree. Students delve deeply into their selected areas of study by discipline or field. They **write extensively in the Seminars.**

Students are supportive of each other. For the most part, they tend to form strong ties and become a closely-knit community. They are not over the top on athletics, more often taking enjoyment from their own performances in the arts, community service and each other's company.

Compatibility with Personality Types and Preferences

Sarah Lawrence is a campus for those who like to imagine and deliberate (N). They are caring folks (F) in a casual but compelling way. They accept responsibility for designing their curriculum, but are also very grateful and cooperative with the faculty support and programs that help them. Here undergraduates must choose coursework that is tailored to their interests, so most students arrive on campus without a favorite subject in which to major. If they did favor one subject over the other, it may only serve as a spring board to move in another academic direction.

Sarah Lawrence faculty expect students to develop individual perspective giving direction to study within academic disciplines. A student might read *The Sound and The Fury*. That student may decide that William Faulkner understood mental illness better than most literary figures of the 20th century. Therefore--the student decides to concentrate in the field of psychology. A realization like this may evolve over two to three years on campus. Actually, one year is required just to read that book. Undergrads here may not always be passionate, but they do take on the shades of conviction. With that in place, its not a giant step toward declaring their Conference studies and careers upon graduation.

The student body at this university flexes in academic interest, is somewhat restless (P) and attracted to novel interpretation. What could be more attractive to these students than this educational approach that demands introspection and reflection? Here students will be able to spin a strong thread between individual interests, curriculum and future careers.

In the following listing of college majors it is important to remember that students can fit into any college and can be successful in any major. We have found that the Personality Types below fit very well at this college. The course-of-study chosen for each Personality Type corresponds to MBTI® research and is presented as one of many examples favorable for that type.

INFJ and introspective speculation go together like hand in glove. There will be no shortage of conversations to prompt this activity. The Conference System pairs student and professor, biweekly, to discuss the most

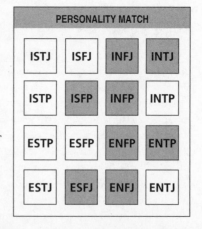

PERSONALITY MATCH

ISTJ	ISFJ	INFJ	INTJ
ISTP	ISFP	INFP	INTP
ESTP	ESFP	ENFP	ENTP
ESTJ	ESFJ	ENFJ	ENTJ

meaningful way to complete the course. The INFJ who often explores in depth will find the first year course in **Writing** perfect for this. The course titled Autobiography in Literature: Self/Life/Writing will familiarize them with the academic philosophy at SLC.

INFP can be quiet and is very often passionate. On campus, they are likely to reach for a personal understanding of a subject by discussion with other students. Equally observant SLC peers are willing to join their conversation. INFPs will admire the wide-ranging focus in the **Biology** department where they can explore the limits of human health while preparing for graduate study in physical therapy.

INTJ who is analytical and future-oriented will want to take advantage of the Conference Courses for advanced students. This type will precisely prepare for approval from their Don. The Division of Science and **Math** curriculum expands INTJ's options for tackling big problems. This type can process knowledge in two modes, a fuzzy gestalt or clear definition; both ways support their passion to find solutions with mathematical concepts.

ENTP thrives on a wide-ranging knowledge and tension in the debating scene. This logical type might bring definition to the conversations on campus. They could also appreciate the SLC tolerance of their sometimes abrupt explanations. The typical interdisciplinary work here meets ENTP's need for variety. **History** courses like The Disreputable 16th Century could really work since their interests often focus on laws and principles. The combination of philosophy and historical events is dynamite.

ENFP might get the greatest of benefits from the Don system at SLC. The Don must provide the structure necessary for this type's free-roaming intellect, yet the Don will be pleasantly surprised and rewarded by ENFP's typical warmth, enthusiasm and caring. SLC's **Early Childhood** Center will fire up their imagination. Interaction with the children comes naturally for this fun-loving type. The required meetings with ENFP's Don will help bring insight and personal meaning to the experience.

ISFP will accept introspective debate at SLC when the subjects are centered on serving others or nature. Their strong practical bent approves of community partnerships and service learning. The **Chemistry** department at SLC combines course readings with volunteering in the surrounding community. ISFPs secure personal worth during life's travels, often by action and hands-on activity. Sarah Lawrence provides some stepping stones for that life journey.

ESFJ is usually orderly and down to earth. This type may be surprised by the expansive ideas that float through and around conversations on campus. It is ideal for Seminars and Conferences in **Sociology.** Faculty focus on how current social issues affect the individual. Recession economics and political power wielded by governments can be the focus of intense study here. The Don will be quite important for affirmation and solid feedback in an original investigation such as this.

ENFJ is another good bet for this campus. This imaginative idealist may demand harmony and prefers pluralistic environments. They weave imagination and options together by listening to all perspectives with objectivity and caring. The concentration in **Public Policy** at SLC offers a wealth of sociology courses that start with the exploration of difficult societal themes like promoting peace. ENFJs graduating in this discipline will excel at verbal presentations, often changing the perspectives of their audience.

STANFORD UNIVERSITY

520 Lasuen Mall
Stanford, CA 94305-3005
Website: www.stanford.edu
Admissions Telephone: 650-723-2091
Undergraduates: 6,980; 3,706 Men, 3,274 Women
Graduate Enrollment: 8,897

Physical Environment

Imagine 8,000 acres in northern California, eye-pleasing Spanish architecture and a lake with walking, biking and hiking trails. Stanford appeals to students who like the outdoors, which is not hard to do in this **moderate climate** south of San Francisco Bay. Easy to get to from the airport, a student can take the BART to an above-ground train with a stop at the campus. **Bicycles**, however, are the transportation vehicle of choice for those who want to make the most of their time. That is virtually everyone at this very selective institution. Those on their bikes create vehicle jams along with the skateboard crowd and other wheels at the rotunda, jokingly dubbed "the death circle." We can attest to the fact that it is wise to stay out of their way.

Students typically live on campus. Not bound to any house systems, they can live in any of the resident halls. Bike parks are a social meeting place. Sorority and fraternity houses offer residential options for their members. The **outdoor café** by the main library is another social stop for students who need a perk in between the long hours of study. The Arillage Family Dining Commons features a Culinary Studio and cooking classes. Not to be undervalued for lack of rarities, the library houses a **huge, invaluable research collection** of books in the humanities and social sciences. Did we write about the bicycles?

Social Environment

Stanford students look together, **sporty** and sociable. They dress well, on the preppy side, and look good on their skateboards, with iPods, attired in shorts. No doubt students from cold climates feel unencumbered and relaxed here. Sixty percent of students who attend Stanford come from states other than California, however there is little time for state and home town banter. These students are **serious** about their studies and their future. They understand the **research culture** that prevails here. After getting accepted, students must be focused on taking advantage of the research opportunities especially in the social sciences, either by researching an idea of their own or helping professors with their research. This may be why students are up at two in the morning discussing an idea, whether or not it will ever see the light of day. For Stanford undergrads, it's important to get these **ideas out in the open** and subject them to light of other bright intellects in the dorm. Students mix and match various classes to define their major here. For example, a student who studied Product Design also enrolls in an interdisciplinary program called "IDEA." It requires **connective thinking** to link design with that student's Biology major. If their idea is beyond the current interest of faculty and ongoing research, they work through the Hasso Plattner Institute of Design that serves as an organized, accessible platform for undergrads who want to participate in IDEA. Bravo Stanford - and the other 20 universities in our book that elect this approach to educating tomorrow's leaders.

Compatibility with Personality Types and Preferences

Stanford University is a superb educational institution for the undergraduate student on a mission to excel. Since all students on campus seem to fit this definition, the determination in the air is more than considerable. Fast-moving undergrads on wheels mirror the precise, linear thinking on this campus (T). The typical high school graduate arrives at Stanford with a well-developed passion for a special topic or subject. Within that idea, undergrad students ask "How does this occur?" and "What next is important to discover?" As juniors and seniors in high school, these students were incurably curious. Now at Stanford, they actively jump into the chance to experiment, study and inundate their minds with knowledge. As students on this casual but intense campus, they are likely to be open and excited about exploring (N) while accumulating a solid foundation of hard facts (S) in their chosen field. The faculty and administration expect and enhance this daily, weekly, semester after semester investment (J) of personal/physical energy. Who fits in well here? The bright student who packs the day with class, study, research, student activity meetings, professor appointments, more classes and guest lectures and tops it off with roomie dialogues on that last lecture of the evening. Flexibility and individual choice highlight residential planning by the administration. Stanford loyalties are to the ideas and the knowledge forged within the student body or campus organizations, not to the residence hall.

Underlying the campus energy and productivity is confidence. Students do not second guess their interests, commitment or ability to secure that exceptional knowledge emerging at Stanford. Professors pursue their directed research at the graduate level and welcome the interested, prepared undergraduate who inquires about it. At the same time, there are seemingly endless options to imagine up and execute mini-research with the curriculum of the undergraduate degree. Research grants and other resources needed to pursue and define new knowledge are available to the motivated undergraduate. It can often be accomplished within a quarter or two and suits the young, confident learner who wants to cram as much as possible into those four short years.

The university takes the mini-research a step further by offering a rather unique co-term program. Co-term allows undergraduates to apply for graduate school and take grad course work during the last semester of undergraduate studies. The distinct advantage is flexibility and freedom (P) to pursue an academic research strand to its logical graduate level home. The productive, determined

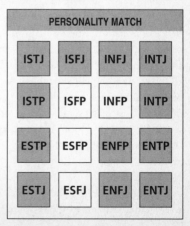

PERSONALITY MATCH

ISTJ	ISFJ	INFJ	INTJ
ISTP	ISFP	INFP	INTP
ESTP	ESFP	ENFP	ENTP
ESTJ	ESFJ	ENFJ	ENTJ

Stanford undergraduate is met with a willing administration and a faculty dedicated to expanding knowledge, utilizing student curiosity and perseverance as the primary tools.

In the following listing of college majors it is important to remember that students can fit into any college and can be successful in any major. We have found that the Personality Types below fit very well at this college. The course-of-study chosen for each Personality Type corresponds to MBTI® research and is presented as one of many examples favorable for that type.

ENFP with their broad range of interests might enjoy the freedom that exists within **Material Science and Engineering**. The degree puts exceptional research options at the disposal of the undergrad. ENFPs are passionate about their sense of the possible. They apply their gut instincts to just about any subject. The elbow room within this discipline and emerging application of materials calls loudly to persuasive, fun-loving ENFP. This department especially concentrates on nanotechnology. It also calls up the need for dreamers and those who brainstorm or invent their way through to solutions and discovery.

ISFJ can mix together their fabulous factual memory and ability to accurately recall the context of a social activity. The **Linguistics** major will make use of both assets. It also doesn't hurt that language systems are highly structured which appeals to this type. Learning in this discipline tends to take advantage of language labs where sensory activity like computer-assisted instruction and audio/visual presentations are typical and also favored by ISFJs. Students must concentrate in an area such as Language Structures, Language and Society, General Linguistics or Language Specialization. ISFJs will explore the extensive body of research housed in the Humanities Center through the lens of their typical social acumen.

INFJ typically hopes to delve into complex projects that benefit others and the major in **Symbolic Systems** at Stanford fits the bill. This major seems packed with abstract possibilities, yet it is a grounded degree growing out of the disciplines of language, mathematics and objective information. INFJs will be successful at extracting meaning from language systems and creative in transferring those meanings to computational theory and utility. This type is both competent and comfortable crossing boundaries into new territories.

INTJ with high school or community experience in theater could find the Bachelor of Arts in **Drama** very compelling. It includes a considerable component of theory, critical study and production. INTJs who declare this major must also select one of seven emphases. This type likes the freedom and integration found in the Directing emphasis. The in-depth study of theater's role will very likely appeal to INTJs. Given the considerable coursework in production, staging, performing and directing, they will have the tools to let their fertile minds fly while creating original performances, possibly for the senior project.

ISTP could find the **Art Practice** major at Stanford calling out to the maverick side of their personality. This type often wants to push technical, mechanical boundaries. ISTPs have loads of creativity when it comes to their interests. The artistically-talented ISTP working with metals, glasses and solid materials will likely utilize the laboratory equipment available on this research campus. Their thoughts can be transformed into art media through innovation with common or rare earth elements.

Stanford's engineering, geology and chemistry labs stand at the ready for the budding ISTP three-dimensional artist. The new arts building, McMurty Building, opens in 2015 and ISTP will be there.

ISTJ looks with interest and appreciation at the objective nature of the Stanford major in **Geophysics**. The curriculum is arranged so that graduates can directly enter the work force or move on to graduate studies. The discipline will make good use of their spectacular memory for details and admirable powers of concentration. ISTJ will gladly step up individual research utilizing facilities in the Center for Computational Earth and Environmental Science. Step aside for the ISTJs, they are up for Rock Physics. They do not leave much to chance and their data banks of factual knowledge is notable, if not amazing.

INTP has the patience and insight to secure solutions to the technical problems which compose much of the advanced curriculum in **Product Design**. Stanford offers this unusual major within the School of Engineering. The course work is an interesting blend of art, psychology, math and mechanical engineering. The Product Design coursework focuses on adaptable practices, systems and equipment. The graduate with this degree will have knowledge and skills to plow through dilemmas in work and living environments. Products in this sense can be revolutionary; think of LEDs. INTP is just the type to get absorbed and come up with a winning patent.

ESTP has a set of skills primed for action. ESTPs are driven to be productive in the present time frame. Although the major in **Aeronautics and Astronautics** will require a focus on the future, the day-to-day work environment is stimulating and oriented toward observable events. Observable dilemmas such as how to recycle life sustaining chemicals or how to move around in light gravity on a planet surface are the stuff of this study. These "how" questions are a specialty of Stanford's approach to education and a favorite ESTP word. The department assumes that each student will pursue a graduate degree in the field. Research equipment at Stanford is extensive and will support ESTP's penchant for troubleshooting.

ENTP with an interest in politics will jump right into the problem solving offered by the senior seminar in **Public Policy**. This major appeals to ENTPs because of the high stakes decision making. ENTPs are comfortable with the world of power and influence. Stanford's curriculum specifically engages the bay area community to provide policy analyses for community issues in commerce, public services and social services. Undergraduates get firsthand experience with success or not so successful analytic problem solving. Bright, quick ENTP will be right at home sitting at the table, generating concepts for the group to review.

ESTJ will bring their strong reasoning and practical approaches to the curriculum in **Energy Resources Engineering**. Stanford has carved out a research niche in the search for energy production utilizing evolving engineering methods. The intersection between geology, energy and engineering is a firm yet emerging discipline. ESTJ has an administrative mind and will strongly identify with the focus for efficiency in this career field.

ENFJ is inclined to gather up large views of historical movements as well as the reasons behind them. The Stanford degree in **History** is a broad three-dimensional approach taking in time, the world's geographical regions and a selected topic. Undergraduate research will center on the amazing social science research archives at the Green Library. ENFJ will forge personal relationship with librarians as they secure a foundation in this concentration. All this prepares ENFJs to move forward with the graduate degree. Idealists at heart, ENFJs will seek out careers with educational impact or interface that also capitalizes on their engaging, compelling style.

ENTJ will probably like the **Earth Systems Program** that is chock full of complexity and relevance. Both should dominate the discipline if this type is going to be happy. ENTJ's competitive, sharp instincts will hone productive thoughts between human activity and the earth environment. Stanford shapes this degree with the critical question, "What should be measured within the air, land and organisms of the planet?" This seems to comprise the first two undergraduate years of study. Thereafter the question of "How to measure and gain relevant meaning?" launches the ENTJ on a demanding quest for the remaining two years on campus.

SWARTHMORE COLLEGE

500 College Avenue
Swarthmore, PA 19081-1390
Website: www.swarthmore.edu
Admissions Telephone: 610-328-8300, 800-667-3110
Undergraduates: 1,526; 751 Men, 775 Women

Physical Environment

The Swarthmore campus is located within a beautiful **arboretum**. Collegiate buildings call out to their Quaker foundations with **clean lines and simplicity**. The college takes advantage of this setting with an outdoor amphitheater and white Adirondack chairs randomly located on lawns and in nearby woods. At Swarthmore, endless discussions about **life and injustice** take place. With the college's Sesquicentennial celebration underway, there is much focus on views of the former campus, interior spaces and alumni.

The ethos of Swarthmore pushes through and is conducive to thinking about drinking in knowledge for a purpose. Students eat together in Sharples Dining Hall. Dining services caters to undergrads who want to picnic before the weather closes in with delightful, delicious-looking picnic baskets to go. Almost all students live on campus or in school-sponsored housing. The **Tri-College Consortium** doubles the course offerings available through cross-registration with two other similar colleges in the area. Indoors or outdoors, **observation/discussion/consensus** are pretty much ongoing day and night. When students want a break, the nearby train runs to the "city of brotherly love," Philadelphia, where some volunteer with initiatives to benefit the inner city.

Social Environment

Students here write well and write quite a bit. Even students enrolling for engineering, an unexpected major at this liberal-arts college, write a great deal and learn engineering within the context of a liberal arts education. Public speaking is an important skill to acquire and surfaces throughout the curriculum. The Peaslee **Debate** Society is well-known for winning many parliamentary debates. Swarthmore students must have or develop the ability to think on their feet and come up with a reply to an argument as it is being made. Students here are **absorbed in soaking up knowledge** and focused on sharpening their minds.

Undergraduates generate **intense investigation** so that they may comprehend and impact contemporary society. Students are highly motivated to join **cause-related clubs** and organizations that range from the Swarthmore Progressive Action Committee to the Kick Coke/Conscious Consumers. The Swarthmore Conservative Union, a former student organization and Swarthmore Republicans seem to have little presence on this campus. Swarthmore students tolerate some level of dissent among themselves. There are two opposing political activist clubs on campus now, representing differences within the feminist agenda. Some service projects, emanating out of political activism for change, reach into local underserved neighborhoods. The students put most of their efforts into **their campus environment**, supporting a daily campus newspaper and a campus radio station with simultaneous webcast. It is a huge task and responsibility as the content includes both entertainment and political news.

It goes without saying that students are up to the academic rigors. The relationship between a student and professor is like the meeting of two bright lights. Students take the intellectual risks inherent in pursuing a challenging course of study.

Compatibility with Personality Types and Preferences

Swarthmore College is thorough and studied. Critical discussions form around the concepts of education, purpose and country. These conversations among faculty and students evolve and reformulate within the whole student body. The college environment places high value on humanistic concerns (F) by connecting citizenship to purpose and utility within society for a common good. This transcends the curriculum and activities on the campus. Random activity has little use at Swarthmore and spontaneity is measured (T) and judged by its outcome or product. The minds of the students are frequently in overdrive as a result. Education is truly the winding path that you travel (P) and knowledge is information that you gather along the way to advocate for change. Swarthmore educators really fine tune the art of the question. In fact, there is a sequence of courses offered that center on the process of interpretation (N). To minimize excessive wear and stress on physical and emotional stamina, the administration maintains a very functional environment. Directions and expectations are clear and simple in reference to curriculum requirements and major advising. Residential life is quite community-oriented and intimately connected with learning. Relationships within the college culture are key learning vehicles also.

In the following listing of college majors it is important to remember that students can fit into any college and can be successful in any major. We have found that the Personality Types below fit very well at this college. The course-of-study chosen for each Personality Type corresponds to MBTI® research and is presented as one of many examples favorable for that type.

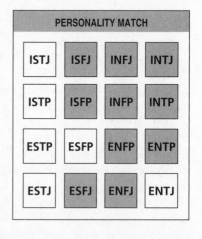

PERSONALITY MATCH

ISTJ	ISFJ	INFJ	INTJ
ISTP	ISFP	INFP	INTP
ESTP	ESFP	ENFP	ENTP
ESTJ	ESFJ	ENFJ	ENTJ

INFP has iron will and iron values to persevere in the tough courses of **Chemistry** at Swarthmore College. They will need to apply some of that iron in Physical Chemistry: Energy and Change. Wow, even static chemicals are demanding to comprehend, let alone chemicals that are dancing to hip hop in the test tubes. Yet bright INFP can handle it along with an outlet that is non-academic, perhaps volunteering in an animal shelter.

INFJ is thoughtful and can be reserved, yet also quite aware of others. The major in **Psychology** will allow this type to delve into the feeling states that all experience such as happiness, depression, joy and anger. On this campus of political activism, INFJ only has to take a walk along the beautiful campus pathways to encounter these emotions in passing.

INTJ has the focus and determination to study a language of which there are few active linguists. So the study of **Latin** when combined with advanced degrees, is ideal. They are original, novel thinkers and will pull plenty of meaning out of Roman-carved inscriptions during study abroad to Italy and Greece.

ISFJ especially likes the facts and can handle a great volume of information. The major in **Mathematics and Statistics** at Swarthmore can also serve up an orderly approach. Their fabulous memories will come in very handy as they seek to recall those mathematical formulas while analyzing quantitative problems.

ISFP can get lost in the study of the **Japanese** language on this campus. The department offers chat hours with native speakers and language tables for this highly visual, design-intensive language. This type is also very astute with visual space and sometimes can be found in design careers. ISFP will enjoy study abroad and relate well to the calming, contemplative Japanese gardens.

INTP is likely to enjoy the degree in **Engineering.** The course in Truss Bridge is a competition and an annual tradition that this type can relate to. Using wood and glue, prospective engineers build small scale bridges that are put to the test. It is a nice break from the typical intellectual work that comprises much of the engineering focus. That is just the type of extracurricular activity for INTP.

ENFP usually has a soft spot for the arts. The major in **Music** here is a good bet. There are quite a few ensembles and a Swarthmore favorite is the jazz ensemble that performs on campus. Beyond the practiced faculty instruction, the department also includes teachers from New York City and eastern metropolitan enclaves, rich in the performing arts.

ENTP will like the study of **Biochemistry** on this campus. After the sound training in foundational knowledge, ENTP gets excited for the upperclass work which switches over to seminars. In these later studies, exchanges and discussion take over between student and faculty as they acquire skills involved to pursue research in the campus laboratories.

ESFJ may enjoy the **Biology** major here. The curriculum focuses on students observational skills. Also students design and perform their own experiments. ESFJ will enjoy working in the local fields and streams, perhaps to craft exciting high school lesson plans. They will likely support traditional college service activity like Saturdays of Service.

ENFJ is a bit of an idealist and may enjoy the major in Asian Studies with a focus on **Chinese Language, History and Culture**. A fair number of courses will be offered through the Tri-College consortium and will give this friendly type an opportunity to generate more friendships. It is pretty likely they will also enjoy the database that includes Chinese movies as an opportunity to connect with the culture prior to studying abroad.

SYRACUSE UNIVERSITY

200 Cruise-Hinds Hall
Syracuse, NY 13244
Website: www.syracuse.edu
Admissions Telephone: 315-443-3611
Undergraduates: 14,422; 6,448 Men, 7,974 Women
Graduates: 6,170

Physical Environment

An aerial view of Syracuse University shows a large campus within greater Syracuse, New York. The university has a variety of both historic and new buildings that are spread out over 200 acres. Chartered in 1870 by the Methodist Episcopal church, there is a **functional** element in design across the campus. At times, it feels like a large, state university. The renovated residence halls are **multi-story towers of brick** and cinderblock built in the 50s and 60s. Just recently, the front doors to the Carnegie Library opened for the first time in decades with renovation of the reading room. Prior to that access was from other directions and sufficed.

There is much outward enthusiasm and a **charging spirit** at Syracuse University evident in the Carrier Dome. The largest physical structure on any college campus it seats 50,000 fans indoors. Usually painted in orange and blue cheering on the 'Cuse sports teams, students are protected from the fall winds and winter snows. Basketball, football and championship playoff games are really the starter soup for the social life here. But most intramural and fitness sports require additional fees. Without extra charge, however, students can sign up for a reserved time in one of several fitness gyms.

These students have the **stamina** to walk back and forth to in heavy blankets of snow, but also use the **shuttle transportation** around campus. The new Syracuse Connective Corridor is a seamless transportation that facilitates the cooperation historically present between university and city. Both graduate and undergraduate students work in conjunction with city organizations to promote economic development.

Social Environment

Syracuse University has **12 schools and colleges**. Students identify with the **practical nature** of the curriculum. Most freshman students are admitted to the College of Arts and Sciences. The other Divisions and Schools can be quite competitive with very limited transfer options especially into the Newhouse School of Public Communications. Certain segments of this collegiate community tend to be **first among equals**. It is not unusual to find 'Cuse involved with investigative research on international and national newscasts, although this feature does not often impact the day-to-day undergraduate experience.

There are many **different types** and groups of people at Syracuse. With 15,000 undergraduates, multiple affiliations of like-minded students form within the undergraduate student body. The university has multiple **administrative programs** in place that seek to support undergraduates adjusting to college life. Approximately,

20 percent of the students join a **Greek organization**. Students tend to be **service-minded**. Each school and college has a connection to specific areas within the city's infrastructure. The Center for Public and Community Service oversees a strong service learning program for the surrounding neighborhoods.

Students must live on campus the first two years in one of the 21 dormitories with freshmen together in dedicated halls. The university offers Learning Communities that function essentially as activities clubs. In this large setting, students tend to fall into two groups, those who are focused and admitted to the selective Colleges and those who benefit from the process of searching for a major, often enrolling as undeclared, in the College of Arts and Sciences.

Compatibility with Personality Types and Preferences

Since Syracuse University is larger than most private universities and colleges, it has distinct social environments within its richly resourced campus community. Some schools, appeal to the creative types focused on possibilities (N). However, other schools and colleges tend toward guided logical practice (T) in preparation for graduation and the coming world of work. Certainly there is a hardy soul in the Syracuse undergraduate who emerges to conquer both the weather and the intellectual demands of the curriculum. The administration's educational philosophy predisposes the curriculum to meet the needs of the American workplace. The students are not expectant of wrap-around services. They step forward with determination seeking to secure their degree and skill sets. Undergraduates who want to develop skills and acquire a specific knowledge base (S) will not be disappointed with the Syracuse curriculum.

The administration provides undergraduate services at the campus level. Campus-wide programs emanate from the different departments organized to support undergraduate residential life. A key feature of this is the strong emphasis on serving others (F), especially the citizens and businesses of greater Syracuse along with communities in New York State. The resilient Syracuse undergrads are very comfortable extending their helping hand in a myriad of innovative ways developed by the schools and colleges at the university. Above all, the Syracuse administration encourages Syracuse undergraduates to become civically engaged (E).

In the following listing of college majors it is important to remember that students can fit into any college and can be successful in any major. We have found that the Personality Types below fit very well at this college. The course-of-study chosen for each Personality Type corresponds to MBTI® research and is presented as one of many examples favorable for that type.

ISTP with an interest in design or arts definitely is going to smile when they see that Syracuse offers a minor in **Jewelry and Metalsmithing**. ISTPs will be in their element as they construct and weld that last

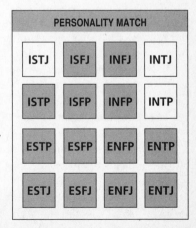

PERSONALITY MATCH

ISTJ	ISFJ	INFJ	INTJ
ISTP	ISFP	INFP	INTP
ESTP	ESFP	ENFP	ENTP
ESTJ	ESFJ	ENFJ	ENTJ

piece of silver in the senior portfolio for graduation. The major has a cap of five students per semester and requires an interview, but ISTP may just meet the challenge for this course of studies.

ESTP is pretty realistic and the minor in **Forensic Science** will be interesting. This robust curriculum interfaces well with majors in chemistry, biology or psychology. Study in this discipline offers ESTP career options in medicine, science, engineering and the social sciences. This type might move forward into the exciting world of investigating criminal behavior.

ESFJ fits well into the world of business when the career involves direct, daily interaction with customers. The major in **Real Estate** at Syracuse will likely support many of ESFJ's inclinations. The newly emerging mixed use commercial/residential villages appeal to this type. The curriculum assures financial astuteness with a solid management core in finance, marketing, accounting and corporate mechanisms.

ESTJ likes to be organized and that works well for today's classrooms at all levels in the public schools. The **Educational Studies** major at Syracuse prepares graduates with a solid understanding of the profession. Limited time will be spent in classrooms since this curriculum is designed to prepare for graduate programs. The city offers excellent opportunities to intern in educational programs supported by federal and state initiatives.

ENTP might enjoy declaring a minor in **Entrepreneurship and Emerging Enterprises**. Naturally drawn to new business ventures, ENTPs are quick to spot a trend and could enjoy looking at start ups in business or hybrid strategic partnerships. Undergrads in Introduction To Entrepreneurship create a venture plan and secure resources. Guest lecturers round out this reality-based curriculum. ENTP, sometimes overly optimistic, will benefit from this considered approach.

ISFJ could look closely at the **Music Education** major. Five emphases within the major allow for classic instrumental emphasis or a choral/elementary emphasis. This type is well-suited for a faculty position in public or independent schools. The school of music also offers degrees in music industry and music performance/composition, all of which support this type's dedication and thorough preparation for a career in music.

ISFP with a flair for apparel should look into the **Fashion Design** degree in the College of Visual and Performing Arts. It is well-complimented with the course offerings in fashion merchandising. This type enjoys both independence and handiwork. Piecing together their own creations on paper through to production and sale in clothing stores is just the ticket for ISFPs. Syracuse has an exceptionally rich curriculum in the hand-crafted arts.

ESFP will surely want to look at the **Retailing/Management** degree. This curriculum allows for elective courses outside of the management curriculum and ESFP is likely to pursue design courses also. ESFP's ease with persuasion and dynamic, fast-moving environments could mean a smooth transition into retail business on graduation.

INFP always seeks meaning and a connection between their educational studies and personal growth. The degree in **Social Work** has good bones for this type. INFPs are quite comfortable getting close to those in distress when providing help or guidance. Graduates have administrative and policy knowledge as well as a grounding in promoting human dignity.

ENFP will probably enjoy the **Advertising** degree in the selective School of Communication. This type is drawn to possibilities in the fast-paced, dynamic world of marketing. The facilities in the school are over the top with the latest digital equipment. ENFP can create a larger artistic community to collaborate with during undergraduate studies by enrolling in the visual arts also. The advertising major leans one of two ways, management or creative design.

ENTJ is usually a great team member and often a team leader. The degree in **Marketing Management** utilizes project teams in many of the courses. This is ideal in that it replicates the professional environment of large corporate firms providing these services to even larger corporate firms. All this largeness will work for ENTJ who is a natural in powerful positions.

INFJ has that ability to juggle complicated ideas and connect them in a meaningful way with people. The degree in **Linguistics** at Syracuse pulls together knowledge from many areas in anthropology, geography, sociology, languages and psychology. This degree is excellent for the INFJs about to pursue graduate studies. It can be paired with a minor in **Classics** studying a nation's culture, institutions and underlying values. INFJs will be adept at these two abstract, interdisciplinary fields. The degree could lead to study in law or with international NGOs.

ENFJ is very well-suited for the Syracuse **Inclusive Elementary and Special Education** Teacher Prep program. This type is fulfilled when performing activities that help others grow and succeed. The education field has several key features that appeal to ENFJs. Diversity is high on this list with ENFJs placing harmony within the environment as their first priority.

TUFTS UNIVERSITY

Office of Admissions
419 Boston Avenue
Medford, MA 02155
Website: www.tufts.edu
Admissions Telephone: 617-627-3170
Undergraduates: 5,148; 2,471 Men, 2,677 Women
Graduate Students: 2,702

Physical Environment

Tufts University is located on a slight rise in the Medford-Somerville area and is accessible by the subway that travels to and from Boston. From the subway stop, it is a bus or 20-minute walk to campus. The heart of campus is encircled with mostly red-brick buildings around "the green" and "President's lawn" which students cross regularly on their way to class. On a sunny and warm day students lay on the grass or sit by a tree in the quad studying. In winter they may be studying in the Tisch Library or sledding down the hill in front of it, or taking in the **view of Boston** from the roof. Tufts' outdoor monument is a **cannon** that changes colors and messages overnight. Some are social and political in nature while others are more lighthearted.

The residence halls are assigned by lottery each year with preference given to freshmen and sophomores. Upperclassmen are likely to live off campus. Additionally, there are 16 special interest houses for students of like interests and 13 Greek chapter houses with off-campus housing. There are many great eateries adjacent to campus for undergraduates, such as Buddy's Truck stop, a diner in a silver 1929 Worcester lunch-car that brings back the 60s era with all the nostalgia. This environment appeals to students who want **sophistication** and a top name university near a large city, without the intrusive impact of traffic and congestion. The surrounding neighborhoods primarily consist of modest houses built in the mid 19th century to house the growing labor market for American industrialization.

Social Environment

High achieving, intellectual students are attracted to Tufts' rigorous academics in the arts and sciences, engineering and pre-professional sciences. Entering freshman score at the top range on standardized tests. A Tufts' education is for those who enjoy analyzing facts, observing what is and imagining what can be. Administration and faculty seek to connect this new found knowledge with civic engagement. There is an emerging emphasis within the curriculum on combining 'what can be' with civic engagement opportunities. Education for Active Citizenship is a course which instructs select students on how to implement and complete local community projects. At the conclusion of the instruction, they follow through with a project with support by professional staff. Students at Tufts are typically motivated to take risks in conjunction with faculty guidance while searching out something new that offers value. **Practice** will mix with **imagination** and these graduates will be responsive to emerging frontiers in their fields.

Developing and stretching concepts is a primary tool to improve **reasoning** ability on this campus. Students who like **visual imagery** will enjoy Tufts' propensity to communicate via photographs and artistic design. It is formally part of the curriculum through the partnership between Tufts and the **School Museum of Fine Arts** in Boston. The new Center for Scientific Visualization allows researchers from multiple disciplines to reimagine their own work in this different medium. Students here find value in presenting what they observe. The Department of Visual and Critical studies also exercises reasoning abilities across their arts curriculum.

Many undergraduates arrive on campus with well-developed **leadership** abilities and will move on to graduate studies. Many will seek professions in medicine, allied health and veterinary science where they will apply their learning in a practical way. There is a fun line of traditional collegiate social activity like the Winter Ball, potlucks in the dorm and snacks with the university president. There is a vibrant musical and **theatrical core** of campus performances for and by undergraduates. They may pick up their wind instrument on a spring day and sit outside the student center playing old eastern European melodies. Undergraduates have **unique talents and hobbies** which they exercise for relaxation.

Compatibility with Personality Types and Preferences

Tufts University is taking scientific research into the emerging world (N) of visual imagery and visual utility. The lines are blurring between technology, art, science and visual applications on this university campus. To be sure, a lot of Tufts research remains oriented to the fundamental properties of basic molecular research. However, within their laboratories there seems to be an outward momentum (E) directed by the faculty and administration. New initiatives, like the study of water in the Middle East and Bridge Professors continue to reform disciplinary knowledge which then finds its way into the undergraduate experience. Tufts research results are frequently translated for the general community of citizenry through stunning visual expression. Video, photography and manipulated images produced by faculty and students seem to carry the weight of an essay about newfound knowledge. The website and university publications readily present compelling messages about emerging technology and ideas (P) that can address current day problems in America.

Six schools on campus have recently been directed to work on water problems in the Middle East, conjectured by the administration to be the underlying source of problems within that geographic region. There is a Department of Religion at Tufts University that is small in comparison to other well-resourced programs and departments. Undergraduates travel off campus to observe and understand other ethnic groups. Internships and co-ops here are oriented to comprehend and document other cultures. Visual record keeping (S) is a favorite choice

PERSONALITY MATCH			
ISTJ	ISFJ	INFJ	INTJ
ISTP	ISFP	INFP	INTP
ESTP	ESFP	ENFP	ENTP
ESTJ	ESFJ	ENFJ	ENTJ

to capture and bring home the meaning of experiences abroad. Undergraduates of Tufts are precise observers, confident in the knowledge of their discipline and ready to move forward into their professional careers with hyper awareness of social and technological currents in their discipline.

In the following listing of college majors it is important to remember that students can fit into any college and can be successful in any major. We have found that the Personality Types below fit very well at this college. The course-of-study chosen for each Personality Type corresponds to MBTI® research and is presented as one of many examples favorable for that type.

INTJ can be oriented to creative design. This type is very good at dreaming up new systems that solve three-dimensional problems. Tufts University offers a curriculum that includes the elements of engineering with the functional elements of human habitation. The BS degree in **Engineering in Architecture Studies** prepares graduates for advanced study in architecture or design. The very thorough and often technically competent INTJ will be drawn to state-of-the-art innovation seen in much modern architecture. Metals, glass and polymers are all rather exotic substances to use in construction. Their use requires engineering expertise and a distinct absence of conventional models. INTJ has these both in abundance.

ISTP could hook up with the **Computer Engineering** degree almost like a robot being connected to a joystick. The two simply go together. Tufts University offers an excellent environment for getting prepared to tackle computer applications for the next 30 or 40 years. On this campus, ISTP will be nudged toward experimentation as well as ethical application. Undergraduates work in teams and also solo. ISTP is fine with either approach. This type brings a desire for efficiency to their work and study. They avoid fussy stuff and will find the tools, logic and principles they seek to get to the end of the tunnel with the least effort expended. This is a nice trait to have in the workplaces that direct and control our limited resources through software.

ISTJ will find the second major in **Biotechnology** suitable for pairing up with a traditional major in the social or physical sciences. The precise nature of the physical applications in biotechnology appeal to this type. They can bring their tremendous concentration and retention powers to bear in the lab experiments. The ISTJ can also explore several career tracks through this coursework. ISTJs could be attracted to medical practice, health administration, research or diagnostic skills in the realm of the pure sciences. At Tufts, this type will be surrounded by innovative thinking and novel internships. This will provide the encouragement they need to continue exploring options until it is clear which direction they will pursue.

ESTP loves to solve a problem that requires people plus machines as elements of the solution. They are pretty good at it too. Tufts University offers the very unusual **Human Factors** major. It is a very versatile degree, also titled engineering psychology. This type often boasts a good sense of the aesthetics, likes to move into the center of action and typically is very much at ease with people. All of these skills will become major strengths as they design products for work, recreation or daily living. Both client and ESTP will enjoy the projects focusing on safety, appearance and efficiency.

ENFP is naturally enthusiastic and Tufts is a place of optimism and dreams. Both this type and their enthusiasm will be a wonderful gift to bring to the studies in **Child Development**. It is an exceptionally strong program with its research foundation, history of children's studies and many options for internships. ENFPs love to help other people and they are quite creative in this art. They are excellent long-range thinkers, comfortable and happy with big abstract ideas, ready with a smile or a bit of humor. They are ideal for spontaneous work with children in stressful environments like inner city neighborhoods, refugee camps or disaster areas. This degree nicely prepares ENFP, who demands a satisfying lifetime career, for graduate work in child studies.

ENTP is one who likes to predict future trends. The major at Tufts University in **Community Health** is just right for this. It draws together collected knowledge from very different fields like political science and engineering plus others. ENTP is a big thinker, ready to embrace these concepts and reformulate them into health perspectives. This type will especially be attracted to the side of the major that deals with policy and planning for large health systems. Faculty in all majors at Tufts will encourage undergraduates to visit and observe other cultures. ENTPs with their boundless need for new experiences can learn to trust their intuition and creativity in distant locations while pondering mass delivery of preventive health care.

ESTJ likes to organize and analyze. This type is comfortable with systems of logic and fact. They could excel at using systems to bring products to the market, straighten out unproductive organizations or develop a technological interface that advances medical practice. The degree in **Biomedical Engineering** is a good choice because it offers the option of developing technology for emerging medicinal procedures. This type prefers to work toward objective goals. How much more logical and objective does it get than developing assistive devices for surgical insertion in the human body? Tufts extensive presence in the health care field provides the needed prompting for this traditional, conservative type to keep exploring this growing field.

ENTJ can productively ponder the future of continental Africa after educational study of its many distinct regions. Attracted to the complexity and hugeness of the continent, ENTJ is fine with pulling that knowledge from several departments on campus. **Africa in the New World** is a minor that would easily combine with majors in the physical or social sciences. This type has long term vision to help human communities move forward. Tufts' approach to off-campus learning experiences is ideal for African study. The faculty embraces observation and places much faith in research technology. The confident ENTJ doesn't need much more than this to launch a rewarding international career.

TULANE UNIVERSITY

Office of Admissions
6823 St. Charles Avenue
New Orleans, LA 70118
Website: www.tulane.edu
Admissions Telephone: 504-865-5731
Undergraduates: 6,487; 2,740 Men, 3,747 Women
Graduate Students: 5,110

Physical Environment

Few people can think of **New Orleans** and not conjure up images of the Super Bowl and French Quarter. Yet beyond the obvious lies a very intricate culture with strong French influences in architecture, cuisine and ethnicity. Tulane University has strong connections with city. The trolley line travels straight from the front campus right into the heart of the city. A short few blocks from there and undergraduate students are in the French Quarter. Yet the real connection with the city is through the student body's remarkable commitment to volunteer service throughout the city. Direct service for others in local residential neighborhoods is a staple at Tulane University. To honor the retiring university president, the student body, faculty, staff and alumni pledged 750,000 volunteer hours to be completed by his Spring 2014 retirement.

Gibson Hall is distinguishable by its **Romanesque architecture** of stone over brick, built in the 1800s. This campus mixes modern and historic together quite comfortably. Sidewalks and lawns are marked by tropical vegetation and it is a delight to walk through campus in mild weather. Another building that competes for attention on this campus is the eco-friendly Lavin-Bernick Center, an impressive modern structure that is the hub of campus and central meeting place for students. **Environmental practices** are an ever-present feature at Tulane University just a few blocks from the Mississippi River and adjacent to the **Arboretum**. RecycleMania is a practical and recent initiative to address the easy over-consumption of plastic and cardboard that collects in university facilities. Faculty reached out to volunteer student building captains in each residence to organize a day long toss out of the stuff.

Tulane continues to invest in **research**, especially at the graduate level. The research energy quickly seeps down to undergraduate courses, thus exposing undergrads to challenging concepts early on. Research spans across the many divisions in biology and especially concentrates on human medical advances.

Social Environment

Tulane University has a large variety of housing options each with a fairly distinct atmosphere. They serve to improve communication and usually offer **leadership opportunities** for the residents. Weatherhead Hall and Butler Hall are honors living and learning communities for freshmen and sophomores. First and second-year students must live on campus. It is not uncommon for faculty members and their families to get involved with students, an extension of the campus/city community feel at

Tulane. Eager undergrads refine leadership skills that tend to be service oriented, not in the activist orientation. As such, they generate community support and success. CACTUS is in its 42nd year on campus and spearheads much of the student-led service success at Tulane. **Elected student leadership** within the collegiate community is very active on this campus.

An important statistic here is that about 80 percent of students come from outside the state of Louisiana. Many come from the **Northeast, followed by the South Atlantic and the Midwest.** They can be seen walking in flip-flops and reveling in the warm weather. Today's students are attracted to the campus for the quality of the education, the opportunities for student involvement and the opportunity for direct service to nearby communities. These are the same attributes that are prevalent on their high school resumes. They are highly sociable and seek to build a wide community experience. At Tulane they are able to interface with others of different cultures. After all, that is the distinguishing mark of the city itself. **Literacy work** is a popular choice and garners much commitment from the university and community. As a result of the required student leadership, communication and follow through, these undergraduates grow in professional skills much needed in pluralistic America today. Tulane's message is clear: be a leader, **be engaged and be successful**. Those students with **emotional power and resiliency** do well here. It comes in most handy as students readily join the Mardi Gras celebrations and the vibrant, sophisticated city life as often as studies and commitment will allow.

Compatibility with Personality Types and Preferences

Tulane University is very much a reflection of its unique association with New Orleans, a city that blended cultural influences for centuries and carries a European aura. Alongside this fascinating historical culture, Tulane's well-regarded graduate schools developed and mirrored the organization of formal European universities in past centuries. This academic philosophy prompts the graduate school research perspectives to translate downward to the undergraduate curriculum. Students at Tulane quickly get a wide exposure (N) to advanced concepts and observation of how those ideas travel in today's mainstream organizations. The university's emphasis on utilization of knowledge also moves into the concepts of leadership for the undergraduate student population. Undergraduate students prepare, through active leadership on campus and in the New Orleans neighborhoods, to translate their recently accrued knowledge out into the larger American community of business and government.

Freshmen happily adopt the casual dress needed for the climate while they prepare for the formal, corporate worlds of policy, business, government and the professions. For this reason, there is a precise order (T) to the coursework in the educational majors and minors. There also is a clear set of core courses designed to assure competencies (S) for all graduates of the university. These competencies in writing, foreign language, public service, mathematics and humanities drive the message home that graduates should aim to accomplish much within their post graduate spans of influence.

There is a natural alliance between Tulane's curriculum and the demands of an advanced economy. Social and extracurricular activity at this university very much prompts connection to the outer world. (E). Undergraduates do not suffer from tunnel vision on this campus. The university mirrors the experience of city life and complex city politics. It can do so because minutes away one finds the professional sophistication of New Orleans and the socio-economic needs of its neighborhoods. Tulane administration is mindful of these juxtapositions (F). It seeks to prepare graduates for transition within all societies for the purposes of leadership and progress. Successful Tulane students are typically characterized by their predisposition to thoughtful reflection and leadership.

In the following listing of college majors it is important to remember that students can fit into any college and can be successful in any major. We have found that the Personality Types below fit very well at this college. The course-of-study chosen for each Personality Type corresponds to MBTI® research and is presented as one of many examples favorable for that type.

INFJ could be enthusiastic about developing strategies to address health issues within neighborhood communities. The five-year BS/MS degree in **Global and Community Health** is ideal for this occupational interest.

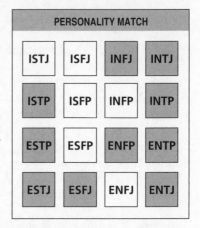

INFJ might easily commit to the nature of this field and appreciate the demand to create new approaches to communicable disease. The need for this work is increasing as fast as the population is growing on Earth. INFJ is most satisfied working in career fields such as this. The major is unusual and receives robust support in tandem with Tulane's perspective toward graduating accomplished professionals.

INTJ prefers to be involved with original, emerging activities. Creative occupations such as architecture and design can easily work for this type if they have artistic talent. Tulane University offers a minor in **Architectural Studies**. The major in **Engineering Physics** would make a nice companion for this minor if INTJ has tolerance for additional semesters beyond the four years. As 21st century design calls for cantilevered structures with glass, metal and the use of new materials, it will be the INTJ who understands their strength and physical properties. This major and minor combination is quite attractive for application for advanced study in Architecture School. This is all very appealing stuff to INTJ whose vision works handily with large, complicated systems.

ISTP will enjoy the **Biomedical Engineering** degree at Tulane University because of the independent research options. The graduate programs reveal many strands of research in this growing field. Undergraduates are required to design a year-long research project of their own. This type lights their own fire once they identify their mechanical passion somewhere within the research labs. At the same time, the school requires students to work on a team-designed project. This, too, fits in well with ISTP who enjoys working with others of similar interest and often becomes the go-to person when the project hits a snag.

INTP will need to satisfy their curiosity in reference to the **Health Informatics** major offered at Tulane University. They like to mix, match and invent computer programs that might constructively organize the millions of data files associated with public and private health service. There really is no level of information management that is too complex or vast for this type as long as they have access to powerful computing resources. This major is well-situated in Tulane's School of Public Health and undergraduates have access to a wealth of knowledge resident in the faculty at this prestigious, forward-thinking medical school. This is an emerging career field with the troubled reorganization of American health care in 2014.

ESTP can find the finance world enticing with its inherent elements of risk and investment. The major in **Finance** at Tulane University has a good selection of coursework that surveys these two critical concepts. The focus on professional preparation also appeals to ESTP who is usually socially savvy. This type can successfully promote products or services with ease through their negotiation skills at the conference table. Tulane's strong graduate programs in the business school will pique the interest of undergraduate ESTP.

ENFP isn't often drawn to business careers but the major in **Management** in Tulane's business school could really appeal to this type. Social issues mix with business concerns as products and services move to market. Within this major, ENFPs must select one of two career tracks, consulting or entrepreneurship. The consulting track is the likely ENFP choice since it focuses on ethics, negotiations and conflict resolutions. It will be valuable for sorting through corporate mergers and acquisitions. As such, it is a skill needed by major consulting firms and this would offer ENFP plenty of travel and excitement.

ENTP could be attracted to the course sequence in **Environmental Health** at Tulane because it introduces disaster management along with toxicology. Preparation for any number of environmental crises is appealing to ENTP who instinctively improvises. Throw in their typical confidence and you have the potential for a very capable disaster manager. ENTP prefers to be in the power circles while focusing on policy planning for the future. This sequence of courses will fill up their disaster skills tool box. Regional and state governments will offer multiple internship options and career options which are stimulating for this type. The focus is an option in the Bachelor of Science Public Health.

ESFJ will delight in combining two fields not often paired together at the undergraduate level. The major in **Psychology and Early Education** is so appealing to this sensitive, caring type. The curriculum in psychological development is an excellent companion to educational studies and the elementary classrooms. Tulane University pairs the major with the option for teacher certification. This type will find career satisfaction in traditional community organizations such as preschools and outreach programs for children. Tulane's strong interface with the city neighborhoods provides excellent service learning options also.

ESTJ often moves into positions of authority during their career. Tulane University is an excellent undergraduate environment for this purpose. ESTJ often has a realistic career plan and commonly utilizes the undergraduate degree to gain access to professional studies for their chosen field. The major titled **Legal Studies in Business** has several advantages for this purpose. It is a curriculum that offers specific, realistic preparation for quite a few fields such as real estate and insurance. ESTJ could also use it to enter law school or as an operations manager in a legal firm. Regardless, this type is excellent at focusing on goals: theirs and the firm's!

ENTJ is quite comfortable in leadership positions. Tulane's emphasis on leadership in extracurricular activities will give this type a chance to secure several positions of authority during the four years on campus. The degree in Management with a major in **Consumer Behavior/Marketing** will allow them to move into the business world they typically enjoy. Coursework emphasizes planning and management of products or services in retail markets. This curriculum has the added benefit of preparing ENTJ for their long term career options. This type has vision that extends far forward so consulting to national and international companies might be on a career horizon for ENTJ. Their natural networking ability also comes in very handy in this field.

UNION COLLEGE

Office of Admissions
Schenectady, NY 12308
Website: www.union.edu
Admissions Telephone: 518-388-6122
Undergraduates: 2,225; 1,199 Men, 1,026 Women

Physical Environment

Union College has a remarkable history with its founding shortly after the American Revolutionary War in 1795. This college has educated **historical figures** such as William H. Seward, Abraham Lincoln's Secretary of State and U.S. President Chester A. Arthur. The beauty of this campus dates back to the late 1700s, when it was founded as a non-denominational college. A most unique building on campus is **Nott Memorial**, a site for many cultural events, and easily recognizable for its **16 sides and Russian-like architecture.** Located in Schenectady, a 30-minute drive from the Albany airport, the city is not in the Snow Belt so it gets an average of **three good snow storms** each year and the rest is just northeastern windy, coolish weather, except maybe in 2014, the year of the polar vortex.

Dedicated May 2011, the Peter Irving Center seeks to increase the **interface between teaching and research** with IBM's donation of Intelligent Cluster computing capabilities. This exceptional facility and the Butterfield Hall renovation, including a scanning electron microscope, reveals the confidence and expectation by the administration for their undergraduate students. It is hard to overestimate the value of the **research equipment** in the Center since no other small liberal arts colleges possess this expansive computing potential. All the more remarkable is the undergraduate student body's original research under the tutelage of Union faculty. The sophomore research seminar and two decades of the Steinmetz Symposiums channel the **excellent undergraduate research programs** on this campus.

The Lippman Hall renovation, completed in 2011, supports the social sciences on campus with the Henle Dance Pavilion, opened in 2013, providing a beautiful setting for rehearsals and small performances. A popular campus hub is Reamer Center which is home to many student organizations. It is one of several dining options on campus, each with distinct menus.

Social Environment

The social environment at Union College can be described in one word: **community**. This campus is for students who want to connect with their peers and their professors, learn a lot and form a warm, welcoming community. They enjoy the cave-like Old Chapel, where there's a coffee bar with internet access, games and room for dances. Students here like their sports, the gymnasium, ball courts, hockey rink and pool. These are very **social students** who get involved in many activities. Each student is assigned to a **"Minerva house"** which puts on event after event. Students have opportunity to both lead and relax at the end of the academic day since the Minerva houses develop student initiative, collaboration and accomplishment. There are also Socials held by fraternity and sorority houses. Undergraduates form a tight-knit community that supports one another's differences and invites discussion. The Union educational experience **includes a study abroad period** and approximately 75 percent of the students will travel and learn off campus.

Union is one of a select few liberal arts colleges with an **engineering** program grounded in intellectual discourse. The core curriculum includes history, science, math and study abroad to gain exposure to other cultures. Union College also attracts students who have an interest in **pre-professional fields** such as medicine. Many students graduate with a Bachelor's degree and pursue a joint program of advanced study in business, education, public policy or medical administration. These degrees are completed on campus in conjunction with other nearby universities. Other students participate in **service learning** facilitated by the curriculum which often is in tandem with research. Most recently the study of dementia was at the center of an undergraduate project. Interviews with local seniors were followed by technology that allowed students to experience seniors' cognitive impairment - temporarily.

Compatibility with Personality Types and Preferences

Students and faculty at Union College reach out, intending to latch on to the future (N) of ideas and concepts. Together, they form a community that prefers to integrate current knowledge with every day common social and physical reality. As a result, personal connections are quite vital at Union College. Friendships and mentoring are viewed as a primary foundation for learning (F). Integrating knowledge through analysis and discovery is the other side of the balanced coin. Undergraduates here carry the responsibility to be prepared for change in the coming century and thus must remain open (P) and able to respond to evolution in their chosen field. The individual departments offer a wide selection of coursework for exploration. This breadth in the curriculum encourages students to continue sampling the field beyond the foundation, often into the junior and senior years. The curriculum always interfaces the social and human context with the technical and scientific concepts. Student-centered research is designed to teach undergraduates how to interpret data and concepts. It features traditional mentoring, advising and investigative methodologies. Therefore, undergrads assertively seek out concepts that can attain success in the marketplace of ideas.

Similarly, the residential life here is vibrant and thoughtfully planned (J). Education invariably crosses the boundary with the residential life programs. International study is designed for overseas academic study that reveals foreign cultural perspectives as applied to the undergraduate academic major. The international sites are selected for this purpose and not chosen to meet other objectives such as travel or service. Integrated knowledge is uppermost at Union College and the administration's humane perspective is very much a part of this integration.

PERSONALITY MATCH			
ISTJ	ISFJ	INFJ	INTJ
ISTP	ISFP	INFP	INTP
ESTP	ESFP	ENFP	ENTP
ESTJ	ESFJ	ENFJ	ENTJ

In the following listing of college majors it is important to remember that students can fit into any college and can be successful in any major. We have found that the Personality Types below fit very well at this college. The course-of-study chosen for each Personality Type corresponds to MBTI® research and is presented as one of many examples favorable for that type.

INFP is one to join up and support a cause or select a career field that advances a particular social issue. The degree at Union College in **Psychology** is nicely tailored to the needs of this type. The curriculum provides a survey of this evolving science. It is really important for INFP to interface their work with their ideals. INFP can focus on human behavior in any of several areas: learning, personality, developmental, language and the list keeps growing as this field matures. INFP is likely to seek and gain admission for the Honors degree in this major.

INFJ is a thoughtful type and a darn good fit for Union College. A degree in **Philosophy** allows for study in history of mankind's expanding knowledge over time. It can help refine the student's own ethical beliefs. The curriculum in philosophy is constructed in a sequence that grows in complexity right along with the undergraduates. INFJs will consider the honors thesis in preparation for graduate study in law, health or the social sciences.

INTJ is an ideal type to declare a minor within an emerging field. It will be the INTJ who can connect precision and imagination in **Nanotechnology** at Union College. As could be expected, this department developed a curriculum that is representative of Union's academic philosophy. Students will acquire basic information about the properties of matter. They will also spend considerable time in relationship with peers and faculty supporting research studies and searching for resolutions. It is a complex thinking activity. However, INTJ is up to it.

ISFP usually can handle change and in fact enjoys changing it up for a good reason. Union College, of the same predisposition, incorporates the inevitability of change within their curriculum. The degree in **Computer Science** at this campus has several attributes that are attractive to ISFPs. Since the college values the concept of social responsibility the technical knowledge in this major will reside with humane perspectives. This also works for values driven ISFP.

ENFP has a very large horizon when it comes to selecting subjects of interest, however, the major selected by this type must offer abstraction and variety. The major in **Geology** can deliver both. At Union College, the current state of the art in understanding Earth's geographic formations is paired with world news of tsunamis and earthquakes in the Pacific Rim. This major is very much about connecting the past, present and the future with abstract, big pictures. ENFP is all for that.

ENTP might be intrigued by the thought of a career in teaching astronomy. Should ENTP have mathematical acumen and interest, the major in **Astronomy** at Union College explores career options for this discipline. This ingenious type might by pass teaching astronomy in high school to reach for a law career in patent work for space hardware. On the other hand, an advanced degree in human health research oriented to the human body in space is a career option. ENTP is attracted to possibilities and Union College is devoted to preparing graduates for the innovative future.

ESFJ wants to support productive partnerships within a community through current business and government practice. The curriculum in **Science, Medicine**

and Technology in Culture is available as a minor or major that could support any of ESFJ's favored career choices in the health sciences, education or social sciences. For the ESFJ captured by the physical sciences, the minor will provide perspective that points to a pure science major such as physics.

ESTJ has the tenacity and determination to deal with the issues surrounding worldwide demands for energy. Union College has just the program to prepare ESTJs for this challenging environment with their unique minor in **Energy Studies.** The course Heat, Light and Astronomy will alert Union graduates to the possibility of future energy production in space. This type will like the recommended mini winter term in New Zealand, touring energy production on the island.

ENFJ is rewarded by understanding and helping others to realize individual potential. The major in **Anthropology** at Union College surveys specializations within this discipline. ENFJs are decisive and organized. The help and mentoring of faculty will be critically important as ENFJ chooses a focus within this expansive curriculum. This type will want the advantage of a warm, mentoring relationship to craft a postgraduate plan. The department curriculum includes coursework in anthropological medicine, environmental anthropology, economic anthropology, urban anthropology, anthropology and religion, psychological anthropology and several more.

ENTJ will find the major in **Neuroscience** at Union College offers three tracks in studying the human brain: bioscience, cognitive or computational. Should they like the idea of moving toward psychiatry, the cognitive track will work. If they like the idea of becoming a medical researcher or medical doctor, the bioscience track will work. If its computational neuroscience, careers in artificial intelligence are calling. With any choice, this type will bring a flair for the corporate world to their career through private practice or consulting work. ENTJ always has that little touch of entrepreneurship buried within their career plans.

THE UNIVERSITY OF CHICAGO

Office of Admission
5801 S. Ellis Avenue
Chicago, Illinois 60637
Website: www.uchicago.edu
Admissions Telephone: 773-702-8650
Undergraduates: 5,369; 2,738 Men, 2,630 Women
Graduates: 6,928

Physical Environment

The University of Chicago is located on the south side of Chicago in the **Hyde Park** area, which flanks Lake Michigan. In this neighborhood of approximately 45,000 residents there are aging residential structures and historic edifices under the care of the local preservation society. Many of the 31 residential houses are located in 11 dormitory halls that are spread across the campus. Prospective students may not be aware of how the physical layout of the campus affects the daily experience. Some dormitory halls are located off campus with a 15-minute walk to reach the academic quads. **Bus service** delivers students to and from campus. The South Campus Residence Hall serves somewhat as a student center with its late night quick-stop market and gathering spaces. Midway Pleasance bisects the campus along with the many busy, bustling avenues delivering products and services to the community. The campus shuttles move students in and around the campus. The projected North Residence Hall is in current construction phase through opening in Fall 2016. Taken together, the construction, congestion and inner city nature of the setting calls out to students who are alert and resilient.

The University of Chicago's circa-1890s original campus consists of a **neo-Gothic rectangular** structure, replete with gargoyles and all, built along several city blocks that enclose a large rectangular yard, the main quadrangle. The campus has and is undergoing a comprehensive update to its infrastructure. In the past 15 years, a new, **minimalist architecture** has spread throughout. The Mansueto Library is modern to the extreme and the architectural space reminds one of the Apple store in New York City. Like all new structures on the campus it sports the **latest convenience and technological design** with its automatic book retrieval in shelves 50 feet high. The new architecture forms an interesting juxtaposition of layers and heights, geometric lines composed of glass and steel abound in vertical and horizontal planes with occasional curves thrown in for variety. The Logan Center for the Arts is another example. The university elects to often raze dated historical structures like the Research Institutes for the construction of new facilities housing the same departments but with a new name.

Social Environment

The campus environment is a bastion of **rational thought**. Here there is everything for the **brilliant, reserved** student. For curious, intellectually-aggressive first year students, knowledge and **pursuing research** are tandem activities. The **Core** of required courses consumes approximately one-third of a student's undergraduate study. It is comprehensive across nine large academic subdivisions including health fitness. Within these first year studies, there is discussion and more discussion over the primary texts. In this challenging way, students forge a deep level of inquiry that opens multiple academic paths for the upperclass studies. Students quickly generate connections among bright peers and **stimulating professors**. Many of them already know their academic major.

Intellectual inquiry can lead to single-minded pursuit on this campus. The vast majority of students will pursue graduate study and look to craft their undergraduate efforts toward a particular research field. Recently, a second year student studied the Syrian crisis and its effect on higher education. His research led him into an international project of the same agenda and will likely form his further postgraduate studies. Others may study problematic trends in American legislative bodies and the current executive office usurpation of powers. Here there may be potential for a broad base of inquiry after studies in foundational knowledge. Yet connections with powerful agendas in Chicago politics may exist and bring influence to bear on inquiry.

With that said, sports don't dominate the social scene but intramural teams do and they are robust. Each residence hall has multiple teams supported by frequent scheduling of competitions, multiple locations to play and plenty of equipment. It is all very accessible. Each of the Halls forms its own environment with approximately 100 or so students, faculty and professional staff to direct residential life within. Active fraternities and sororities contribute to the social and service activities. These students enjoy **occasional breaks off campus** visiting artistic, blues and jazz clubs, but a lot of the action is on campus with interesting student clubs and active residential life components.

Compatibility with Personality Types and Preferences

University of Chicago is an analytical machine (T) with fuzzy edges. It's a nice combination actually. They honor tradition (J) and history in a number of ways which can serve to inform logic on this campus. However, the graduate research relentlessly seeks new truths that seem to pop up with the passing of each decade. The list of scientific discoveries at U Chicago, such as carbon-14 dating, attests to this. University of Chicago students are cool with reading historical texts and speculating on what was meant by the author of those texts (N). This interesting way of looking in the past for possibilities is a hallmark of the university, as well as a contradiction. These students arrive as freshman with the belief that the next four years will intensely look to the future to develop their understanding of the world, yet U Chicago sees much wisdom in the past. Undergraduates will learn to look for novel ideas (P) in all time and space mediums. They will come to connect this personal understanding with the past and the future forming a starter soup for intellectual endeavors in graduate school. The curriculum pulls from across disciplines, seeking wisdom, no matter the era. University of Chicago draws students who may be conservative in some ways and always anxiously curious and driven.

In the following listing of college majors it is important to remember that students can fit into any college and can be successful in any major. We have found that the Personality

Types below fit very well at this college. The course-of-study chosen for each Personality Type corresponds to MBTI® research and is presented as one of many examples favorable for that type.

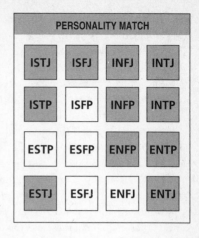

PERSONALITY MATCH

ISTJ	ISFJ	INFJ	INTJ
ISTP	ISFP	INFP	INTP
ESTP	ESFP	ENFP	ENTP
ESTJ	ESFJ	ENFJ	ENTJ

INFJ who has a spiritual bent will very much be interested in the **Religion and Humanities** major at University of Chicago. The thoroughness with which this major is designed is pretty impressive and definitely appeals to INFJ's attraction to philosophy and human values. Four major areas help build a foundation for upper level courses. First, U Chicago approaches the basic complexity of studying religion. Second, the department helps the student acquire one of several strategies to comprehend historical religious texts. Next, students focus on the community of believers and how they self-interpret their religion. And lastly, specific religious texts are reviewed. With this preparation, INFJ will find many satisfying days of study throughout the four years.

ENFP smiles broadly when they see that U Chicago offers a program of study in **Big Problems**. It is not a major but combines nicely with the many interests typical of the wide ranging ENFPs. As foretold, Big Problems are essentially defined as unsolvable. U Chicago brings together courses that help undergraduates learn how to approach the enormous complexity with optimism and skill intended to make a positive difference. ENFPs will have no trouble stretching their imaginations wide enough to comprehend the enormity and love the long-range projections that go along with the program.

INFP sometimes has a chivalrous streak. By studying past successful civilizations, INFPs ferret out questions and answers that led to progress within an ancient society. Study abroad at U Chicago offers a 10-week course on location with departmental faculty in that field. The **Civilization Studies** program is held in Europe, the Far and Middle East and South America. It provides a good opportunity to explore academic fields in the social sciences for follow on research back at U Chicago.

ENTJ who likes numbers is going to really enjoy the **Applied Mathematics** major at U Chicago. This department is at the forefront of leading edge mathematics. Faculty actively promote the evolution of modern day math usage in disciplines across society. ENTJs with their visionary mind and interest in reality will like the three-course requirement in one of the physical sciences. By combining the efficiency of advanced math with a physical science, ENTJ will access and secure leadership positions within industry. This type might otherwise exercise leadership as a professor of mathematics who mentors and organizes graduates to solve industrial problems.

INTJ will find lots of room to maneuver with the **Physics** major at U Chicago. The administration and department philosophies strongly support interdisciplinary application. INTJs will first get grounded in the fundamental studies of matter, energy and force. This can be followed with further technical courses that move in the direction of medical, atmospheric or environmental sciences. INTJs love the rapid, spontaneous nature of discovery in technology and will likely be inventing stuff themselves after further graduate studies.

ENTP might initially find the **Law, Letters and Society** major at U Chicago revealing a very structured view of society. It could bump up against this type's wish for spontaneity with intellectual competence. As ENTP moves through the sequence of coursework and research, they will gain clarity on how society is organized, shaped and controlled through the application of laws. This very abstract nature of study is sufficiently complex to keep ENTP from getting bored. The required course selection will also be a good lesson in control for the freewheeling ENTP.

INTP absolutely likes to come up with something original. It really gets their juices going. The interdisciplinary program in **Creative Writing** here is a perfect approach to writing for this type who is passionate about their major. U Chicago expects those who take these writing courses to apply their writing expertise to their major field of study. INTP is just fine with this idea and will approve of new writing styles designed to turn the apple cart around, whatever apples are in their major.

ESTJ has a penchant for seeking out and doing away with the illogical and inefficient. This is a great characteristic if you intend to major in **Economics.** The math and the modern economy are the focus. The marketplace is explored through mathematical theories of supply and demand such as game theory, auctions and econometrics. Since this type is a natural administrator with the toughness needed to run regulatory offices, the course Regulation of Vice is a fine preparation for careers in government and its interface with the corporate world.

ISTJ is going to get the facts straight and every one of the facts will be in that straight line. You can count on it. The major in **Geophysical Sciences** is a good bet with its scientific data that ISTJs can apply with their tremendous powers of concentration. This type may struggle with the individualized nature of the curriculum. Undergraduates in this department at U Chicago start tailoring their studies immediately by following their interests. Inclined to survey all approaches to education, they can count on congeniality with peers and faculty while identifying that niche of interest that will become their major focus. Once determined, ISTJ's strengths come back into play big time.

ISFJ who is attracted to nursing, as they can easily be, can pursue the major in **Biological Sciences** here. It will be an ideal preparation for the medical field or perhaps a professor of nursing. The department does not introduce studies from other disciplines into this major, beyond the general education requirements of the university itself. Rather there is a sound commitment to educate undergraduate students with a realistic understanding of the physical nature of this science.

ISTP is often accurate with the numbers and always likes to add reality to whatever they study. The major in **Statistics** is a good choice for this type, yet ISTPs with their little touch of humor will need more than just numbers to keep them engaged. At U Chicago, there is choice to combine the statistics major with any other field in the natural or social sciences. This type is likely to move toward the physical sciences, however, since they are often technically quite competent.

UNIVERSITY OF MIAMI

Office of Admission
P.O. Box 248025
Coral Gables, FL 33124-4616
Website: www.miami.edu
Admissions Telephone: 305-284-4323
Undergraduates: 9,979; 4,886 Men, 5,093 Women
Graduate Students: 5,582

Physical Environment

University of Miami is only a few miles from downtown Miami and less than **20 minutes from South Beach**. This inviting, pleasant campus is surrounded by the residential neighborhoods of Coral Gables. Students get down town quickly by hopping the metro at the stop adjacent to campus. The Coral Gables campus houses graduate and undergraduate studies and features Lake Osceola at its center. Recent and current construction has enhanced the Student Activity Center which is perched on the edge of the lake. Architecture is cohesive and identifiable with function, warding off the direct sun and its energy demand on air conditioning equipment.

With excellent fall and winter weather, students get around by bicycles, pedestrian sidewalks or the shuttle system which is a must since the campus is quite large. **Benches and outdoor chairs** abound on campus in lovely outdoor landscaped places. There are two main dining halls located on opposite sides of the campus. Most first year students are on the meal plan while many upper class students go off campus more often or rent an apartment with friends. Sprinkled throughout are plenty of small snack shops like Subways, Wendy's, etc. Students can experience beach life at its best, along with vibrant night life and outdoor restaurants, yet the action on campus is equally vibrant and well-provisioned by an attentive administration.

Undergraduates may declare majors within any of the nine academic schools at the university. There is a flexible policy for double majors and interdisciplinary majors. The graduate academic departments and research laboratories at University of Miami are imposing in size, presence and national importance within their disciplines. Administration philosophy for undergraduate participation within these national research facilities is channeled into a few select service learning projects in the greater Miami area.

Social Environment

Slightly less than half of the students on campus are from Florida with the other half coming from large Midwestern states, the eastern seaboard and California. Students who attend U of Miami are academically **high achieving** and arrive with outgoing attitudes and extracurricular interests to match. First-year classes can be large, especially the **general education classes**. Upper-level classes have fewer students, some with as few as 20 students or less. Academic advising is handled differently within each of the schools. The Business School utilizes **peer counseling** whereby selected upperclass students advise freshmen on classes, schedules and adjusting to college life. In the College of Arts and Sciences, freshmen are assigned a first year advisor in the department of their declared majors or meet with counselors serving those who remain undeclared in the first year.

University of Miami has a very active and well-resourced **Student Government**. It is patterned after the United States government with a Senate, Executive Office, Courts, etc. Much of the informal social environment is organized and channeled through this group of elected undergraduate students. Social events and campus wide entertainment are excellent as a result. Greek fraternities and sororities also are active in generating social options on campus.

Resident faculty and professional staff are in each of the dormitories. They provide academic and recreational programming in conjunction with student representatives of their dormitory. Juniors and seniors can apply for housing in the Villages which is apartment style. First year students must live on campus together in designated dormitories with staff attuned to their transition from home towns hundreds of miles distant. Most Residence Halls are coed and operate traditionally with men and women on alternate floors, singles and doubles with common restrooms. Visiting hours for guests and Quiet Hours lend stability to the dynamic daily experience on campus. This arrangement acknowledges the many off campus diversions within minutes of an international playground. In its way, University of Miami is cognizant of the challenges involved with each incoming freshman class and their successful transition to university life and greater Miami.

Compatibility with Personality Types and Preferences

University of Miami in Florida is a large presence in the collegiate liberal arts world. It is a large campus and has the big undergraduate student numbers to rival a regional state university. The educational curriculum boasts many majors not frequently found at independent institutions. U Miami has the extra advantage of appealing to single-minded high school grads who know exactly what they want to be when they grow up. Undergraduate energy on this campus tends to move in two directions: one is negotiating the demanding, dynamic curriculum and the other is the big, wide city life. Students who like this university come to terms with the city's social intensity in their own way. Some embrace it with vigor, others sample it as needed for a break from the demanding academics. Regardless of social inclinations, students here are on the ball, paying attention, pursuing a goal (S). The campus is geared for analytic learning with expectations for precise content (T) by both the professors and students in the classroom. Fuzziness is reserved for pillows in the dormitory. It is an ideal campus for the socially adept who can take advantage (E) of the exciting international culture, yet show up in class the next day prepared. It is also just right for the socially quieter types who often keep their nose in the books, yet want to experiment with new social venues in college. For these latter types, it is great to drop into the city anonymously for an evening of observation with a friend or two. Undergraduates who keep their academics as the first priority do quite well at this energetic, well-connected university. They become productive, astute citizens in the workforce which is a pretty darn good paraphrase of the U Miami mission statement.

In the following listing of college majors it is important to remember that students can fit into any college and can be successful in any major. We have found that the Personality

Types below fit very well at this college. The course-of-study chosen for each Personality Type corresponds to MBTI® research and is presented as one of many examples favorable for that type.

INTJ sometimes finds higher education in academia an enticing career goal. This type thrives in educational atmospheres where peers are also interested in tough subjects. The INTJs really love to pull together theoretical, abstract information and throw it into an operating system or useable concept. U Miami offers a double major in **Marine Science** that is paired with one of the other physical sciences: geology, biology, chemis-

PERSONALITY MATCH			
ISTJ	ISFJ	INFJ	INTJ
ISTP	ISFP	INFP	INTP
ESTP	ESFP	ENFP	ENTP
ESTJ	ESFJ	ENFJ	ENTJ

try, physics or computer science. Visionary INTJs will have no trouble seeing the connections between these disciplines during their undergraduate years. After graduation, advanced degrees for academic teaching/research posts or government and industry might call out to this type.

ISTP loves to discover the how and why of things. The **Audio Engineering** degree at U Miami is an accredited degree and comes with all the demands and privileges of a bachelor of science in engineering. The fun part for ISTP is that this option is highly integrated with the robust School of Music at this university. ISTPs will secure the code or get a door key for access to the audio labs at all times of night. The options for utilizing this degree are greater than one might think: medical instrumentation, analog/digital industrial applications and the obvious music entertainment industry.

ISTJ can utilize the curriculum track in **Health Science General** to explore and possibly prepare for a career in the medical field—perhaps veterinary services. This type is outstanding at noticing the facts and details, including listening carefully to the owners or their four-legged patients. ISTJs are typically conscientious, thoughtful, competent and possess fabulous memories for techniques and procedures. They are comfortable in offering services that require repetitive use of the skills. Mastery of content is their forte and they will be prepared for admission to professional schools.

INTP could like the major in **Ecosystem Science and Policy**. This curriculum also requires a second major selected from the physical sciences or math. The senior capstone course interfaces science and policy as it applies to a verifiable ecosystem, perhaps the Everglades. INTPs on our planet earth will not back away from such heavy, theoretical and critical issues. In fact, this type is energized by problems of this complexity. They typically need time to think over their reaction/answer. Identification of their second major will evolve out of this introspective process. Fast-paced, fact-based University of Miami may put a little rush on them, yet this major and the campus social life are ideal for this type. INTPs often become absorbed in study and only occasionally want to head out for a social break.

ESTP is often a natural at promoting goals through spontaneous, quick-thinking action in their lighthearted way. This predisposition might become a full-blown career after completing the major in **Public Relations** within the very strong School of Communication at University of Miami. ESTPs accurately read the tea leaves and will enjoy learning the craft of developing a consistent, targeted message. Spontaneity once again comes into play as ESTP dreams up all the various vehicles to get the message out to the audience.

ESFP might dust off their fifth grade recorder or hang onto that marching band horn to look closely at the unusual major, **Music Therapy**, offered at U Miami. This type is often attracted to the helping professions in education and health care. At the same time, many have proficiency or at least an interest in the performing arts. Therefore, this major should click with a few ESFPs. The requirement for good communication skills needed in this field also comes naturally to this type. The well-provisioned School of Music at U Miami is also accredited through therapeutic organizations, giving the graduate strong credibility in the marketplace. This growing discipline is exploring treatments for difficult personality constructs such as autism and Alzheimer's.

ENTP tends to be a risk-taker who might look favorably at going into business. A few courses in **Entrepreneurship** selected together with the professional advisors at the business school is ideally situated with nearby international, dynamic Miami. The school encourages a competitive focus with the annual business plan competition. Naturally assertive, ENTPs will be comfortable looking for partners to enter this contest. Likely ENTP will pair up with a peer in their major discipline and put an entrepreneurial angle to a research study. Although not known for their practicality, their creativity often sparkles.

ESTJ and the concept of authority go quite nicely together. It is a serious and honorable business for this type to make decisions, supervise and issue guidance with a solid foundation of skills and knowledge. The major in **Management** at U Miami is well-positioned to sharpen that foundational set of skills. The international flavor of Miami alerts traditional ESTJs to new possibilities in commerce. ESTJs will study the thorough business curriculum, but note that internships and professional mentoring seem to be reserved for the graduate students. After consideration, this type may opt for a minor in business which is also possible.

ENTJ likes to be high on the list for efficient on-time arrivals. This often capable administrator likes to develop an innovative and on-time leadership style. University of Miami School of Business is well paired with the School of Nursing in offering the major in **Health Sector Management and Policy**. ENTJs will recognize that this degree would give them entry points to executive positions in medicine, health insurance or health administration. The troubled overhaul of the American health industry from insurance to medicine is fertile ground for future careers with this major.

UNIVERSITY OF PENNSYLVANIA

Office of Admissions
1 College Hall
Philadelphia, PA 19104-6376
Website: www.upenn.edu
Admissions Telephone: 215-898-7507
Undergraduates: 9,374: 4,711 Men, 4,663 Women
Graduate Students: 10,521

Physical Environment

U Penn is located in busy and bustling West Philadelphia, a few blocks from the Schuylkill River. The university's surrounding neighborhoods have many **ethnic shops and restaurants** along narrow streets. Upperclass students with confidence in their city skills ride their bikes to and from off-campus apartments should they decide to rent a room in these neighborhoods. Once on campus, they are assisted by the Penn Connect design that 'friendlies' this urban campus for pedestrians. The campus offers a park-like setting and an interesting **mélange of historic buildings** in Federal, Colonial, Romanesque and Modern vertical style. The extremely varied architecture, representing several periods on this campus, is visually delightful. Within the last five years, it has also been dressed up with planned ecological green lawns. It all calls out to students interested in applied art and classical studies. The libraries are housed separately by subject and are clearly designated for either undergraduate or graduate use. U Penn is a very organized place indeed.

Shoemaker Green, completed in Fall 2012, is a reclaimed open space on campus that will serve to improve ground water and reduce heat intensity during the summer months. College Hall was the first building in 1872 to be constructed on U Penn's campus and the statue of Ben Franklin in front of the entrance was there to witness it. An immediate sense of **American history** attracts high school students who may have elected American history over European history in their advanced high school classes. The planned Neural and Behavioral Sciences building will truly impact the undergraduates arriving on campus when completed. It will house undergraduate studies in psychology and biology, facilitating emerging research and interface between these two disciplines.

Most students live in the College Houses, essentially **tall dormitory towers**. New College House opens in 2016 and will bolster on campus occupancy which currently accommodates about 60 percent of the student body. The inside perimeter of these residences and the evolving campus design provide a comfortable enclosure and contrast to the city. The nearby Penn track is handy enough for most students to exercise on campus. U Penn students arrive comfortable with the **city landscape** or become quickly attuned to it.

Social Environment

The very large majority of U Penn students are valedictorians of their high school graduation class. They were likely to be athletes and/or **student leaders** who initiated service projects through their high school clubs for their hometown community.

They tend to come from all over the U.S. and around the world. Their well-developed inclination to be **goal-driven** can be accommodated in the residential dormitories too. The university has approximately 50 optional residential living programs with a common academic theme. Incoming freshmen may apply by essay for selection to one of these programs.

Once on campus, undergrads move through the first two semesters fulfilling core and general course requirements. Each of the Schools of Business, Nursing, Engineering and Arts and Sciences sets their own core distribution. However, there is flexibility and classes may cross over into any of the other undergraduate schools. With basic study completed, undergrads will move into majors and minors including **undergraduate research**.

University of Pennsylvania is over the top in their **encouragement** for undergraduates who want to tackle research in addition to their basic studies. The national laboratories and noted national faculty are not held out separately from the undergraduate academic departments. There are multiple advisements that initiate and help students find the right research for their study. Equally desirable, there seems to be no overriding university philosophical agenda narrowing options in which political direction to pursue research.

Many students will want to continue volunteering in service clubs and activities and curriculum offers a significant number of service learning courses in West Philadelphia. Students will also find social outlets in the performing arts, athletics, and residential programs. Fraternities and sororities continue to provide social and leadership options for those who join.

Compatibility with Personality Types and Preferences

University of Pennsylvania is unique among the most prestigious American universities in a number of categories. Probably the singular and most important factor is that of their founder, Ben Franklin. On this campus, the American Founding Fathers have a presence and appreciation. His lifetime achievements influenced a foundation of practicality and innovation that is holistically in place today. Three hundred years later, as one looks closely at the course of studies available to undergraduate students, you will see a curriculum of which he would likely approve.

Undergraduates at U Penn like the concept that you gather all the known information and then see how it can be applied. This type of knowledge can be advanced into the near future for the benefit of society as well as the bank account of the innovator. It is most important to understand how things work and how they will be used at U Penn. The favorite learning tool for this is logical analysis (T). Students drawn to U Penn are exceptionally fine logical thinkers. The happy student knows that the universe is predictable (J) and will be evolving for the better as soon as they graduate and get out in the marketplace.

U Penn excels at real world applications of knowledge (S). The sciences are stellar at Penn and crossing academic boundaries is facilitated with an emphasis on integrated knowledge. The new Translational Research Center is more than over the top, gathering the biomedical research departments under one roof. Undergraduates may find their way into it should they be interested. The educational philosophy is also viewed in part as a "repository of knowledge." Between these two perspectives, the university continues to play a much-needed, pivotal role in the well being of the nation.

In the following listing of college majors it is important to remember that students can fit into any college and can be successful in any major. We have found that the Personality Types below fit very well at this college. The course-of-study chosen for each Personality Type corresponds to MBTI® research and is presented as one of many examples favorable for that type.

ISTJ at U Penn will want to look into the Huntsman Program to utilize their excellent memory for foreign languages in an environment that requires accuracy and efficiency. A language like **Russian** combined with the **International Studies and Business** curriculum is an excellent choice for the business world, a comfortable place for ISTJ. This type can make the tough decisions and cut through to the core with precision. That includes summoning up amazing concentration while conducting business in a second language with aggressive, savvy East European entrepreneurs. Sounds a little like training for the Sochi Olympics, doesn't it?

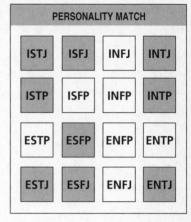

PERSONALITY MATCH

ISTJ	ISFJ	INFJ	INTJ
ISTP	ISFP	INFP	INTP
ESTP	ESFP	ENFP	ENTP
ESTJ	ESFJ	ENFJ	ENTJ

ISFJ can work one-on-one and do very well at satisfying a client's needs. Add this to their natural appreciation for fine design and you have a concentration in **Real Estate.** U Penn's Wharton School of Business and Management is always in the top five national ranking. Undergraduates reap the benefits of its presence on campus. Upon graduation, ISFJ is likely to join a brokerage and pick up the experience needed to move into top firms. An alternative might be to branch out and serve the real estate market in the U.S. or internationally. This reflective type prefers to serve others and might be found developing affordable housing in third world countries in a few years. Ben Franklin, an international at heart, would approve.

INTJ is quite the visionary and prefers to work in areas where originality and new ideas rule. U Penn's major in **Digital Media Design** could be a good one if paired with some level of artistic talent. This four-year degree resides in the Engineering School of Applied Science. INTJs have the determination to create new expression and ways of communication. They love to work independently and often hold themselves to a very high standard. Only a few types would be willing to secure a Bachelor of Science in Engineering with the goal of going into graphics. Yet when you throw in virtual reality, then INTJs are on board. The U Penn graduate in this field will probably move toward virtual programming that helps apply practical knowledge without the risk of physical failure. Ben Franklin has a smile on his face.

ISTP might want to take up a career in the military. As a member of the Navy Reserve Officer Corps at U Penn, there will be rewarding financial scholarships to apply to tuition. This type is a natural troubleshooter when it comes to practical problems. The Economics degree with a concentration in **Actuarial Science** might open up challenging and rewarding career tracks in weapons development. This type's comfort with machines and moving parts supplements their pragmatic accuracy with numbers and details. This degree and those characteristics are true assets while evaluating risks inherent to billion dollar weapon system contracts or reducing their budget lines to numbers in the high millions.

INTP likes to take on studies that might seem beyond the pale to others. Neuroengineering and genetic engineering fit nicely into the category of possible majors for this type. They possess a rampant curiosity for new fields. U Penn's research facilities in the **Bioengineering** field are more than pretty special. Once again we have the Ben Franklin perspectives influencing the curriculum. After all, how much more practical does it get than working on the artificial heart that could become reality in the near future? No abstractions here, it either beats on time or it's not working. INTPs could spend years perfecting the instrumentation with their exceptional skills in long-range planning.

ESFP absolutely gets the real world of "what's happening now." There is no fuzzy-headed, wanderlust thread through their observation of the day. U Penn's Wharton School of Business concentration in **Insurance and Risk Management** will take advantage of this skill. It also provides this type with people interaction which they thrive on. The variety of risk assessments within the field of insurance also work perfectly for ESFPs who are excellent communicators. Their ability to recall and juggle large amounts of data allows them to be productive in this exacting science. The major in economics with this concentration prepares ESFP to tackle citywide assessments such as those generated in New Orleans as a result of Hurricane Katrina.

ESFJ easily travels well in the world of **Nursing.** U Penn's objective within the nursing school is to activate research designs that improve nursing practices. ESFJ values this goal because it involves serving patients as individuals. Priority one for this type is maintaining a healthy, well-functioning, caring environment. U Penn's degree in nursing has an interdisciplinary nature with human health decisions viewed through ethical, wellness and community perspectives, as well as treatment regimes. This type has the curiosity to touch base with all patients and staff during their nursing daily routines. The U Penn nursing graduate is surely headed for decision making at the most encompassing levels of health in our society.

ESTJ is very good at spotting inefficient and impractical habits. With this natural inclination, they function well as civil servants in city, state or national government. Implementing policy while interacting with the public is a critical skill. Fortunately, competent decision making tends to be ESTJ's work style. They simply cut through confusion or inefficiency if at all possible. With the U Penn major in **Urban Studies** this type has the knowledge and credibility to wield authority in some of the most demanding municipal environments. It would be ESTJs, with a U Penn degree in this major, that possess the competence to excel at city planning for Detroit, Philadelphia or Washington, DC.

ENTJ could look at the fine management degrees in U Penn's Wharton School and settle on **Health Care Management and Policy**. This field offers the complexity and big picture that ENTJs need for satisfaction. It also offers the potential for a spiraling climb to the top in an industry that seems to be very good at spiraling. This type has the acumen to develop successful plans in complex environments. The medical fields of today include artificial hearts, indigent services, technical diagnostics, knowledge of litigation and above all, execs who bring a sense of honesty. ENTJs, with a U Penn degree in this field, will have each and every one of these skills and talents.

UNIVERSITY OF REDLANDS

1200 East Colton Avenue
Redlands, CA 92373
Website: www.redlands.edu
Admissions Telephone: 800-455-5064
Undergraduates: 3,452; 1,518 Men, 1,934 Women
Graduates: 1,504

Physical Environment

Located in the **small town** of Redlands, inland about 60 miles east of the Pacific Ocean, this campus was founded by the American Baptist Convention in 1909. The surrounding ecological environment visually encourages students to focus on the delicate balance between nature and man. Students quickly access the semi-arid mountains for recreation, leaving behind the lush campus landscape. Spacious but not remote, the university has always sought to connect with the larger American scene opening its doors to those of all faiths. A similar ethos exists in the adjacent small town which offers the only memorial shrine to Abraham Lincoln in the western half of the United States. Despite the sesquicentennial of the American Civil War, there have been a very few museums in the country responding with exhibits educating the public about emancipation and this critical time period. It seems to be replicative of public schools driven by agendas resulting in little time available for our founding history.

U Redlands founder located the main campus buildings with striking views of the San Bernardino Mountains and much appreciation for the potential of America. The administration understood then and now the **nature of space** and how it plays a critical factor in **shaping human activity.** The **Hunsaker University Center** has three dining areas, located in the middle of the campus next to the new science quad, library and sports complex, it gets a lot of traffic. Renovation of the library in 2011 included the much desired 24-hour study lounge. The sports complex is extensive and includes an outdoor pool for water polo. At this university many students are athletically-inclined and talented. The new Center for the Arts expands the artistic and creative spaces on campus.

On one side of the quad by the chapel, the Johnston School for Integrative Studies is almost a second college within the Redlands campus. Students selected for this program are comfortable with forgoing grades and designing their course of studies in lieu of a major. The Johnston School is a cohesive living-and-learning community since Johnston students take classes in the same residence halls where they live and self-govern their educational experiences. Their studies are interdisciplinary in nature as well as highly individualized. The school's curriculum is designed for its own undergraduates, although Johnston students take many courses at the university also.

Social Environment

Student life is integrated with academic life. The aim of the university is to develop students capable of making wise choices in a complex social world. The university hosts a vibrant **Greek community** with chapter houses for the local sororities and fraternities on campus. Students are **physically fit, comfortable and enthusiastic** to be at Redlands. Students want the emphasis on service learning much as they did in their hometowns during high school. At the same time there is an **entrepreneurial focus** that seeps down from the business school encouraging undergraduates to be successful as well as passionate. As a result, students tend to be responsible, seek traditional security and hope to benefit society.

The **student government** is very active and well-resourced with a judicial structure and executive functions which generate on-campus arts, entertainment and cultural programming. The residence halls are very active also with programming for students. Each is staffed with professional support whose purpose it is to gather the community and prompt them to develop a **Community Standard**. It is an active process which builds fellowship and collaboration within the small groups in the dormitories. There is a wide variety of housing including California Founders Hall with all female and all male communities. The prevailing activist view here is to work in conjunction with regional and national humanitarian organizations. Ideally, students here seek to promote awareness and policy for those across the world living in poverty. There is also an underlying and quiet tolerance of all world religions. Most Redlands students care about **social order,** and finding new solutions to old problems.

Compatibility with Personality Types and Preferences

University of Redlands does a great job blending order, structure (S), creativity and openness into a strong, consistent campus culture. The environment is comfortable and feels healthy and optimistic. The administration and faculty devote most of their effort and resources toward the learning experience. The social experience or social fabric on this campus takes its direction (J) from the academic life. Students socialize "early and often" while their gatherings (F) are also likely to have more than a shade of beneficial activity within. This nicely reflects part of the college mission to develop "circular diversity." There is just a hint of the Quaker morality on this campus, along with the emphasis on what and how it should be. The lovely cream stucco buildings and red tile roofs at this college speak to that standard. In decades past, the founders hoped to educate students who would come to appreciate other cultures by studying established formal belief systems from around the world. The administration and faculty hold this cross-cultural foundation as uppermost while guiding the student population through their educational studies. At the same time, American culture and heritage is valued and studied for its historical richness and underlying national strength.

In the following listing of college majors it is important to remember that students can fit into any college and can be successful in any major.

PERSONALITY MATCH			
ISTJ	ISFJ	INFJ	INTJ
ISTP	ISFP	INFP	INTP
ESTP	ESFP	ENFP	ENTP
ESTJ	ESFJ	ENFJ	ENTJ

We have found that the Personality Types below fit very well at this college. The course-of-study chosen for each Personality Type corresponds to MBTI® research and is presented as one of many examples favorable for that type.

ENTP should like the mix of finance and economics. This could lead to a career in investments and U of Redlands offers a BS in **Financial Economics**. There is a strong math requirement for this degree which includes freshman level calculus and one sophomore level math class, followed by a junior level elective in Mathematical Economics. With this preparation, ENTP will attain the skills to move across the spectrum of the financial markets, following their keen intuition and entrepreneurial spirit.

ENFJ is an excellent fit on the Redlands campus. The major in **Government** is particularly rich with national perspectives, reflecting Redland's comfort level with American heritage. Learning outcomes for undergraduates seem to pop with freshness throughout this curriculum in this major. You can get your head around this statement taken from the major's website - "Discover the origins of government and how they are structured."

ENFP might enjoy the unusual major in **Environmental Business** in the School of Business at this university. The emphasis is to explore how large established companies can improve their ecological practices while manufacturing goods or providing services. This is rather a niche in the business world and likely to be well received with increasing municipal and governmental directives.

INFP is another excellent fit at University of Redlands. In **Creative Writing**, the English department focuses on the creative process rather than a specific genre such as poetry, short stories or writing for the theater. Exceptionally vision-driven, INFPs seek to find their own tune to march to in the collegiate years. The major in creative writing offers an avenue to express their closely held values. The department regularly bumps up its visiting speakers lecture series. INFP will incorporate their thoughts with noted writers and that is just fine with INFP.

INFJ, the deep thinker, may wonder why a minor in **Human Animal Studies**? However, the answer comes fairly quickly if they intend to follow a career in wildlife conservation, veterinary medicine, therapy, zoos or wildlife rehabilitation centers. The program is unusual and this original thinker will enjoy the Johnston School curriculum and its emphasis on writing in lieu of grades.

ESFJ wants to efficiently help others, preferably with direct or at least tangible results. The degree in **Communicative Disorders** here fits this description. At Redlands there is a carefully defined curriculum within each major. In addition to the speech and hearing body of knowledge, students must also have interpersonal skills to gain admission to the major and be successful on the job. It is likely that ESFJ will pass these requirements with flying colors since they are warm and enjoy situations where they can better get to know individuals.

ESFP would find the degree in **Business Administration** at U Redlands just the right mix between objective study and humane perspectives. This campus is remarkably encouraging of experiential learning through the internship, study abroad and travel abroad options in May and the summer. The business curriculum presents the basic business skills in a thorough manner. ESFPs need and crave action so their typical gift of gab with sound business practices might make for VP of Sales within five years at local or regional business concerns.

ISFP can definitely find a place at U Redlands and it might just be the **Biology** major which includes a more formal approach to premed advising than many small liberal arts colleges offer. The course titled Observations in the ER allows ISFP students to watch others excel at their own talent—taking quick decisive action in crisis situations. Since this type is also a free spirit and prefers freedom of action in the work place, perhaps they would rather be outside, not quite so confined as an emergency room. U Redlands department in biology is also helping undergrads explore the nature of insects and the diseases they carry to our food crops. Small scale research projects in the California fruit orchards are so doable here and supportive of the growing need for PhDs in this field populated now by retiring Baby Boomers.

ISFJ can be generous, giving, helpful and thoughtful which serves them well in the health care fields. The major in **Biochemistry and Molecular Biology** is excellent as an introduction to this ever-growing discipline. At Redlands, there will be a strong interface with community well-being perspectives also. The service clubs on campus like Roots and Shoots bring sciences to local elementary school and ISFJ will enjoy the time to engage others in service learning.

UNIVERSITY OF RICHMOND

28 Westhampton Way
Richmond, VA 23173
Website: www.richmond.edu
Admissions Telephone: 804-289-8640
Undergraduates: 2,983; 1,393 Men, 1,549 Women
Graduates: 548

Physical Environment

The University of Richmond is nestled into forest and hills with Westhampton Lake at the center of the campus. The campus grounds reveal a **landscaped valley** reminiscent of a country club. The Tyler Haynes Commons is not only a student center, but also functions as a bridge over the ten-acre lake. Essentially in the middle of campus, students travel through it daily. In this building students exercise or eat at Tyler's Grill while taking in the views of the water and woods through floor-to-ceiling windows. It's no surprise why this campus is often cited as one of the most beautiful in the U.S.

U Richmond was founded as a Baptist seminary in the 1800s with Westhampton College for women added in 1914 on the opposite side of the lake. In the late 1980s, the university opened the **Jepson School for Leadership** which sought to define leadership through the lens of the humanities. Queally Hall, an important addition to the Robins School of Business, includes a finance trading room. Similarly, the Gottwald Science Center gathered the biology, chemistry and physics departments together offering a remarkable opportunity for research with advanced electronic instruments.

There are many **athletic** fields and a sports complex supporting 17 NCAA Division I teams. Men's Lacrosse opened its first season on campus in 2013, responding to a national high school trend toward this sport.

Social Environment

The **Honor Code** is a defining experience for a U Richmond student. First year women sign an honor contract during a public ceremony called Proclamation Night, while first year men are similarly "incorporated" on Investiture Night. The administration supports these **historic collegiate traditions** in several ways including the male and female separation of student governments, dean of student offices and honor code administration for each. Students, well prepared by their gender specific residential colleges, have the luxury to explore societal roles without distraction. Generally, the student body is fine with observing this traditional organization since all education and extracurriculars are totally coed.

The U Richmond bubble can be an affirming intellectual cocoon. Although most enter without a declared major, they have a deep love for the liberal arts. Students here have the ability to take an idea and the **abstraction** of it and move it forward. They examine many concepts from different perspectives and then fit their understanding together within their declared major of study. The university prepares students for this starting with the First Year Seminars in which they will utilize critical reading, thinking and communication avenues to explore a topic within the 30 or so offered. The university expects to **pull down the barriers** between the liberal arts subjects and pure science and research as was evident with their approach to leadership several decades ago. The business and journalism majors, however, are viewed as academic disciplines that are comprised of **skill and craft preparation** for a career. Students in these disciplines experience a different educational perspective, a bit outside of the humanities undergraduate student population. Their studies are more finely tuned for competence in a career field. Yet critical thinking is more than evident in their premier publication, *The Collegian*. It analyzes and evaluates the good and the bad on campus with precision. In fact, there is admirable precision across the student body and student leadership for honesty and sincerity. Perhaps the best example is the student-authored *Plain English Guide to the Honor Code*.

Academics within the three undergraduate schools are interdisciplinary in nature and students are encouraged to double major and double minor. It all adds up to a rather intensive collegiate experience intertwining ethics, reality and life on a small yet vibrantly connected campus.

Compatibility with Personality Types and Preferences

University of Richmond can be viewed as a study in contrast. Warm, southern grace coexists with a classical, time-honored format for education, yet the administration reacts quickly to the pulse of emerging trends in modern America. The Jepson School of Leadership offering leadership studies is a good example. Richmond's overall academic philosophy also leans toward acquiring evolving knowledge (N) even if it requires rewiring institutional agendas. Yet with internal guidance they value their traditions established in rational thought on university founding (T). It is reflected in the two residential colleges—Richmond College for the men and Westhampton College for the women. And so it goes, back and forth, two distinct educational philosophies ruling, depending on the particular department. Some majors are best described as transformative, bold and innovative. Others are conventional in their course curriculum. Here, journalists report the information, aggressively and boldly reporting facts that do not look or smell pleasant. Yet, they also avoid forcing the reader to adopt a specific viewpoint. It's admirable and uncommon journalism.

Above all, U Richmond is an intellectual environment that places the highest priority on acquiring knowledge with traditional respect for the historical institutional practices and codes.

In the following listing of college majors it is important to remember that students can fit into any college and can be successful in any major. We have found that the Personality Types below fit very well at this college. The course-of-study chosen for each Personality Type corresponds to MBTI® research and is presented as one of many examples favorable for that type.

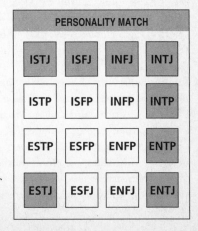

PERSONALITY MATCH

ISTJ	ISFJ	INFJ	INTJ
ISTP	ISFP	INFP	INTP
ESTP	ESFP	ENFP	ENTP
ESTJ	ESFJ	ENFJ	ENTJ

ISTJ who appreciates the tried and true could go for the **Accounting** major. The mind of a typical ISTJ is almost computer-like. Their ability to take in and utilize data will be perfect for this traditional discipline. ISTJs often are rather private individuals who appreciate the confidentiality required in the objective world of accounting. This type sees the asterisks and actually reads the fine print at the bottom of the page. U Richmond undergraduate study in the business curriculum is equally precise.

ISFJ talented in the arts will do well in Richmond's strong **Studio Arts** department. Undergraduate students will be exposed to a broad spectrum of art techniques and mediums. At the conclusion of four years, ISFJs entering career tracks in the arts will have a strong collection of work for their portfolio. U Richmond's thoroughness appeals to ISFJ's nature to answer the call of duty and be mindful of good design in their surroundings.

INFJ can be attracted to business if the emphasis is people-oriented in actual practice on the job. Because of this, the **Management** concentration in the Robins School of Business works for them. The curriculum allows the INFJ to acquire concepts and skills in organizational development and organizational design. Combined with a major in business administration, INFJs are likely to excel as a consultant or specialist in the people end of enterprise, including marketing on occasion.

INTJ is an independent, quiet leader more often than not. Richmond has two rather nice options for this type who likes to think both big and original. The **Military Science and Leadership** program allows INTJ to explore the art required to lead military forces without military commitment. At the start of the junior year, this type can accept or decline a second lieutenant commission in the Army Reserves, complete with government financial aid. The INTJ who also chooses the **International Studies Concentration in Africa** has an eye to the future. The strategic value of this continent to the world will assure either a military or civilian career with decades-long fascination and opportunity.

INTP gets the intellectual freedom they need in the study of **Economics** at Richmond in the Arts and Sciences program. They can opt for the standard course work or specialize in business economics, international economics, economic history, public policy or quantitative economics. This wide-ranging discipline really suits independent, pattern-oriented INTP with plenty of options and wiggle room to exercise their global curiosity. This major is viewed from two different perspectives and falls right into line with the university's academic philosophy by offering both.

ENTP who looks closely at the **Rhetoric and Communication Studies** just may declare the major immediately. The coursework should be very attractive to this type. Argumentation and Debate alone will pull them in. Add in a minor in **Leadership Studies** and you will have a very competent, powerful ENTP change agent. The major is rarely offered and harkens back to the traditional educational perspectives of the university. Courses will be invaluable to ENTPs who can experience difficulty expressing their original thoughts.

ENTJ will find the **Marketing** concentration very handy for their entrepreneurial spirit. Richmond's robust school of business is nicely supplemented with the school of leadership and students are eligible to pursue a minor in leadership. ENTJs will find this combination very attractive because of their inclination to take charge.

The refined business practices explored in the Richmond curriculum will give ENTJ the finesse to secure lead assignments after arriving on the job.

ESTJ has what it takes to make an effective parole officer, and Richmond has the corresponding **Criminal Justice** degree. This type likes to manage with gusto. The degree objectively focuses on the goals of supporting society and helping the troubled individuals within the penal system. ESTJ has the personality to serve both of these "clients" at the same time. The Victim Assistance Academy in downtown Richmond is an unusual resource not often available to students entering this career track. As an undergraduate degree, the major can lead to immediate employment or be a strong stepping stone to graduate study in criminal justice, public administration, social work, sociology or law. Ever mindful, practical ESTJ will narrow down the choice early in their studies at U Richmond.

UNIVERSITY OF SOUTHERN CALIFORNIA

University Park
Los Angeles, CA 90089
Website: www.usc.edu
Admissions Telephone: 213-740-2311
Undergraduates: 18,315; 8,791 Men, 9,524 Women
Graduate Students: 21,642

Physical Environment

The USC undergraduate campus is in the **center of Los Angeles**. This humming and thriving city pulses at an eclectic pace. To love USC is to love Los Angeles and all that it offers, and Los Angeles loves the USC Trojans. This setting pulls in students who can step with zest into the very large USC campus and the glitzy L.A. city life. The many nearby diversions like the beaches and high end shopping, the giant legendary film-production houses and much more require prospective students to become familiar with **public transportation options**. It takes approximately one-and-a-half hours to travel by metro train and metro bus from the LAX airport to the campus. Once on campus, the **compact**, modern, multi-storied academic buildings demand a similar familiarity with transportation routes for pedestrian and bike paths.

Modern residence halls have created guaranteed space for every freshman and returning sophomores. The campus is jam-packed with **bicycles** and those with cars experience traffic jams and a dearth of parking spaces in this compact metropolitan environment. The Greek houses embody the exceptional school spirit on this campus. Sports facilities, as well as the new sports complex, support their national reputation as an **athletic powerhouse**. The weather and emphasis on sports encourage lively activity on campus at all hours of the day and night. This 155-acre enclosed campus gives students fertile ground to mature into young adults and develop a **vibrant**, smart social life.

The research labs are designed for a faculty that is **innovative** and **independent**. The university's fundamental purpose of **searching for knowledge** received a facelift in 2011. The Board of Trustees adopted a **USC Strategic Vision** which emphasizes knowledge as translational research performed by a transformative faculty for the purpose of global citizenship. To accomplish this lofty goal, the university kicked into high gear with securing finances. The second half of this decade finds **multiple, multimillion dollar projects** kicking into gear across the campus in the schools of business, cinema, dance, sciences, journalism and more. USC is a leader in digital records and digital representations of information and that also is going to be a recipient of multimillion dollar investment. Just in 2011, the Broad Center for Regenerative Medicine opened with 11 research labs and 200 researchers.

Social Environment

The 18,000+ undergraduates on campus make up a **dynamic** student body. The large majority, 60 percent of the undergraduate student body, identify as an ethnic minority. It is an ideal climate for interdisciplinary studies and the university is well acquainted with their position as a **Pacific Rim** powerhouse of ideas. The pre-professional programs and business school pull in practical types who value traditional careers that are in demand. Here also, the student who ran his own scientific experiments in the basement is rewarded with access to USC's **amazing research labs**. USC has an admirable program for undergraduate research considering the large campus and the extensive nature of research across so many disciplines. It is well administered by the Undergraduate Research Associates Program.

This campus attracts those who get along well in a large community filled with very different talents and social styles. There are "geeks" in the best sense of the word and "party animals" in the funniest sense. There are quiet and withdrawn students who find hiding places in the labs where they go to chill and chase after knowledge.

This university is **exceptionally well-managed**. The 1994 Strategic Plan is remarkable for its foresight in respect to the campus and the Pacific oceanic basin. The strategic plan doesn't get stale either, with updates in 2004 and 2011. Service staff, faculty and administrators seem to support a humming campus. The undergraduate student body responds to this exceptional environment. The dormitories are contemporary in design with **utility.** The residential life policies are clear and simplify this high-density living environment. There is a PDF file on all topics at USC. The administration channels student emotional energies for learning and playing. In the evening, students are outside, talking, walking and playing pickup games. Students are **optimistic** and healthy to the casual observer. Those who gain the most out of this USC experience are independent learners, **self-directed**, imaginative and goal-driven.

Compatibility with Personality Types and Preferences

Wow is the word that comes to mind when thinking of this large university. Also independence, dynamic and invention crowd into a good description. At USC, intellectual and physical energy combine and the product mirrors thriving, spontaneous Los Angeles. In some ways, the city and the campus are the same since the USC community proudly admires and frequently interfaces with the culture and resources of the city (E). In addition to this distinct LA influence, educational philosophies also drive and definitely impact this huge collegiate community in a studied way. USC academic philosophies include a magnetic-like attraction to the unknown (N). There seems to be an institutional mandate to push the boundaries of human knowledge. The mandate is naturally achieved through the exceptional research resources on the several USC campuses that include the physical laboratories and the world class faculty. It is all increasing notably in size under the 2011 strategic plan.

The undergraduate students themselves are expected to actively push forward. Their vehicle for this process is through the coursework of the undergraduate degrees (S) which are unique and large in number. At the same time, the majors are dwarfed by the extraordinary list of minors offered, many of them also unusual. A review of the catalog reveals that critical thinking (T) and logical disciplined approaches to learning are primary vehicles of energy. Of equal importance, the undergraduate student body mirrors the administrations concern for others within the larger community. The new Engemann Student Health Center is both caring and rational in its delivery of services to the young undergraduate students. This predisposition for noticing and caring about others seems to extend to visitors, employees, scientists, inventors and other individuals who find themselves on this campus for a few hours or a career (F).

In the following listing of college majors it is important to remember that students can fit into any college and can be successful in any major. We have found that the Personality Types below fit very well at this college. The course-of-study chosen for each Personality Type corresponds to MBTI® research and is presented as one of many examples favorable for that type.

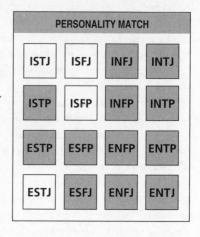

ESFJ will readily understand the purpose of the degree in **Health Promotion and Disease Prevention Studies**. This type is typically very responsible and readily supports following the rules. As they learn more about preventative health through the course Theoretical Principles of Health Behavior, they will relate to the "shoulds" and "should nots." Their empathy for others encourages them to seek answers in courses like Social Exclusion, Social Power and Deviance. Their loyal natures will likely assure them of continued upward momentum within larger health organizations.

INFJ is quietly persistent and powerful with their gift of insight. The **Biophysics** undergraduate degree on this campus is going to utilize each of these INFJ talents. Introduction to Quantum Mechanics and Its Applications is a course that challenges and launches INFJs into the world of graduate school. Follow on graduate classes could be in biology, physics or medical school. INFJ will summon up the hours, personal drive and values needed to select the most productive graduate program.

INTJ who is attracted to both the creativity of computer science and the unforgiving nature of physics won't have to choose between the two with the USC undergraduate degree in **Physics/Computer Science**. Its solid coursework in math, computing and physics nicely prepares the senior for the Final Project. This particular area of study also helps INTJ refine their scientific insight while reality reins in their most out-of-this-world ideas.

INFP can drop into the **Health and Humanity** undergraduate degree and search for life's meaning throughout the four collegiate years. They can clarify their personal contribution to the field by taking courses in the modules of bioethics, aging, ethnicity, the mind and biology. This type might select the thematic module titled Health and Aging or Health and the Mind. The very abstract nature of these topics allows INFPs to focus on human potential and that is very comfortable for this type.

INTP is drawn to complicated patterns. They seek out complex, large systems with data and hope to further develop a particular strand within that knowledge. They think about riddles and word puzzles a lot. The unusual minor at USC in **Operations and Supply Chain Management** introduces this type to the world of numerical volume. Think what could happen if all 4,000 fuel pumps on all the 737 airliners started leaking in the same month across the nation. How should you then make repairs and prevent a possible airplane crash, without disrupting the airline schedules? INTP can handle this type of crisis scheduling and also stand up to the intense pressure that always surrounds these decisions.

ENFP is loath to make a decision too early for their undergraduate degree. In the **Policy, Planning and Development** degree they will take elective coursework among the fields of health, sustainable planning and real estate development, law and social innovations. After graduation, this type might just work in each area through multiple career progressions. This will keep ENFP's need for variety and interest appropriately satisfied.

ENTP with a flair for business will position themselves well with the interdisciplinary minor in the **Pacific Rim**. It might pair up with a major in communication or business and give this type the elbow room they typically like to have as they charge into their studies with abandon. Their ability to see into the future is spot on if they have developed the intellectual discipline to support their insight. USC will help them with the discipline part. ENTP will reciprocate with originality in essays for courses like Global Strategy.

ENTJ who is not majoring in business but wants to pick up the basic tools will like the minor in **Organizational Leadership and Management** at USC. There are three classes this type will like: Power, Politics and Influence, Designing and Leading Teams and The Art and Adventure of Leadership. This last course is probably their motto and they should wear it on a T-shirt.

ENFJ has a vibrant humor that connects easily with their audience. The undergraduate degree in **Communication** will allow ENFJs to discover and develop their natural charisma. Their fine sense at verbally reaching out to people through formal presentations is an advantage. The course in Public Speaking reflects USC's acknowledgement of the importance and art of presentation. Formal, traditional curricula combined with the most modern and evolving techniques will be enticing for this future-oriented type.

ESFP is going to love the Bachelor of Science in **Arts, Technology and Business Innovation** at USC. It is a prime example of the university's transformative and translational knowledge. OK, forget those words. It means that the curriculum will come from the departments of venture management, design, engineering and computer science. It is team taught and interdisciplinary. At this university, this degree, this location, career possibilities are exciting and numerous.

ESTP is going to thrive with the day-to-day action of a career in real estate. USC has a specialty in **Real Estate** among its many useful specializations within the Business Administration major. The city of Los Angeles offers a natural extension to the campus and this curriculum. An hour drive around L.A. reveals the many, many different types of human habitats that fit within the definition of real estate. It will take a GPS, good driving skills and about 10 months to understand this metropolis. ESTP can handle the drive with skill, acquire LA acumen and professionally move on to any other American metropolis.

ISTP can select a minor in **Management Consulting** and be successful in certain business environments. They would be good at helping businesses that offer practical services or products. This type will make a judgment by using their strong logical, analytic skills. They will work hard, seeking solutions in a production environment. Although they are not natural business consultants, ISTPs can be exceptionally effective in an industrial setting.

UNIVERSITY OF TAMPA

401 West Kennedy Boulevard
Tampa, FL 33606-1490
Website: www.ut.edu
Admissions Telephone: 813-253-6211, 888-MINARET
Undergraduates: 6,398; 2816 Men, 3582 Female

Physical Environment

Imagine leaving the business district of Tampa, crossing the bridge of **the inter-coastal waterway** and then coming upon a palace with wrap-around verandahs, honeycombed archways and minarets on the roof that evoke images of Arabian Nights. Historic Plant Hall, U Tampa's admissions and administration center, is striking for these architectural features. This is Florida, where vacations and surprises come together. Students, returning from Thanksgiving break, want to wear flip-flops in November as they board a plane for Florida. The latest dormitory, West Kennedy, is **minimalist** in design, yet also boasts displays of historical artifacts from other cultures in glass showcases, akin to a museum.

Modern residential halls that were completed in the first decade of 2000 include suite-style halls reserved for upperclassmen. Dormitories are spacious and similar to that aspired to by young urban professionals. Brevard Hall is one of the most popular and much coveted by upperclass students because of this community-style living and the views of the **waterfront** and the minarets.

The campus is well into a major construction phase of new facilities. The Student Health Center is a bonus not easily matched by most colleges of similar size. The newest UT nursing laboratories include sophisticated simulation equipment. The new academic building completed in 2010 dramatically expanded the life science curriculum. The athletic complex remodeled in 2012 functions as a sports showcase for past and present UT athletes, medical clinic, training facility, conference and banquet space, not to mention the indoor courts for team play. The College of Business has a **financial trading room** and brings in students seeking to get the low down on Wall Street investment.

Social Environment

University of Tampa is a good fit for those students who want to continue their solid high school academic and extracurricular experience in high school. Students are mindful of social media and outgoing here. Ready for the next level of education, they are expectant and ready to **absorb instruction**. Students get in on the **latest trends** in arts and culture. They come from New England and the Midwest, about one half are from Florida and approximately 40 percent identify themselves as a minority. The Greek fraternities and sororities are popular on campus, providing outlets for service, leadership and socials. Many activities are held on campus since the immediate surrounding neighborhood is comprised of conference hotels. Division II athletics, intramural and fitness facilities are modern and well-provisioned.

AT UT the faculty and administration carefully shape programs and policies which lead to a cohesive, safe learning environment. First year students experience an intensive, solid program in **writing** that introduces the reasoning skills needed on this **reality-based**, hands-on campus. Faculty is careful to impart informational content that can be mastered and recalled in professional settings after graduation. There are many excellent experiential learning classes and service learning projects within the curriculum. Professors and undergraduates interface in **strong mentoring relationships** on this campus. It is a primary vehicle for learning alongside the actual curriculum.

Compatibility with Personality Types and Preferences

The students at U Tampa are just a bit more on the city sophisticate side than the typical first year student in college. The international presence of the city draws students from many differing backgrounds and they blend their outlooks and expectations giving a trendy, energized feel to this campus. At U Tampa, there is a strong focus on attaining work experience and skills to move successfully and directly into the future workplace. As a result, practical yet cutting-edge knowledge (S) is quite the fashion at U Tampa. The faculty is devoted to providing high quality experiential learning. To this end, there is an attraction to technology and the faculty assertively introduces its use within the curriculum.

With a greater number of cultural perspectives on this campus, there is easy awareness and sensitivity that translates into serving the community. The faculty is very mindful of the global marketplace of ideas and employment. They bring this perspective to the curriculum, infusing technology and seminars by outside experts early and often. The educational atmosphere is expansive as it monitors society-at-large and responds with carefully designed campus infrastructure and policy. It all serves to encourage orderly (J), methodical perspectives and pragmatic academic majors at U Tampa.

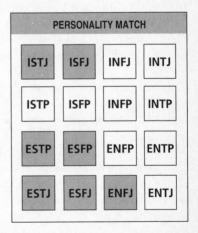

In the following listing of college majors it is important to remember that students can fit into any college and can be successful in any major. We have found that the Personality Types below fit very well at this college. The course-of-study chosen for each Personality Type corresponds to MBTI® research and is presented as one of many examples favorable for that type.

ISTJ will like the direct nature of instruction in the **Criminology** major, especially the Criminology Scholars' Program. This very exacting type prefers to cover all the bases. The annual Scholars Seminar presented by a respected practitioner in the field could find this type sitting in the front row, diligently taking notes. The department also offers a full curriculum in **Forensic Science** which, as with most majors on this campus, has excellent job prospects on graduation. UT is ideal for the investigative sciences with its strong international presence and environment.

ESTP with an interest in athletics could excel in the field of **Sport Management**. This career field will exercise their talents in problem solving. Tampa's Sport Management curriculum provides undergraduate students with a good exposure to all of the academic disciplines that intersect the billion dollar sports industry—finance, economics, media, fund raising, event management, stadium management, legal issues and the list goes on.

ESFP will like the variety and action in the **Marine Science** major. U Tampa is alert to employment trends in this major and requires a double major. Students must add either biology or chemistry. ESFPs, often possessing a vibrant personality, would be ideal ambassadors for endangered animals or exceptional animal trainers at Sea World. This combination of science, education and entertainment plays to their strengths.

ESTJ could be very comfortable with the major titled **Financial Enterprise Systems**. At U Tampa, the focus is toward a comprehensive exposure to the markets and regulating institutions. As is typical, the UT faculty is well aware of the growing executive functions that accountants are stepping into within the corporate world. So it is not surprising that this new major features accounting principles and practices as well as finance. Since ESTJs are natural administrators, they will be more than capable of directing action in the fast-paced financial world.

ESFJ could go for the **Human Performance** degree. It is centered on individual physical fitness. This type's strong sense of responsibility and genuine caring for others fits in nicely with this degree. It is ideal for immediate, meaningful employment as wellness directors, private trainers and fitness technicians at exercise centers across the country. The degree can also be a solid stepping stone for graduate studies in allied health fields, also a favorite occupation for this type.

ENFJ often builds consensus with ease. Their attraction to the possible and their strong people-based values interface nicely with the major in **Government and World Affairs**. Nongovernmental organizations will tap ENFJs' strengths sending them out to serve in underdeveloped countries. Turning the Possible into the Probable is the motto on their T-shirt.

ISFJ often appreciative of design, could be a good match for the certificate in **Arts Administration and Leadership** at U Tampa. This type's fine sense of space and color will be an asset in design worlds. With this certificate and a major in **Management of Information Systems** multiple careers and employers emerge such as the Smithsonian, Caesars Palace in Las Vegas, Disney World, Hilton Hotels and architectural firms. Each of these organizations has heavy reliance on design and computers to maintain and operate their client-centered environments. This is good because ISFJ is client-centered too.

VALPARAISO UNIVERSITY

Office of Admission
Valparaiso, IN 46383-6493
Website: www.valpo.edu
Admissions Telephone: 219-464-5011; 888-468-2576
Undergraduates: 2,855; 1,354 Men, 1,501 Women
Graduates: 800

Physical Environment

Valparaiso means "Vail of paradise." Students refer to their school as simply "Valpo." This university is surrounded by a **1960s neighborhood** of simple homes, each different than the other, and well-cared for yards. The campus buildings are **striking, functional and flat** on the horizon. Its straight lines remind us of Frank Lloyd Wright's architecture. The Fites Engineering Innovation Center, opened in fall 2011, is primarily designed for undergraduates with labs and learning spaces. A new, functional student union centralizes student services and is a fave campus meeting spot.

The nearby, large new library sends a clear message about the **importance of academics** and intellectual work. Students arrive with an appreciation for the traditional visual arts and the center for the arts encourages them to continue their creative work. The Chapel of the Resurrection, built on a rock, has a Midwestern, prairie-style architecture to it. It's a clear **moral reference point** on this campus, where the chapel marks the physical and emotional center. Many students attend the optional daily services since about one-third are Lutheran and 20 percent are Catholic.

Midwestern values of efficiency and hard work are alive and well at Valparaiso University. Two-thirds of the student body is from the Midwest and plains states with many from New York, California, Colorado and Texas. Students must live on campus the first three years. Fraternity and sorority members live in chapter houses off and on campus. About 20 percent of the undergraduates are affiliated with **Greek organizations** and take on very large community service initiatives. Athletics are really big at Valpo. They strongly support their sports teams in time-honored collegiate style. About 20 percent of the students here are involved in competitive athletics at this Division I University. When the campus starts to close in, students take the bus to Chicago or travel to the near-by beaches of Lake Michigan in the early fall or late spring.

Social Environment

Students here want a big school experience with lots of professional and club sports while still learning in small classrooms with attentive professors. Valpo pulls in students who will pay close attention to securing a job on graduation. Students are attracted to the **pre-professional** programs in business, engineering and nursing, yet students also like the core of liberal arts classes which allows for more abstract discussion. If they did not have it in high school they will certainly get abstraction and searching for human purpose in their first two years at this campus.

Two required courses in theology and the student administered Honor Code support the **ethical underpinnings** on this **Lutheran** campus. The global leaders living and learning community brings ongoing awareness of other cultures and values to the campus. The core curriculum also includes study of cultures within the United States and internationally. The elected student government leaders and council have responsibility for administering the Honor Code and Student Activities budget. Student athletes are also in charge of the intramural and recreational teams on this campus. The **Arts** play an equally important role, especially in the fun, enjoyment category. Many of the students are **musically talented** and continue to perform joining campus ensembles with widespread attendance. Professional musicians from the Chicago metropolis are commonly performing on campus also.

Initiative and leadership tend to be in good supply within the overall student body. Volunteering and service very much are in the forefront. The faculty within each department develop tailored initiatives for their undergraduates to take on, occasionally overseas but often for the benefit of the local Indiana neighborhoods.

Compatibility with Personality Types and Preferences

Two abstract principles consistently hover over the Valparaiso University campus. Faith and learning move together within this realistic community and within each individual student. Learning takes off for first year students with expectations that undergraduates will ethically define their understanding of the world. Despite this very conceptual expectation, Valparaiso is quite grounded in the here and now. The educational philosophy strongly supports out of classroom learning experiences (S) where students participate directly in field experiences. Technology is embraced and ever present on the campus along with faith. Student organizations and student behavior adopt a consistent emphasis on service and caring (F), yet the campus is full of activity and fun also. At Valpo, students are interacting with each other on a continual basis (E). The arts, athletics, service, learning, spiritual study and dorm confabs can all be silly or serious. In this lighthearted and honest environment, the administration expects both faith and learning will develop serving both the graduating students and the Valpo campus that they will shape in the passing four years. Valpo is not static in any sense of the word.

In the following listing of college majors it is important to remember that students can fit into any college and can be successful in any major. We have found that the Personality Types below fit very well at this college. The course-of-study chosen for each Personality Type corresponds to MBTI® research and is presented as one of many examples favorable for that type.

ENTJ is busy preparing for leadership at reality-based Valparaiso. The major in **American Studies** orients itself to the philosophical underpinnings of American society. The ENTJ who wants to move into a

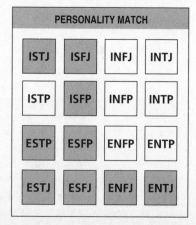

PERSONALITY MATCH

ISTJ	ISFJ	INFJ	INTJ
ISTP	ISFP	INFP	INTP
ESTP	ESFP	ENFP	ENTP
ESTJ	ESFJ	ENFJ	ENTJ

career associated with government will have a very sound understanding of America. Course electives are considerable once the core is fulfilled. Three elective courses in particular address critical turning points in the nation: the Revolutionary Period, Civil War and Reconstruction plus the Depression and War 1929-1945. It seems so evident that this would be available to students at all liberal arts colleges electing to study America. But it is not the case. Many colleges fashion this major through a particular lens of choice - be it ecology, ethnicity, gender or economics. ENTJ will benefit applying those critical and needed lenses at the graduate level of study with their solid foundation gained at Valpo.

ESTJ could use the knowledge gained in Valpo's **Actuarial Sciences** major with a career in corporate finance or insurance. This type is comfortable with environments that combine facts with the expectation of decision. The world of high finance definitely fits this description. ESTJ is not fatigued by the responsibilities of supervising others. In fact, they are quite comfortable with traditional settings that require decisive action.

ESTP is a natural for Valpo's **Sports Management** major. The element of entertainment in professional sports fits this dynamic personality type well. This major requires a minor or double minor in **Fundamentals of Business** or **Business Administration**. Two classes in particular, the Psychology of Sport and Sport and Society, will help ESTPs understand their role in management as a promoter or as the organizational guru within the multimillion dollar professional teams. Yet the strong business curriculum keeps ESTP grounded in financial detail.

ESFP takes kindly to helping others through mentoring and informal advising. The concentration in **Criminology** is a good choice for this type who is sympathetic to young children and adolescents. The course in Urban Sociology is going to find on-the-go ESFPs wandering the streets of nearby Chicago. Here they will find excellent opportunities for internships with Chicago's many ethnic populations and value systems. ESFP is often especially skilled at reducing tensions within troubled relationships which is perfect for this field.

ISFP has a technical side to their personality and Valpo has the right degree and approach for this type who would like to get a degree in **Civil Engineering**. ISFPs enjoy being out of doors. The practical courses in geotechnical, structural transportation, water resources engineering and environment protection appeal to this type. ISFPs prefer to leave abstraction stuck between the pages of books located on library shelves.

ENFJ, not often attracted to the discipline of economics, might look twice at the Valpo major **International Economics and Cultural Affairs.** The senior research project can interface the distribution of resources with the social outcomes. This should appeal to ENFJs who would enjoy championing altered systems of distribution to achieve positive outcomes. At Valpo, there will be a solid discussion on exactly what a "positive outcome" looks like. Millennials will come to understand, as each generation does, the results of social engineering are not predictable, nor always positive. Valpo especially will help undergraduates search for solutions through theological, moral reasoning while exploring the limits of courts, government, business and nongovernmental organizations.

ISTJ will like the field of accounting because it is so very fact-based. This type is literally a mastermind with data. They can excel in this profession because of their own thoroughness and follow through. The Bachelor of Science in **Accounting** has room for more electives since it requires additional coursework beyond the fourth year of study. For impatient ISTJs, although there are few, the Bachelor of Business Administration with an accounting major is more focused and is completed in four years.

ISFJ has the touch to be empathetic with the people they supervise. When you combine this with their wry sense of humor, the **Management** major in Valpo's college of business is a nice choice. After all who wouldn't want a boss like this? The ISFJ brings these special talents to the world of business. It is likely to move them toward staff positions where they are advising employees on the nature of their performance or work output. Valpo will bring much in the way of ethical thought and practice within the undergraduate studies. This will appeal to ISFJ.

ESFJ is often gifted with the art of communication and a strong desire to pay attention to organize and retain facts. The major at Valparaiso in **Marketing** has a nice element that is not always emphasized in this highly persuasive field – that of loyalty. This university is strong in weaving values and the ethical perspective throughout its campus and curriculum. Caring ESFJs will find this is just the right approach to marketing and business for their style.

VANDERBILT UNIVERSITY

2201 West End Avenue
Nashville, TN 37325
Website: www.vanderbilt.edu
Admissions Telephone: 800-288-0432
Undergraduates: 6,835; 3,349 Men, 3,486 Women
Graduate Students: 5,960

Physical Environment

At the edge of a vibrant city, a mile from downtown Nashville, **Commodore Vanderbilt** started this institution that students call "Vandy." His mission was to "strengthen ties between geographical areas" at a time when the world seemed larger. Vanderbilt embraces the American nation as well as its historic and dynamic role in the world. The Commodore wanted this college to be intellectually at the center of the region and a thriving nation, with powerful **connections** to industry. With its **relentless drive for excellence**, Vanderbilt remains within a number of fine universities that continue to respect traditions from the American past yet incorporate innovative 21st Century attitudes and knowledge. Vanderbilt's 'Region' is now well extended across the oceans and to the third world. With the same drive for excellence, the mission fosters mini independent initiatives and opportunity in developing countries, the same American grass roots philosophy that previously served our growing nation. True to its founder, the university is a bold institution seeking to advance the fruits of its infrastructure and intellect throughout national and international economic spheres and spheres of impoverishment.

The university campus is an **arboretum** with beautiful trees, huge magnolias and oaks, tying together a varied architecture, from Victorian to the 60ish and to the modern. The **sprawling campus** encourages students to form smaller, cohesive communities centered around their school or major field of study. The new Recreation Center has its own version of sprawling, with a place for intramural games from squash to spinning and the inbetweens.

All freshmen live in the Ingram Commons within one of 10 houses. For sophomores, juniors and seniors, the university supports learning-living communities often based on academic interests and sponsored by academic departments. Others are theme-oriented residence options like the Mayfield learning lodges which afford the opportunity to live and work together on service learning projects. Vanderbilt has successfully reversed the trend of under representation among men within the student population. Students are warmly welcomed in the many off campus restaurants, pubs and coffee shops with lattes and ice-cream by the curb-side. The Grand Ole Opryland influence is strong in town and students never know which famous country singer they might run into.

Social Environment

Vandy undergraduates often come from well-funded public or independent schools. They bring a resume that is characteristic of students who were quite active outside of their high school environment in the arts, service or athletics. One-third of the students are from the southern states and the student body is equally defined by the same number of Midwesterners with the remaining third from the east and west coasts. **Bright, high-performing and expectant** of a professional career, they are capable of stepping up to the considerable **academic demands** of this curriculum. The large majority intend to pursue advanced graduate studies.

The Blair School of Music echoes the overall Vanderbilt heritage, providing an education that is functional, artistic and rational. Calling out to those who want to pursue **music performance**, teaching or composition, the Blair School connects well with Nashville's booming music industry. Prospective students gain admission directly to Blair School, the College of Arts and Sciences, College of Engineering or the School of Education and Human Performance. The popular major, Human and Organizational Development in the Human Performance curriculum, is a stepping stone to advanced studies in most disciplines. Extensive faculty research establishes an ever-present educational standard that seeps into the undergraduate curriculum. **Research laboratories** across the campus are remarkable and students may complete senior capstone projects while pursuing national research. Archives are equally remarkable, as in the **Vanderbilt Television News Archive** with abstracts of all network newscasts since 1968 and open to the public. The Commodore would approve.

All students find affiliation initially in the First Year residential dormitories which take on individual identities that reflect the faculty and residents through their common interests. Many students will also identify with the faculty in their departments and seek service learning opportunities there. **Independence, resilience and perseverance** are good descriptors of Vandy students. The Honor code and university regulations are well understood and operate within judicial structures. There is a **predisposition to go Greek** and Vandy social life offers a traditional atmosphere with many social and cultural activities. The students strongly support the 'Dores who are winning games in the tough SEC football conference. The mild winter weather, handsome campus, recreational activities and Nashville's social vibrancy make for a memorable, productive undergraduate experience.

Compatibility with Personality Types and Preferences

Vanderbilt students often move through their four years of studies on campus expecting to acquire a rational, all-encompassing knowledge of their chosen discipline. The Vanderbilt educational philosophy supports this drive for excellence. Acquiring and refining knowledge (T) is critically important and these students understand and appreciate this goal. The pursuit of excellence will also squeeze out time for a broad survey of global issues; many will seek to impact issues of poor education and poverty closer to home in America also. All seek to be competent graduates, watching for opportunity to take that competence farther afield. The faculty and student body is supportive of strength and power emanating from knowledge. In this way Vandy graduates will become pillars within many influential institutions.

The student body is quite energized (E) and well-organized around their selected disciplines. Service learning and academic work that expands beyond the foundational knowledge is well-supported by the administration. Vandy students may support causes which tend to reflect traditional American values such as registering voters in the immediate neighborhoods or studying microloans for the destitute lower castes in India. Their service will be direct and realistic more than likely. The predominant feeling on campus supports the American historical perspective toward human community. This is reminiscent of those values raised in the ancient texts and held by Commodore Vanderbilt. It certainly supports the unique Peabody College of Educational and Human Development. Classic, (J) traditional values really mesh within the student body of civically-minded young adults who were active in high school service and will remain so throughout life.

In the following listing of college majors it is important to remember that students can fit into any college and can be successful in any major. We have found that the Personality Types below fit very well at this college. The course-of-study chosen for each Personality Type corresponds to MBTI® research and is presented as one of many examples favorable for that type.

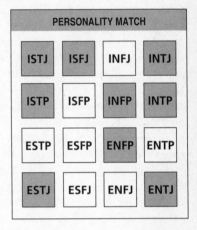

ISTJ is a natural administrator who will want to secure an exceptionally fine preparation for leadership should they pursue a career in the K-12 schools. The ideal major for this purpose is at Vanderbilt. **Human and Organizational Development** looks at public policy and human development. It gives this type needed practice and experience with broad-based approaches to problem solving in demanding career paths such as school principal or superintendent of schools.

ISTP could find the **Biomedical Engineering** curriculum at Vandy to be full of fascinating lab courses. The Foundations of Medical Imaging course will be a fun challenge for this type through its study of technical absorption, reflection and scattering of energy. The precise nature of this degree and its technical methods appeals to the unemotional side of ISTPs. The utility of diagnosing and treating illness speaks to the real life practicality that is necessary for this type to stay interested.

ESTJ can pick up management credentials at Vandy through the minor in **Scientific Computing**. It combines with the **Biomedical Engineering** degree and prepares this type to follow their inclination to take charge while clearing up shades-of-gray thinking. Given this, the course in Program and Project Management is going to be excellent for their other inclination to root out inefficiency and remember virtually all aspects of a project.

ISFJ is a gentle soul and will be most welcome in the **Child Studies** major. At Vandy, students study the entire world of the child from developmental psychology, language and learning to the family. Fascination with human development will engage the very rich inner world and personal perspectives of this type. Their dependability is also spot on for a career in this field, lending an element of stability to the intense, variable activity of American childhood. A second non-educational major is required. Take a look at the suggestions on page 378 for the many other majors ISFJ prefers.

INFP is often considerate as well as adaptable. They may be drawn to the field of education and especially to children struggling in the classroom. The degree at Vanderbilt in **Early Childhood Education** could appeal to INFP's desire to seek out and support human potential. As a double major with **Communication of Science and Technology,** INFP will pick up skills in the natural sciences, engineering, and statistics. With their penetrating insight, they will thrive looking at the TV network broadcasts on child rearing since the 1960s. As the Commodore would know, there is wisdom in the past and this combination of majors has the potential for a skilled educator who has the perseverance and ingenuity to side track politically-motivated trends in public school education.

ENFP with a resume that notes private music lessons or school band, may enjoy the **Musicology and Ethnomusicology** major in the Blair School of Music. It offers an intense study of several areas from choir chants to Broadway musicals to, of course, the blues. With New Orleans about six hours by car, an internship is in the making. Music in the French Quarter, played on the streets by the local musicians, is brilliant and replicates the level of excellence in the Blair School of Music.

INTJ will find the **Mathematics** department at Vandy offering a great preparation for advanced study in a demanding profession like astronomy and upper level undergraduate courses with enticing course titles like Error-Correcting Codes and Cryptography. This will come in handy when America finally returns to the moon, assuming we do not wish to share our advanced technology under globalization paradigms.

INTP has characteristics reminiscent of the triple "i"—intense, internal, intuition. They will help this type move rather smoothly through a degree in **Chemistry** at demanding Vandy. The physical facilities and labs are outstanding, prompting free thinking and conceptual schemes, one after the other. INTPs will need to be mindful of the very structured nature of the science departments at Vandy. Creativity is fine here, accidents that could have been prevented and being late are not so well appreciated.

ENTJ will jump right into Game Theory with Economic Applications. This course has the entrepreneurial bent and is sufficiently complex to keep ENTJ's busy mind engaged. This course is an elective in the **Economics** degree which might also fit into Vandy's unusual concentration in Economics and History. Leave it to this type to understand the intriguing nature of combining these two subjects.

WABASH COLLEGE

P.O. Box 352
Crawfordsville, IN 47933
Website: www.wabash.edu
Admissions Telephone: 765-361-6225
Undergraduates: 904 Men

Physical Environment

Wabash College is located in **rural Indiana** but only 45 miles from Indianapolis. The college is remarkable for its place as an all men's institution and the loyal alumni who keep a strong hand in this college community. The Eli Lilly Endowment for Wabash helps project this small campus outward through the **Center of Inquiry in the Liberal Arts**. The center conducts research to strengthen liberal arts education supporting national assessments of the independent schools and colleges. As is often the case, students at Wabash benefit directly from emerging practices in academic practice. The new President arriving on campus in summer 2013 spoke to the ongoing negative trends for men in American society. Four decades of centering educational energy and resources on women who were poorly represented in most occupations and careers during the 1960s has flipped this unhealthy statistic. It is time for American liberal arts colleges and universities to step up, acknowledge and actively seek solutions as Wabash College continues to do.

Thursday mornings can find **legendary Wabash alumni** speaking at the weekly Chapel gathering or the students themselves presenting on topics or raising support for a cause. The **Athletic Center** is nothing short of spectacular with its **Olympic-size pool**, lots of exercise equipment and weight rooms. It is a magnet for athletic students who also realize that Wabash often wins conference championships within competitive sports. In March 2011, the new baseball stadium propelled the Little Giants to send four players to the All Conference Baseball team. The **Fine Arts Center** is also a big draw for artistically-inclined guys who want to do big art in the outdoor classroom space.

Social Environment

Tradition is important here and social organizations compete to see who can belt out the **Old Wabash refrain** the loudest in front of the Chapel. Many young men seek out Wabash College because they had **traditional,** active lifestyles at home. High school athletes appreciate Wabash. Socially outgoing guys appreciate Wabash. Students who were leaders in high school clubs appreciate Wabash. Eagle scouts appreciate Wabash. Guys who want to study physics by building and throwing armored spears appreciate Wabash. They see the Wabash community holding these same values.

Professors engage students in **pointed discussions** that often become enthusiastic, **ongoing debates**. Successful students prepare carefully for class. Especially in the first year there is a lot of talk on **character development**, such as what it means to be a **Wabash man** and **The Gentlemen's Rule** which calls for students to act with responsibility at all times and to be accountable at all times. At Wabash, college boys will become men over the course of the four years along with an appreciation of the **role of men** in the larger American society. It spills over into ethical behavior within the student body and with extracurricular activities with women. Casual conversation on this campus ranges from sports to women to ethics. The Wabash chapter of College Mentors for Kids, nationally recognized, is one of the most active service clubs helping local elementary youth. This is an intentional collegiate community with professors who take an earnest interest in advising.

Athletes are the central focus of the campus during the week and some weekends too. Forty percent of students who come here play one or two varsity sports in the NCAA III conference. Wabash college football, wrestling, baseball and basketball teams are hotbeds for young men intent on toning up their muscles and physical agility. Lacrosse was added in 2013. Three-quarters of all students play in intramurals. **Friendly competition** is an ethic and a reality on campus. The college also supports an impressive drama department and large performing theatre where the men can experiment with **forms of expression through the arts**. Wabash College has many **fraternities** with campus houses that function as residential halls. Fraternities and clubs spur friendly rivalries and the men generate a great deal of camaraderie within the student body as a result of those Greek social traditions.

Compatibility with Personality Types and Preferences

Wabash College has done a great job of incorporating learning styles with moral behavior into a strong mix that serves a variety of undergraduate men. The administration of this guys-only college really understands the perspectives of their entering freshmen. Professors promote the idea of abstract thinking and its value to the incoming students in first year courses. New students quickly hear about humane concepts (F), awareness and analytic thinking. The values associated with athletics, sportsmanship and giving-it-your-best are in practice across the campus. Faculty and administration carefully build the Wabash community through these moral codes and expectations of personal behavior.

As undergraduates progress toward graduation, they learn through trial and error (T) how one is expected to honor the Wabash community and prepare for citizenship in (E) the larger society. Faculty in all departments elect to make considerable use of experiential (S) learning. Undergraduate students travel frequently to locations within the U.S. and overseas through their courses. Professors make great use of immersion learning on short four-to-five day trips to connect students to the world beyond campus. This observation and fact-based learning is featured in foreign language and political science courses especially. The faculty also invokes use of abstract conceptual learning (N), which is featured in Wabash's classics curriculum. The curriculum nicely meets the educational preferences of these two opposite learners: the hands-on, give-me-the-facts student and the abstract discussion-based learner. Students who are attracted to Wabash are confident that this single-gender environment will give them the best of both worlds—the caring world that builds community and the traditional guy world that loves athleticism and power.

In the following listing of college majors it is important to remember that students can fit into any college and can be successful in any major. We have found that the Personality

Types below fit very well at this college. The course-of-study chosen for each Personality Type corresponds to MBTI® research and is presented as one of many examples favorable for that type.

INFP pretty much has to have their personal values lined up with daily living. They rarely bend their behavior code. Wabash College is a brilliant light when it comes to ethical awareness. As a result, INFPs are likely to feel good about this campus. The major in **Philosophy** can offer this type the chance to bring congruence to their inner values. The curriculum includes a wide range of topics with unfamiliar perspectives. Students refine their own points of view through discourse and intense study of the classical texts. The Pre-Law advising on campus supports the philosophy major who might want to pursue a legal career in advocating for the disadvantaged. This surely meets the needs of INFPs. They will find like-minded guys to have fun with and probably get active in campus publications.

PERSONALITY MATCH			
ISTJ	ISFJ	INFJ	INTJ
ISTP	ISFP	INFP	INTP
ESTP	ESFP	ENFP	ENTP
ESTJ	ESFJ	ENFJ	ENTJ

INFJ is a creative type, supporting change for improving the lives of others. The **German** major with pre-professional advising in **Health and Allied Sciences** at Wabash College offers INFJs uncommon career possibilities. They love to think about the future and will carefully review the decision as to which path to follow after their years at Wabash. The familiarity with a foreign language further expands their linguistic thinking as well as opens up research options in Europe and around the globe. All of this sounds downright exciting to the typical INFJ interested in the sciences. They are likely to find a fraternity or club or both that share their values and jump right in connecting their ideals with service projects.

ISTJ is going to love studying **History** at Wabash College because it clearly points to five areas of competence for its graduates. This makes good sense for this type who values accuracy. The History major combined with **Pre-Law** advising provides a clear career track for this realistic type. The department offers a curriculum that focuses on analytical skills, interpretation and oral/written expression. These are the tools of the historian and the lawyer. The former seeks to recover meaning from documents and the latter seeks to change a current practice or event. ISTJs are likely to find like-minded friends on campus, revealing their wry humor while participating in select social activities on campus. Expect the homecoming float to sport some humorous feature.

ISFJ with their typical well-developed sense of color and space might go for the major in **Studio Art** or **Art History.** ISFJs who may be lacking the talent but possess the artistic sensibilities can elect the Art History major. It will be bolstered by the strong curriculum in the classics. Both majors concentrate on visual expression of abstract ideas. Not to worry about how to translate this concept into a career because Wabash has a pre-professional concentration in **Business**. ISFJs can gain both of these skill sets here. They might join the Malcolm X Institute on campus for discussion with visiting alumni and pizza.

ISFP likes to work with their hands and enjoy the outdoors. ISFPs can get out the shovels for the major in **Classics** at Wabash College with archeological digs in Greece and Jordan. The curriculum focuses on Greek and Roman ancient literature, history, art and archeology. With this major, ISFPs might want to look into the **Teacher Education** minor. Wabash assures undergraduate students have multiple experiences in the classroom early and reflect on the experience by submitting a sophomore portfolio for admission to the program. The emphasis on fun at this college is also ideal for this type who will look for organizations to join with a solid record of service activities.

ESTP likes to take calculated risks for the most part and this translates into spontaneity on the Wabash campus. It comes alive on the weekends with full-hearted fun and activity associated with the athletic teams and the social fraternities. Academically, ESTPs are brilliant observers of what is, i.e. reality. The major in **Physics** is a strong possibility for this hands-on type. The conceptual thinking on this campus may be a bit off-putting for this type. However, the athleticism, ethnic perspectives, social community and alumni presence are very appealing to this natural straight shooter. The major in physics can smooth ESTP into the graduate world of law, engineering, teaching and computer programming. This type will be in the first row at athletic events cheering and leading the fans. They also might be on the various teams since they are often physically coordinated.

ENFP can be a very compassionate soul and the study of **Religion** just might appeal. The department has an excellent national reputation. Theology professors come from across the country each summer to explore methods of religious study with the financial support of the Lilly Endowment. At Wabash, enthusiasm for the classics easily supplements comprehending ancient religious texts. Professors actively mentor students in this major that can lead to further theological studies and the worlds of medicine, law and business. ENFP's insight will find a home in the Wabash curriculum. They will also find plenty of fun which is a daily requirement, similar to a vitamin supplement, for ENFPs. They are likely to join one of the fraternities and may join the Sphinx Club of students supporting the historical, social traditions of Wabash.

ENTP will be front and center when it comes to discerning conversation. They crave the social debate and can become stressed without this source of energy. The classic major in **Rhetoric** with a concentration in **International Studies** is ideal for this type. The major explores how the mass media impacts citizen consciousness. In doing so, ENTPs will seek understanding of social institutions and organizations as they pressure society to adopt their peculiar version of reality. As a spontaneous thinker, ENTPs must guard against articulating their unformed thoughts. The coursework in this major rewards time spent in deconstructing positions put forth in the public square. As ENTPs master this time delay processing, they can become powerful personalities with their creativity and long-range thinking in play. The additional work in international studies will open doors for possible careers. Ingenious ENTPs will spot lots of career options. Their difficulty will be in selecting one or two.

ESFJ will like studying **Biology** at Wabash College. The science building has all the bells and whistles to support an experiential, lab-driven curriculum. The department has a particular interest in molecular biology which well prepares students to move forward to graduate study. ESFJs want to find harmony and companionship in their environment. Wabash College works socially and academically for this type. The immersion and experiential learning options on and off campus offer practical skills. The large number of spirit-filled organizations offer traditional options to participate and lead and ESFJ will be in the mix.

ENFJ will like the independence that comes with a career in **Psychology** and the opportunities to help others one-on-one. The department in psychology at Wabash College has well incorporated the leaps in psychological therapy over the past 30 years. Their curriculum focuses on the scientific research that is becoming critical as the field moves forward with new discoveries about behavior and the brain. ENFJs will find the preparation needed for admission to the increasingly competitive PhD studies in this field. ENFJ has a natural inclination toward generating concepts. Faculty in this department push students to generate and answer significant questions. There is emphasis in the department to select undergraduate research that is meaningful to the larger community and the undergraduate. It all works for ENFJ.

ENTJ will find the sequence of courses in **Business** to their liking as generally this type has an entrepreneurial side. Their desire for leadership and long-range planning seems to naturally fit into the business world, yet much of leadership today, even in the business world, requires political acumen. At Wabash College the **Political Science** major is a solid choice for an ENTJ looking to read the political tea leaves. The department gives good exposure to four areas: American politics, comparative politics, international politics and political theory. With a foundational heads-up in the political world and business world, this type is ready to enter any number of challenges in the post-graduate world of academia or work. ENTJs will support Wabash athletic events and likely be a leader in any number of other organizations that provide them leadership opportunities such as the fraternities.

WAKE FOREST UNIVERSITY

1834 Wake Forest Road
Winston-Salem, NC 27109
Website: www.wfu.edu
Admissions Telephone: 336-758-5201
Undergraduates: 4,591; 2,253 Men, 2,488 Women
Graduate Students: 2,617

Physical Environment

Wake Forest University exemplifies the values associated with success in America, both economically and individually. Founded by the Baptists in the early nineteenth century, there is scant reference to that heritage now. The surrounding forests of Winston-Salem frame the many new attractive buildings on this campus. Very student-centric, **The Barn**, opened in Fall 2011 with its classic A-frame structure and metal roof, is reminiscent of the one story mid-1800s Appalachian feed barns. It is perfect for its location and well-used for student-hosted parties and events.

Residential living on campus is enhanced by the tons of planned social events. South Hall, a new dorm opened in Fall 2011, is part of a construction program on campus that is generating new spaces and renovating older facilities. Magnolia and Dogwood Residence Halls opened in 2013 and feature software to monitor utilities usage by the residents. The university has an **extensive, content-laden intranet** that serves multiple purposes. Farell Hall opened its doors in 2013 also. It is home to the business school. With occupancy for over 1,000 students and faculty, it is more than spacious. The new Administration building is light and airy with its two-story glass atrium but retaining that classic, homey red brick architecture. Ribbon cutting and dedications seemed to be a monthly event and certainly provide **many new study and social spaces** on campus.

Social Environment

The university appeals to students who want to belong to a cohesive, forward-looking community. Wake Forest attracts students seeking to secure an education and career path. Students here were likely to be very active in their hometown communities in athletics, performing arts and service. They continue these same activities with gusto on campus at Wake Forest. They really value educational studies, **attend classes with purpose** and manage their time well. They look for strong career advising to help them with electives, internships and job opportunities. Most students are quite **ambitious** and hope to address problems in society. They respect the professors who support them in this and look to be mentored in their plans for research and **career exploration**.

Coming primarily from the eastern seaboard, undergraduates are also quite socially savvy and fun-loving. They are confident, **gregarious** and physically active. They enjoy pranks and are not above wrapping trees with toilet paper to celebrate a sports victory. They bring this **spirit to athletic games** and love their mascot the Demon Deacon, who is very distinctive in a black and yellow tie. Wake social events are plentiful with guidance provided by the multiple student development offices on campus. There is a club sport for most extracurricular interests from bass fishing to karate and all in between. Intramurals are similarly expansive with inner tube water polo, all the in betweens and table tennis. Service and politics have a large presence here also. Students develop skills and interface with established local and national organizations with political and civic agendas. Wake Forest has a chapter of the Roosevelt Society which models itself after a think tank and addresses ecological issues.

Compatibility with Personality Types and Preferences

Wake Forest is a campus where the curriculum has evolved to support current day economics with an underlying humane vision. The administration and faculty have strongly focused curriculum development and advising at the academic department level for undergraduate students. Independent thought and analysis is a vehicle for reaching truths within introductory and advanced course work. Through study and discussion undergraduates look to secure skills and knowledge. Logical analysis (T) and an emphasis on service for others interfaces this academic community.

Faculty encourage students to prepare for difficult issues that will be raised in the senior year courses. The first year curriculum features critical reading, thinking and writing. It pushes students to develop personal values and explore ethical positions. Students often learn through inquiry that utilizes inductive reasoning. This process requires the movement of particular information to general understanding. Think of Wake Forest as a well-balanced community of learning with room for big picture folks (N), the here-and-now reality types (S) and those orderly planners (J). The strong social and athletic traditions in residential life on campus help the undergraduate's transition from high school to successful collegiate student. In fact, the campus honors many of the vibrant, fun collegiate stuff of the old classic movies.

In the following listing of college majors it is important to remember that students can fit into any college and can be successful in any major. We have found that the Personality Types below fit very well at this college. The course-of-study chosen for each Personality Type corresponds to MBTI® research and is presented as one of many examples favorable for that type.

ENTJ will feel comfortable with the wide range of financial courses in the **Economics** major. The Economics of Entrepreneurship course studies economic theory in comparison with the actions of successful entrepreneurs, past and present. This type will be at ease in the uncertain world of economics.

PERSONALITY MATCH			
ISTJ	ISFJ	INFJ	INTJ
ISTP	ISFP	INFP	INTP
ESTP	ESFP	ENFP	ENTP
ESTJ	ESFJ	ENFJ	ENTJ

The curriculum will give ENTJs practice at applying their insight and strategic planning. It will be an invaluable learning experience for this type who will likely move into a professional environment such as law, business, medicine or government as an expert advisor.

ISTJ will really appreciate the extensive course selection in the **Biology** Department. There are just a few survey courses in the freshmen and sophomore year. ISTJs will approve of the variety and intensity of subjects offered in junior and senior year. The course in Insect Biology might appeal to this type because the level of detail would be distinct, voluminous and organized. ISTJs are attracted to comprehensive, demanding classification systems in the animal kingdom. The career field is in need of Millennials to come on board since many Baby Boomers are presently retiring.

ESFJ places well being high on any priority list. The course in Physiology of Exercise could easily be an elective of choice for this reason. This curriculum will affirm ESFJ's people-centered focus and prepares undergraduates for entry into professional schools in the health sciences. It examines both the benefits and potential risk as the body responds to various exercise programs. Wake Forest has a strong emphasis on all aspects of safety across the campus. It shows clearly in this **Health and Exercise Science** degree.

ISFJ should look at the courses in the **Anthropology** department at Wake Forest. The curriculum could be preferable for this type who is patient with the details and empathetic. Students have the opportunity to volunteer or secure work study at the WFU Museum for Anthropology. This hands-on learning allows ISFJs to examine the process of exhibit preparation. Their sense of loyalty will ensure the exhibit's worthiness in serving the membership and public. The course Feminist Anthropology would be well-informed when its counterpart, Masculine Anthropology, is added to the department.

ISFP often has affinity with nature and the interdisciplinary minor in **Environmental Studies** could easily draw attention from ISFPs. This minor has a social policy tract that could lead to a satisfying career where idealism is honored in conservancy organizations. The second tract in the minor explores scientific paradigms as applied to the physical environment.

ESTJ will be drawn to the business school major in **Finance**. Among the several management courses, Strategic Management will appeal to their drive for setting goals and making decisions. Competition will be acceptable to this type with their ability to make tough calls when necessary. ESTJs are likely to enjoy the computer modeling of business competitions.

ENFP will relate to Wake Forest on the very first day. Outgoing, active participation is the norm on campus and this type will be first in line on game day. Should the **Psychology** major draw them in, a favorite class could be Altered States of Consciousness. This course offers the novelty that captures ENFP's attention. Their exceptional insight will be an advantage in this course. The study of dreams, meditation and hypnosis could also help them with self-introspection as opposed to exclusively focusing on friends.

ENTP is often drawn to concepts in **Political Science**. At Wake Forest, the major examines this unpredictable field—just think of the United Nations. Nevertheless, the subject is likely to be fascinating for ENTPs. On this campus they will be rewarded with both variety and intensity of study—American Politics, Comparative Politics, International Politics and Political Theory. Choosing one of these specializations will make for a difficult decision for ENTPs. The introductory course in each should help with the decision.

INFP just might sign up for the minor in **Linguistics** at Wake Forest. The overview, history and structure of romance languages will be of interest to many students of this personality preference. WFU is a little gregarious for this type, however, with all the new buildings now, there will be multiple, comfy nooks and crannies to hide out in.

INFJ values independence and social harmony. It is a perfect fit for Wake Forest. Within the Department of **Religion,** INFJs will find a solid foundation of survey courses in the major world religions. Beyond this level, INFJ will find a fascinating selection of topics viewed through religious perspectives. The department offers a rich study in Christian texts and history. The inquiry will surely trigger personal introspection by INFJs.

INTJ often will find idle speculation leads to something definite in the way of an idea that can be put into action. This consistent thinker often excels in research. The major in **Chemistry** at Wake Forest is ideally oriented toward research. Put this together with a follow on career path that includes research and development in the pharmaceutical industry and the whole picture could be intriguing for many INTJs.

WASHINGTON AND LEE UNIVERSITY

116 North Main Street
Lexington, VA 24450-0303
Website: www.wlu.edu
Admissions Telephone: 540-463-8710
Undergraduates: 1,834; 928 Men, 906 Women
Graduates: 464

Physical Environment

Washington and Lee University is located in the **quaint and historical town** of Lexington, population 7,000. Surrounded by farm land, picturesque horse pastures and the Appalachian Mountains, the university appeals to students who are comfortable with traditional venues. However, nearby Washington, DC is of greater importance to students who typically are looking for **power internships** in communications, business and politics.

Campus architecture is all the more remarkable because George Washington bequeathed his 20,000 shares of James River canal stock for seed money. Mindful of history, the entering class walks through traditional southern wrought iron gates framing a beautiful green lawn that is flanked by red brick academic buildings. Each of these have their front porticos decorated with massive **white columns**. **The Colonnade**, on the National Historic Register since 1972, was the recent focus of a careful and much needed technological rehabilitation that included internet access, air conditioning, etc. Confederate General Robert E. Lee is buried with his horse within sight of the buildings.

The newer section of campus on top of the ridge reflects the futuristic side of Washington and Lee with up-to-date everything. Accomplished high school athletes are attracted to the university because of the excellent sports facilities. Students socialize in the Elrod commons, the library, the ivy-covered classroom buildings and Greek houses. Freshmen and sophomores are required to live on campus. Thereafter students rent apartments or houses in town which are readily available.

The profound sense of American tradition and community is apparent to all who walk the campus. This university is one of two educational institutions in this book that featured a speaker or referenced the Civil War Sesquicentennial and Abraham Lincoln's Emancipation Document on its 150th anniversary in February 2014. Is there not something about knowing your past before you can know your future? Hurrahs to W&L.

Social Environment

W&L students are eager to learn the concepts, knowledge and expectations that give them a head start in **pivotal career fields**. They are high-achieving, expressive, ambitious and hard-working. Some will come from socially and historically influential families. Students like to be challenged by a **rigorous academic** curriculum and faculty at W&L is more than happy to oblige. The educational experience is **intense and individualized.** It starts prior to arrival on campus in the fall. Faculty and administration are well aware that much will be required to attain the expected level and quality of academic production. Each newly-arriving student is well advised to be ready, already possessing reasonable time management, good study skills and **attention capable of discernment**. **Conversational engagement** is a favorite teaching practice and it must kick in by the end of the first semester. In many ways the cliché, "It's time to put your big boy/girl pants on" applies to W&L. As graduates, they will have intellectual poise and acumen to interface with the distinguished W&L alumni network often leading to further opportunity.

Successful students take advantage of the academic peer tutoring and several other supports on campus. Some students will settle into academic mentoring with their professors that goes beyond the course curriculum. The speaking tradition and Honor System point to individual and community accountability. Both are taken very seriously on the campus. Service learning is typically focused on issues of poverty and sustainability and interfaced throughout the curriculum.

The student body here forms close ties. The First Year Experience settles all freshmen into small sections of about ten individuals within the residence halls. They each have an upper division student to help them adjust to college life. The **Greek system** is exceptionally strong on this campus with close to 90 percent student participation. They hold many parties and events, socials and formal dances that keep the town's drycleaners busy. Student organizations tend to take an **intellectual bent** and often a political bent. The administration developed a four-week **Immersion Term** in addition to the two regular semesters, seeking to push fun into the learning syllabus. The club sports, intramurals, fitness and outing club also provide counterpoints to the intellectual life.

Compatibility with Personality Types and Preferences

Clarity of thinking, originality (N), analysis, precision and attention to current societal trends do a good job of characterizing the Washington and Lee academic environment. Logic and the art of concentrated thinking (T) are in demand on this campus. Incoming undergraduate students are encouraged to adopt the W&L value of honoring intellectual inquiry. Seminars, courses and clubs all offer guideposts in respect to current day practices and issues. The Mock Convention is an intense two-year effort by the student body to predict the presidential candidate of the sitting national minority political party. On this campus, the undergraduate student interfaces knowledge with the persuasive communication abilities needed to place it in the public square. Successful students here are keen and assertive. The Johnson Symposia and Shepherd Program offer leadership opportunity and initiative at the regional and national levels.

W&L offers many sophomore level courses with advanced level content and broad expanse across the disciplines. There is some ability for students interested in a particular topic to enroll in sophomore courses. As is the case with most American universities, courses within the Americas are narrowed to offer increased content of other continents. At W&L undergraduates are grounded in the leading-edge present. Students here don't often miss new trends in society or find themselves unaware of academic or social movements.

In the following listing of college majors it is important to remember that students can fit into any college and can be successful in any major. We have found that the Personality Types below fit very well at this college. The course-of-study chosen for each Personality Type corresponds to MBTI® research and is presented as one of many examples favorable for that type.

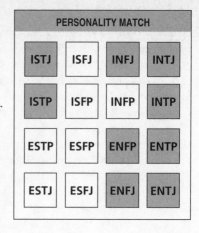

ENTJ is an exceptionally fine fit for Washington and Lee. Direct, decisive and conceptual, they will be drawn to the Williams School. Among the exciting entrepreneurial projects within the school is the **W&L Student Consulting**. This group of business students advises client companies on a variety of strategies to increase market profitability. A current project is advising villagers in the Amazon with their difficulty of bringing craft goods to international markets. These students would find a sympathetic ear with Pope Francis, who has also waded into South American economic and social paradigms.

ENFJ would likely approve the program in **Teacher Education** at W&L. The department offers course work in conjunction with two other nearby universities. This really expands the exposure to many different types of public and private schools for ENFJ. It is critical in this discipline which is not one size fits all. The administration's attempt, in Common Core, to standardize the curriculum is admirable yet profoundly inlaid with disagreement, as is the Bush Initiative No Child Left Behind. This type has the savvy to listen and respond to school board queries.

ENFP who is stimulated by difficulties and enthusiastic in solving them is quite welcome on this campus. ENFPs can usually excel in any major that captures their imagination. The interdepartmental program in **Neuroscience** could serve a couple of functions for this type who likes to carefully examine all the exciting possibilities. The major offers research in the several disciplines of biology, chemistry, psychology, mathematics and the computational sciences. Once the research concentration is selected, ENFP will be passionate with their chosen subject.

INFJ could quietly bring metaphor and symbolic representation to some of the nuts and bolts logic that travels so easily on this campus. Should they disagree with a particular statement or direction of discourse, which they are likely to do, it may be done with a touch more grace than some of their more direct and dispassionate classmates. The **Medieval and Renaissance Studies** program is ideal for this student's exceptional insight that can be riveted on human populations of the 1300s to the 1600s. If any type can find purpose and meaning in medieval customs and society, it will be the INFJ.

INTJ brings skeptical analysis to the classroom and will challenge any information that doesn't fit into their emerging perspective. Of all the types, this one will have the least appreciation for the tradition and custom that W&L emphasizes. The INTJ takes nothing for granted. If this type needs to rearrange the principles of

Physics and the basics of nature, so be it. W&L faculty would likely permit and enjoy the ensuing mayhem—for a short time.

ENTP can be comfortably assertive on this campus. With strong ideas and big personas in abundance at W&L, ENTPs will receive the intellectual stimulation they crave. The **Mock Trial** might provide ENTPs the jury box and audience to which they will put forth their courtroom litigation strategies. Quick thinkers, assertive and outspoken, this type will likely perform well and perhaps win the competition if they do not procrastinate.

INTP is intellectually curious and contemplative. Their powerful minds may be underestimated when they are typically reserved in the classroom. However, faculty at W&L will spot intellectual potential and draw out this type. INTPs and the courses in **Philosophy** are likely to connect and become a minor or possibly a major. This type will push for personal clarity and truth through their individual study when examining philosophers. The faculty will support them in the truest sense once past the foundational courses.

ISTJ comfortably masters large volumes of fact and they take whatever extra steps necessary to be accurate. ISTJs won't be overwhelmed with the intensity of the W&L free flow of ideas; rather, their natural tendency is to endure until all is said and done. They gain well-deserved respect for their perseverance and mastery of study in their major program. The **Pre-Law program** is an additional sequence of elective courses that present political issues primarily from a progressive perspective.

ISTP is likely to find a good home in a technical and statistical field of interest like the W&L **Environmental Studies** major. It requires direct observation of phenomena in the field. This type would identify with environmental capstone projects that involve redeveloping the degraded slopes along stream beds. W&L practicality and technology is featured in this major. Technical gadgets involving measurement will appeal to the university and the ISTPs.

WASHINGTON UNIVERSITY IN ST. LOUIS

One Brookings Drive
St. Louis, MO 63130-4899
Website: www.wustl.edu
Admissions Telephone: 800-638-0700, 314-935-6000
Undergraduates: 6,445; 3,223 Men, 3,232 Women
Graduates: 6,693

Physical Environment

Washington University is located in St. Louis approximately five miles from the mighty Mississippi River and famous Arch. The campus is just west of city limits and is accessible by Metro from the airport. Students board at Skinker station and go shopping or out to Forest Park, cite of the 1904 World's Fair, now host to museums, the zoo, planetarium and many athletic fields. The weather here can be unpredictable. Students say they may go to class at 8 AM in shorts and T-shirts and by the time they get out of class it's snowing. Wash U built on top of a hill gets windy and there are many places on campus where students can warm up. The modern library with rectangular glass panels is often packed with students who are studying or hanging out between classes. Another favorite place on campus is the Holmes lounge, because of its comfy leather chairs and its **gorgeous ceiling,** heavily inlaid with carvings. The **Danforth University Center** also has an interesting ceiling with colored panels. Make sure you notice ceilings across this campus.

The university has expanded the perimeter of the undergraduate Danforth campus with development of the Delmar Loop. Fall 2014 brings the opening of a retail and undergraduate student residence known as **The Lofts**. It features many demonstrable concepts in sustainability including dramatic sun screens. Brookings Hall houses Wash U's admissions office and is the most photographed edifice on campus. Appearing much as a European castle with its gates open, it influences other structures on campus to follow in the same **Gothic** design. The **classical buildings along with modern technology** house national research laboratories that are continually charged with advancing knowledge by the powerful alumni and Board of Trustees. Recent construction finds two new business buildings connected by a three-story glass atrium. Above ground the atrium allows light to stream down below ground into an amphitheater. Much of the campus is built into the side of natural sloping ground and architects have taken advantage with delightful facilities like the new Olin Business complex. Together with two new engineering buildings housing the chemical, biomedical and systems engineering, they each fuelled the amazing growth in infrastructure.

Social Environment

When first-year students arrive at Washington University's Danforth campus, they come with **stellar high school accomplishments**. The majority will come from the eastern half of the United States. They may ponder the optional Wash U pass/fail grade options but each department sets its own guidelines. There is some academic competition on campus since the university attracts many pre-professional students.

The university's own prestigious schools of law, medicine and business call out to those interested in advanced study. Students arrive on campus expecting to find new pursuits and there are tons of invitations for tons of pursuits.

Enrolling in first year courses and possibly deciding on a major is just one level of involvement here. **National initiatives and national research labs** offer ongoing points of entry for undergraduates who wish to apply for a position in established studies. There is also an extensive Office of Undergraduate Research that mentors students with selecting and presenting research findings of interest to them. It is not surprising to understand the Wash U predisposition to send out graduates who are highly skilled in developmental research. The **Undergraduate Council** conducts continuous assessment and makes regular adjustments based on input from across the campus. The **Interfaith Campus Ministries Association** is another example of the university's commitment to disseminate knowledge and encourage dialogue. Again, there are multiple points of exploration on this campus all with pretty much with the same open doors.

There is a nice and easy flow of interaction between students. One-quarter join **Greek life** and become really involved in it. After the first year on campus, undergrads can choose from a large variety of housing options. It is difficult to identify a residence type that this university does not offer, especially with the opening of the new residence/retail complex on Delmar Loop. **Strong friendships** form during this first year that remain in place through graduation on this campus. For some, it's hard to break out of that bubble and get to know other students.

Compatibility with Personality Types and Preferences

Washington University consistently ensures its academic environment supports discovering and disseminating knowledge. The university is really exceptional at both activities and commended especially for their efforts to bring knowledge into the public square of usefulness. Their research and outreach within the social realms of American metropolitan and suburban life have taken a page from South America's Open Streets and introduced it to American benefit. We must say this is the first time we have noticed this type of reversal. Simple, uncostly effort like Open Streets, is helping communities across our nation support public health in these difficult, recessionary years. Thank you Wash U.

Like-minded students at Wash U seek to be part of this vibrant energy. It reflects their wish to grow in understanding of themselves (I), become active and be appreciative of giving back. Faculty and administration support a stable community with a strong undercurrent that highlights the responsibilities inherent in teaching and learning - the two-way street. Teacher and student collaboration is common on campus.

Exceptionally bright students who are predisposed to analysis and objective thinking (T) excel here. Academic activity is ever present in the classes, in the extracurricular clubs and the social gathering of friends. Faculty soften the academic edges with individual encouragement, collaborative and team learning. Mentoring students is a high priority for faculty. The student-professor relationship often moves into the research labs and grows within the academic structure (J) of research. Graduates are focused on achievement and move easily onto prestigious advanced studies as well as influential positions in business.

In the following listing of college majors it is important to remember that students can fit into any college and can be successful in any major. We have found that the Personality Types below fit very well at this college. The course-of-study chosen for each Personality Type corresponds to MBTI® research and is presented as one of many examples favorable for that type.

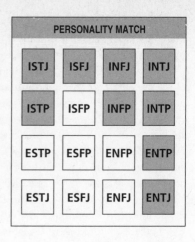

INFP will find the major in **Urban Studies** at Washington University absolutely in synch with their desire to work for a greater cause. This major offers a broad curriculum cataloging ills and issues within American urban settings. The department is vigilant in review of difficulties surfacing in large American metropolitan cities. Juniors are encouraged to apply for the senior honors program. INFP is likely to do this and naturally develop a well-supported thesis proposal. It will be presented in good written form and likely get approval from one of the core faculty members. Wash U social life is sufficiently intellectual for this type, too.

INFJ is drawn to creating new ideas to say the very least. The minor in **Bioinformatics** is an unusual course of study offered within the engineering department. It is an emerging field that will afford this type with many opportunities for pushing the envelope. This minor combines nicely with a degree in computer science, biology or engineering. Creative INFJ will likely choose one of these three by honoring their inclination to help others. INFJ might zero in on implanted electronic devices that monitor diabetic levels in the blood stream.

INTJ is attracted to complex, tough problems. The major in **Operations and Supply Chain Management** offers a peek at the complexity of moving parts around the globe to support manufacturing and service operations. Business competition is intense under free trade and globalization trends. These types of competitive environments get INTJ enthusiastically in the game. They may appear quiet but the reality is that their participation is evident after they generate a solution. Their self-contained nature adds all the more power to their internal thinking.

ISTP likes investigation and the major in **Archeology** requires a good bit of speculating. Students in this major learn about the nature and meaning of artifacts as they travel to study collections in major museums across the country. This type also likes to be outdoors because of the freedom and activity that comes with leaving the desk and iPad behind. At Wash U, they can expand their preparation for this career by selecting a study abroad experience that takes them into active archeological digs. The emphasis on academics over social learning on campus appeals to this type.

ISTJ relates well to the goals of the **Health Care Management** major. Graduates are expected to think precisely and develop useful frameworks that address problems. Both easy for ISTJ, they prefer to gather all the facts and assess them objectively to reach an overall position. The financial mechanisms in the troubled national health care roll out of 2014 are under constant scrutiny and it is the ISTJ who can answer the numbers questions. This type has a quiet humor and will find themselves in demand with friends who also hit the books and need a break occasionally.

ISFJ should not be surprised by the intellectual approach to **Fashion Design** at Wash U. After all, this is a very intense academic environment. The graduates of this major bring skill and confidence to fashion creation in the rapidly changing apparel industry. ISFJ, typically aware of design, could easily focus on fashion apparel. Work after graduation will be developing and delivering desirable clothing lines that serve busy Millenials. This career honors the type's own value for a pleasing, comforting human environment. Their typical attention to detail is perfect and they can handle the repetitive routine in the seasonal delivery of spring and fall fashions.

ENTP is ever ingenious and looking to come up with original ideas and will find plenty of room for each in the **Earth and Planetary Sciences** major at Wash U. This type is constantly available for intellectual discussion and that fits so well on this campus. The department encourages students to participate in research studies, including geobiology. This appeals to ENTP who prefers a challenge and normally feels up to just about any challenge that comes their way. This demanding subject and equally demanding university will not disappoint them. The political advocacy on campus will delight this type who is always ready to debate—on either or both sides!

ENTJ attracted to the idea of business will find the major in **Economics** at Wash U quite interesting. The department infuses the curriculum with mathematical models applied to national problems such as inflation and government decision making. This university is very much focused on the social issues that are reported in the national media and national debates. ENTJs have an objective mindset which they can put to use while moving through the curriculum in this major. It will be this type who sees through the confusion and searches out the facts in order to form their own perspective.

INTP has the curiosity and time to speculate about the unusual elements to be found in the **Geobiology**. This discipline is primarily an advanced graduate level of study. However, INTP can take advantage of the Open Doors on this campus and speak directly to faculty conducting research. The unknowns within the planet's historical record will definitely catch their attention and generate ponderings of sorts. INTPs will approach those unknowns as if they were puzzles to be solved and time is no obstacle, there will be decades to find the answers. Wash U competes in National Geographic's FameLab, a type of science quiz and reality show which features research across the country in the earth sciences. It's fascinating because in only three minutes you get a layman's description of what's happenin' on Earth.

WESLEYAN UNIVERSITY

237 High Street
Middletown, CT 06459
Website: www.wesleyan.edu
Admissions Telephone: 860-685-3000
Undergraduates: 2,932; 1,415 Men, 1,517 Women
Graduates: 203

Physical Environment

Named in honor of John Wesley, the founder of the Methodist Church, Wesleyan University is located mid-way between Hartford and New Haven, off old Route 66, which weaves though the quaint town of Middletown. The university spreads out on a hill with a mixture of eighteenth century **New England brownstones** and modern buildings. It creates an eclectic feel, with continuous buildings blended and connected to each other in a pleasing style. The Andrus quad is a common meeting place for students who want to play a casual game of Frisbee, barefoot, on a sunny day, and it's also where intercollegiate games of football and baseball are played.

The Arts Center is a series of modern buildings that are startling in their presence compared to much of the gentle 1800s reddish architecture on campus and the surrounding town. The 41 Wyllys Ave Project renovated the 1930s squash courts, opening new digs for the College of Letters and the Art History department. The **Usdan Center** is central to the campus energy. It is the meeting place for all who spend their days in this intellectual environment. Students have many quirky architectural spaces for gathering, dining and learning within Usdan.

The residences are a mixture of **Victorian homes,** cottages and **contemporary dormitories** from the 60s. Numbering over 100, they form a **unique foundation for social life** across the campus. Although students are required to live in campus housing all four years, they do not identify strongly with their residences here. Rather, they quickly form small groups of like-minded friends, assisted by incoming room assignments within the dormitories. During the first year on campus, they easily identify with others with common threads of interest. Students look to find their next residence as a group and scout out the multiple housing options that will work best for their small group during sophomore year. Junior and senior year finds most living in off campus college housing which is comfortably mixed in the surrounding residential neighborhoods. In this manner, undergrads are also neighbors of the campus. They get familiar with living in multigenerational communities, yet their residences are managed by the college.

Social Environment

Wesleyan students mirror the population of New York City, with near half identifying as an ethnic minority. **Discussion-prone,** Wesleyan students love that small cadre of friends that share their several interests. They are supportive of each other, appreciating the freedoms that brought them to this campus that plays host to students of atypical rhythms. In the classroom there is no excessive competition for grades. Greatly involved in the life of the mind, they have life experiences and values which they hope to mesh with others **in the larger community.** AP and IB high school coursework only served to whet their appetite and spike their GPAs.

Passions are accepted, supported and expected within the student body. Undergrads spend time **developing the communication finesse required to advance their** finely-tuned opinions. Students here might ask questions like: How can this current biological research study here at Wes be meshed with research studies elsewhere? What question should I be asking now that will lead this work into an avenue for my advanced graduate study? How can this work radiate outward off of the campus and into the larger world?

Students here intend to be informed about current local and national politics and will put in time searching their favored websites for that purpose. They tend to mirror the progressive politics of New York City, seeking answers to problems through collaborative agendas of like-minded people. However, activism is just one of many pursuits and not the most popular. Rather undergrads here are usually in casual conversation, cheering for the Cards on the field while sporting their red hoodies.

Compatibility with Personality Types and Preferences

Wesleyan is a college for the creative (N) students who want to search for truths through exact and precise dialogue. The student who arrives on campus with a questioning predisposition will find plenty of company. Though these opinions are likely to be tested as contemporary events impact society, the campus culture is comfortable with that process. Students are encouraged to develop their own core beliefs about the world around them, albeit there is little support for conservative conceptual understanding. Armed with information, introspective Weslies must apply it to their own life and their own activity in leisure or business. These people-centered folks (F) will find much energy directed toward the state of humanity. Practical considerations are put aside to value abstraction and ideals on this campus. The undergraduate curriculum explores human endeavor in the pure sciences, efficient use of national resources and progressive social constructs in society.

In the following listing of college majors it is important to remember that students can fit into any college and can be successful in any major. We have found that the Personality Types below fit very well at this college. The course-of-study chosen for each Personality Type corresponds to MBTI® research and is presented as one of many examples favorable for that type.

INFJ is often well-prepared in the labs and will be rewarded for remaining glued to the microscopes in the **Molecular Biophysics** certificate at Wesleyan. The field is advancing by genetic leaps and bounds due to the recent advances in gene mapping. INFJ will appreciate the emphasis on discussion at the meeting of the Molecular Biophysics Journal Club. Deep conversation is a preferred learning method for this type.

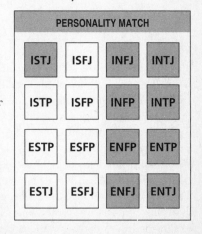

PERSONALITY MATCH

ISTJ	ISFJ	INFJ	INTJ
ISTP	ISFP	INFP	INTP
ESTP	ESFP	ENFP	ENTP
ESTJ	ESFJ	ENFJ	ENTJ

INTJ applies analytical power to find new information. The major in **Astronomy** at this university is very good at developing passion in this precise, yet remote science. That combination of adjectives is just fine with this type who is prone to ruminate on the improbable with facts in place prior to any rumination. Here INTJ will be able to take courses and conduct research in the professional observatory on campus.

ENTP will gain much needed presentation tools in the certificate program for **Informatics and Modeling**. This type often has original, creative concepts but also struggles with getting them into the conversation in a productive way. This sequence of courses introduces the use of computational science to set a framework for analysis. There are two approaches within the program and ENTP will do well to discuss the best approach in consultation with their major advisor on campus.

ISTJ at Wesleyan is likely to appreciate the **German Studies** minor at Wesleyan because it surveys the political culture of the recent past and present day politics. This type likes to collect information in factual form and then rearrange it to fit into larger concepts. Wesleyan is an ideal campus for this and ISTJ will enjoy getting lessons in the abstractions from fellow high flyers on this campus prone to conceptualization.

INFP interested in writing will apply their demanding expectations of analysis to the certificate in **Jewish and Israel Studies** at Wesleyan University. Over a three-year period, courses are offered covering the biblical Israel, Diaspora, Spanish Expulsion, Jews in Eastern Europe, the Hebrew Bible and the various forms of Judaism. It is a great companion study to any degree, especially the physical sciences since it involves no labs.

ENFP will find the **Art History** major at Wesleyan ideal because it approaches art through cultural history. Rather than overly focusing on the visual art techniques and style, this type will prefer to take advantage of their strong insight while finding the human story in paintings. The course Art and Identity in the U.S. previously offered would draw in ENFP. Perhaps Frank Lloyd Wright: Myth and Fact can do the same.

ENFJ will appreciate the nature of team work used in archeology. The program in **Archaeology** requires ENFJ to design their own curriculum within the major which is interdisciplinary at Wesleyan. The combination of mentored encouragement and enthusiasm is a favored learning experience for this type. It is offered as a minor or major which can be nicely paired with studies in the physical sciences required to interpret the archeological dig sites.

INTP will like the pure pursuit of science in the **Molecular Biology and Biochemistry** major. This type could easily be attracted to study which focuses on the transmission of genetic information. Despite the yawning title of this project, Transcriptional Regulation of rRNA Metabolism Related Genes in Yeast, INTPs could be absorbed in the lab, arriving late to dinner and oblivious to the clean up clatter in the dining hall. INTP can also find the real verb in that last sentence too.

ENTJ is a strategic planner and might enjoy **Economics** at Wesleyan University. This major prepares for post-graduate study in business, law and the public sector. ENTJs like these active professions. Much of the curriculum is devoted to quantitative methods and analysis in the worlds of finance. This practical type will be ready to delve into senior level thesis and tutorial. Students critique their own economic perspectives while seeking practical applications during the course of their studies.

WILLIAMS COLLEGE

Office of Admission
800 Main Street
Williamstown, MA 01267
Website: www.williams.edu
Admissions Telephone: 413-597-2211
Undergraduates: 2,013; 965 Men, 1,048 Women

Physical Environment

Nestled at the base of the Berkshire mountains in the north-west corner of Massachusetts, Williams College tends to feel remote. With quiet time and imagination one can hear the clip-clopping of 19th century horses and buggies. Now the area and campus appeals to hikers, snowboarders and those who value history. The campus architecture proudly reveals a record of its three centuries from 1700 to present. **Kellogg House,** over 200 years old, has a rarely documented history with decades of useful purpose. It was renovated and reopened in 2014 as a Living Building. That means it will be self-sufficient with its own water, energy, materials, agriculture and health performance characteristics. It serves the environmental policy studies at the college and demonstrates truly aggressive sustainable concepts such as water recirculation. It is a clear indication of the academic philosophy for **valuing history and conserving the present with purpose** at Williams College.

The new Sawyer Library, also opened in 2014, features space and utility designed for **archival study**. The university has rich historical documents and has brought those documents forward, off the shelves and into the current day curriculum. The Williams College Art Museum also holds many **original paintings and artifacts**. The collection offers pieces from several specific points in time. The extensive Science Complex pulls in many pre-med, pre-vet and science-loving students and houses nine departments of the physical sciences. The new **Student Center** of soaring, arching glass windows is the major hub for socializing and dining. The undergraduates remain long after finishing their meal, next to their forgotten dishes piled up on tables. Hollander and Schapiro Halls are also new academic buildings opened in 2010 for the humanities and social sciences

In fact, Williams College is completing much renovation planned and executed over the past decade. The town itself, a short way down Mohawk Trail, may offer the best chance now to hear those horses and carriages. Students and faculty more than likely take their zip cars into the small establishments that also cater to visiting parents and Williams' employees.

Social Environment

Students who arrive at Williams College quickly move toward one of the **varied social groups** on this campus. The community changes as the classes and individuals pass through reflecting their **individual and collective values**. It is a small campus in feel, yet intellectually large and rich in academic presence. A good number are drawn to the college's prominent reputation in New England. Intellectual boundaries are pretty permeable when it comes to ideas and debate here at Williams College.

Students share their extracurricular experiences and teach one another with frequent presentations given to small campus audiences gathered at the student center. It is also a favored form of collegial entertainment and often with cookies and beverages.

Professors **labor devotedly** over their disciplines and share their academic passion with the undergraduates. **Tutorials** are an example of this social construct. Two students work together with a professor and forge ahead seeking exceptional clarity while critiquing their own work. It's intensive and sometimes fatiguing as students challenge each other to improve each week over the semester-long tutorial. About one-half of the students participate in Tutorials. But all students engage in time-honored winter conversation, fashioning their thoughts during **long evenings** on campus.

For recreation there's the excitement of the games and their purple cow mascot. Students here are exuberant at game time and very comfortable painting their faces purple. Many students here were comfortable in their demanding academic high schools and bring that confidence with them. All in all, Williams College appeals to students who value tradition and want to continue an intellectual journey that connects community with responsibility.

Compatibility with Personality Types and Preferences

Williams College can offer a time capsule of American history as no other liberal arts college does. This concept has novelty in the charged up world of 21st century young adults. Students come to campus who want to move through the four years with traditional mentoring and a buffer distancing them from the contemporary scene. Here at Williams, the more reserved undergraduates excel with the one-on-one faculty-student relationship (I). Many are also expecting a close (F), directed experience with their professors and department advisor. The campus becomes larger through excellent service learning programs both local and abroad. They tend to be experiential and hands-on, also giving an alternative to the heavy dialogue on campus.

In addition to their major educational studies, students find some of the colonial New England ideals quietly in place on campus, like community participation. Education at Williams College is a process (P) rather than a goal. The process is very much paired with an educational community of discussion, collaboration and earnest exploration (N). Students bring a lot of energy (E) and intensity. Faculty across the physical sciences are engaged with peers at other research universities across the country. Speakers in the Biology Colloquium offer undergraduates a window across the discipline that is timely and provocative. Each of the natural science departments are well-connected with leading research institutions through Williams' own research. Intensity is balanced with the many Williams College traditions that lighten the atmosphere with fun.

PERSONALITY MATCH			
ISTJ	ISFJ	INFJ	INTJ
ISTP	ISFP	INFP	INTP
ESTP	ESFP	ENFP	ENTP
ESTJ	ESFJ	ENFJ	ENTJ

In the following listing of college majors it is important to remember that students can fit into any college and can be successful in any major. We have found that the Personality Types below fit very well at this college. The course-of-study chosen for each Personality Type corresponds to MBTI® research and is presented as one of many examples favorable for that type.

ENFP would do well to take advantage of the varied, in depth offerings of the **History** department. Williams College is abundantly informed of historic American tradition and foundation. The advanced courses in United States history offer some illuminating lenses through which to survey our nation during its founding decades. They also offer penetrating historical perspectives less often encountered in smaller liberal arts colleges. ENFPs love to be inspired and creative. How about combining this major with a journalistic career in historical perspectives and current social trends?

ENTP would do well to pursue the **Leadership Studies** track at Williams College. The faculty offers a collection of courses that explore the power relationships between leaders and followers. Since ENTPs are drawn to the worlds of power, they often find themselves in positions of authority and they seek rapport. At the same time, these creative thinkers can become tongue-tied when trying to express their vision. The course in Art of Presidential Leadership exposes ENTPs to strategies and they will likely select a few for their own tool box.

ESFJ frequently moves into the world of health care. At Williams College, the **Biology** department offers a balanced course of studies that prepares graduates for advanced degrees in the life sciences. This type's strong organization skills and the close advising on this campus will assure that ESFJs sample all the career options prior to graduation. This is important because this type makes decisions with careful deliberation and with a desire to be of value to others and society. The Williams tutorial is also likely to really appeal to this type who values harmony and close working relationships.

ENFJ can be a compassionate personality, so the study of **Psychology** is likely to resonate. The field has expanded considerably within the last 30 years. The department has a increased its curriculum interface with the physical sciences and Williams laboratories are well equipped to develop research options for the growing fields pairing brain and behavior. ENFJs could develop a course of study at Williams that replicates the national trend of pairing the disciplines of biology and psychology with interdisciplinary study.

ISFJ often is a stickler for technical accuracy. They can put this skill to good use in a scientific career and Williams College has a unique concentration in **Maritime Studies** that combines easily with another science major of choice. This concentration offers several perspectives on maritime naval power, ocean studies and literature welling up from the literary depths. If ISFJs would rather major in the social sciences they can still sign up for Maritime Studies and enjoy the study of the classic epic *The Old Man and the Sea*. Williams College is just the place to value and study literary classics of all ages.

ENTJ has the characteristics and style needed and necessary to be a credible expert and consultant. Their propensity for long-range planning is just the right stuff for a degree in **Geosciences.** The department offers a focus on interacting global systems and really hones in on the oceans' circulation. Since geosciences is so wide-ranging and requires exacting resources, faculties at liberal arts colleges will often select areas of specialization beyond the foundational course work. At Williams College, one of the specializations moved toward oceanography and is nicely supplemented with the unusual concentration in maritime studies.

INFJ likes to study complex problems very closely and at a steadied pace that is free of the pressures of strict time schedules. The degree in **Political Economy** at Williams College certainly offers both. It ties public policy together with economic resources. INFJs are likely to thrive with the tutorials that pair a professor with student in debate and elocution for the semester. This unusual degree requires a willing, powerful thinker and INFJ often is both these, but they also possess a dose of stubborn once in a while. INFJ may chaff at the structured curriculum in this major, but will hear that undergraduate passion does not necessarily lead to mastery of a major or discipline.

INFP will possibly be drawn to the **Theatre** major at Williams College. This department views dramatic performance as an interpretive tool that utilizes the story line for a purpose. Aside from their typical appreciation of the arts, INFPs love to tell their story and present their original thoughts through another medium. They are not figuratively or literally "talking heads." With their creative spirit in overdrive a combination of drama and therapy could emerge. Williams College students in theater typically double major. INFPs might go for a double major: theater/psychology.

ESFP has the enthusiasm and spontaneity to spin a degree in **Classics** into a high end service in floral landscapes and floral interior design in cities like New York City, London or Los Angeles. ESFPs will stretch their imagination and refer to classical concepts of design with interior and exterior botanical landscapes. The classics department is exceptionally credible since it pairs up with Williams College's deep appreciation for historical tradition. The college's own art museum supplements the on-campus courses in this major. Williams offers a nice selection of coursework in botany to add the practical knowledge need for such a career goal.

YALE UNIVERSITY

38 Hillhouse Avenue
New Haven, CT 06520
Website: www.yale.edu
Admissions Telephone: 203-432-9316
Undergraduates: 5393; 2,710 Men, 2,683 Women
Graduate Students: 6,347

Physical Environment

Yale is the **second oldest private institution** of higher education in the nation and has been at its present location in downtown New Haven since 1716. Yale and New Haven have evolved together over the centuries. The neighborhood next to the campus is a mixture of clothing stores, museums, art galleries, city offices and ethnic restaurants. City streets and campus tend to blur together and Yale students remain aware of their surroundings. The Yale campus displays **three centuries of architecture**, from the red-brick, Georgian style of Connecticut Hall to the Gothic Harkness Memorial Tower to the ultra-modern glass-and-metal Malone engineering building. The campus and its facilities are extraordinary, best understood as a mid-size regional city. Undergraduate students are **cradled within**.

Dormitories as this university are always referred to as residential colleges and more specifically by their individual names. It is appropriate in many senses since each of the 12 has its own budget, facilities and a staff similar to smaller liberal arts campuses. The Yale residential colleges have been in continuous renovation since 1996. Most recently, Morse College finished its redo featuring a small theater, an underground courtyard and other fab spaces for dance, exercise, art and music. Renovation of the final dormitory, Ezra Stiles College, moved forward slower than anticipated and earlier plans to add two more Residential Colleges are not in the news at present.

To comprehend the Yale **national research laboratories** is to imagine one of the disciplines, let's say biology, and realize that Yale Biology is akin to all of the hospital research institutions in, lets say, the city of Boston. It is an allegory but likely to be a true allegory. The Yale **literary archives** might best be understood if one thought of the literary holdings at the British Museum. So do undergraduates have access to these? Yes, they do.

Social Environment

Yale students are **very aware.** Period. Of many things--politics, zip cars, art, math formulas, space, history, cancer, wealth, power, networks, ibuprofen, zinnias, the Mississippi River. Not a conclusive list, it is best understood of as an infinitive recitation of important nouns. Three recent United States presidents graduated from Yale. Circles of power and feedback enhance and re-enhance the institution. Politically, Yalies have traditionally leaned to the right except for the last decade, when the Iraq war and economic downturn have made this side less appealing to Millennial sensibilities. Perhaps more importantly than political centers, Yale academics live within the umbrellas of what is known as **Moral Relativism**. Faculty academic resources, emotional resilience and energy are directed squarely at the student body and all residential experience and individual student perspective becomes knowledge, even so if it is contradictory.

Undergraduate students reside at one of **the 12 residential colleges**, located in the most central and well-traveled areas of the campus. Each become **cohesive communities** of approximately 300 students. The Master of each house facilitates student **social and academic gatherings** at weekly afternoon English teas. Most teas feature a noted speaker or authority and are designed for smaller groups of 10-40 students with similar interests. The financial resources are not limited in securing speakers who can be antagonistic of American values of freedom or may be offering the latest instruction on knitting stitches and yarns, all are presented within the envelope of academic freedom.

There are many opportunities for learning via research projects and networks within the Hartford nonprofit community. In fact there are over 90 student-led programs. This does not include the Senior Project and Senior Capstone. Both individual and group led projects are managed by **Dwight Hall, a nonprofit organization** independent of Yale. Adopting the **Community-Based Learning** system, undergraduates can extend their research projects with local citizen participation or international community inclusion. Funding and administrative support is included and about 3,500 students are utilizing the system to enhance their study.

Undergraduates are **socially sophisticated** for the most part. Much Yale residential life revolves around the **performing arts, club/intramural athletics and their 500 student organizations.** These are each student-led organizations and activity tends to be at the semi-professional level. The Yale Symphony Orchestra is composed of about 80 undergraduates who audition for a position within the orchestra. It performs on campus and off campus and enters soloist and other off campus symphonic competitions, squarely placing it the semi-professional category, yet it is composed of students. It is the same for each of the 500 clubs. Their undergraduate members practice with near professional standards. They are also supported with considerable financial and administrative resources. One could say, students entertain students on this campus. Here it is about growing talent, and students will receive accolades and encouragement beyond expectation.

Aside from formal clubs, tradition plays a big role on campus as could be expected at an institution approaching its 400th anniversary. There is folklore and fact about the secret societies such as skull and bones, to which many American politicos belong. More, however would be aware of the **Yale Sex Week**, an odd and recent addition to annual campus traditions. It has been dramatically opposed by some within the undergraduate student body for its agenda of sexual innuendo featuring much video and content considered pornographic. Four other campuses in this book, Harvard, Brown, Duke and Northwestern, have adopted sex week for their campuses. The latter had to address an angry constituency with a public apology, making the *Wall Street Journal* in March 2011. We are unaware if the three other universities have constituencies who find it symptomatic of decay. On answering protests, Yale administration has cited academic freedom which is consistent with their Moral Relativist position.

Compatibility with Personality Types and Preferences

Yale University assigns its premier role for undergraduate students. The educational experience at the college is tailored for the aggregate student body and tightly structured. With less focus on finding a common thread within the individuals admitted, there is effort to admit unique talents and personal perspective. The vast resources at Yale College are positioned to meet all academic interests. Each student is assured that the materials and educational resources are in place to develop their talent and undergraduate study. Students are brought into the academic fold and expected to become part of Yale's short and long term intellectual community. However, undergraduates must scramble within the curriculum availability for the combination of the studies they will need. They must invoke flexibility (P) when Rarified Underwater Basket Weaving 201 is filled for the semester. Serendipity has a place on this campus.

The Yale environment includes academic philosophy and practice for all 16 personality types. Strands of study and knowledge that occur as discussion (T) or independent study at smaller fine liberal arts colleges become full-fledged programs or courses at Yale. The private students (I) will find it possible to select programs and studies with small numbers of like-minded peers. Faculty within their major will happily collaborate in studied research offering that isolated, preferred single point focus. In this way and other educational practices, the campus is looking inward. Yet the student who derives energy from others (E) will find that Yale educational philosophies demand interaction and collaboration. This mixing it up is honored as the best way to advance the whole student body of aggregate knowledge. Yale faculty expects and intentionally benefits from this collaboration with students. The resultant reciprocal learning with students brings knowledge of current trends within society to the campus gestalt.

The student who arrives expectantly looking for relationships to replace hometown friends now dispersed across the collegiate landscape (F) will find solace in 12 residential colleges, essentially small communities. Friendships quickly develop within each of these residences which are populated to be more or less identical in makeup. Upper class students will find encouragement to interface their evolving knowledge through research with local, national or international communities. Yale provides that encouragement also through professorial mentoring within the residential colleges. Students must use their imagination (N) to propose and identify the experiences that will push them forward in their discipline. As a result, there is considerable informal interface with the exceptional faculty within the residences.

Yale resources include collections of specimens and artifacts that mirror world class museums. Three centuries of collecting has positioned their historical archives to be topped only by the collections of advanced nation states while equal to or beyond their peer institutions. The archival vaults have to be a delight for the student who prefers to see, touch, listen and smell (S) while learning. Nevertheless, it is hard to believe that an undergraduate student will leaf through the pages of the Tyndale Bible, 1534, acquired by Yale in 2014. The science laboratories are equipped beyond wild wishes to support undergraduate proposals with a disciplined approach (J) in research design. Indeed, there is not a learning preference that is not very well-supported at Yale.

In the following listing of college majors it is important to remember that students can fit into any college and can be successful in any major. We have found that the Personality Types below fit very well at this college. The course-of-study chosen for each Personality Type corresponds to MBTI® research and is presented as one of many examples favorable for that type.

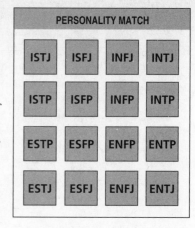

INFP can be driven by their personal beliefs. Often this is a private journey that leads INFPs down some pretty creative paths. During their upperclass years, this type will want to move ahead in spite of any scheduling or limiting obstacles. They are likely to be relentless in pursuing knowledge for their vision of how the world could be improved. The **Yale Summer Session** gives them a little lagniappe, Louisiana talk for an extra slice of bread, to squeeze in a needed course prior to graduation. Their ease with writing can be put to good use in these more concentrated summer classes. INFPs can be creative at the art of overachieving.

INFJ occasionally enters the dynamic world of national or international corporations. At Yale, INFJs can combine knowledge of their undergraduate major with the program of study in **Engineering and Applied Sciences**. It offers three educational tracks for the non-science major who wishes to move into the world of business. INFJs will have their big-picture-glasses on during all the course work and can quickly spot an opportunity to bring advanced engineering applications into the practical world. This program is perfect for INFJs who can major in any social science of their choice.

INTJ will probably ponder the **Special Divisional Major** at some point through the first years at Yale. INTJs are bent on translating their visions into reality. At the same time, they are pretty original and their novel ideas can be difficult to understand. It is possible that even Yale may not have the direction of academic study they require. In this case, INTJs can present their request to the appropriate faculty committee and hopefully be given the go ahead. This type has the persistence and personal strength to follow the process through to the decision. Should it not come out in their favor, the vision will still live on, perhaps, now altered to assure success next time.

INTP will constantly be delighted and absorbed with the major in **Physics and Philosophy**. How much more complicated could it get? For this type, that is just what they need to keep their intense search for clarity at bay or at least occupied. INTPs see the world through patterns and expect those patterns to provide utility at some level, even if it is an abstract level. When they find others interested in their philosophical patterns at the residential college soirees, it will be hard to get in a word edgewise.

ISTP is going to be a first class participant in the **Yale Robotics Undergraduate Student club** at Yale. This club plays around with machines that are directed and powered by computers and people on the ground. ISTPs will only play with machines if they do something practical or interesting. This type will see that the group fulfills both qualifications; ISTP may also want to look closely at the **Environmental Engineering** degree which requires monitoring of air and water. Of course, mechanical devices affixed in odd locations on Earth must be controlled by folks who like robotics.

ISTJ is swell at picking up huge amounts of specific data and storing it for immediate or future use. Once gathered, this type enjoys analysis and formulation in useful categories and concepts. ISTJs are a natural for **Archeological Studies** at Yale. Their senior thesis, required for this major, will be a comprehensive study through logical analysis of their individual observations on an archeological find. ISTJs will devote months to this work and it will likely have practical implications for further research in the field.

ISFJ with an artistic talent has the dedication, starting with day one, to develop a portfolio of studio art work in the freshman and early sophomore years. This reflective, gentle type will find the art department assertively moving into new expressive forms such as Art Wiki—interactive web art for all. The **Art** major explores all modern day and traditional studio arts. ISFJs will bring their excellent visual memories to the forefront in any medium they choose. Their typical sensitivity for others will find a home within this community of fellow students and faculty. They will thrive in the residential house system and support the house Master's efforts to bring the arts into their residence.

ISFP prefers to actively and directly work with information. The major in **Near Eastern Languages and Civilizations** has a component of archeology mixed into the studies. Visits to Egypt for immersion learning and the chance to visit sites of ancient civilizations enliven the major for this type. ISFPs also really appreciate the chance to gather information off campus away from traditional academic environments. It is very relaxing for this type. The artistic nature of much Egyptian archeology also appeals to ISFPs. They relate to this discipline which carries visual meaning as do many of the familiar ancient hieroglyphics incorporated through the centuries into current day symbols.

ESTP is quick to get the picture and will like the courses of instruction centered on **Operations Research**. These courses teach elements of optimization, efficiency and calculation as applied to complex systems in business and government. ESTPs can pick from four subfields within the course work: mathematical programming, stochastic processes, game theory or production/inventory control. This whole arena has elements of risk within the reality of day-to-day operations. This type is right at home and ready to jump in, armed with a Yale education, and there will be solutions—with fun added in to relieve any boring moments.

ESFP will be sporting a smile after a few hours of introduction to the residential colleges. The options for fun and friends will be pretty enticing for this social type. Along the same lines, the program of study in **Sociology** department should be quite appealing. This discipline meets their need for variety and activity. Students quickly become involved in researching behavior and outcomes. ESFPs actually like to move into disorganized environments to bring order and meaning. Therefore most study in this discipline makes sense to them.

ENFP who likes science and math might get the nod to enter the world of finances. The **Economics** program at Yale looks at the wealth of nations, its production, exchange and allocation among the citizens. Many of the research approaches to this discipline are analytical and statistical, yet this type is more often found in counseling and teaching, people-centered careers. ENFP might find careers with NGOs whose purpose is to distribute resources through statistical analyses of needs within the population, similar to the Dwight Hall set up.

ENTP is fascinated by the world and quite capable of finding multiple shades of meaning through their expansive insight. The language courses in **Polish** hold multiple advantages for this creative type. Their interest in political science will likely come to surface at Yale also. Their comfort level in big settings with important players is an asset when leveled with a little needed humility. Fortunately, Yale offers multiple lessons in humility. ENTPs only have to think about the resurgent Russia and its former satellites to see the utility in speaking a little Polish on the international stage.

ESFJ is forever curious about others. This type is more than capable of collecting and cataloging information for future benefit on behalf of people and their organizations. The course in **Study of the City** at Yale has advantages for this type. American cities are attempting to serve all populations and they have multiple programming needs. This course offers a look at those in need.

ESTJ often hones in on challenges, preferably those that exist in the real world rather than an Ivory Tower. They will be right at home here at Yale. The dynamic, hard to predict field of economics can be paired with a second discipline. At Yale, the major is called **Economics/Mathematics** and it offers formulaic solutions for the somewhat chaotic environments they like to straighten out. This type could specialize in the methods and skills that capture data trends within the national economies around the world. ESTJs will especially enjoy the department's Seminars that emphasize class interaction, writing and reading professional articles. ESTJ's natural inclination for leadership in this active environment will likely come forth.

ENFJ will find the **Agrarian Studies Program** at Yale University intriguing because it approaches land study through the lens of human potential. The courses focus on the third world and less developed, emerging nations. Undergraduate students learn through discussion and conversation with members of many different departments at the university. Development of agrarian communities forms the foundation for this program. ENFJs will likely find plenty of support and funding to finish their research overseas in destitute areas of the globe. After graduation, this gifted public speaker will likely bring forward their new found understanding to interested audiences at regional and national levels.

ENTJ has the competitive drive to hang in there for the valuable fifth year of the **Public Health** degree at Yale. This type will be happy with the combination BA-BS and the Masters level degree awarded on completion. ENTJ may seize the opportunity to analyze the troubled roll out of the national health plan in 2014. They have the strategic thinking to do this and the leadership skills to get it into the public square.

CHAPTER 6

THE TABLES OF COLLEGES AND MAJORS RECOMMENDED FOR PERSONALITY TYPES

In this chapter you will see a comprehensive listing of the colleges and majors assessed in this book that are compatible with your Personality Type. It is important to understand that this list is not exclusive and students can be successful at any college. Our basic premise is that the colleges within these tables represent collegiate environments that are excellent fits for the indicated Personality Type and characteristic learning style.

The reader is reminded within each of the 82 college descriptions that the Personality Type information provided is supplemental and it is best used in conjunction with other factors such as size, distance from home, social environment, admission and financial considerations, etc.

Sixteen Personality Types and Colleges

ISTJ

American University
Amherst College
Beloit College
Boston College
Boston University
Brandeis University
Butler University
California Institute of Technology
Claremont Colleges–Pomona
Claremont Colleges–Scripps
College of Charleston
College of Wooster
Columbia University
Connecticut College
Dartmouth College
Davidson College
Denison University
Duke University
Emory University
Florida Southern College
Furman University
George Washington University
Georgetown University
Georgia Institute of Technology
Hamilton College
Harvard University
Johns Hopkins University
Kalamazoo College
Kenyon College
Lynchburg College
Marquette University
Massachusetts Institute of Technology
Middlebury College
Northeastern University
Northwestern University
Notre Dame University
Oberlin College
Princeton University
Roanoke College
Rollins College
Saint Louis University
Stanford University
Tufts University
University of Chicago
University of Miami
University of Pennsylvania
University of Richmond
University of Tampa
Valparaiso University
Vanderbilt University

Wabash College
Wake Forest
Washington and Lee University
Washington University
Wesleyan University
Yale University

ISFJ

Amherst College
Bates College
Beloit College
Boston College
Brandeis University
Butler University
Case Western Reserve University
Claremont Colleges–Pitzer College
Claremont Colleges–Scripps
Colby College
Colgate University
College of Wooster
Columbia University
Connecticut College
Davidson College
Denison University
Elon University
Emory University
Florida Southern College
Furman University
Georgetown University
Georgia Institute of Technology
Guilford College
Harvard University
Haverford College
Johns Hopkins University
Kalamazoo College
Kenyon College
Lynchburg College
Marquette University
Muhlenberg College
Northeastern University
Notre Dame University
Occidental College
Pepperdine University
Princeton University
Redlands University
Roanoke College
Rollins College
Saint Louis University
Salve Regina University
Stanford University
Swarthmore College
Syracuse University
Tufts University
University of Chicago
University of Pennsylvania

University of Richmond
University of Tampa
Valparaiso University
Vanderbilt University
Wabash College
Wake Forest
Washington University
Williams College
Yale University

INFJ

Agnes Scott College
Amherst College
Bates College
Beloit College
Bowdoin College
Brown University
Carleton College
Case Western Reserve University
Claremont Colleges–Claremont McKenna
Claremont Colleges–Harvey Mudd
Claremont Colleges–Pitzer College
Claremont Colleges–Pomona
Colgate University
College of Charleston
College of Wooster
Columbia University
Connecticut College
Davidson College
Denison University
Duke University
Emory University
Florida Southern College
Furman University
Georgetown University
Guilford College
Hamilton College
Hampshire College
Harvard University
Haverford College
Hendrix College
Kalamazoo College
Lawrence University
Massachusetts Institute of Technology
Middlebury College
New York University
Oberlin College
Occidental College
Princeton University
Redlands University
Salve Regina University
Sarah Lawrence College
Stanford University
Swarthmore College
Syracuse University

Tulane University
Union College
University of Chicago
University of Richmond
University of Southern California
Wabash College
Wake Forest
Washington and Lee University
Washington University
Wesleyan University
Williams College
Yale University

INTJ

Agnes Scott College
American University
Amherst College
Bates College
Bowdoin College
Brown University
California Institute of Technology
Carleton College
Case Western Reserve University
Claremont Colleges–Claremont McKenna
Claremont Colleges–Harvey Mudd
Claremont Colleges–Pomona
Claremont Colleges–Scripps
Columbia University
Connecticut College
Dartmouth College
Duke University
Emory University
George Washington University
Georgetown University
Hamilton College
Hampshire College
Harvard University
Hendrix College
Johns Hopkins University
Lawrence University
Massachusetts Institute of Technology
Middlebury College
New York University
Northwestern University
Oberlin College
Occidental College
Princeton University
Sarah Lawrence College
Stanford University
Swarthmore College
Tufts University
Tulane University
Union College
University of Chicago
University of Miami

University of Pennsylvania
University of Richmond
University of Southern California
Vanderbilt University
Washington and Lee University
Washington University
Wesleyan University
Yale University

ISTP

American University
Amherst College
Boston College
Boston University
Bowdoin College
Brandeis University
California Institute of Technology
Carleton College
Case Western Reserve University
Claremont Colleges Harvey Mudd
Claremont Colleges–Pomona
Claremont Colleges–Scripps
Columbia University
Connecticut College
Dartmouth College
Davidson College
Emory University
George Washington University
Georgia Institute of Technology
Hamilton College
Harvard University
Johns Hopkins University
Kenyon College
Marquette University
Massachusetts Institute of Technology
New York University
Northeastern University
Princeton University
Saint Louis University
Salve Regina University
Stanford University
Syracuse University
Tufts University
Tulane University
University of Chicago
University of Miami
University of Pennsylvania
University of Southern California
Vanderbilt University
Washington and Lee University
Washington University
Yale University

ISFP

Bates College
Beloit College
Boston University
Bowdoin College
Brandeis University
Brown University
Butler University
Case Western Reserve University
Claremont Colleges–Pitzer College
Colby College
College of Charleston
College of Wooster
Davidson College
Denison University
Elon University
Florida Southern College
Furman University
Guilford College
Hampshire College
Harvard University
Haverford College
Hendrix College
Kalamazoo College
Kenyon College
Lynchburg College
New York University
Northeastern University
Pepperdine University
Princeton University
Redlands University
Roanoke College
Rollins College
Saint Louis University
Salve Regina University
Sarah Lawrence College
Swarthmore College
Syracuse University
Union College
University of Southern California
Valparaiso University
Wabash College
Wake Forest
Yale University

INTP

Agnes Scott College
American University
Amherst College
Bates College
Bowdoin College
Brown University
California Institute of Technology
Carleton College
Case Western Reserve University

Claremont Colleges–Harvey Mudd
Claremont Colleges–Pitzer College
Claremont Colleges–Pomona
College of Wooster
Columbia University
Connecticut College
Dartmouth College
Davidson College
Duke University
Emory University
Georgetown University
Hamilton College
Hampshire College
Harvard University
Haverford College
Hendrix College
Lawrence University
Massachusetts Institute of Technology
Middlebury College
Northwestern University
Oberlin College
Occidental College
Princeton University
Stanford University
Swarthmore College
Tufts University
Tulane University
University of Chicago
University of Miami
University of Pennsylvania
University of Richmond
University of Southern California
Vanderbilt University
Washington and Lee University
Washington University
Wesleyan University
Yale University

INFP

Agnes Scott College
Bates College
Beloit College
Bowdoin College
Brandeis University
Brown University
Carleton College
Case Western Reserve University
Claremont Colleges–Harvey Mudd
Claremont Colleges–Pitzer College
Claremont Colleges–Pomona
Colgate University
College of Wooster
Columbia University
Davidson College
Denison University

Duke University
Elon University
Florida Southern College
Guilford College
Hampshire College
Harvard University
Haverford College
Hendrix College
Lawrence University
Massachusetts Institute of Technology
Oberlin College
Occidental College
Pepperdine University
Princeton University
Redlands University
Saint Louis University
Sarah Lawrence College
Swarthmore College
Syracuse University
Union College
University of Chicago
University of Southern California
Vanderbilt University
Wabash College
Wake Forest
Washington University
Wesleyan University
Williams College
Yale University

ESTP

American University
Boston College
Boston University
Butler University
California Institute of Technology
Case Western Reserve University
Claremont Colleges–Claremont McKenna
Colby College
College of Charleston
Columbia University
Dartmouth College
Denison University
Elon University
Florida Southern College
Furman University
George Washington University
Georgetown University
Georgia Institute of Technology
Hamilton College
Harvard University
Johns Hopkins University
Kenyon College
Lynchburg College
Marquette University

Massachusetts Institute of Technology
Muhlenberg College
New York University
Notre Dame University
Northeastern University
Princeton University
Roanoke College
Rollins College
Saint Louis University
Salve Regina University
Stanford University
Syracuse University
Tufts University
Tulane University
University of Miami
University of Southern California
University of Tampa
Valparaiso University
Wabash College
Yale University

ESFP

Agnes Scott College
American University
Boston College
Boston University
Brandeis University
Brown University
Butler University
Case Western Reserve University
Claremont Colleges–Harvey Mudd
Claremont Colleges–Pitzer College
Colby College
Colgate University
College of Charleston
College of Wooster
Denison University
Elon University
Florida Southern College
Furman University
George Washington University
Georgetown University
Georgia Institute of Technology
Guilford College
Hampshire College
Harvard University
Kenyon College
Lynchburg College
Marquette University
Massachusetts Institute of Technology
Muhlenberg College
New York University
Northeastern University
Northwestern University
Redlands University

Rollins College
Saint Louis University
Salve Regina University
Syracuse University
University of Miami
University of Pennsylvania
University of Southern California
University of Tampa
Valparaiso University
Williams College
Yale University

ENFP

Agnes Scott College
Bates College
Beloit College
Boston College
Boston University
Bowdoin College
Brown University
California Institute of Technology
Carleton College
Case Western Reserve University
Claremont Colleges–Harvey Mudd
Claremont Colleges–Pitzer College
Claremont Colleges–Pomona
Colgate University
College of Wooster
Columbia University
Dartmouth College
Denison University
Elon University
Florida Southern College
Furman University
George Washington University
Georgetown University
Guilford College
Hampshire College
Harvard University
Haverford College
Hendrix College
Johns Hopkins University
Lawrence University
Massachusetts Institute of Technology
Muhlenberg College
New York University
Northwestern University
Occidental College
Princeton University
Redlands University
Salve Regina University
Sarah Lawrence College
Stanford University
Swarthmore College
Syracuse University

Tufts University
Tulane University
Union College
University of Chicago
University of Southern California
Vanderbilt University
Wabash College
Wake Forest
Washington and Lee University
Wesleyan University
Williams College
Yale University

ENTP

Agnes Scott College
American University
Amherst College
Bates College
Boston College
Bowdoin College
Brown University
California Institute of Technology
Carleton College
Case Western Reserve University
Claremont Colleges–Claremont McKenna
Claremont Colleges–Pomona
Colgate University
College of Charleston
College of Wooster
Columbia University
Connecticut College
Dartmouth College
Duke University
George Washington University
Georgetown University
Georgia Institute of Technology
Guilford College
Hamilton College
Hampshire College
Harvard University
Haverford College
Hendrix College
Johns Hopkins University
Lawrence University
Massachusetts Institute of Technology
Middlebury College
New York University
Northwestern University
Notre Dame University
Oberlin College
Occidental College
Princeton University
Redlands University
Sarah Lawrence College
Stanford University

Swarthmore College
Syracuse University
Tufts University
Tulane University
Union College
University of Chicago
University of Miami
University of Richmond
University of Southern California
Wabash College
Wake Forest
Washington and Lee University
Washington University
Wesleyan University
Williams College
Yale University

ESFJ

Agnes Scott College
American University
Bates College
Beloit College
Boston College
Brandeis University
Brown University
Butler University
Claremont Colleges–Claremont McKenna
Claremont Colleges–Pitzer College
Claremont Colleges–Pomona
Claremont Colleges–Scripps
Colgate University
College of Wooster
Columbia University
Davidson College
Denison University
Elon University
Florida Southern College
Furman University
Georgetown University
Guilford College
Harvard University
Haverford College
Kalamazoo College
Lawrence University
Lynchburg College
Marquette University
Muhlenberg College
New York University
Northeastern University
Notre Dame University
Occidental College
Pepperdine University
Princeton University
Redlands University
Roanoke College

Saint Louis University
Salve Regina University
Sarah Lawrence College
Swarthmore College
Syracuse University
Tulane University
Union College
University of Pennsylvania
University of Southern California
University of Tampa
Wabash College
Wake Forest
Williams College
Yale University

Saint Louis University
Syracuse University
Stanford University
Tufts University
Tulane University
Union College
University of Chicago
University of Miami
University of Pennsylvania
University of Richmond
University of Tampa
Valparaiso University
Vanderbilt University
Wake Forest
Yale University

ESTJ

American University
Amherst College
Boston College
Boston University
Brandeis University
Butler University
California Institute of Technology
Claremont Colleges–Claremont McKenna
Claremont Colleges–Pomona
Claremont Colleges–Scripps
Colby College
College of Charleston
Dartmouth College
Davidson College
Duke University
Elon University
Emory University
Florida Southern College
Furman University
George Washington University
Georgetown University
Georgia Institute of Technology
Hamilton College
Harvard University
Johns Hopkins University
Kalamazoo College
Kenyon College
Lynchburg College
Marquette University
Massachusetts Institute of Technology
Muhlenberg College
New York University
Northeastern University
Northwestern University
Notre Dame University
Pepperdine University
Princeton University
Roanoke College
Rollins College

ENFJ

Agnes Scott College
Amherst College
Bates College
Beloit College
Bowdoin College
Brandeis University
Brown University
Butler University
Case Western Reserve University
Claremont Colleges–Claremont McKenna
Claremont Colleges–Harvey Mudd
Claremont Colleges–Pitzer College
Claremont Colleges–Scripps
Colby College
Colgate University
College of Wooster
Columbia University
Connecticut College
Dartmouth College
Davidson College
Denison University
Duke University
Elon University
Emory University
Florida Southern College
Furman University
Georgetown University
Georgia Institute of Technology
Guilford College
Hampshire College
Harvard University
Haverford College
Hendrix College
Kalamazoo College
Lawrence University
Lynchburg College
Marquette University
Middlebury College

Muhlenberg College
New York University
Northeastern University
Notre Dame University
Occidental College
Pepperdine University
Princeton University
Redlands University
Roanoke College
Saint Louis University
Salve Regina University
Sarah Lawrence College
Stanford University
Swarthmore College
Syracuse University
Tufts University
Union College
University of Southern California
University of Tampa
Valparaiso University
Wabash College
Washington and Lee University
Wesleyan University
Williams College
Yale University

ENTJ

American University
Beloit College
Boston College
Boston University
Bowdoin College
Brandeis University
Butler University
California Institute of Technology
Carleton College
Claremont Colleges–Claremont McKenna
Claremont Colleges–Pomona
Claremont Colleges–Scripps
Colgate University
College of Charleston
Columbia University
Connecticut College
Dartmouth College
Duke University
Elon University
Emory University
George Washington University
Georgetown University
Georgia Institute of Technology
Hamilton College
Harvard University
Johns Hopkins University
Kalamazoo College
Lawrence University

Lynchburg College
Marquette University
Massachusetts Institute of Technology
Middlebury College
Muhlenberg College
New York University
Northeastern University
Northwestern University
Notre Dame University
Oberlin College
Occidental College
Pepperdine University
Princeton University
Roanoke College
Rollins College
Saint Louis University
Stanford University
Syracuse University
Tulane University
Union College
University of Chicago
University of Miami
University of Pennsylvania
University of Richmond
University of Southern California
Vanderbilt University
Wabash College
Wake Forest
Washington and Lee University
Washington University
Wesleyan University
Williams College
Yale University

Personality Types and College Majors

Operations & Supply Chain Management 326

Product Design 281

Philosophy 100, 175, 351

Physics 41, 49, 131

Physics and Philosophy 366

Psychology 100

Theater 225

INFP

African American Studies 53

Architectural Studies 77

Art 89

Biochemistry 208

Biology 277

Chemistry 284

Civilization Studies 305

Communication of Science & Technology 338

Comparative Study of Religion 185

Creative Writing 318

Drama & Theater Arts 118

Early Childhood Education 338

Educational Studies 41, 136

English 115

Environmental Economics 106

Fine Arts 191

Forensic Accounting 172

Geology 57

Gerontological Studies 93

Health & Humanity 326

Irish Studies 233

Jewish & Israel Studies 358

Language & Culture 258

Linguistics 347

Linguistics and Cognitive Science 100

Marine Science 179

Multimedia Design 255

Music 68

Neuroscience 130, 247

Nutrition and Dietetics 270

Philosophy 341

Physics 100

Psychology 139, 193, 301

Religion 151

Religious Studies 93

Science, Technology & Society 220

Social Work 288

Sociology 251

Studio Art 72

Theater 362

Theater and Dance 100

Urban Studies 354

ESTP

Accounting 236

Advertising 65

Aeronautics & Astronautics 281

Asian & Middle Eastern Studies 127

Athletic Training 264

Aviation Management 270

Broadcast & New Media 143

Business Administration 333

Business Economics & Management 85

Civil Engineering 168

Civil & Environmental Engineering 221

Computer Science 233

Construction Engineering and Management 216

Criminology 82

Cultural & Historic Preservation 274

Dance 135, 267

Economic Crime Prevention & Investigation 212

Environmental Science & Public Policy 184

Environmental Studies 175

Exercise Science 159

Finance 229, 297

Financial Economic Sequence 98

Financial Markets 104

Forensic Science 288

Gnarly Waves 98

Human Factors 292

Information Technology 155

International Business 164

Landscape Horticulture 151

Landscape Horticulture Production and Design

Law and Society 45

Logistics & Transportation 110

Management 93

Management Entrepreneurship 244

Mechanical & Aerospace Engineering 260

Operations Management 62

Operations Research 367

Physics 342

Pre-Athletic Training 159

Public Health Studies 198

Public Policy 205

Public Relations 310

Real Estate 327

Sports Management 329, 333

Theater 267

Urban Studies 119

ESFP

Advertising 216

Animal Behavior 180